BISON
BOOKS

JESUS OF NAZARETH
AND OTHER WRITINGS

Richard Wagner

TRANSLATED BY
William Ashton Ellis

University of Nebraska Press
Lincoln and London

Manufactured in the United States of America

♾ The paper in this book meets the minimum requirements of American National Standard for Information Sciences—Permanence of Paper for Printed Library Materials, ANSI Z39.48-1984.

First Bison Books printing: 1995
Most recent printing indicated by the last digit below:
10 9 8 7 6 5 4 3 2 1

Library of Congress Cataloging-in-Publication Data
Wagner, Richard, 1813–1883.
[Literary works. English. Selections]
Jesus of Nazareth and other writings / Richard Wagner; translated by William Ashton Ellis.
p. cm.
Originally published: Richard Wagner's prose works. Vol. 8, Posthumous, etc. London: Kegan Paul, Trench, Trübner & Co., 1899.
Includes index.
ISBN 0-8032-9780-7 (alk. paper)
1. Wagner, Richard, 1813–1886—Political and social views.
2. Music—19th century—History and criticism. I. Title.
ML410.W1A12668 1996
780—dc20
95-24315
CIP
MN

Reprinted from the 1899 translation of volume 8 (*Posthumous, Etc.*) of *Richard Wagner's Prose Works*, published by Kegan Paul, Trench, Trübner & Co., Ltd., London.

CONTENTS

PAGE

Translator's Preface vii

Errata xxii

"Siegfried's Death" 1

Discarded 53

On German Opera 55

Pasticcio 59

Bellini 67

Parisian Amusements 70

Parisian Fatalities for the German . . . 87

Letters from Paris, 1841 108

Halévy and "La Reine de Chypre" . . . 175

Jottings on the Ninth Symphony 201

Artist and Critic 204

Greeting from Saxony to the Viennese . . . 215

On E. Devrient's "History of German Acting" . 218

Theatre-reform 222

Man and Established Society 227

The Revolution 232

Invitation to the production of "Tristan in Munich" 239

PAGE

POSTHUMOUS 249

"THE SARACEN WOMAN" 251

SKETCH FOR "THE APOSTLES' LOVE-FEAST" . . . 277

"JESUS OF NAZARETH" 283

SKETCHES AND FRAGMENTS 341

SUMMARY 399

INDEX 409

GENERAL CHRONOLOGICAL TABLE OF THE CONTENTS OF THE EIGHT VOLUMES 433

TRANSLATOR'S PREFACE.

IN this closing volume of Wagner's Prose, for which I have chosen the title "Posthumous" as most in keeping with its general character, we have a survey embracing all but half a century, from the first æsthetic criticism of the youth just verging on majority, to the last philosophic reflection of the master within two days of immortality. The order of succession may not exactly give that survey with chronologic accuracy, but it has been dictated by my wish to group the writings according to the degree in which they had received the author's final imprimatur. For instance, "Siegfried's Death" comes in point of time immediately before the sketch of "Jesus of Nazareth," but to have introduced it in that part of the collection would have been to wedge in the only contribution from the *Gesammelte Schriften* between works not published until after Richard Wagner's death. Moreover, this *Siegfried's Tod* being as much of a poem, in the original, as those dramas which Wagner finally clothed in the melody and harmony of tone, it seemed more fitting that it should take the place of a proem to the rest of the book. Though not legitimately entering into the scheme of a series of "Prose Works," it had to be included with them, as it otherwise would have been left out in the cold entirely, through its not falling under the marketable category of "operatic textbooks."

That brings me to a fact the importance of which cannot be exaggerated, namely that Wagner included this poem in the standard edition that contains the finished drama of the *Ring des Nibelungen*. Scene after scene of *Götterdämmerung* is identical, down almost to the least significant word, with the corresponding scene in *Siegfried's Tod*; so that the very fact of the author's having printed the earlier version at a date (1871) when the whole tetralogy had already once been published (1863) may be taken as proof of his desire to mark the far-reaching differences between the work of 1848 and that of 1852. In the *Fortnightly Review* of last March I pointed out those differences in so far as they concern the plot and tendency: here to go into the minutiæ of change in *style* would occupy too much of my available space,—in fact, it would demand a lengthy critical essay; but an example or two may faintly indicate the line which such analysis might profitably pursue:—

It will be observed at once that the scene for Brünnhilde and Waltraute in the first act of *Götterdämmerung* is represented in the earlier work by a scene for Brünnhilde and the eight Walküren. When Brünnhilde is left alone again, Siegfried's horn is heard: she now cries, "Siegfried!—Siegfried zurück? Seinen Ruf sendet er her!—Auf!—Auf, ihm entgegen! in meines Gottes Arm!"; but in *Siegfried's Tod* she had cried, "Siegfried, Siegfried ist nah'! Seinen Gruss sendet er her!—Verglimme, machtlose Gluth! Ich steh' in stärk'rem Schutz!" Even the note of interrogation after the third word, in the more recent version, lends dramatic force to the situation, by reducing the apparent interval of Siegfried's absence; but the replacing of the stilted "Fade out, ye feeble flames! I stand in stronger guard" by "Up—Up! to meet him. To the arms of my god!" shews an advance in power of stroke almost as characteristic as the revolution effected in this drama by its altered close. Then take the scene that ensues with Siegfried: how much more energy it gains by the omission of all that "Trembling thou fleest from me, like the cowering dog that feareth its master's chastising" etc., etc.; while the action of Siegfried is made both far less brutal, and far more tragic, by leaving out the lie put into his mouth about his sitting in the boat below, "trying his tunes."—Another interesting point in this *Siegfried's Tod* is the antiphonal chorus at its end, so prophetic of the temple scene in *Parsifal* act iii.

But I must leave this subject, and pass on to the group of writings which, for convenience of classification, I have called the "Discarded." All of these were published in Wagner's lifetime, in various journals, and for the most part above his full name. Why were they not reprinted in the *Gesammelte Schriften*? An answer that would cover the whole group cannot be given: some of them, such as the jottings on the Ninth Symphony and the polemical articles of the Dresden period, he may have either forgotten or considered too ephemeral to reproduce, though they hold a fund of valuable matter; others may have proved inaccessible, whilst the three short articles that commence this series he would probably have discarded for reason of their preceding the epoch at which he really entered public life. Only with regard to one subdivision has he afforded us an answer himself, namely the bright and humorous articles written in Paris 1840-41. At the end of that section of vol. i. of the *Ges. Schr.* which he calls "A German Musician in Paris," he refers to "various Reports from Paris, whose flippant style I can only account for on the supposition that they were attempts of my poor friend to procure subsidies from some German journal through amusing contributions. Whether he succeeded at the time, God only knows! One thing is certain, that a bitter feeling has kept me from here reprinting for a critical posterity the Correspondence-articles dictated by his want" (see Vol. VII. of these translations, page 150). After such a pronouncement it may be disputable whether those articles ought to be unearthed for "posterity;" but the position of Richard Wagner at the present day is very different from what it was a generation back. We must not forget that that first volume of the Collected Writings was published in 1871, i.e. at the very time when their author was straining every nerve to get his Bayreuth theatre founded, in the teeth of venomous opposition by "critical" contemporaries. Having given a selection from these "amusing contributions," he may well have deemed it prudent to restrain his hand and hasten onward to reissue of those works which clearly state his serious aims; moreover, he then had at his side a most fastidious young literary friend, F. Nietzsche, who appears to have found "the merry, joking Wagner not quite to his taste" (see my preface to Vol. VI. p. xix). But the original German of these entertaining articles is quite accessible to the inquisitive critic, even in our own British Museum, and I therefore think that no profound apology is due to Wagner's shade for including them in a "posthumous" volume, and thereby rescuing them from chance and fragmentary resuscitation.

As to the articles that come immediately before and after this subdivision in the present arrangement, a word or two may not be out of place. So far as ascertainable, "On German Opera," "Pasticcio," and "Bellini" are the only prose-writings by Richard Wagner previous to his first Paris period; more than that, all three were written before *Rienzi* was commenced. Now, it is curious to note in these three articles the literal repetition of one or two sentences; on page 64, in "Pasticcio," we have the reproduction of a sentence that occurs on page 55 in "German Opera," and on pages 65 and 66 the facsimile of sentences on page 58: these two articles were published within five months of one another, but it is still more curious to find in the "Bellini" of the end of 1837 a sentence (p. 68) which had actually appeared in "German Opera" at the middle of 1834 (p. 55). In the article last named, and earliest written, for a wonder we have an unsympathetic allusion to Weber; to account for it, we must bear in mind that Wagner was on the point of writing his full-blooded youthful opera *Das Liebesverbot*, in which he temporarily threw himself, as he himself confesses, into the arms of the younger French and Italian schools. However, even in these somewhat anti-German articles we find the greatest stress laid on the necessity of cultivating a new, as yet unheard-of form of Opera, "for he will be master who writes neither Italian nor French—nor even German." In that expression, repeated from one to another of these articles, we may detect the true note of the future universalist as much as in this other, from *Pasticcio* (p. 66), "If the librettist has the true poetic spirit, in him there lies the universe of human moulds and forces, his figures have an organic core of life; let him unroll the heavenly, or the earthly chart of human characters, we shall always find them lifelike, even though we may never have met their like in actual life"—a remark as characteristic of the later Wagner as in *German Opera* is the epigrammatic turn of "In the genuine scholar one never marks his learning" (p. 57).

I need not descant on the feuilletons sent to Germany from Paris, for their airy wit will speak for itself; whilst it would take too long to pick out from that pair of twins, the "Parisian Amusements" and "Parisian Fatalities," the passages which really bear a half-cloaked autobiographic interest. But the French essay on "Halévy and the Reine de Chypre" is an absolute treasure trove, whose history may therefore be given at greater length. It will be remembered that the semi-facetious Report on Halévy's *Reine de Chypre* printed in Volume VII. originally appeared in the Dresden *Abendzeitung* of Jan. 26 to 29, 1842, but in his *Leben Richard*

Wagner's Herr C. F. Glasenapp informs us that a totally different article was written for the *Gazette Musicale* with a view to obtaining, or assisting to obtain, the requisite funds for Wagner's migration to Dresden, where his *Rienzi* was presently to be produced. Herr Glasenapp shall now be called upon for the history of the original German MS. of this French article: "Long afterwards it was offered for sale as 'a pièce in splendid preservation,' and disposed of to an unknown collector for 150 marks; a sum which can scarcely have been much exceeded by the fee once paid the youthful master for its contribution. On the back of the twelfth page was a note, 'Authorised by Herr Schlesinger, I send to Herr Düesberg the continuation of my article on Halévy, as it is to appear in the next number. . . Paris, 26th February 1842. Richard Wagner.'" Glasenapp conjectures, and I should say correctly, that Düesberg was the French translator (probably of the other *Gazette* articles as well); but, since the MS. has passed out of reach, it is quite impossible either to fill in the words omitted from the note, or to be certain that the whole MS. was thus disposed of, for the "continuation" obviously refers to the second section of the article, that published on March 13. It is most exasperating that precisely this MS. should have been snapped up and hidden away by the private collector, since it is the very one to which Wagner refers in his article on Auber in Vol. V. (pp. 37-8) as having led to a wordy war with his editor, necessitating the omission of a certain passage about Rossini (see p. 191 *infra*),—which would probably account for the second section's having been delayed beyond the "next number" of the half-weekly *Gazette*. That article on Auber of 1871 contains so many points of resemblance to this essay of 1842 on French music, that I should almost imagine the author to have employed the earlier work as foundation for the new.—Before dismissing the subject, perhaps I may be forgiven for recording my own mild adventures in unearthing the article. In my preface to Vol. VII. I referred to the kindness of a correspondent in Paris who had procured me the volumes of the *Gazette Musicale* for 1840 and 1841, and thus enabled me to trace a number of more or less important variations: unfortunately my request does not seem to have been sufficiently explicit; the volume for 1842 was actually obtainable at the time, but had slipped past our fingers before the mistake could be rectified. From no other quarter could I make good the loss, until at last I appealed to Professor Joseph Kürschner, curator of the Richard Wagner Museum at Eisenach, who courteously had a manuscript copy of the article made for me from the files of the *Gazette Musicale* originally collected by Herr Nicolaus Oesterlein, founder of the Museum. As Prof. Kürschner himself has certified this MS. copy, we may accept it as a perfectly accurate reproduction, and to him I therefore owe a very valuable addition to our knowledge of Richard Wagner's Paris period.

As regards the remainder of the articles etc. included under the general heading "Discarded" I have to thank Herr Glasenapp for either the suggestion that I should include them in this volume, or the actual information where to find them. With two exceptions, they do not call for any comment beyond those added to them in the text. These exceptions are formed by the two articles contributed early in 1849 to Roeckel's *Volksblätter*. If any further proof were needed, that these two articles sprang from Wagner's pen, it should suffice to note the parallelism between the sentence beginning, "A prodigious movement," on page 370, and the opening sentence of "The Revolution" (p. 232); and between the main paragraph of p. 369, taken in conjunction with the passage on pages 310-11, and the main paragraph of page 229 in "Man and Society."

Passing to the Posthumous publications proper, *Die Sarazenin* has an instructive history, half related and half suggested in the *Communication to my Friends*. Its author had already completed his *Flying Dutchman* when he first conceived the subject; but he abandoned it for the idea of *Tannhäuser*. This was at the end of 1841, in Paris. At Dresden in 1843, after the *Flying Dutchman* had been performed, he returns to *Die Sarazenin*, and writes the full text, as here presented; but again he abandons it, and this time definitely, for *Tannhäuser*, to the composition of the poem and music for which work he devotes himself with heart and soul. Now the significance of this lies not only in Wagner's temporarily reverting to a historic subject after so thoroughly launching out into the legendary sea with his *Dutchman*, but in his also harking back to the five-act form of *Rienzi*. I cannot help thinking that his preoccupation with the *Reine de Chypre*—of which he was to have made "arrangements," in addition to his critical review—may in the first instance have influenced him to take this step, and that he was following his own half jocular advice to operatic librettists to "go to the great book of history and find a half or whole page that tells you of some strange event," then "draw three or even five bold lines across it, which you may call *acts* if you please," etc., etc. (Vol. VII. 211). This might account for the first conception, whilst the resumption of the idea would probably be due in part to the comparative coldness with which the *Flying Dutchman* had been received at Dresden, after the phenomenal success of *Rienzi.* Worldly wisdom would certainly have been consulted by his adhering to the "Saracen" plan; for it had a far more spectacular basis than *Tannhäuser* (in common wherewith it nevertheless breaks through the operatic convention by relegating the ballet to the opening scene), and Manfred's character would have presented no such difficulties to the ordinary tenor as are offered by the impulsive Heinrich. On the composing, or not composing, of *Die Sarazenin* hung the decision of Richard Wagner's whole career. Had he produced this opera, there is little doubt that it would have had a success as brilliant as *Rienzi's*, and the composer's fate would have been sealed: it would have been wellnigh impossible for him to turn his back on the Grand Operatic path after *two* such productions.

However, *Die Sarazenin* is in some respects an advance beyond the *Dutchman*: though Manfred has little of the impressiveness of Vanderdecken, Fatima is a more human creation than Senta; she is the first of Wagner's flesh-and-blood women, and for her sake we can regret that nothing came of this operatic project. One charming scene at least it offers, a picture by which this draft will always be kept alive in the reader's memory; this occurs at the psychologic moment in the third act, where Fatima keeps watch with Ali and Nureddin at the gate of Luceria, and may be recommended to any artist in search of a new Wagnerian subject for his canvas. As to the diction, it would not be fair to judge *Die Sarazenin* by its existing form; for not only had Wagner not yet turned his libretto into verse, but the MS. is an imperfect copy by another hand, with several manifest omissions: for instance it lays the scene of the first and fourth acts at "Laxua," for which Herr Glasenapp most plausibly suggests the substitution of "Capua."

Whether the full sketch of *Die Sarazenin* closely followed, or immediately preceded the composition of *Das Liebesmahl der*

Apostel, it is impossible to say; but the year that saw the drafting of three such heterogeneous works, as these two and the *Tannhäuser*, must have been a year of considerable mental activity. Again we seem to hear the author addressing his question to fate, "Zu welchem Loos?" But the path of Oratorio, or "biblical scene," is renounced equally with that of Historical Opera.

The next posthumous publication is that of a work drafted at what might be termed the vernal equinox in Wagner's life. Six years have elapsed since the *Liebesmahl* was written, the *Sarazenin* abandoned; six years that have added immensely to the author's grasp of the problems of life. He now has written and composed his *Tannhäuser* and *Lohengrin*. Per contra, he has had the chagrin of finding it impossible to get the latter work produced at the very theatre for which it was destined, the theatre where he long had been one of the two appointed musical conductors; he has had to suffer unspeakable insults from his chief, the Intendant, and to combat jealous machinations started by his colleague; the publication of his first three operas has involved him in the cruelest financial embarrassments, which have been taken advantage of by the court to read him lectures on the crime of poverty; revolution is in the air, and—were it not—the stifling atmosphere of Dresden is becoming unbearable to him. Here he stands at the very parting of the ways, and writes his *Jesus of Nazareth*; a work which he soon recognises as containing so much Revolution in itself, that its performance would be impossible before that general cataclysm, and meaningless thereafter.

Let us see the exact position occupied by this work in the author's evolution, and we shall be better able to fathom its import. Wagner has written the last bar of *Lohengrin* (end of March 1848) while Vienna and Berlin were going through the first act of that abortive revolution which was soon to convulse the whole of Europe—and to lead to so little. He has handed in his scheme for reforming the theatre, and has sent that Greeting to the Viennese which appears on page 215. He has delivered his "Vaterlandsverein Speech" (see Vol. IV.) and been warned against any further meddling with politics. He now is seized once more with the creative afflatus, and sets about the drafting of another drama: its subject is Barbarossa, whose "rewakening is so longed for by so many." The actual date of this as yet unpublished draft is immaterial; suffice it for us to know that it was somewhere between the early spring and summer of 1848, i.e. in the thick of the revolutionary movement that was advancing toward the gates of Dresden. Here he has again returned to history, though with the object of making it read a lesson to the modern world. He finds that History, however idealised, will not comport with Music: ergo, this Barbarossa, or *Friedrich Rothbart*, must become a five-act spoken drama. But the spirit of Music is too strong within him to permit of his abandoning her just yet, and he takes up another subject, conducted to it by Jakob Grimm's assertion that this Friedrich is, so to speak, a reincarnation of Siegfried. So *Siegfried's Tod* is drafted in the summer of 1848, and its full poetic text completed by November: some "fugitive attempts at its musical composition" are also made, but the solitude of his position is so borne in on Wagner by fresh contact with his lyre, and the social agitation all around him seems to accord so badly with the harmonies of tone, that he lays Siegfried also on one side, "burning to write something that shall take the message of his tortured brain, and speak it in a fashion to be understood of present life." He says in 1851 (*Communication*) "I saw afresh that the sole redemption lay in flight from out this life," and that it was this that led him to "Jesus of Nazareth the *Man*." But we must remember that these words were written nearly three years after the event, and I am strongly inclined to believe that it was *music* from which he then was fleeing—music to which he did not return till five years later. The great crisis in his artistic life had arrived: after *Lohengrin*—the effect of which he was not even allowed to hear—a pause must necessarily follow; a pause in which to meditate on those new lights the music of his *Lohengrin* had brought him, and, yet more important, to discover what it was that *Siegfried's Tod* still left untold in Drama.

However that may be, there can be little doubt that *this* "poetic sketch" of *Jesus of Nazareth* was not intended for a musical setting. I am aware that on August 9, 1849, Wagner writes to Uhlig about a passing notion of offering this subject to Paris,—an idea which he has already dismissed before he writes to Liszt on Oct. 14 of the same eventful year; but the sketch itself had been written about six months prior to the first of these two references, and neither of them betrays any antecedent thought of music for it. In the *Communication* on the other hand we have three whole pages

(I. 378-81) devoted to an account of the *Jesus of Nazareth* and its author's state of mind at the time of writing it: it is there expressly designated as "the sketch of a drama," without a word to suggest that it was meant to be a *musical* drama; so that the whole project of offering it to Paris appears to have been a stupendous stroke of irony, perhaps dictated by the five-act form of the work. That five-act form in itself, as I believe, excludes all original intention, at least, of turning this work into an "opera." Wagner had definitely adopted the three-act form, for operatic works, when he abandoned his *Sarazenin*; his *Tannhäuser*, his *Lohengrin* and the immediate precursor of his *Jesus*, the *Siegfried's Tod*, had been written in three acts; whereas the five-act *Friedrich Rothbart* that preceded *Siegfried's Tod* was the draft for a spoken drama. Incidental music may well have been intended to accompany certain situations, in the manner of *Egmont*; but the only suggestion of music in the sketch itself occurs in the second scene of its third act, the Entry into Jerusalem, where we read of the strewing of carpets and flowers, "music and cheering, nearer and nearer." Had this work been intended for regular musical composition, I cannot conceive the omission of such obvious indications as "And when they had sung an hymn, they went out into the mount of Olives" (Matt. xxvi., 30, and Mark xiv., 26); for Wagner had not yet ostracised the chorus, as may be seen in his *Siegfried's Tod*. Yet another argument against this being the probable sketch for a musical drama may be found in the elaborate working out of social and metaphysical problems in its second part, forming an exact parallel to the supplementing of the (unpublished) *Rothbart* drama by that "world-historical" essay "The Wibelungen" (see Vol. VII. p. 258): in this respect the two dramas for unadorned word-language stand apart from any other of Wagner's poetical works. Though I cannot imagine his having meant the longer disquisitions in Part II. of the *Jesus of Nazareth* as actual speeches to be delivered by the principal personage, yet they cannot but be regarded as scaffolding for the dialogue; and the idea of setting these Feuerbachian hermeneutics to music must be rejected at once as incredible.

As to the dramatic merits of the sketch, it is so rare to find an English man of letters taking the smallest notice of Richard Wagner—due perhaps to the nonsense heaped upon his head by amateur scribblers and half-informed critics,—that I will reinforce my own opinion with that expressed by Mr George Moore in *The Musician* of May 12, 1897: "There is only one thing to say—viz., that neither Shakespeare nor Sophocles could have contrived a nobler or a more dramatic telling of the story. Quite naturally every incident falls into its place, and advantage is taken of every hint. . . It is doubtful if Shakespeare would have conceived the opening scene with the massive purpose that marks the opening lines. Barabbas says the Roman forces are unusually weak, and that success is certain if the people can only be stirred to a decisive rising. This is the key of the dramatic action. In the fifth act . . . Pilate's anxiety increases. 'Is the Syrian legion at hand?' . . . I know not how far the incident of [the delayed] Syrian legion is derived from history; I fancy it must be Wagner's own: or to express myself more accurately, I believe that in this incident Wagner has divined a lost fragment of the history of the time. But how exquisitely it fits with the known facts, how it completes and explains! For without the Syrian legion, how can we reconcile Pilate's consent to the crucifixion with his well-known repugnance to the condemnation? The washing of the hands is the symbol of a man's last horror of a deed of blood, which he would avert if he could. The washing of the hands is the act not of a weak but of a strong man who is overborne by circumstances.—The beauty of Wagner's music has shadowed his genius as a writer."

And now for another aspect of *Jesus of Nazareth.* In my preface to the first volume of this series (Dec. 1892) I referred to Dr Hugo Dinger's promise to complete his work by furnishing us in a second volume of his *Richard Wagner's geistige Entwickelung* with the proofs of numerous assertions contained in the first. That promise has not yet been redeemed, but I should much have liked to see how Dr Dinger supports his contention that this sketch betrays the influence of D. F. Strauss, the author of the well-known *Leben Jesu,* as stated in a footnote to page 257 of the work just named, and again on page 321 *ibidem,* where a footnote says that "Wagner appears to have derived the concept 'Mythos' from Strauss; a matter with which I shall deal in the second volume by a comparison of Wagner's 'Jesus von Nazareth' with Strauss's ideas." Now, as to the source whence Wagner derived his general ideas of "Myth," one has only to consult the rubric "Jakob Grimm" in Glasenapp's *Wagner-Encyclopædie.* That he had closely studied Grimm, must be obvious to all who know the origins of *Lohengrin*; but if Wagner had studied and followed David Strauss, it would be incomprehensible that the first time he ever makes mention of the "Christian mythos"—namely in the second chapter of Part II. of *Opera and Drama*, written in December 1850, i.e. about two years after *Jesus of Nazareth*—he should have used this expression, "The enthralling power of the Christian mythos consists in its portrayal of a *transfiguration through death*," whereas Strauss confines the concept, so far as it applies to the history of Jesus Christ, to what he calls the "Messianic myth," i.e. the constant reference of *earthly* Messianic prophecies to Jesus Christ by his disciples or later followers. True, Strauss saw reason to modify his Messianic hypothesis in his "popular edition" of the *Leben Jesu*, the edition to which Dr Dinger refers in his list of books consulted; but, unfortunately for the Doctor's assertion, that popular edition was not published until 1865!

However, is there any internal evidence in *Jesus of Nazareth* that Strauss's work (first published in 1835-36, and in its fourth edition by 1840) had been read by Wagner? One striking feature will at once be noted in this sketch, the omission of every miracle save that of the raising of Jairus' daughter, and Jesus' explanation of this event as a natural recovery: but the Rationalists had already endeavoured to account for all the miracles in a natural way long before Strauss came on the scene; and their omission, to my mind, s merely an additional argument in favour of the theory that Wagner intended this work for a non-musical, i.e. a more realistic setting (see his chapter on the Miraculous in art, *Opera and Drama* pp. 213 *et seq.*). It surely did not need any inspiration by Strauss, to discard the miracles, as stated on page 298, from a work whose purpose it was to display the Son of Man, and not the mystic Christ.

On the other hand, the evidence *against* a Straussian derivation is overwhelming. In the first place we find Jesus, as portrayed by Wagner, continually prophesying his violent death and the destruction of Jerusalem: these sayings are all attributed by Strauss to the imagination of the disciples *after* the Redeemer's death. Secondly, we have stress laid on Jesus's descent from David in the very first line of Part II.; whereas the opening section of the *Leben Jesu* treats the "Genealogies" as the rankest fiction. Thirdly, Wagner makes Bethlehem the birthplace (p. 290), whereas Strauss had conclusively proved that it was Nazareth. Lastly, and most significant of all, the whole colouring of the work is borrowed from the Fourth Gospel: not only does Wagner make Jesus pass over the brook Kidron, which "St John" alone mentions, but he takes the date of the trial and crucifixion, with many of the details connected therewith, from that evangelist—who is at variance in this respect with the synoptists, whilst Strauss prefers *their* statement; moreover, in Part II. he cites text after text, and on page 338 six whole chapters, from the "Gospel according to St John." To me it is inconceivable that anybody who had come even indirectly under the influence of Strauss should lay so much emphasis on passages taken from the very evangelist whose authority that celebrated critic was the first to impugn; whereas earlier bible-critics, and the body of orthodox believers, had always given their preference to this Fourth Gospel.—We may therefore dismiss Dr Dinger's theory of a Straussian derivation as quite incompatible with the internal evidence supplied by the *Jesus of Nazareth* itself, even were it not contrary to all probability that the study of a minutely reasoned piece of destructive criticism should leave the student with sufficient enthusiasm to take the subject of that criticism for the hero of a drama. No: to any but determined hunters after mare's nests it must be clear as noonday, that the imposing figure of Jesus of Nazareth is a figure seen by Richard Wagner with his inner vision after a prolonged study of the New Testament itself; a study to which he may well have fled for comfort in the trouble of that agitated time.

It would be instructive to establish the exact date, or dates, of the writing of this *Jesus of Nazareth*, in view of the Feuerbachian cast of various portions of its second part; but unfortunately the manuscript is undated, nor is it possible to say with any certainty even whether all the three sections were written before Wagner left Dresden in May 1849. For my own part, I am disposed to assign at least a portion of Part II. to the early Zurich period, owing to its resemblance to certain pages of the *Artwork of the Future*; but I offer this hypothesis for no more than it is worth as a personal impression. The handwriting cannot be called upon to settle the point, for the distinctive change had already taken place in the late autumn of 1848. In an article contributed to the *Bayreuther Blätter* for September 1885 by its editor, Baron

Wolzogen informs us that the MSS. of *Friedrich Rothbart* and *Siegfried's Tod* were written throughout in German hand, but a few additions to *Rothbart* were already in what the Germans call "Latin" and we "Italian" character, which thenceforth was adhered to by Wagner for the rest of his life. For the next year or two he also discarded the German use of capitals for the initial letters of nouns, and largely even for the commencement of sentences, but gradually resumed their use from about the beginning of 1852, until in 1853 he had entirely reverted in this respect to the ordinary German usage. So that it is quite easy to assign any document of this period to within a year or so of its exact date, but closer than that we cannot go with any dateless paper on the evidence of handwriting alone. The *Jesus of Nazareth* being a work practically complete for publication, the German editor has reasonably left out of sight this peculiarity as regards the capital letters; but it has been strictly observed in the case of the posthumous Fragments, in keeping with their more intimate and personal character. This fact I mention in order to avoid the attribution of carelessness to my printers wherever a sentence in these Fragments begins with a "lower case" letter, or a bracket appears to have lost its mate, and so forth: the idiosyncrasy in setting-up is deliberate and intentional.

That brings me to another point in connection with the Fragments. It would have been to destroy their character of fugitive jottings, had I attempted to trim them into shape where the sense is incomplete: in many cases they must be viewed as quasi short-hand notes, for working out on a plan of the author's own; and this will explain the marginal glosses often having nothing at all to do with the passage in the text to which they are appended, —they were evidently flung down on paper just as and how the thought occurred, frequently in the midst of another reflection. However, there need be no difficulty in the comprehension of all but two or three of the most enigmatic of these jottings, if the reader will deign to consult the countless references in the footnotes, which in themselves almost constitute a key to the whole series of prose-works; I only wish I were allowed to name the compiler of this priceless aid, that honour might be given where honour is due.

And now I have a farewell to take. For nine years, through

thick and thin, I have been permitted to enjoy the companionship of Richard Wagner as a prose-writer. To myself it has been an unalloyed enjoyment, whatever obstacles may occasionally have stood in the way of my seizing his precise intention. Echoes from outside have crossed my path at times, echoes of the journalist who would fain see even the greatest master compelled to talk in journalese. Those echoes, I rejoice to say, are dying down; though I sometimes feel a little lonely without the harmless amusement they afforded me in the good old days when the road before me still appeared so long. But that road is covered now, and I can have no other thought save of gratitude, first to the genius who constructed it, and next to those who have encouraged me to pursue it to its happy end. Some future day there may yet be opened up the prospect of following Richard Wagner's footsteps through his own life-history, but that cannot be for several years to come. Meantime I have the honour to invite my readers to accompany me for the next two or three years to the most trustworthy Life of Richard Wagner ever penned by another, the fruit of the untiring zeal of C. F. Glasenapp. So that my Farewell may really prove, I hope, "Auf Wiedersehen!"

WM. ASHTON ELLIS.

October 1899.

ERRATA.

Page 29, line 3 from bottom, *for* "?" *read* "!"

,, 44, ,, 1, *for* "woodbirds'" *read* "woodbirds."

,, 290, ,, 7, ,, "them" ,, "him."

,, 314, ,, 8, ,, "indivuality" ,, "individuality."

,, 358, ,, 7 from bottom, *for* "un-understable" *read* "un-understandable."

,, 383, in note after third paragraph *omit* the words from "Glasenapp" to "but it" (inclusive), and *read* "This jotting" etc.

SIEGFRIED'S DEATH

(November 1848).

Siegfried's Tod.

CHARACTERS.

SIEGFRIED.
GUNTHER.
HAGEN.
ALBERICH.

BRÜNNHILDE.
GUDRUNE.
THREE NORNS.
THREE WATER-NIXIES.

VALKYRIES.

BY THE RHINE.

PROLOGUE.

(After a very brief musical prelude the curtain is raised. The stage represents the summit of a rocky mountain : on the left the entrance of a natural stone-chamber. The brink of the precipice is free toward the back ; on the right, high firs.—Bright starlight.)

THE THREE NORNS

tall female figures in dark, flowing garments, are spinning a rope of gold. The First, the eldest, binds the rope to a fir-tree on the extreme right. The Second, younger, winds it round a rock on the left. The Third, the youngest, holds the end in the middle of the background.

The First Norn. In the east I wove.

The Second. In the west I wound.

The Third. To the north I cast.

(to the Second). What wound'st thou in the west?

Second (to the First). What wov'st thou in the east?

The First (loosing the rope from the fir-tree).

Alberich robbed the Rhine-gold,
bent therefrom a ring,
bound thereby his brethren.

The Second (unwinding the rope from the boulder).

Thralls the Nibelungen,
thrall too, Alberich,
since his ring was stolen.

The Third (throwing the end of the rope to the extreme background).

Free the elves of darkness,
free too, Alberich :
Rhinegold rest in the waters!

(She throws the rope to the Second, the Second throws it to the First, who binds it anew to the fir-tree.)

First. In the east I wove.

The Second (who has wound the rope once more round the boulder).

In the west I wound.

The Third (holding the end aloft as before).
To the north I cast.—
what wound'st thou in the west?
Second. What wov'st thou in the east?
The First (loosing the rope once more).
The Giants built the Gods' burg,
with threats they asked the Ring in pay:
the Gods bereft it from the Nibelung.
The Second (unwinding the rope once more).
In fear I see the Gods' race,
in bonds the depths are groaning:
the free alone give peace.
The Third (throwing the end once more).
Gleefully dareth a glad one
freely to fight for the Gods:
through triumph a hero brings peace.
(They handle the rope as before.)
First. In the east I wove.
Second. In the west I wound.
Third. To the north I cast.—
What wound'st thou in the west?
Second. What wov'st thou in the east?
First. A Worm did the Giants beget them,
the Ring's all-murderous warder.
Siegfried hath slain it.
Second. The hero won Brünnhild,
broke the Valkyrie's sleep:
loving, she teacheth him runes.
Third. Her runes unheeding, faithless on earth,
yet faithful for ever, he tricketh his dear one:
but his deed she hath wit to unravel,
freely to finish what glad he began.
(They throw the rope once more.)
Windest thou yet in the west?
Second. Weavest thou yet in the east?
(Day begins to dawn.)
First. Wotan draws near to my fountain.
Second. His eye bendeth down to the well.

Third. Wise be his answer!
The Three (while they coil the rope completely up).
Roll up the rope, guard ye it well!
What we have spun, bindeth the world.

(They embrace, and vanish from the rock.—Day breaks.—Siegfried and Brünnhilde step out of the cavern. Siegfried is in full armour, Brünnhilde leads a horse by the bridle.)

Brn. To seek new deeds, beloved hero,
how lov'd I thee—sped I thee not?
One only care yet bids me falter,
that too little thee my worth hath won.
What Gods had taught me, gave I thee,
of hallow'd runes a rich-fed hoard;
of mine own strength the maiden hold
the hero stole 'fore whom I bend me:
of wisdom bare, of wish o'erflowing,
of love full rich, yet reft of force—
flout thou not the empty-handed,
who grants thee all, no more can give!
Sieg. More gav'st thou, wonder-wife,
than I have wit to guard:
yet chide not, if thy lessons
have left me all untaught!
But one thing know I surely;
that Brünnhild lives for me:
one lesson learnt I lightly;
of Brünnhild aye to think.
Brn. Wouldst yield me all thy heart's love,
think thou but of thyself,
remember but thy deeds!
Think of the seething fire
that fearless through thou strodest
when round the rock it raged.
Sieg. Brünnhild alone to win!
Brn. Think of the shielded woman
whom in deep sleep thou found'st,
whose close-lockt helm thou clov'st.
Sieg. Brünnhilde to awaken.

Brn. Think of the oaths—that make us one,
think of the troth—each bears to each,
think of the love—that is our life:
Brünnhilde then thou'lt ne'er forget.
Sieg. This ring, behold! I reach thee
in barter for thy runes:
what deeds soe'er I've done,
their virtue it enfolds.
I slew once a loathly Worm
that long o'er it had watched:
now guard thou all its strength
as guerdon of my troth.
Brn. Be it my only good,—
for it take thou Grane my horse!
If erst with me he dauntless leapt the tempest,—
with me hath he lost that might;
o'er the clouds away, on paths of lightning,
no more may he take his flight.
Yet to thee, my hero, shall he hearken:
ne'er rode a warrior nobler horse!
Heed'st thou him well, he hears thy word:
o bring him oft Brünnhilde's greeting!
Sieg. Through might of thine alone
shall deeds of mine be done!
My warfare shalt thou choose,
my victories turn to thee!
On back of steed of thine,
'neath shelter of thy shield—
no longer am I Siegfried,
I'm but Brünnhilde's arm!
Brn. O were Brünnhild thy soul!
Sieg. Through her my heart is fired.
Brn. So wert thou Siegfried and Brünnhild?
Sieg. Whither I go, fare they twain.
Brn. So bare my rock-abode?
Sieg. Nay, both of us it holds.
Brn. O holy Gods, ye heavenly rulers!
Feed ye your gaze on the hallowed pair!

Sunder'd—who shall e'er part it?
Parted—'tis ever at one!
Hail Siegfried, light of the world!
Hail, hail! Thou joy of the Gods!

Sieg. Hail to thee, Brünnhild, brightest of stars!
Hail, hail! Thou sun of heroes!

Both. Hail, hail!

(Siegfried leads the horse down the mountain; Brünnhilde long gazes after him, in rapture. From below are heard the merry notes of Siegfried's horn.—The curtain falls.)

(The orchestra takes up the horn's theme, and develops it into a forcible movement.—Thereon the First Act begins at once.)

FIRST ACT.

(Hall of the Gibichungs by the Rhine: it is open at the back, which is occupied by the shore of the river; rocky heights surround the scene.)

FIRST SCENE.

(Gunther and Gudrune are seated on a dais; before it stands a table, at which sits Hagen.)

Gunther. Come tell me, Hagen, moody man!
Firm is my seat on the Rhine,
as fitteth the Gibichungs' fame?

Hagen. In thee a Gibich true I envy:
Queen Grimhild taught it me of old,
who both of us once bore.

Gunt. 'Tis mine to envy—envy thou not me!
Was mine the right of firstborn,
wisdom fell but to thee.
Half-brothers' strife ne'er ended better:
thy counsels alone I extol,
ask I how stands 't with my fame.

Hag. Then bad the counsels, bad the fame,
for higher goods I wot of,
the Gibichung ne'er yet has won.

Gunt. Hast thou held silence, thine's the blame.

Hag. In fairest summer-tide
I see now Gibich's stem,
thee, Gunther, un-bewifed,
thee, Gudrun, still unwed.
Gunt. Whom wouldst thou I should woo,
our fame full well to fit?
Hag. One woman lives—the crown of the world:
on mountain high her seat,
a fire burns round the hall:
but he who through the fire breaks,
durst Brünnhild's wooer be.
Gunt. My heart, would 't stand the test?
Hag. Still stouter than thine must it be.
Gunt. Tell me the fearless one's name.
Hag. Siegfried, the Wälsungen scion:
he is the hero of strength.
From Wotan sprang Wälse,
from him a twin-pair—
Siegmund and Siegelind:
the truest of Wälsungs begat they,
his father's blood-sister
gave him birth in the forest:
who there so manfully throve,
him wish I for Gudrune's mate.
Gudrune. What deed so glorious hath he done,
that highest of hero's he's praised?
Hag. On the Neidhaid the Nibelung's Hoard
was watched by a giant-got Worm;
Siegfried closed its ravenous maw,
slew it with conquering sword.
Such deed unheard-of
sounded the hero's high fame.
Gunt. Of the Niblungen-hoard have I heard;
it harbours the richest of wealth?
Hag. Who knew how it rightly to use,
o'er the world would he verily rule.
Gunt. And Siegfried hath wrested it?
Hag. Thralls are the Niblungs to him.

Gunt. And Brünnhild but he can e'er win?
Hag. No other could venture unscathed.
Gunther (rising petulantly).
Thou shew'st thine evil breed!
A thing beyond my reach
thou fain wouldst make me long for.
Hag. Were Siegfried to win her for thee,
were Brünnhild less thine own?
Gunther (striding impatiently to and fro).
And what could move the wilful man
the maid to woo for me?
Hag. Thy bidding soon would move him,
bound him Gudrune before.
Gud. Thou wicked mocking Hagen!
How could poor I bind Siegfried?
Is he the highest of heroes,
the earth's most winsome women
have long ere this been his!
Hag. Forget not the draught safeguarded,
and trust me, who it got:
what hero e'er thou long'st for,
it binds in love to thee.
Comes Siegfried hither,—
tastes of the spicéd drink,—
that ere thee he saw a woman,
or e'er a maid approached,—
'twill make him clean forget.—
Come say: how deem ye Hagen's word?
Gunther (who has returned to the table and, leaning on it, listened raptly).
All praise to Queen Grimhilde,
who us this brother gave!
Gud. Would I could see my Siegfried!
Gunt. How set about his quest?
Hag. Drives him afield the lust of deeds,
the world he'll find a narrow belt:
his hunt will surely bring him
to Gibich's strand by the Rhine.

Gunt. Glad welcome would I give him.

(Siegfried's horn is heard from the distance.—They listen.)

Gunt. From the Rhine sounds the horn.

Hagen (has gone to the shore, peers down the river, and shouts back).

In a skiff come hero and horse!
'Tis he who blithely blows the horn.—
The mighty stroke of a hand at ease
drives swift the skiff against the stream:
such toilless strength in ply of oar
is his alone who the Worm once slew.
Siegfried it is,—sure, no other!

Gunt. Is he hasting by?

Hagen (shouting toward the river through his hollowed hands).
Hoiho! Whither bound, my stalwart?

Siegfried's voice (from the river).
To Gibich's sturdy son.

Hag. To his hall I bid thee.
Hither! Lay to!—
Hail Siegfried, hero bold!

SECOND SCENE.

(Siegfried lays to.)

(Gunther has joined Hagen on the shore.—Gudrune catches sight of Siegfried from the dais, fastens her gaze on him in joyful wonder, and, as the men draw nearer to the hall, retires in visible confusion to her chamber through a door on the left.)

Siegfried (has landed his horse, and now leans placidly against it.)
Which is Gibich's son?

Gunt. Gunther, I—whom thou seek'st.

Sieg. Thy fame I've heard, far down the Rhine:
so fight with me—or be my friend!

Gunt. No fighting: welcome here!

Sieg. Where stall I my horse?
Hag. Mine be its care.

Sieg. Thou call'dst me Siegfried,—hast seen me before?

Hag. I knew thee but by thy strong arm.

Sieg. Deal well with Grane! Ne'er hast held
the bit of horse of nobler breed.

(Hagen leads the horse off behind the hall on the right, and soon returns.—Gunther advances into the hall with Siegfried.)

Gunther. Glad welcome, hero,
to my father's hall:
where'er thou stepp'st,
whate'er thou seest,—
thine own I bid thee hold it.
Thine is my birthright,
land and lieges,—
help, Wotan, this mine oath!—
myself I give as vassal.
Siegfried. Nor land nor lieges pledge I,
nor father's house and home:
his only heirloom,
venger's right—
already have I voided.
But weapons have I,
self-won gear—
help, Wotan, this mine oath!—
myself and them I bond thee.
Hagen (standing behind them).
Of the Nibelung's Hoard
the tale makes thee master?
Sieg. The treasure I wellnigh forgot,—
so low I rate its lordship!
In a cave I left it lying,
where once a Worm was warden.
Hag. And naught thou took'st of it?
Siegfried (pointing to a piece of mail that hangs from his belt).
This trinket, knowing not its virtue.
Hag. The Tarncap is it,
the Niblungen's cunningest work;
it serves, when covering thy head,
to give thee any shape thou choosest;
wouldst travel to the farthest spot,

it forthwith sets thee there.—
Of naught besides thou stripp'dst the Hoard?

Sieg. A ring.

Hag. And that thou'st kept?

Sieg. A lordly woman keeps it.

Hagen (aside). Brünnhild!

Gunt. Nay, Siegfried, we'll not barter.
Dross would I deem thy trinket,
gave I all my goods therefor:
unpaid I gladly serve thee.

(Hagen has moved to Gudrune's door, and now opens it. Gudrune comes forth; she bears a filled drinking-horn, and approaches Siegfried with it.)

Gud. Welcome, our guest, to Gibich's hall!
His daughter reaches thee the draught.

Siegfried (makes an obeisance, and grasps the horn; holding it musingly before him, he murmurs).

Forgot I all thou ever gav'st,
one lesson ne'er shall leave me:
the earliest draught to truest love,
Brünnhild, I drink to thee!

(He drinks and returns the horn to Gudrune, who, in an access of bashful confusion, casts down her eyes.)

Siegfried (gazing at her in emotion).
Why sink'st thou so thy glance?

(Gudrune, blushing, raises her eyes to him.)

Sieg. Gunther, how call'st thy sister?

Gunther. Gudrune.

Sieg. Good runes, i' faith,
her eye now redes me.

(He takes her gently by the hand.)

To thy brother I bade myself as man,—
the proud one then forbade me:
Wouldst thou, as he, prove haughty too,
bade I myself thy bondsman?

(Gudrune modestly inclines her head, and with a gesture implying that she is not worthy of him, she staggers from the hall.)

Siegfried (gazes after her, as if spellbound, attentively observed by Hagen and Gunther;—then, without turning round, he asks).

Hast thou, Gunther, a wife?

Gunt. Ne'er wooed I yet, and woman's charms
would find me loth to cherish:
on One have I set my mind
whom scarce myself can leap to.

Siegfried (turning sharply round to him).

And what shall be gainsaid thee,
stands but my strength by thy side?

Gunt. On mountain high her seat,
a fire burns round the hall:
but he who through the fire breaks,
durst Brünnhild's wooer be.

Sieg. Ne'er fear thou her fire;
I'll woo her for thee.
For thy man am I,
and thine is my might,
gain I Gudrune to wife.

Gunt. Gudrune gladly I give thee.

Sieg. Brünnhilde bring I thee.

Gunt. How wilt thou entrap her?

Sieg. Through the Tarnhelm's craft
I cross my look with thine.

Gunt. So pledge we oaths, and swear!

Sieg. Blood-brothership shall seal the oath.

(Hagen fills a drinking-horn with fresh wine. Siegfried and Gunther notch their arms with their swords, and hold them for a few moments above the drinking-horn.)

Siegfried and Gunther.

Wotan, hallow the draught,
troth-plight to drink to the friend!
All-ruler, ward thou the oath
binding two brothers in one!—
The bond that blooms from our blood,
ever broken—avenger be thou!—
Breaks it a brother,
tricking the trusty,

dread be thy wrath
wreaked on the traitor,
call down thy curse
the caitiff to track,
hurl him to Hellja's
bottomless gulf!
Wotan, hallow the draught!
All-ruler, ward thou the oath!

(They drink, one after the other, each his half; Hagen, who has stood aside during the oath, then breaks the horn; Siegfried and Gunther clasp hands.)

Siegfried (to Hagen).
Why took'st thou no share in the oath?
Hag. My blood would curdle the drink;
not blithe and noble as your own,
it halts too cold within my heart
and will not flush my cheeks:
so, far I bide from fiery bond.
Gunt. Leave the man to his mood.
Sieg. Forth on our way! There lies my skiff;
to Brünnhild's rock 'twill swiftly bring us;
one night on shore thou'lt wait for me,
the woman then I'll lead thee.
Gunt. No rest wilt thou before?
Sieg. To be back I'm afire. (Goes to the shore.)
Gunt. Thou, Hagen, guard the hall! (Follows Siegfried.)
Gudrune (appears at the door of her chamber).
Whither so haste they away?
Hag. Aboard, to woo Brünnhilde.
Gud. Siegfried?
Hag. See, how he burns
for wife to win thee quickly.

(With shield and spear he takes his seat before the hall. Siegfried and Gunther push off.)

Gud. Siegfried—mine! (Retires to her chamber in great agitation.)

Curtains are drawn across the stage, shutting in the scene.—After this has been changed, the curtains are drawn completely up.

THIRD SCENE.

The mountain-peak as in the Prologue.—Brünnhilde sits at the entrance of the rock-chamber, plunged in deep thought. From the right comes the song of the Walküren (Valkyries), gradually approaching from the distance. After their first call, Brünnhilde springs up, and listens attentively.

The Walküren.

Brünnhild! Brünnhild! Long-lost sister!—
Gone is the fire from thy rock-abode!
Say who hath routed it! Who thee awoke?

Brn. My greeting, whilom sisters!
Seek ye for her ye have lost?
Gone, of a truth, is the fire
since e'er he routed it who me awoke:
Siegfried, the hero unmatched.

Wlkn. Brünnhild! Brünnhild! Now art thou his wife.
Thy horse, no more wilt thou ride it,
never hie thee to rush of the fight.

Brn. So Wotan doomed the never-daunted
who shielded Siegfried's sire in strife
against the god's behest:
no peace there was, at Frikka's word,
since wedlock he broke, the truest son
to win from his own sister.

Wlkn. Brünnhild! Brünnhild! Long-lost sister!
who taught thee the ruler of warfare to flout?

Brn. The light-streaming Wälsungs he ever had taught me
to shelter in stress of all fight;
to Siegmund I would not be traitor:
beneath my own shield he was drawing his sword
on Hunding, his sister's wed master;
but on Wotan's spear the weapon broke,
which the god himself once gave him:—
he fell in the fight,—I was outlawed.

Wlkn. Brünnhild! Brünnhild!
Then wast thou thrust from the Wish-maidens' host,

to this rock wast bann'd, in slumber sunk,
foredoom'd to be wife to the man
who by the way thee should find and awake!

Brn. That the manfulest only should win me,
so meted me Wotan my wish,
that raging fire the rock should ring:
for Siegfried, I knew, alone would leap it.

The Walküren (drawing nearer and nearer, as the stage grows darker).

Brünnhild! Brünnhild! Long-lost sister!
Gav'st thou away thy godlike might?

Brn. To Siegfried, who gain'd me, I've lent it.

Wlkn. Gav'st thou away, too, thy holiest lore,
the runes that once Wotan had taught thee?

Brn. I taught them to Siegfried, whom love I.

Wlkn. Thy horse, that o'er clouds truly bore thee?

Brn. Now Siegfried leads it forth to fight.

The Walküren (still closer).

Brünnhild! Brünnhild! Long-lost sister!
Ev'ry craven now can bend thee,
to cowards an easy booty!—
O burnt but the fire anew round the fell,
from shame the fenceless bride to shelter!
Wotan! All-giver! Ward off the worst!

(Heavy thunder-clouds gather thickly in the sky, and sink to the ridge of the mountain.)

Brn. So stay, my sisters! Stay, ye dear ones!
How leaps my heart to see your strength!
O stay! O leave the lost one not!

The Walküren (quite near, while a blinding light breaks through the black clouds from the direction whence they come).

To the South we are hieing, hosts to set striving,
mettlesome warriors to mete out their lot,
for heroes to fight now, heroes when fallen
to Walhall to lead in the flush of their might!

(In shining armour and seated on white horses, the Walküren, eight in number, ride over the edge of the leaden cloud in the light, with din of storm.—At brink of the crag a wall of fire springs up.)

Brünnhilde (in solemn exaltation).

Wotan! Wotan!
Wrath-gracious God!
The lordliest hero to love,
thine anger hath taught me:
who fondly in Walhall
the mead-horn oft bore thee,
thou wilt not vow her to shame.
The hallowed fiery herald
gladly now grants me thy grace:
of strength and wisdom widow'd,
thy greeting still live I worth.
The fire burns round Brünnhild's fell!
Thank Wotan! Ruler of all!

(Siegfried's horn-call is heard from below: Brünnhilde listens,—her expression changes to one of utmost joy.)

Siegfried! Siegfried is nigh!
His greeting hither he sends!—
Fade out, ye feeble flames!
I stand in stronger guard!

(She joyfully rushes to the background.)

FOURTH SCENE.

Siegfried—wearing the Tarnhelm, which conceals half his face, leaving the eyes alone free—appears in form of Gunther, springing out of the flames on to a jutting boulder.—The fire at once burns lower, and soon fades out entirely.

Brünnhilde (shrinking back in alarm).

Betrayed! Betrayed! Who storms my rock?

(She flees to the front, and thence directs her gaze in speechless horror upon Siegfried.)

Siegfried (remaining on the stone in the background, and leaning upon his shield, regards her for awhile: then with disguised voice—deeper—he slowly and solemnly addresses her).

Art thou Brünnhild, the mettlesome maid
who scares all heroes far and wide

by the scorn in her heart?
Trembling thou fleest from me,
like the cowering dog
that feareth its master's chastising?
The goblin wile of wizard fire
to thee was gain indeed,
since it shielded the weakest of women.

Brünnhilde (muttering to herself).
The weakest woman!

Siegfried. Flared up thy wrath
but while the fire was flaming?
See, it dies down, and the weaponless woman
I conquer through her craven heart.

Brn. (trembling). Who is the man who dared a deed
for the mightiest only foredoomed?

Siegfried (still on the stone in the background).
Of heroes one among many
who harder toils have torn through
than here I've found to face.
Soon shalt thou pay me in full
for that our men thou'st scared by mouthing tales
of ruin to whoe'er would Brünnhild woo.
To all the world will I shew
how tame at home in my hall
a woman spins and weaves.

Brn. Who art thou?

Sieg. A better than he
whom for husband thou fitt'st.
A Gibichung am I,
and Gunther's called the man
on whom thou wait'st as wife.

Brünnhilde (falling into despair).
Wotan, thou grim and gruesome God!
Woe's me, I see what thou hadst willed:
to taunts and jeers thou huntest me hence!
(Recovering herself.)
Yet heard I a horn—Siegfried's horn?

Sieg. The merry hero mans the skiff

wherein thou follow'st me to-morrow:
his tunes he'd sooth be trying.

Brn. Siegfried?—Thou liest!

Sieg. He shewed me the way.

Brn. No!—Never!

Sieg. (stepping closer). Night is falling:
within thy bower
with me thou now must mate thee.

Brünnhilde (threateningly stretching forth the finger on which she wears Siegfried's ring).

Avaunt! This token fear thou!
To shame thou shalt not bow me
what time this ring's my shield.

Sieg. Husband's-right gives it to Gunther:
by the ring to him be wed!

Brünnhilde. Stand back, robber!
Dastardly thief,
dare never to draw nigh!
Stouter than steel
makes me the ring,
ne'er—robb'st it from me.

Sieg. Thus teachest me to tear it from thee.

(He closes with her: they wrestle. Brünnhilde breaks away and flees. Siegfried catches her,—they struggle afresh: he seizes her, and snatches the ring from her finger.)

Siegfried. Now art thou mine!
Brünnhilde, Gunther's bride,
grant me the grace of thy bower!

Brünnhilde (almost swooning).
What couldst thou ward thee, hapless woman?

(Siegfried drives her before him with a despotic gesture: trembling, she staggers into the cavern.)

Siegfried (drawing his sword).
Come, Balmung, guard thou well
my brother-plighted oath!

(He follows her.)

The curtain falls.

SECOND ACT.

Shore before the Hall of the Gibichungen : on the right the open forecourt of the Hall, on the left the bank of the Rhine, from which a rocky eminence ascends diagonally across the stage towards the right. —Night-time.

FIRST SCENE.

Hagen, his spear in his arm, his shield by his side, sits sleeping in front of the hall. Suddenly the moon casts a vivid light on him and his immediate neighbourhood : in it we see Alberich, the Nibelung, with his arm resting on Hagen's knee.

Alberich. Sleep'st thou, Hagen my son ?—
Thou sleep'st and hear'st me not,
the harbourer of sorrow ?

Hagen (softly and without moving, so that he still appears to sleep).
I hear thee, elf of evil ;
what com'st thou now to tell me ?

Alberich. Now must thou hear
what might thou hast—
art thou so strong and manly
as erst thy mother bore thee.

Hag. (as before). Tho' gave she strength and manhood,
no thanks to her I bear,
that to thy wiles she fell :
soon aged, wan and sere,
I hate the glad,
I have no glee.

Alb. Hagen my son, ne'er hate thou me,
for greatness give I to thy hand !
The ring for which to strive I taught thee,
know now what it enfolds !
From Death and black Night in Nibelheim's depths
once sprang the Nibelungen ;
cunning in smith-craft, ceaselessly shaping,
fret they the bowels of earth.

The Rhine-gold I reft from the waters' bed
welded therefrom a ring:
through spell of its all-compelling power
swayed I the busiest folk;
for lief of their lord I bade them labour;
mine own brother I held in bonds:
the Tarnhelm Mime needs must make me,
through it o'er my kingdom watch I kept.
The brimming Hoard I heaped so high
that the world ere long it should win me.
Then envy seized the Giant brood,
the fools were plagued with care;
to the upstart Gods they bade their help,
a burg did the dullards build them,
whence the Gods now rule in safe array:
yet the Hoard the Giants asked for their toil.—
Hear'st thou, Hagen my son?

Hagen. The Gods? . . .

Alb. With tricks and lying trapped they me,
in ransom I left them the Hoard;
the Ring alone I thought to save,
but of that they robbed me too:
then cursed I it, to farthest days
to bring but death to him who wore it.
For himself would Wotan fain ward it,
but the Giants defied him: to word of the Norns bent Wotan,
of his downfall warned.
Fruitless now were my pains,
by the Ring was I bann'd, as my brothers it bound;
unfree were we all thenceforward.
Restlessly striving, nothing we reach:
sank e'en the Giants' boast-breathing race
long since 'fore the glittering light of the Gods—
a sluggish Worm, whom as warder they bred,
yet held in fetters all our freedom:
the Ring! the Ring! the Ring!—
Sleep'st thou, Hagen my son?

Hag. But Siegfried now the Worm hath slain?
Alb. Mime the false one fared with the hero,
the Hoard through him to win him:
so wise a fool! For his trust in the Wälsung
his life he left behind him.
Offspring of Gods I trusted ne'er,
their blood is bred of treason:
thee, changeless one, begat I myself;
thou, Hagen, troth wilt cherish!
Yet, strong though thy thews,
the Worm I durst not let thee strike:
but Siegfried that could venture,—
so vengeance wreak thou on him!
Fool eke he!
Plaything to him is the Ring,
whose power he cannot fathom.
By craft and onslaught now wrest thou the Ring!
By craft and onslaught Gods robb'd it from me.
Hagen. The Ring thou shalt have.
Alberich. Swear'st it me?
Hag. First of the Niblungen, free shalt thou be!

(Hagen and Alberich are shrouded in deeper and deeper shadow. From over the Rhine the day begins to break.)

Alberich (as he gradually vanishes from sight, his voice becomes more and more inaudible).

Be true, Hagen my son!
Trusty hero, be true!
Be true!—True!

(He has completely disappeared. Hagen, who has never changed his attitude, remains staring fixedly towards the Rhine.—The sun rises, and is mirrored in the stream.)

SECOND SCENE.

Siegfried (suddenly appears from behind a bush, hard by the river: he is in his own form, saving that he still wears the Tarn-cap on his head; he takes it off, and hangs it to his belt).

Hoiho! Hagen, watch-weary man!
Seest thou who cometh?

Hagen (rising slowly).
Hei! Siegfried, swift-footed hero!
Whence speed'st thy way?
Sieg. From Brünnhild's crag:
there drew I first the breath
with which I called thee now:
so quick my feet have fared!
Slower there follows a pair,
aboard they wend their way.
Hag. Thou'st master'd Brünnhilde?
Sieg. Is Gudrun yet awake?
Hag. (shouts). Hoiho! Gudrun! Come forth!
Siegfried is back, the bustling warrior.
Siegfried (turning toward the hall).
You both I'll tell how Brünnhild I bound.

(Gudrune meets them in the forecourt.)

Welcome give me, Gibich's lass!
A harbinger of good am I.
Gud. May Freija greet thee,
in honour of all maidens!
Sieg. Freija, the winsome, that art thou:
Frikka waits for our calling,
Wotan's hallowed wife,
may she e'er shield our wedding!
Gud. Then Brünnhild follows my brother?
Sieg. Light was the woman to woo.
Gud. Singed him the fire no whit?
Sieg. Ne'er would it have harmed him;
yet for him I went through it,
since thee I fain would win.
Gud. And thee it left scatheless?
Sieg. It glided from me, and was gone.
Gud. Held Brünnhild thee for Gunther?
Sieg. I looked him to a hair:
the tarnhelm lent me that,
as Hagen taught before.
Hag. I gave thee good advice.

Gud. Thou forcedst the haughty maid?
Sieg. She fell—to Gunther's might.
Gud. And mated she was to thee?
Sieg. Brünnhild obeyed her husband
throughout a bridal night.
Gud. As her husband passedst thou?
Sieg. Siegfried abode by Gudrun.
Gud. Yet by side of him was Brünnhild?
Siegfried (pointing to his sword).
Between East and West—the North:
so far—was Brünnhild nigh.
Gud. How gav'st her to Gunther thereafter?
Sieg. In the morning-mist she followed
my footsteps down the mountain;
by the shore—in a trice
changed Gunther with me;
in virtue of this trinket
a wish brought me swiftly here.
A steady breeze now drives
the plighted up the Rhine:
so ready make their welcome!
Gud. Siegfried, man of all might,
fear takes me at thy tale!
Hagen (peering down the Rhine from the rising ground at the back).
I see a sail in the offing.
Sieg. So yield the herald thanks!
Gud. Come give her bounteous greeting,
that blithely and glad she may bide!
Thou, Hagen, call the clansmen
to wassail at Gibich's court;
the women I myself will call,
to weddings they willingly come.

(To Siegfried, as she passes to the hall.)

Wilt thou not rest, sir rogue?
Sieg. In helping thee is my rest.

(He follows her.—They pass into the hall.)

THIRD SCENE.

Hagen (on the rising ground, facing toward the inner country, blows a great stear-horn with all his might).

Hoiho! Hoiho! Hoiho!
Ye men of Gibich, gird you up!
Through all the hillside, arms to hand!
Weapons, weapons! Goodly weapons!
Sturdy weapons! Sharp for strife!
Want! Want calls loud! Want! Hurry! Hurry!
Hoiho! Hoiho! Hoiho!

(He blows again: war-horns answer him from different quarters of the countryside. From the hills and valley men armed in hot haste rush on.)

The Clansmen (now singly, now together).

Who winds the horn? What calls to war?
We're coming to aid, we're coming with weapons!
With stout good weapons, with sword and spear!
Hoiho! Hoiho! Hagen! Hagen!
What want doth call? What foe is nigh?
Who fights with us? Is Gunther in fray?

Hagen (from the rising ground).

Ready you well, and rest you not!
Gunther waits for your cheering,
a wife the chief hath wooed.

Men. Threatens him harm? Harries the foe?
Hag. A vixenish wife he brings him home.
Men. Him follows the venging kith of her kinsmen?
Hag. Only comes he, with her alone.
Men. So he 'th bested the want, beaten the foe?
Hag. The Worm-killer warded the want,
Siegfried, the hero, wrought him his weal.
Men. What's left for us, then, to help him?
Hag. Sturdy stears shall ye slaughter,
on Wotan's stone let flow their blood!
Men. What then, Hagen? What bidd'st thou do next?
Hag. A boar shall ye fell, and offer to Froh,
a strong-horn'd buck let bleed for Donner;

sheep will ye slay then for Frikka,
    that good she grant the wedding!

The Clansmen (in more and more boisterous glee).
Slaughter'd the beasts, what bidd'st thou do then?

Hag. The drink-horn take from women fair,
with mead and wine brimm'd to the full.

Men. Drain'd to the dregs, what next shall we drive?

Hag. Swill ye so long till your speech runs aslant;
    all to the glory of Gods,
    that happy wedlock they give!

The Clansmen (breaking into roars of laughter).
High days and hale must laugh on the Rhine,
when the grim-grudge Hagen so gleeful can be!
The blackthorn its stab has lost,
as wedding-bidder, look you! it stands.

Hagen (who has maintained his seriousness throughout).
    Now leave your laughter,
    mettlesome men!
Welcome Gunther's bride!
Brünnhild nears with him there.

(He descends.)

True to your lady, help her in trust:
suffers she wrong—swift be to wreak it!

FOURTH SCENE.

Gunther has arrived, in the boat, with Brünnhilde. Some of the men leap into the water, and drag the skiff to shore; while Gunther lands with Brünnhilde the Clansmen clash their arms and shout. Hagen holds aloof, in the background.

The Clansmen. Hail! Hail! Hail! Hail!
    Be welcome! Be welcome!
    Hail thee, Gunther!
    Hail to thy bride!

Gunther (leading Brünnhilde by the hand).
Brünnhild, the woman unmatch'd,
hither I bring to the Rhine;
a nobler wife was never won!

Hath Gibich's proud race
erst been blest by the Gods,
to height of fame it reacheth to-day.

The Clansmen (beating their weapons).
Hail! Hail thee, Gunther!
Happiest Gibichung!

(Brünnhilde, pale and with eyes cast to the ground, follows Gunther, who conducts her by the hand towards the Hall, whence Siegfried and Gudrune are advancing at the head of a train of women.)

Gunther (halting with Brünnhilde before the Hall).
My greeting, faithful hero!
My greeting, sister fair!
I see thee willingly by side
of him who makes thee wife.
Two blissful pairs all here see blooming:
Brünnhilde and Gunther,
Gudrune and Siegfried!

(Brünnhilde starts, raises her eyes, and beholds Siegfried: she drops Gunther's hand, takes a hasty step toward Siegfried, falls back in horror, and mutely stares at him.—All are astounded.)

The Clansmen and Women. What ails her?

Siegfried (quietly advancing a few steps toward Brünnhilde).
What trouble cause I thee, Brünnhild?

Brünnhilde (scarcely mistress of herself).
Siegfried . . . here! . . . Gudrune?

Sieg. Gunther's winsome sister,
wed to me, as thou to Gunther.

Brn. Wed? . . . Gunther? . . . Thou liest!—
The light fadeth out . . .

(She is about to fall: Siegfried, standing nearest, supports her.)

Brn. (murmuring, clasped in Siegfried's arms).
Siegfried . . . knows me not?

Sieg. Gunther, thy wife is ailing.

(Gunther approaches them.)

Good woman, wake!—Lo here thy husband!

(As Siegfried points to Gunther with his finger, Brünnhilde sees on it the Ring.)

Brünnhilde (in passionate horror).

Ha! The ring—on hand of his!—
He— Siegfried—!

The Clansmen and Women. What is't?

Hagen (leaving the background, and mingling with the men).

Mark well now what the woman saith!

Brünnhilde (recovering herself, and violently repressing her emotion).

A ring I saw upon thy hand,—
not thine it is, 'twas torn from me—
(pointing to Gunther) by *this* man:—
How cam'st thou by the ring from him?

Siegfried (intently regarding the Ring on his hand).

The ring I never had—from him.

Brn. (to Gunther). Won'st thou from me the ring
whereby to thee I'm wed,
uphold thou now thy right,
claim back from him the pledge!

Gunther (in great confusion).

The ring?—I gave to no one.—
Yet—know'st thou it right well?

Brn. Where hast thou hid the ring
which thou from me hadst wrested?

(Gunther holds silence, in utmost embarrassment.)

Brünnhilde (in an outburst of wrath).

Ha!—He it was,
who tore the ring from me,—
Siegfried, the treacherous robber!

Siegfried (who has been lost in meditation on the Ring).

From no woman came I by it,
no woman was't
from whom I won it.
Full well I know the wage o' the fight
that on Neidhaid once I fought
when the fearsome Worm I slew.

Hagen (stepping between them).

Brünnhild, woman bold,
Know'st thou aright the ring?

Was't it to Gunther thou gav'st,
then is it *his*,—
and Siegfried hath won it by trick,
which the treacherous here shall atone!

Brünnhilde (crying aloud, in agony of grief).
Betray'd! Betray'd!
Most shamefully betray'd!
Treason! Treason,
as never yet was venged!

Gudrune, the Clansmen and Women.
Treason! Vengeance! On whom?

Brn. Holy Gods! Ye heavenly rulers!
Plotted ye this in your plan?
Set ye me suff'rings, as never were borne?
Shaped for me shame, as none in its brunt?
Teach me then vengeance, as never was vow'd!
Kindle me anger, as none e'er hath slaked!
Shew ye to Brünnhild how her heart she may break—
on his whole undoing, who her betray'd!

Gunt. Brünnhild, betrothed! Bridle thy wrath!

Brn. Stand back, betrayer, thyself betrayed!—
Know ye then all: not to—*him*,
to *that* man there am I wed.

Clansmen and Women. Siegfried? Gudrun's husband?

Brn. My lief and love he forced from me.

Sieg. Heedest thou so thy maiden shame?
The tongue that would steal it,
must *I* with lying tax?
Hear an I broke my word!
Blood-brothership
had I and Gunther sworn:
Balmung, my doughty sword,
I drew for the oath's true sake;
its keen edge kept me sunder'd
from this unhappy wife?

Brn. Thou trickster, see how thou liest,
how ill thou call'st thy sword in proof!

Its edge know I well, but know too the sheath
wherein its ease upon the wall
took Balmung, the trusty friend,
when his lover its lord did woo.

The Clansmen (closing up, in lively indignation).
What? Broke he his bond?
Harmed he Gunther's honour?

Gunt. Dishonour'd were I, branded with shame,
answer'dst thou not so burning a tale!

Gud. Faithless, Siegfried, faithless couldst be?
O swear that false is all she says!

Clansmen. Clear thyself, art in the right;
silence her charges, swear thou the oath!

Sieg. To clear the charge, to swear the oath,—
which of you dareth his weapon to lend?

Hag. The point of my spear be the wager;
Wotan guide it aright!

(The Clansmen form a ring round Siegfried; Hagen extends to him the point of his spear; Siegfried lays two fingers of his right hand thereon.)

Sieg. Wotan! Wotan! Wotan!
Help and enhallow my oath!
Help through the weight of the weapon,
help through the spear's sharp spit!
Where keenness can cut me,
keen may it cut;
where death can strike me,
strike through it death;
hath that woman said true,
broke I my brother's high trust!

Brünnhilde (storms into the circle, dashes Siegfried's hand from the spear, and seizes its point with her own).
Hear thou me, hallowed Goddess!
Keeper of holiest oaths!
Help through the weight of the weapon,
help through the spear's sharp spit!
Hallow its weight
that him it lay waste,

guide thou its keenness
that him it may cleave :
for like as all oaths he hath broken,
himself hath this man now forsworn !

The Clansmen (in great commotion).
Help, Donner ! Sound out thy thunder,
to silence the throat of this shame !

Sieg. Gunther, ward thou thy wife
from lying thine honour away !—
Grant her rest awhile,
the wild rock-woman,
to lay the storm of madness
some wizard's trick
by magic's evil spell
against us all hath roused.—
Ye clansmen, come with me,
leave the woman to scold !
Up, haste to make ready
goodly stears for the altar :
follow to Grove of the Gods,
for Froh the boar to fasten.—

(To the women.)

Ye too, give help for the feast,
follow Gudrune, ye women !

(He passes into the hall with Gudrune, followed by the men and women.)

FIFTH SCENE.

Brünnhilde, Gunther and Hagen remain behind.—Gunther, covering his face in deep shame and terrible dejection, has seated himself at the side.

Brünnhilde (standing in the foreground, and staring fixedly before her).
What devil's wile lies hidden here ?
What wizard's spell hath made me its sport ?
Where now is my wisdom, against this tangle,
where are my runes, against this riddle ?

Ah, sorrow, sorrow! Woe, ah, woe!
All my lore to him I lent!
In might of his the maid he holds,
in bonds of his he binds the booty
that, sorrowing in grip of shame,
shouting to others he gives!—
Who beareth me now the sword
wherewith the bonds I may sever?

Hagen (stepping close up to her).
Have trust in me, howe'er betrayed!
Who wronged thee, on him will I wreak it.

Brünnhilde. On whom?

Hagen. On Siegfried, who betrayed thee.

Brn. On Siegfried?—Thou?—

(Laughs bitterly.)

One lightest glance of his glistening eye,
that e'en through the lie of the mask
its lightning shed on me,—
thy manfulest mood would crush to ground!

Hag. Well know I Siegfried's conquering might,
how hard 'twere to meet him in combat:
yet thou wilt teach me crafty toils
in which to trap the warrior?

Brn. O thankless! Shameful reward!
Not an art to me was known,
that helped not to hallow his body!
Unwitting, all my spells were spent
in warding him from hap of wound.

Hag. Can ne'er a weapon harm him?

Brn. In fair fight none!—Yet:—
dealt'st thou a blow from behind.
Never, I knew, would he flee from the foe,
ne'er turn on him a craven back;
so spared I it from the blessing.

Hag. And there my spear shall thrust.

(Quickly turning to Gunther.)

Up, Gunther! Lordly Gibichung!

Here stands thy stalwart wife,—
why crouchest there in grief?
Gunt. (rising). O shame! O stain! O woe is me,
the wretchedest of wretches!
Hag. All stained thy name, deny I that?
Brn. O coward man, false-dealing mate!
Behind the hero hiddest thou,
fame of his deed to safely earn thee.
Deep must have sunk the kingly race
that cravens such could father!
Gunt. (beside himself). Betrayer I—and betrayed!
A trickster I—and yet tricked!
All strewn is my strength,
a-bursting my breast!
Help, Hagen! Help to mine honour!
Help, for thy mother
who me, too, bore!
Hag. Here helps no head, here helpeth no hand:
thy help is Siegfried's death!
Gunther. Siegfried's—death!
Hagen. But that can shrive thy shame.
Gunther (staring wildly before him).
Bloodbrothership swore each to each!
Hag. The bond's foul breach naught heals save blood.
Gunt. Broke he the bond?
Hag. When thee he betrayed.
Gunt. Betrayed he me?
Brn. Thee betrayed he,—
and me, ye all betrayed me!
Claimed I my right, all the blood in the world
never would wipe out your guilt!
Yet the death of one I'll take for all:
Siegfried—falleth
in payment for him and you.
Hagen (aside to Gunther).
Let him fall for thy weal!
Unbounded might is thine,

winn'st thou from him the ring
which but death can make him yield.

Gunther. Brünnhilde's ring?

Hagen. The Ring of the Nibelungen.

Gunther. But so were Siegfried ended!

Hagen. Us all behoves his death.

Gunt. Yet Gudrun, ah! to whom I gave him:
struck we her husband to ground,
how stood we guiltless 'fore her?

Brünnhilde (in an outburst of passion).
What booted my wisdom? What warned me my runes?
In helpless mis'ry clear I see:
Gudrune's hight the wizard
from me my husband witch'd.
Grief take her!

Hag. (to Gunther). Though his death must grieve her,
our deed from her we hide.
To merry hunt we'll hie to-morrow:
the hero brusheth ahead,—
a boar hath laid him low.

Gunther and Brünnhilde.

So shall it be! Siegfried falleth!
Cleanse he the shame, on me he put!
Troth-plighted oaths hath he broken,
his body's blood the guilt atone!

Hag. So shall it be! Siegfried falleth!
Foul let him die, the hero of day!
Mine is the Hoard of the mighty,—
I wrench from him the heir's own Ring!

SIXTH SCENE.

Siegfried and Gunther appear in the hall. Siegfried wears on his head a chaplet of oak-leaves, Gudrune a wreath of many-hued flowers.

Sieg. Why bidest, Gunther, here,
leav'st thou the feast's glad bidding
to me, thy guest, alone?

Host-right I've wielded for thee:
from meadows thine to holy ground
stout droves and herds I've driven;
your women bade I weave fresh wreaths,
to deck the walls right bravely:
 and now, to give the blessing,
 only for thee we wait.

Gunther (recovering his self-possession).
 To whom were better meet
 the blessing's speech, than thee?
 Yet, an thou wilt, I yield
 right gladly to thy bidding.
So long thou livest, know I well
 that I to thee belong.

Siegfried (beneath his breath, to Gunther).
Thou'st tamed the vixen?

Gunther. Tongue-tied.
 Sieg. It irks me
 that so ill I duped her;
 the tarnhelm, truly, but half
 my shape can have hidden.
But women's chiding soon is o'er;
that for thee I won her, she'll thank me yet.

Gunt. Trust me, of thanks—she'll not be chary.

Gudrune (who has drawn near to Brünnhilde, shyly, but kindly).
 Come, sweet my sister,
 with us be soft thy home!
Suffer'dst through Siegfried ever a harm,
 I'll see that he smarts for it,
pays he not love to the full.

Brn. (coldly and calmly). He pays full soon!

(She motions Gudrune to Siegfried with her hand.—From the court the wedding-chant is heard.)

Men. All-father! Ruler of Gods!
All-knower! Hallowed head!
Wotan! Wotan! Hither now wend!

Women. All-soother! Mightiest mother!

All-giver! Fostering Goddess!
Frikka! Frikka! Holiest wife!
The Men and Women together.
Send ye the heavenly watch-keeping host
hither to hark to our hallowing song!
During the chant :—
Sieg. Follow the singers! Thou going first.
Gunther (making way for Siegfried).
Thee, Siegfried, follow I:
to thine own hall thou leadest Gunther,
to thee he owes his lot.

(Siegfried and Gudrune, Gunther and Brünnhilde, pass into the hall. Hagen, gazing after them, remains behind alone.)

The curtain falls.

THIRD ACT.

A gully of wild woods and rocks by the Rhine, which flows in the background at foot of a steep descent.

FIRST SCENE.

Three Water-maidens rise from the Rhine, and swim in a circle during the following song.

The Three Water-Nixies.
Sun-lady sends her light on land,
but night lies in the waters:
once were they bright,
when blest and whole
dear Father's gold in them glanced.
Rhine-gold,
streaming gold,
how brightly shon'st thou once,
glad star of the waters!

Sun-lady, send to us the hero
our gold to give us again!

Gives he it back,
thy beaming eye
never again will we grudge thee.
Rhine-gold,
streaming gold,
how blithe were then thy ray,
free star of the waters!

(Siegfried's horn is heard.)

First Nixy. I hear his horn.
Second. The hero nears.
Third. Let us take counsel!

(They dive swiftly under.—Siegfried appears on the rising ground, in full armour.)

Sieg. An elf hath trick'd my steps,
that so the sleuth I've lost!
Hé, rascal! In what lair
hidd'st thou the prey so swift?

The Water-nixies (rising again). Siegfried!
Third. On whom wouldst wreak thy wrath?
Second. Who's the elf that twits thy sport?
First. Was it a Nixy that did it?
The Three. Say it, Siegfried! Tell it us!
Siegfried (smiling as he watches them).
Was't ye who witch'd to you
the ragged-coated fellow
who cross'd my path?
An he's your lover,
my laughing maids,
I gladly let him go.

(The women laugh aloud.)

First. Siegfried, what gav'st thou us,
if we the game would gain thee?
Sieg. Still am I bootyless,
so bid what I should bring.
Second Nixy. A little ringlet
lightens thy finger.—
The Three together. That give us!

Sieg. Once a Giant-worm
I slew to wrest the ring:
for a wretched bruin's paws
now should I barter the prize?
First Nixy. Art thou so mean?
Second. So niggard of pelf?
Third. Hands-open to women shouldst be!
Sieg. On you did I squander my goods,
'twould bring me small peace with my wife.
First Nixy. Eh! is she shrew?
Second. She strikes, maybe?
Third. He feels her hand already!

(They laugh.)

Sieg. Come, laugh as ye may,
in grief I'll yet leave you:
for, grudge ye soe'er the ring,
to you nixies never I'll give it.
First Nixy. So fair!
Second. So strong!
Third. So good to see!
The Three. What pity, he's so stingy!

(They laugh, and dive under.)

Siegfried (coming farther down the bank).
Why bear I, tho', a niggard's blame?
Why thus be shamed and flouted?—
Came they once more to the water's rim,
the ring, they well might have it.—
Hé, hé! Ye merry water-minxes!
Come quick, I'll give you the ring.

The Three Water-maidens (rising to the surface again, with serious, solemn mien).
Nay, hero, keep and ward it well,
till thou the ill shalt hear
that with the ring thou reapest.
Full glad then wilt feel,
if from its curse we free thee.

Siegfried (calmly replacing the ring).
So sing whate'er ye know!
The Three Water-maidens (now singly, now together).
Siegfried! Siegfried!
Evil tidings we sing.
To thine own worst woe thou wardest the ring!
From the Rhine's sweet gold its hoop was welded:
he who craftily shaped it, and shamefully lost,
his curse is upon it, thro' farthest days
to beckon death to him who bears it.
As the Worm thou felledst, so fall'st thou too,
and that this day—so tell we thee—
barter'st the ring not to us,
in deepest Rhine to be buried:
its waves alone the curse can slake!
Sieg. Ye huckstering women, let me be!
Cared I scarce for your coaxings,
trick me your threat'nings can not.
Nixies. Siegfried! Siegfried! We tell thee but truth!
Flee thou! Flee from the curse!
By waking Norns 'twas woven
in the Ur-law's endless coil.
Sieg. From your curse I never will flee,
nor flinch at the Norn's weird weavings!
On what my heart is set,
Ur-law is that to me,—
and what my mind beholds,
ever is that mine end.
Tell them who you hither sent:
for cowards cutteth no sword,
its edge but the strong ever serveth,—
no one from him may e'er snatch it!
Nixies. Woe! Siegfried!
Where Gods are mourning, thou canst mock?
Sieg. Dawneth the day upon that heath
where heroes in care are forgath'ring,—
leaps forth that fight whose end the Norns
themselves have no wit of foretelling:

to mine own mood
I turn the outcome!
And shall I myself be unmanning,
with the ring cast loose my manhood?
Held it less than my finger's worth,
its hoop I'd not give forth:
for life itself—lo!—
thus do I fling it away!

(With the last words he has raised a clod of earth, and thrown it backwards over his head.)

Nixies. Come, sisters! Back from the booby!
So strong and wise he weens himself,
so bounden and blind he is.
Oaths he swore, and heeds them not:
runes, too, knows he, and redes them not:
one highest good to him was given,
that he's cast it off he knows not;
but the Ring, that dooms him to death,
the Ring but, will he not part with!
Farewell, Siegfried!
A lordly wife
this day will her heirship enter:
she'll lend us better ear.
To her! To her! To her!

(They swim off, singing.)

Siegfried (laughing, as he gazes after them).
In water, as on land
I've learnt now women's way:
who bends not to their fawning,
they threaten him with frowns;
whom black looks cannot scare,
they treat to scolding tongue.
And yet, held I not Gudrun's troth,
one fairest of these sisters
full sweetly had I tamed.

(Hunting-horns call from the height, ever nearer: Siegfried lustily answers with his horn.)

SECOND SCENE.

Gunther, Hagen and the Clansmen descend from the height during what follows:

Hagen (still on the height.) Hoiho!
Siegfried. Hoiho!
Clansmen. Hoiho!
Hag. At last we've found, then, whither thou'st flown?
Sieg. Down to me! Here 'tis fresh and cool!
Hag. Here rest we now, and ready the meal!
Lay out the booty, unbuckle the wine-bags!

(The game is laid in a heap; drinking-horns and wine-skins are brought out. Then all make camp.)

Hag. Who spoiled for us our sport,
now wonders shall ye look on
that Siegfried hath won in hunt!
Sieg. (laughing). Ill stands it with my meal!
From others' booty must I beg it.
Hag. Thou empty-handed?
Sieg. For wood-game fared I forth,
but water-fowl only I found:
had I a mind for such hunting,
three water-birds full wild
had I brought to you bound:
for there on the river they sang me
that slain would I be e'en to-day.

(Gunther shudders, and looks stealthily at Hagen.)

Hag. That were a sorry hunt,
where the bootyless himself
fell prey to lurking booty!
Sieg. I'm thirsty!

(He has seated himself between Hagen and Gunther; filled drinking-horns are handed to them.)

Hag. I've heard it said, friend Siegfried,
the speech of wild birds' singing
thou understood'st:—was true the tale?

Sieg. Since long I ne'er have given them heed.
(Drinks, and hands his horn to Gunther.)
Drink, Gunther, drink!
Thy brother brings it thee.
Gunther (thoughtfully and moodily looking into the horn.)
Thou'st mix'd it sad and faint:
thy blood alone's therein!
Sieg. (laughing). So mix it well with thine!
(He pours from Gunther's horn into his own, till it runs over.)
See! mixt it bubbles over,
to all the Gods an off'ring meet!
Gunt. (sighing). Thou over-mirthful man!
Siegfried (aside to Hagen).
Has Brünnhild unmann'd him?
Hag. If he but knew her moods
as thou the wild birds' song!
Sieg. Since women have been my singers,
the birds I've clean forgot.
Hag. Yet once thou knew'st their meaning?
Sieg. Hei, Gunther! gloomiest man!
Thank'st thou my lay, I'll sing to thee marvels
of mine own youthful days.
Gunt. I'll hear them gladly.
Hag. So, noble warrior, sing!

(All draw closer round Siegfried, who alone sits up, while the rest recline on the ground.)

Sieg. Mime was call'd a manikin old,
sharp was his work, neat at the stithy;
Sieglind, my own sweet mother,
he helped in the wild waste forest:
me, whom dying there she bore,
to strength he brought me up
with all a dwarf's best craft.
Of my father's death he told me then,
gave me the pieces of the sword
which in last fierce fight he had broken:
as master, Mime taught me his smith-work,

the sword's rent sherds I melted down,
and Balmung made I anew.
Balmung hammer'd I hard and fast
till no fault in the blade we could find:
with its edge I clove through an anvil.
Then fit and meet thought old Mime the sword,
that with it a Worm I should slay
who on evil heath had his lair:
"They'd laugh aloud—said I—the sons of Hunding,
did they hear such a tale,
that Siegfried's weapon with Worms had fought
or ever it venged his father!"

Hag. Right well was it said.

Clansmen. Health to thee, Siegfried!

(They drink.)

Sieg. Then Balmung hailed, my hard good sword,
the Hundings all sank before it.
I follow'd Mime, the Worm to fell,
and slit up the hulk of its belly:—
now hearken to wonders!
With the Worm's hot blood afire were my fingers,
I set them to cool at my mouth:
scarce dripp'd a little the drops on my tongue,
when lo! what the birds were singing
I understood forthright;
they sat on the boughs and they sang me:
"Hei, Siegfried is lord of the Niblungen-hoard!
No trust in Mime, the false, let him put!
He wish'd him its wealth but to win him,
and lurks now with wiles by the way;
for the life of Siegfried he's thirsting.
O trust not Siegfried in Mime!"

Hag. And well they warned thee.

Clansmen. Thou paid'st it on Mime?

Sieg. Short work I made of the treacherous dwarf:
his head to Balmung was forfeit.

The words I heard of the woodbirds' again,
as blithely they sang while I hearken'd :—
"Hei, Siegfried has slain him the wicked old dwarf;
the hoard in the hollow O would that he found!
Would he the tarnhelm but win him,
'twould help him to happiest deeds;
but might he the ring's might unriddle,
'twould make him the lord of the world!"

Hag. Ring and tarnhelm took'st with thee home.

Men. The wood-birds thou heardst yet again, eh?

Hagen (who has pressed the juice of a herb into his drinking-horn).
Drink first, hero, take my horn!
I've spiced thee a goodly draught;
to the past shall it help to awake thee,
and far-away things 'twill bring back.

Siegfried (after drinking).
The words of the woodbirds I heard yet again,
as blithely they sang while I hearken'd :—
"Hei, Siegfried is lord of the helm and the ring,
now would we might shew him the lordliest wife!
On lofty fell is her sleep,
dread fire engirdles her hall:
strode *he* through the flame, awoke he the bride,
Brünnhilde then were his own!"

(Gunther listens with growing amazement.)

Hag. And follow'dst thou the woodbirds' call?

Sieg. Swifter than saying, sped I aloft
till the fiery fell I had climbed;
through the burning I strode, and found for pay
sweetly a woman asleep
in glittering weapons' bright garb:
by side of her rested a horse,
in slumber sound as hers.
Her helm I loos'd from the heavenly maid,
my kiss was bold her to wake:

O with what blessing claspt then my neck
bountiful Brünnhilde's arm!

Gunther. What hear I?

(Two ravens rise from a bush, circle above Siegfried, and fly away.)

Hag. And redest thou too these ravens' croak?

(Siegfried rises hastily, and, turning his back on Hagen, gazes after the ravens.)

Hag. They haste to Wotan thee to herald!

(He plunges his spear into Siegfried's back; Gunther clutches at his arm—too late.)

Gunther and the Clansmen.
Hagen, what doest thou?

(Siegfried swings his shield on high, with both hands, to fell Hagen to the ground: his strength fails him, and he falls on the shield with a crash.)

Hagen (pointing to the fallen man).
Treason veng'd I on him.

(He moves quietly aside, and mounts alone the hill, where he slowly passes from sight.—Long silence, as of deepest consternation.—Gunther sorrowfully bends down by Siegfried's side; the Clansmen stand round the dying man in pity.—Twilight had already begun at the appearing of the ravens.)

Siegfried (once more flashing open his eyes, in solemn tones).
Brünnhild! Brünnhild!
Thou shining child of Wotan!
Bright-beaming through the night,
the hero I see thee draw near:
with holy earnest smile
thou saddlest thy horse,
that dew-dripping
cleaveth the clouds.
Hither the war-swayer!
Here is a warrior to choose!
Thrice happy me, whom for husband thou chos'st,
to Walhall lead me the way,—
that to honour of all heroes

All-father's mead I may drink,
which thou, wish-pledging maid,
fondly to friendship there reachest!
Brünnhild! Brünnhild! Thy welcome!

He dies. The Clansmen place the body on the shield, and bear it slowly and solemnly over the rocky height. Gunther follows first. The moon breaks through the clouds, and lights the train of mourners as it reaches the height.—Then mists arise from the Rhine, and gradually fill the whole of the stage.—So soon as the mists have dispersed again, we see—

THIRD SCENE.

—the Hall of the Gibichungen with the river-bank, as in the first act. —Night. Moonbeams are reflected from the Rhine. Gudrune steps from her chamber into the hall.

Gudrune. Was that his horn?

(Listens.)

Nay! Not yet hies he home.—
Evil dreams have haunted my sleep!—
Wild was the neigh of his horse,—
laughter of Brünnhilde woke me at last.
—Who was the woman
I Rhine-wards saw her footsteps turn?
I've fear of Brünnhild;—is she within?

(She listens at a door on the right, then gently calls.)

Brünnhild!—Brünnhild!—art awake?—

(She timidly opens the door, and peers in.)

Empty her room!—So she it was,
to the Rhine I saw go forth?—

(Shudders, and listens toward the distance.)

Heard I a horn?—No, all is hushed.—
Would that Siegfried soon came home!

She takes a few steps towards her chamber: hearing Hagen's voice, she pauses and remains motionless for awhile in terror.)

Hagen's voice (from without, gradually coming nearer).
Hoiho! Hoiho! Awake! Awake!
Lights there! Lights there! Torches burning!

Booty we bring from the hunt!
Hoiho! Hoiho!

(The light of torches is seen, brighter and brighter, on the right.)

Hagen (entering the hall).

Up, Gudrune! Now greet thy Siegfried!
The man of might, he cometh home!

(Men and women, assembling in great confusion with tapers and torches, escort the train of those returning with Siegfried's body, among whom is Gunther.)

Gudrune (in utmost alarm).

What has happ'd, Hagen? I heard not his horn!

Hag. The hero wan ne'er winds it more,—
ne'er storms he to hunt, to strife no more,
nor woos he for fairest of women!

Gudrune (with growing horror).

What bring they there?

Hag. A savage boar's rent booty:
Siegfried, thine own husband dead!

(Gudrune utters a loud scream and falls over the body, which has been set down in the middle of the hall.—General consternation and sorrow.)

Gunther (endeavouring to raise the swooning woman).

Gudrune, dearest sister!
Lift up thine eyes, thy voice let me hear!

Gudrune (returning to consciousness).

Siegfried!—Siegfried—they've slain him!

(Passionately thrusts Gunther away.)

Back, troth-breaking brother!
Thou murd'rer of my mated!
O help there! Help there! Woe! Woe!
Siegfried have they slain, my Siegfried!

Gunt. Lay not the blame on me!
Thy blame be laid on Hagen!
There stands the boar accursed
that rent thy husband's body!

Hag. And thou, art wroth thereat?

Gunt. Grief and evil take thee ever!

Hagen (advancing with terrible defiance).
Know then! 'twas I who slew him,
I, Hagen, dealt him his death:
to my spear-head was he forfeit,
whereon he swore false oath.
Holy avenger's-right
by the deed have I gained me:
so here I claim this ring.

Gunt. Stand back! What falls to me
thou never shalt distrain!

Hag. Ye clansmen, claim me my right!

Gunt. Robbest thou Gudrun's heirloom,
shame-bereft son of Elf?

Hagen (drawing his sword).
The Elf's own heirloom thus claimeth—his son!

(He thrusts at Gunther, who parries: they fight. The Clansmen rush between them. Gunther falls down dead, from a blow of Hagen's.)

Hag. Here the Ring!

(He snatches at Siegfried's hand, which rises with a threatening gesture. All are horrified. Gudrune cries aloud.)

The Men and Women. Woe! Woe!

FOURTH SCENE.

From the background Brünnhilde solemnly advances to the front:

Brünnhilde (still in the background).
Cease your upbraidings, your idle rage!
Here standeth his wife, whom ye all have betrayed.
(Tranquilly advancing.)
Children hear I whining
that mother has spilt their milk:
no cry have I heard yet worthy
the hero ye bewail.

Gud. Brünnhilde, thou evil one,
'twas thou who brought us this ill!
Thou who arousedst the men against him,
woe, that e'er thou set'st foot in this house!

Brn. Poor wretch, hold thy peace!
Ne'er wast thou his wedded wife.
His true wife am I, to whom he swore troth
ere Siegfried e'er thee beheld.

Gudrune (in an agony of despair).
Accursed Hagen! Woe! Ah woe!
that thou the draught badest give him,
which a husband from her robb'd.
O sorrow, grief! Now I know, alas!
that Brünnhild was the treasure
the drink made him forget!

(Shamefacedly she moves away from Siegfried, and, racked by grief, bends over Gunther's body; in which position she remains to the end. —Long silence.—Hagen, leaning on spear and shield, stands in brooding defiance at the extreme end of the opposite side to where Gudrune lies on Gunther's body. Brünnhilde stands by Siegfried's corpse, in the middle.)

Brünnhilde. O he was pure!—
Truer than his,
never oaths were warded:
in troth to his friend, from his own wedded wife
he sunder'd himself by his sword.—
Have thanks, then, Hagen!
As thee I bade,
where thee I shewed,
hast thou for Wotan
marked him out,—
to whom with him I fare now.—
So bring me pine-logs, pile them in heaps
by the waters' brink of the Rhine:
high leap up the fire, the lordly limbs
of earth's highest hero to lap!
Lead hither his horse,
the warrior together we'll follow:
for now in the hero's holiest honour
my body myself to the Gods do I give.
Fulfil ye Brünnhild's last of wishes!

(The men erect a huge funeral pyre on the shore: women deck it with hangings, herbs and flowers.)

Brn. My heritage I take for mine own.

(She draws the Ring from Siegfried's finger, puts it on, and gazes at it in deep thought.)

Thou overbearing hero,
how thou heldest me banned!
Of all my wisdom must I go lacking,
for all my knowledge to thee had I lent:
what from me thou took'st, thou usedst not,—
to thy mettlesome mood thou trustedst alone!
But now thou'rt gone, hast given it free,
to me my lore cometh back,
the runes of the Ring unravel.
The Norn's old saying know I now too,
their meaning can unriddle:
the boldest of men's most mighty of deeds,
through my knowledge it gaineth its blessing.—
Ye Nibelungen, give ear to my words!
your thraldom now I end:
who the Ring once forged, you busy ones bound,—
not he shall its lord be again,—
but free be he, as ye!
For this bright gold I give to you,
wise sisters of the waters deep!
The flames that devour me
cleanse the Ring from its curse:
its hoop shall ye loose, and keep without stain
the shimmering Gold of the Rhine,
to our hurt from you once reft!—
One only shall rule:
All-father! Thou in thy glory!
Have joy of the freest of heroes!
Siegfried bear I to thee:
give him greeting right glad,
the warrant of might everlasting!

(The pyre is already in flames; the horse is led to Brünnhilde: she seizes it by the bridle, kisses it, and whispers into its ear:)

Joy to thee, Grane: soon are we free!

At her command the men bear Siegfried's body in solemn procession to the burning stack: Brünnhilde follows first, leading the horse by the rein; behind the body she then mounts the pyre with it:

The Women (standing aside while the men raise Siegfried's body and bear it in procession).

Who is the hero, now ye raise;
where bear ye him solemnly hence?

The Men. Siegfried, the hero, now we raise,
bear to the fire from hence.

Women. Fell he in fight? Died he in house?
Goes he to Hellja's home?

Men. He that him slew, could conquer him ne'er;
to Walhall wendeth the slain.

Women. Who followeth him, lest hard on his heels
the door of Walhall should fall?

Men. Him follows his wife in the hallowing flame,
him follows his westering horse.

The Men and Women together (after the latter have joined the train).

Wotan! Wotan! Ruler of Gods!
Wotan, bless thou the flames!
Burn hero and bride,
burn eke the true horse:
that wound-healed and pure
All-father's free helpmates
in joy may greet Walhall,
made one for a bliss without end!

(The flames have met above the bodies, entirely concealing them from view. In the foreground, now completely dark, Alberich appears behind Hagen.)

Alberich (pointing to the back).

My venger, Hagen, my son!
Rescue, rescue the Ring!

Hagen turns quickly round, and, preparing to plunge into the fire, casts spear and shield away. Suddenly a blinding light strikes forth from the embers: on the fringe of a leaden cloud (as if the smoke from the dying fire) the light ascends; in it appears Brünnhilde on horseback, helmeted and in the dazzling armour of a Valkyrie, leading Siegfried by the hand through the sky. At like time, and while the cloud is rising, the waters of the Rhine flow over to the Hall: the three Water-maidens, lit by brilliant moonshine, swim away with the Ring and Tarnhelm :—Hagen plunges after them, as though demented, to tear from them the treasure: they seize him and drag him down into the deep. Alberich sinks, with gestures of woe.

The curtain falls.

The End.

DISCARDED.

Under this heading I have gathered several articles from Richard Wagner's earlier years, 1834 to 1842, and a few miscellaneous contributions to newspapers, chiefly of the Dresden period. None of these writings are included in the Gesammelte Schriften, *but some of them have been reprinted in the original German since the master's death. Number I., the article "On German Opera," is held to be the earliest contribution ever made by Wagner to the press; it was written just before the drafting of the poem for* Das Liebesverbot, *i.e. when the young composer had barely come of age, and appeared in Laube's* Zeitung für die elegante Welt *of June 10, 1834. The article has been reprinted in Kürschner's* Richard Wagner-Jahrbuch, *1886. Number II., "Pasticcio," originally appeared in Schumann's* Neue Zeitschrift für Musik *of November 6 and 10, 1834, and was reprinted in the* Bayreuther Blätter *of November 1884. Number III., "Bellini," was written during Richard Wagner's engagement as conductor at Riga in Russia, and appeared, unsigned, in the local* Zuschauer *of December 7 (19), 1837; it, also, was reprinted in the* Bayr. Bl., *of December 1885. These constitute all the prose-works, hitherto discovered, anterior to Wagner's first Paris period. Not to overwhelm the reader with two many dates at once, I reserve the bibliography of the remaining articles for later footnotes.*

TRANSLATOR'S NOTE.

I.

ON GERMAN OPERA.

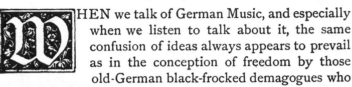

WHEN we talk of German Music, and especially when we listen to talk about it, the same confusion of ideas always appears to prevail as in the conception of freedom by those old-German black-frocked demagogues who curled their noses at the results of modern reforms abroad with just as much contempt as our Teutomaniac music-savants now shrug their shoulders. By all means, we have a field of music which belongs to us by right,—and that is Instrumental-music;—but a German Opera we have not, and for the selfsame reason that we own no national Drama. We are too intellectual and much too learned, to create warm human figures. *Mozart* could do it; but it was the beauty of Italian Song, that he breathed into his human beings. Since the time when we began to despise that beauty again, we have departed more and more from the path which Mozart struck for the weal of our dramatic music. *Weber* never understood the management of Song, and *Spohr* wellnigh as little. But Song, after all, is the organ whereby a man may musically express himself; and so long as it is not fully developed, he is wanting in true speech. In this respect the Italians have an immeasurable advantage over us; vocal beauty with them is a second nature, and their creations are just as sensuously warm as poor, for the rest, in individual import. Certainly, in the last decad or two the Italians have played as many pranks with this second nature-speech as the Germans with their learning,—and yet, I shall never forget the impression lately made on me by a Bellinian opera, after I had grown heartily sick of the eternally allegorising orchestral bustle, and at last a simple noble Song shewed forth again.*

French music acquired its tendency from *Gluck*, who, albeit a German, has had far less influence on ourselves than on the Frenchmen. He felt and saw what the Italians lacked, namely an individuality in their figures and characters, which they sacrificed to vocal beauty. He created Dramatic Music, and bequeathed it to the French as their possession. They have pursued its cultivation, and from *Grétry* to *Auber* dramatic truth has remained a first principle of the Frenchmen.

The talents of the good German opera-composers of modern times, of *Weber* and *Spohr*, are unequal to the dramatic province. Weber's talent was purely lyrical, Spohr's elegiac; and where those bounds were overstepped, art and the expenditure of abnormal means had to supplement what their nature failed in. Thus Weber's best work is in any case his "Freischütz," since he here could move in his appointed sphere; the mystic weirdness of Romanticism, and that charm of the Folk-melody, belong peculiarly to the domain of Lyrics. But turn to his Euryanthe! What splitting of hairs in the declamation, what fussy use of this or that instrument to emphasise a single word! Instead of throwing off a whole emotion with one bold freehand stroke, he minces the impression into little details and detailed littlenesses. How hard it comes to him, to give life to his Ensembles; how he drags the second Finale! Here an instrument, there a voice, would fain say something downright clever, and none at last knows what it says. And since the audience is bound to admit in the end that it hasn't understood a note of it, people have to find their consolation in dubbing it astoundingly *learned*, and therefore paying it a great respect.—O this wretched erudition,—the source of every German ill!

* In March 1834 the young man had heard Frau Schröder-Devrient as "Romeo" in Bellini's *Montecchi e Capuleti* at Leipzig. It should be remarked that the term "Song" (*Gesang*) is used by Richard Wagner throughout to signify the whole manner both of writing for, and of using the singing-voice.—Tr.

There was a time in Germany when folk knew Music from no other side than Erudition,—it was the age of *Sebastian Bach.* But it then was the form wherein one looked at things in general, and in his deeply-pondered fugues Bach told a tale as vigorous as *Beethoven* now tells us in the freest symphony. The difference was this: those people knew no other forms, and the composers of that time were truly learned. To-day both sides have changed. The forms have become freer, kindlier, we have learnt to live,—and our composers no longer are learned: the ridiculous part of it, however, is that they want to pose as learned. In the genuine scholar one never marks his learning. Mozart, to whom the hardest feat in counterpoint had become a second nature, simply gained thereby his giant self-dependence;—who thinks of his learning, when listening to his Figaro? But the difference, as said, is this: Mozart *was* learned, whilst nowadays men want to *seem* so. There can be nothing wronger-headed than this craze. Every hearer enjoys a clear, melodious thought,—the more seizable the whole to him, the more will he be seized by it;—the composer knows this himself,—he sees by what he makes an effect, and what obtains applause;—in fact it comes much easier to him, for he has only to let himself go; but no! he is plagued by the German devil, and must shew the people his *learning* too! He hasn't learnt quite so much, however, as to bring anything really learned to light; so that nothing comes of it but turgid bombast. But if it is ridiculous of the composer to clothe himself in this nimbus of scholarship, it is equally absurd for the public to give itself the air of understanding and liking it; it ends in people being ashamed of their fondness for a merry French opera, and avowing with Germanomaniac embarrassment that it would be all the better for a little learning.

This is an evil which, however ingrained in the character of our nation, must needs be rooted out; in fact it will annul itself, as it is nothing but a self-deception. Not that I wish French or Italian music to oust our own;—that would be a fresh evil to be on our guard against—but we ought to recognise the *true* in both, and keep ourselves from all self-satisfied hypocrisy. We should clear ourselves a breathing-space in the rubble that threatens to choke us, rid our necks of a good load of affected counterpoint, hug no visions of forbidden fifths and superfluous ninths, and become men at last. Only by a lighter and freer touch can we hope to shake off an incubus that has held our music by the throat, and especially our operatic music, for many a year. For why has no German opera-composer come to the front since so long? Because none knew how to gain the voice [? ear] of the people,—that is to say, because none has seized true warm Life as it is.

For is it not plainly to misconstrue the present age, to go on writing Oratorios when no one believes any longer in either their contents or their forms? Who believes in the mendacious stiffness of a Schneiderian fugue, and simply because it was composed *to-day* by *Friedrich Schneider*? [1786-1853.] What with Bach and Händel seems worshipful to us in virtue of its truth, necessarily must sound ridiculous with Fr. Schneider of our day; for, to repeat it, no one *believes* him, since it cannot be his own conviction. We must take the era by the ears, and honestly try to cultivate its modern forms; and he will be master, who neither writes Italian, nor French—nor even German.

II.

PASTICCIO

by

CANTO SPIANATO.*

THE old Italian mode of Song was based on so-called sostenuto singing, demanding a *formare*, *fermare* and *finire* of the vocal tone. It certainly allowed much elasticity, but every passage must conform to the character of the human voice itself. The modern method, on the contrary, only secondarily consists of melodious phrases, whose cut has been so uniformly made upon one last, that we recognise it instantly, for all its trimmings. This odious mania for copying the instruments shews a misunderstanding of both Song and human Voice. Erewhile men deemed the voice the noblest of all instruments and, rightly to enjoy its charm, accompanied it as discreetly as possible; now they bury it beneath a load of senseless instrumenting, and, without regard to the dramatic situation, they make it gurgle arabesques that tell us nothing. These gurglings, sure enough, are often mastered, but they rebel against the throat as obstinately as a hard nut against a worn-out tooth.

That the Singing-voice, like every other instrument, needs schooling, and indeed a very careful schooling, in which the *production* of the voice is dealt with quite apart from the *rendering* (taste and expression), no connoisseur

* *Pasticcio* means a "pasty," an "olla podrida"; it is a term applied to a curious form of entertainment, somewhat common in earlier days, consisting of arias, duets etc., selected from different operas and served up almost at random. *Canto spianato*, the pseudonym adopted by the author, is the Italian for "smooth singing."—Tr.

will deny; but where, in all our German fatherland, are there training-schools for higher vocal culture?—True, we have Singakademieen, Gesangvereine, Seminaries, and may boldly assert that Chorus-singing in Germany and Switzerland has reached a technical perfection to be sought in vain in Italy itself, the land of song; but the higher vocal art, of solo-singing, is in manifest decline, and many a mile might we journey before we could assemble a couple of dozen good singers really worthy of the name, singers who should possess not only a *well-trained organ*, but also a *good delivery*, *correct declamation*,, *pure enunciation*, *sympathetic expression and thorough knowledge of music.* Merely gauge the majority of our celebrated singers male and female by *this* standard!—Certain highly important endowments must be set to the credit of certain individuals, but nowadays we could but rarely and exceptionally convene a whole such as not only our fancy might dream of, and our higher aspirations wish for, but also is humanly realisable, and in former times has actually been realised. To-day one hardly ever hears a truly beautiful and finished *trillo*; very rarely a perfect *mordente*; very seldom a well-rounded *coloratura*, a genuine unaffected, soul-stirring *portamento*, a complete equalisation of the vocal register and perfect maintenance of intonation throughout the varying nuances of increase and diminution in the volume of sound. Most of our singers, so soon as they attempt the noble art of *portamento*, fall out of tune; and the public, accustomed to imperfect execution, overlooks the defects of the singer if he only is an able actor and versed in stage-routine.

> "The tricky roulade, be it neat or a smear,
> Will draw sure applause, as the onion the tear."
>
> C. M. VON WEBER.*

---

* "Auf die Roulade, gut oder übel,
Folgt das Geklatsch wie die Thrän' auf die Zwiebel."—
Wagner would appear to have quoted the couplet from memory, for he has substituted "*die Roulade*" for "*den Laufer*" (runs, or scales), and "*Geklatsch*" for "*Gepatsch*" (clapping, or slapping) — unless the latter be a misprint in the *N.Z.f.M.*, repeated in the *Bayr. Bl.* of Nov. 1884. The original lines appeared in a half humorous, half serious sketch contained in

The German singer gladly sinks himself in the character he has to represent. That deserves all praise, but has its own grave dangers. If the singer lets himself be carried away by his rôle; if he does not stand absolute master *over* the whole of his portrayal: then all, as a rule, is lost. He forgets himself, he no longer sings, but screams and moans. Then Nature none too seldom fleeces Art, and the hearer has the unpleasant surprise of suddenly finding himself in the gutter. If in addition to this, each performer tries to set *his* part in the best and most striking light, without regard for his companions, it is all over with the harmony of play and song. Hence it comes, that our ordinary stage-performances in Germany pitch down from the height of rapt emotion to the depths of fussy dulness, and lack the outward stimulus of sustained artistic charm.

Many German singers regard it, in a certain sense, as a point of honour to be willing to sing *anything*, no matter if it suit their voice or not. The Italian does not hesitate to say right out that such and such a part he cannot sing, since it is ungrateful to his voice through height or depth, its trick of ornament, or other qualities. In this he often goes too far, and as good as demands that all his parts shall be written expressly for him: but the German, whether from free will or force of circumstances, too often and too readily accommodates himself to every rôle, thereby ruining both it and his voice as well. The singer should never attempt a part for which he is not qualified

(a) *physically*—in respect of vocal compass, timbre, and power of lung;
(b) *technically*—in respect of throat-dexterity; and
(c) *psychically*—in respect of expression.

certain fragmentary chapters of a "A Tone-artist's Life" posthumously published in Weber's *Hintergelassene Schriften* (Dresden 1828) and edited by C. G. T. Winkler, the "Councillor Winkler" referred to in Wagner's *Letters to Uhlig*. In the same collection of Weber's 'remains' occurs the following epigram upon "Bravura-singeress" Tembila: "Man muss es gesteh'n, dass ihr Trillern gelingt, Nur Schade, dass sie vor Singen nicht singt."—"One must freely admit that her trills are the thing; Yet with all her fine singing, 'tis sad she can't sing."—Tr.

German dramaturgists say: "The actor should accommodate himself to the rôle, not the rôle itself to the actor." The maxim—as it stands—may be true; but unreservedly applied to the stage-singer, it is downright false: for the human voice is no lifeless instrument, like the pianoforte, and our German vocal composers, alas! too often are very sorry lords of Song.—Every sterling Instrumental composer must have studied the character of the various instruments, before he can produce true instrumental effects. Let a composer write for any instrument in the orchestra a passage against its nature; let him assign it notes the player can but bring out badly, or which do not lie in its register,—his condemnation is pronounced at once, and rightly. "The man," so the verdict goes, "is a musical bungler; he presumes to compose, and knows nothing of instrumentation! These are pianoforte, not clarinet passages; that cantilena is in the compass of the violin, but not of the violoncello." In short, let the composition breathe never so much life and spirit, it is thrown aside; for the man has not learnt his business—"He writes things that nobody could execute!" Hand on your heart, ye song-composers of our latter days, have ye zealously studied the peculiarities of the human voice? Know ye what it is, to write singably? I will answer:—Ye behold the mote that is in your brother's eye, but consider not the beam that is in your own eye; therefore shall ye be doubly judged.

Most truly does C. M. v. Weber say: The singer's individuality is the actual unconscious colorist of every rôle. The possessor of an agile and flexible throat, and he of a volume of tone, will render one and the same rôle quite differently. The first will be several degrees more animated than the second, and yet the composer may be satisfied with both, insofar as each according to his measure has rightly grasped and reproduced the gradations of passion prescribed.

It will always remain the hardest of tasks, so to combine the vocal and instrumental parts of a rhythmic composition that they shall melt into each other, and the last not only carry and relieve the first, but also help its utterance of passion; for Song and Instrument stand opposed. Breath-taking and articulation of the words enjoin on Song a certain undulation in the bar, not unlike the uniform swell of the waves. The Instrument, especially the stringed instrument, divides the time into sharp-cut sections, like the strokes of a pendulum. Truth of expression demands the blending of these opposite peculiarities. The beat, the Tempo, must never resemble a mill-clack in its tyrannical slowing or speeding, but to the piece of music it must be what the pulse-beat is to the life of man. Yet most of our modern vocal composers in Germany appear to regard the human voice as a mere portion of the instrumental mass, and misconceive the distinctive properties of Song. The instruments should form a guard of honour to the voice: with us they have become the singer's catch-polls, gagging him and casting him into chains at his first sign of free expression of feeling.

Mozart has irrefutably proved that, with the most complex, ingenious, and even massive orchestration, one still may leave the singer in full exercise of his rights; nowadays the human voice is degraded to an instrument. What has been gained?—Nothing!—The efforts of the human voice, even that of a Sontag, are outdone by instrumental virtuosi; a whole choir of bravura singers would never be able to bring out a thousandth of the tone-figures which have sprung up in our instrumental music since the time of *Bach*; and with this expansion of the art of instrumenting the inventiveness of our tone-artists has shot heaven-high above the bounds of Song.—The genuine art of Song depends on a Cantabile in keeping with the text and a Bravura in keeping with the voice.

But since we fell into a depreciation of true Italian vocal beauty, we have departed more and more from the path which Mozart struck for the weal of our dramatic music. With the revival of the, in many respects, classical music of the period of Bach, much too little attention is paid to a really singable cantabile. All the masterworks of Sebastian Bach are as rich in invention as possible within the form of Fugue and Double Counterpoint in general. His inexhaustible creative-force ever drove him on to introduce into each of his products the highest and richest of specific tonal figures, forms, and combinations. But with this superabundance of purely musical, or rather, instrumental contents, the word must needs be often thrust into its place beneath the note by force; the human voice, as a special organ of tone, was not at all considered by him; its peculiar office he never sufficiently appraised: and as a vocal composer of Cantabile he is nothing less than classical, however much the blind adorers of this master may cry out "Fie!"

Our worthy opera-composers must take a course of lessons in the good Italian cantabile style, guarding themselves against its modern outgrowths, and, with their superior artistic faculty, turn out good work in a style as good. Then will Vocal art bear fruit anew; then a man will some-day come, who in this good style shall re-establish on the stage the shattered unity of Poetry and Song.

Among us there is an archipatriarchal sect which refuses the name of beauty to any but quite simple singing, and utterly condemns all art of ornament. Let these judges turn back from their wretched one-sidedness, their taking of the choice of *means* as sole object for consideration, praise or blame, often blinding them to the *effect* itself! Art should be free. No school, no sect, must arrogate the title of the only bliss-purveyor. The simple, smooth and metric song has its great value—provided its setter is really a good vocal composer: only, it is not the sole true path of salvation, and the goal—the expression and communication of feeling—may be reached on other roads as well. The solo-singer ought to be an *artist* of song; as such, he may also give vent to his feelings in an enhanced and ornate art-form. Is that passion less true, forsooth, which takes the air with a volley of words, than that which breathes itself in few? Is not now this, now that, included in the individuality of this or that subject? Should not a speech in Parliament be different in form, to boot, from a sermon to a village parish? May not a sumptuous mould of periods, a flowery, decorative diction, a complex and ingenious scheme of verse, a rare but effective rhythm, be conditioned by æsthetic necessity?—We in nowise are opening the door to those meaningless flourishes by which unthinking singers too often, alas! betray their poverty of proper feeling, either to display their nimbleness of throat, or to mask their lack of portamento; but the nobler art of ornament has not yet reached with us its actual bloom; in our modern operatic singing we have merely the stereotyped *volutes of song*, which our singers and composers slavishly copy from the Italians, and wedge in everywhere without taste or psychological necessity.

The Public is at sea with Art, and the Artists have lost touch with the People. Why is it, that no German opera-composer has come to the front of late?—Because none has known how to gain the voice of the Folk,—in other words, *because none has seized true warm Life as it is.* The essence of dramatic art does not consist in the specific subject or point of view, but in this: that the inner kernel of all human life and action, the Idea, be grasped and brought to show.* By this standard alone should dramatic

* It is somewhat remarkable to find the author thus early propounding the Platonic "Idea" as a basis of Æsthetics, and in fact of Life itself. As may be seen upon turning to Vol. VII. p. 134, the thought recurs to him in 1841, with

works be judged, their special points of view and subjects being simply regarded as special varieties of this Idea. Criticism makes a radically false demand on Art, when it requires the art of the Beautiful to do nothing else than idealise. For without all Ideality, so-called, Dramatico-musical art can take many a form. If the librettist has the true poetic spirit, in him there lies the universe of human moulds and forces, his figures have an organic core of life; let him unroll the heavenly, or the earthly chart of human characters, we shall always find them lifelike, even though we never may have met their like in actual life. But our modern Romantic manikins are nothing but lay-figures. Away with them all—give us *passion*! Only in what is human, does man feel interest; only the humanly-feelable, can the dramatic singer represent. You have been often enough told, but refuse to believe it, that *one* thing alone is needful for Opera—namely *Poesy*!—Words and tones are simply its expression. And yet the most of our operas are a mere string of musical numbers without all psychologic union, whilst our singers ye have degraded into musical-boxes set to a series of tunes, dragged on to the stage, and started by the wave of the conductor's baton. The public no longer believes the opera-singer, since it knows that he is only singing it a thing no heart of man can feel. Mark the age, ye composers, and diligently seek to cultivate new forms; for he will be master, who writes neither Italian nor French—nor even German. But would ye warm, and purify, and train yourselves by models; would ye make shapes instinct with musical life: then take the masterly declamation and dramatic power of *Gluck* and combine it with *Mozart's* contrasted melody, his art of orchestration and ensemble; and ye will produce dramatic works to satisfy the strictest criticism.

special reference to Music. Therefore we are perfectly justified in claiming for Wagner an independent insight into one of Schopenhauer's main principles fully twenty years before he made acquaintance with that philosopher's system.—Tr.

III.

BELLINI († 1835):

A WORD IN SEASON.

BELLINI'S music, i.e. Bellini's music for the voice, has latterly made such a stir and kindled such enthusiasm, even in highly-learned Germany, that the phenomenon itself perhaps is worth a closer scrutiny. That *Bellinian* Song enraptures Italy and France, is natural enough, for in Italy and France men hear with their ears,—whence our phrases such as "ear-tickling" (presumably in contrast to the "eye-ache" caused us by the reading of so many a score of our newer German operas);—but that even the German music-scholar should have taken the spectacles from his fagged-out eyes, and given himself for once to reckless delight in a lovely song, this opens us a deeper glimpse into the inner chamber of his heart,—and there we spy an ardent longing for a full and deep-drawn breath, to ease his being at one stroke, and throw off all the fumes of prejudice and pedantry which so long have forced him to be a German music-scholar; to become a Man instead at last, glad, free, and gifted with every glorious organ for perceiving beauty, no matter the form in which it shews itself.

How little we are really convinced by our pack of rules and prejudices! How often must it have happened that, after being transported by a French or Italian opera at the theatre, upon coming out we have scouted our emotion with a pitying jest, and, arrived safe home again, have read ourselves a lecture on the danger of giving way to transports. Let us drop for once the jest, let us spare ourselves for once the sermon, and ponder what it was that so enchanted us; we then shall find, especially with *Bellini*, that it was the limpid Melody, the simple, noble, beauteous Song. To confess this and believe in it, is surely not a sin; 'twere no sin, perchance, if before we fell asleep we breathed a prayer that Heaven would one day give German composers such melodies and such a mode of handling Song.

Song, Song, and a third time Song, ye Germans! For Song is once for all the speech wherein Man should musically express himself; and if this language is not made and kept as self-dependent as any other cultivated Speech, then nobody will understand you. The rest of the matter, what is bad in Bellini, any of your village schoolmasters could better; we admit it. To make merry over these defects, is quite beside the question: had Bellini taken lessons from a German village-schoolmaster, presumably he would have learnt to do better; but that he perhaps would have unlearnt his Song into the bargain, is certainly to be very much feared.

Let us therefore leave to this lucky Bellini the cut of his pieces, habitual with all the Italians, his crescendos, tutti and cadenzas that regularly succeed the theme, and all those other mannerisms which so disturb our spleen; they are the stable forms than which the Italians know no other, and by no means so dreadful in many respects. If we would only consider the boundless disorder, the jumble of forms, periods and modulations, of many a modern German opera-composer, distracting our enjoyment of the single beauties strewn between, we often might heartily wish this frayed-out tangle put in order by that stable Italian form. As a matter of fact the instantaneous apprehension of a whole dramatic passion is made far easier, when with all its allied feelings and emotions that passion is brought by one firm stroke into *one* clear and taking melody, than when it is patched with a hundred tiny commentaries, with this and that harmonic nuance, the interjection of first one instrument and then another, till at last it is doctored out of sight.

How much the Italians are helped by their form and manner, especially with certain operatic subjects,—whatever that form's onesidedness and tawdriness in degeneration,—of this Bellini affords a proof in his *Norma*, beyond dispute his most successful composition. Here, where the poem itself soars up to the tragic height of the ancient Greeks, this form, pronouncedly ennobled by Bellini, does but exalt the solemn, grandiose character of the whole; all the passions which his Song so notably transfigures, thereby obtain a majestic background, on which they hover not in vaguest outlines, but shape themselves to one vast and lucid picture, involuntarily recalling the creations of Gluck and Spontini.

Accepted with this free, untroubled self-abandonment, *Bellini's* operas have found applause in Italy, in France and Germany; why should they not find the like in Lithuania? *

O.

* For his benefit at the Riga theatre (Dec. 1837) the author had chosen the production of *Norma*; the above article was intended as its avant-courière. —Tr.

IV.

PARISIAN AMUSEMENTS.*

SINCE March the Paris winter is at end. The softest winds, the warmest sunbeams, have come before their time, and routed the monstrous muffs and fur pelisses of the fair clothes-world of Paris, turning the Boulevard des Italiens, the garden of the Tuileries and the Champs Elysées into battlefields thronged by the gay-hued legions which Paris knows so well to muster on the advent of fine weather. More valiantly than ever, spring again the giant fountains of the Place de la Concorde, silently and sadly imitated by the brand-new waterspouts beside the spacious causeway of the Elysian fields; more furiously than ever rages Polichinel in his box, and has even gone the length of building himself a fine new theatre, into which a polished dialogue and noble manners have been imported, while it bears in haughty lettering the title: "*Théâtre de Guignac.*" Nevertheless, you must by no means take it that the real Parisian winter is at end. Let not those rays, those breezes tempt you to exorcise the reign of great, almighty Winter. For this Winter is the Paris summer; 'tis he who brings the genuine flowers, the lights and perfumes,—'tis he who brings to the Parisian ear that soft

* The article "*Pariser Amüsements*" and its companion, "*Pariser Fatalitäten für Deutschen*" (No. V.), were contributed by Wagner, under the pseudonym of "W. Freudenfeuer," to Lewald's magazine *Europa*, where they appeared in the second and third quarters of 1841. The strange company they were then to share—coloured fashion-plates of ladies in gigantic crinolines and furbelows, &c.—is foreshadowed by many a sentence. The original German of the pair of articles has been reprinted in the *Bayreuther Taschen-Kalender* for the years 1892 and 1893.—Tr.

sweet murmur which ye outer mortals, ye other dwellers on this earth, associate with brook or thicket,—'tis he who bids sing the merry lark, the passionate nightingale, and God knows what other feathered songsters; for I tell you again—he is the summer of Paris.

To make acquaintance with this summer, you of course must go into the salons of the upper world, to the Italiens, the Grand Opéra, or at least the concert-room of M. Herz; —on the streets it might happen that you still would find the poor a-freezing, freezing just as with yourselves—quite the same as with yourselves. There, however, you may gaze on the loveliest blooms in the raven locks of beauty, deftly gummed by the skilfulest fingers of great Paul de Kock's most able pupils. There your senses will swoon amid the most voluptuous odours that ever floated from the stall of the perfumer. There may you warm and kindle at the rays that beat upon you from the all-too-conscious eyes of countless planets of the drawing-room. There you will find the wondrous swish and rustle of your trees and bushes outvied by the far more mystic whisperings of the costliest satins and the choicest ribbons that ever left the looms of Lille or Lyon. There shall you hear the lightsome larks, pathetic nightingales, and a thousand other songbirds in their highest, most divine perfection; for there shall you hear—ah! I melt away!—the most godlike singers by profession and the most highborn amateurs by grace of God.

To shorten or protract this summer—look you!—lies not in our Creator's power. Here the wise decrees for storks and cranes no longer hold; here Nature has concluded other treaties, and nor Pope, nor Emperor, nor e'er so Holy an Alliance, can tear them up. Only when the last stork of this summer has departed to its second home—in other words, when the last Italian has left for London,—does a drear late-autumn break upon us: then a derelict half-fledged crane will here and there display its antics; then a mystic rustling of the golden foliage of that venerable oak, which men once planted in the hall of the Conservatoire, will draw to it a faithful band of the initiate from time to time,—but those aforesaid blooms and perfumes fade from sight and scent, and sleep until the well-loved storks return. Everyone flees the city, relinquishing its scorching pavements to the "winter of Parisian discontent." Those left behind may trump up revolutions, depose the peaceful Guizot, lift fretful little Thiers upon the shield of war, and try a thousand other ways of whiling the Parisian winter:—the high and mighty world of silks and satins, flowers and fragrance, will not come back until the earliest nightingale decoys it, the earliest lark trills its *air varié*; for I would have you know that this lofty world is most romantic, and cannot live without its larks and nightingales.

You see how they behave in godless France! The little man of Marengo wiped out their unseemly Republican Calendar; nevertheless, and in spite of the vigilant eye of the Alliance, they gradually have managed so to twist about their seasons that they turn Winter to summer, Autumn to spring.—When living in Russia, I was scarcely so bewildered by the old style of dating, as I now am by this hopeless Parisian arrangement; so that I still am not quite sure if I ought to speak of the pleasures of Summer, or of Winter-pastimes, in drawing you a hasty sketch of what the last few months have brought before my eyes and ears.

To come to facts, how am I to keep faith with our ancient, honourable code, when I tell you of those saucy ladies I saw walking on the Boulevards in the month of February with naked arms and neck laid bare? Everything has its limits. Beggars we are used to see go bare, even in winter;—but dainty girls with feathered hats, and gold galoon on their silken dresses?—It's a little too much, and one gets a bit puzzled in February, with the thermometer eight degrees below freezing!—True, it was Carnival time;—still, I could not reconcile the stoic sacrifice of these young ladies with the scant and beggarly rejoicings, here and there, upon the streets This time the huge ox that was led round as *Bœuf gras* appeared to have swallowed all the scarlet bodices and beauty-patches which last year spread a glow of life through all the Boulevards. Moreover the weather was raw and forbidding, and everyone preferred to see the *Descente de la Courtille* * in the Théâtre des Variétés to making merry in the open.

What on earth do the Parisians want with a set Carnival? Have they not carnival and fun enough the whole year round? What are their thirty theatres for? For what are their singers, ministers, composers, peers, virtuosi and deputies?—I should have thought that all these folk exist for nothing but their amusement? Maybe Louis Philippe and the editors of the *National* think otherwise; —maybe Herr Guizot is meditating some profound metaphysical experiment, with all these things:—but I, and some thousands besides me, will never be able to change our opinion.—Or are we wrong after all? What if some recondite meaning were at bottom, beyond reach of our eyes?—Let us inquire.

Ye singers, permit us to commence with you! Since it would take too long, to sift all these things to the bottom one by one, let us begin by singling out a point or two; a rapid glance convinces me that I thus shall come across the very subjects to prove my statement in a trice.

Tell me, ye Singers, for what purpose are ye in the world, or, to put it more aptly, in Paris? Are ye here for a course of speculative philosophy, or to practise philosophic speculation?—Thou smil'st at me, obese Rubini, and simper'st an inaudible B flat by way of answer.—See! how delighted he is, that the Parisians haven't even heard that B flat, yet melt away in bliss before it! †—For you

* The return of the maskers from Courtille, a suburb of Paris. According to Gasperini, it was for a piece with this title that Wagner undertook to write the music figuratively alluded to in the "End in Paris" (see Vol. VII. p. 56), but, after a rehearsal or two, the choristers declared it quite impossible to sing; one chorus from his pen, however, namely "Allons à la Courtille," appears to have passed into the vaudeville as finally given at the Variétés.—Tr.

† See Vol. VII. p. 120.—Tr.

must know that Rubini is the man of negative speculation:—he gets paid for what he once possessed and gives no longer. The less he gives, the more he gets;—the more he leaves to the imagination, the greater wonders do these people hear; the more he withholds in philosophic calm, the more bewitchingly does he amuse the public. He is a great man,—fat, as is proper,—and every year, just before the grand flight of storks to England, he is on the eve of retiring. But the more he talks of retiring, the more franticly is he clung to; and then he rewards his adorers by throwing at their heads a certain shake on A, which deprives them all of sight and hearing.

I ask, is that no amusement?—

Rubini is the crown of joy on the head of Parisian society. Some day he will be getting on for a hundred years old, and created a Marshal of France. Happy mortal, who would not share thy fate?—O Rubini, godlike master, wouldst make a wight thine adjutant!

Enough of him! My eyes are swimming. Who but an eagle could longer gaze directly at the sun?—Farewell; go shine on the happier English, and make them forget that their countryman is to be hanged by the downright Americans.* Thou only, canst do it, for thou alone art transporting enough to make a Briton get himself suspended for thee!—Farewell, quintessence of all tranquil bliss; and let it not disturb thy calm, that the Grisi so untranquilly breathes out her fire divine beside thee! Let not thyself be borne away, and remember that for at least another fifty years thou still wilt have to sing; until, that is, this tattered world is brought once more to rhyme and reason, till France is peacefully reconstituted and knit for evermore with England;—for until then 'tis thou alone, can save this shaky edifice from speedy overthrow. God keep thee,—with the storks' return we meet again!—Amen!

* A dispute had arisen between England and the United States, the latter power having imprisoned a Canadian, McLeod by name, for having boasted that he had killed an American citizen on the occasion of a former inroad by the Canadians; McLeod was liberated in 1842.—Tr.

Whether I have succeeded in worthily besinging the mighty man, I myself cannot judge. In any case I should doubt that my feeble periods could vie with the enthusiasm the worshipped being spreads among the Parisians, and leaves behind him like a shining comet's-tail each time he speeds to where no substitute, alas! could gather in for him the glorious guineas which his mystic art alone can win.

I was obliged to introduce you to Rubini first, because he is the type, the beau-ideal of all this city's Song—nay, of all this city's Art. All that glitters and bewitches now, has issued once from him; he is the wellspring of all that's high and beautiful, the *ne plus ultra* of the sphere in which Parisian Art must move and welter.

Who is Duprez?—What made his fortune? What induced the Parisians to tolerate his shouts and rantings? —This: that he also has understood to close his eyes, to make no sound, and plunge his audience in the bliss of expectation.—Worthy pupil of the great master with the chubby face, I greet thee. After him thou art the first. Sure art thou of the Legion of Honour and a seat among the members of the Institute. Wouldst more? Wouldst thou, too, become Marshal of France? Reflect! for that thou must live to a hundred years old, and for this thou bawlest much too loud and much too often.

To tell the truth, Duprez is foredoomed to a sad and early death. He will perish in the bloom of youth, and be laid aside with pomp in Père-la-chaise. There one will hear atrocious moanings in the moonlight o'er his grave, and weird lamentings such as: "Woe, woe to thee, Auber! Woe to thee, Meyerbeer! Woe to thee, Halévy! Woe, ye cornets-à-piston! Woe, ye trombones!" A soft and yearning echo will take up the cry: "Hail, hail to thee, Rossini! Hail, thrice hail to thee, Bellini! Hail e'en to thee, Donizetti!" And a broken sob, somewhat like: "Marshal's staff—!" will close the spectral ditty.

I grieve to think of the terrible end of so sturdy a man as Duprez; a man of more than three feet high and good tough lungs, with a throat of wellnigh nine-tones compass. I grieve, and yet I know not how to help him; for he is the idol of the Grand Opéra public. And do you know what it means, to be an idol of the sort?—I will tell you: —an idol of the Paris Opéra is the votive victim on whom is bound a fearful burden and not to be cast off. This burden consists in the first place of a Claque, a body of men more expert in the art of applauding than anyone else; in the second, of a Press which night and morning sings the most pathetic hymns and most official psalms to the idol;—in the last place, of a Public to whom anything in the world would sooner occur, than to think its idol had sung to-day or yesterday abominably badly.—You see, this burden must needs so weigh upon a singer who has not attained the philosophic calm of Rubini, that the valiant throat contracts from time to time and squeezes out a horrible death-rattle. Already I often look upon the wretch with horror: poor fellow, his eyes are even now protruding; he soon will no longer be able to close them for that prime manœuvre of Rubini's.* I foresee, as said, his early death, which will probably be the last Amusement he ever affords the Parisians. As the thought of the death of an innocent creature always makes me sad and gloomy, let us stay no longer with Duprez, but look at what revolves around him.

I mean the lady singers of the Opéra. Next to our Duprez we see another victim marked for speedy death. It deeply grieves me to have to speak it out so bluntly; but let the Dorus-Gras compose her blond features in never so melting and entrancing folds, when she sings the celebrated "*Robert, mon âme!*" for the seven-hundredth time, I—as of some experience in this kind of diagnosis—regretfully prognosticate that *she* too will be done for. However, for a long time yet she will be able to conceal her death; she will long have seen her testament executed, ere the Parisians are aware of her

* Duprez, in effect, had to retire from the Opera in 1849, and take to teaching singing. Albert Niemann was one of his many pupils.—Tr.

decease. For years to come a coloratura in mezza voce will go murmuring round the Opéra tiers; long will an amiable, unrivalled sob caress the fine Parisian ears: for none knows so softly as she to murmur and sob, or to gloss the faded freshness of lost youth with so charming a coloratura.* And *she*, too, enjoys the good fortune of being never blamed; for she, too, is a chartered little idol, accorded the unconditional privilege of amusing.

Now for a living one! In that blue and yellow garment of the Jewess, in the suffering "Recha," you have the picture of fresh youth itself. It is a new engagement, and called Cathinka Heinefetter; † she is handsome, strong and full of feeling, with plenty of talent and a powerful voice. She falters, and is not quite finished:—ah! what a charm in that unfinish! On the day she is dubbed consummate, when none can find the smallest fault with her emotional scenes, her boding sighs, her tasteful colorature; in short, when she is licensed unconditionally to amuse—*her* death, too, will be nigh. God shield her from that banal finish enforced on every talent, no matter what its individual stamp! Even now I often wince at seeing her fall into that fatal French quivering of the hands, and consequently of the voice as well; it is a manœuvre asked of every first-class female singer, and the Heinefetter has given in to the demand,—'tis a method of amusing. In very truth she quivers; and notwithstanding that the poor "Jewess" has good enough cause, it could not please me in the Heinefetter: probably because the Falcon, the Stoltz and the Nathan have quivered in exactly the same manner and at precisely the same places. "Yea, all which it inherit, shall dissolve." ‡

* Mme Dorus-Gras had then sung at the Opéra for eleven years; whether from failing powers, or owing to the jealousy of Mme Stoltz, she retired four years later. (See Grove's *Dict. of Mus.*)—Tr.

† C. Heinefetter, who made her début in 1840, was at this time in her twenty-first year. She was the youngest of three sisters, all of whom sang with great distinction on the operatic stages of France and Germany. She died in 1858.—Tr.

‡ A quotation which I have taken the liberty of substituting for "Es erben sich Gesetz und Rechte."—Tr.

For the matter of that, Halévy's work has really admirably held its own. Though the brilliant products of the new French school have already lost their glamour through a much too rapid and exhausting output,—though we see even Meyerbeer's eternal *Robert* appearing now in tarnished, wellnigh colourless trimmings; yet the great costume, ballet and scenery garb of *La Juive* seems determined to stay ever fresh. Those who had only seen this opera in Germany, here and there, assuredly could never comprehend how it came to amuse the Parisians. The riddle is solved at once, when one sees the Paris curtain rise. Where we in Germany took fire at the powerful features of the composition, the Parisian has quite other fish to fry. For what a time have the French machinist and scene-painter known to strain and feed the curiosity of the opera-goer! Verily, he who sees this inscenation, needs long and careful scrutiny before he can exhaust the thousand details of the mounting. Who can take in the rare and lavish costumes at a glance? Who can grasp at once the mystic meaning of the ballets?—But indeed it needs all these attractions, to disclose in time to the Parisians the intrinsic value of an original work; for I tell you again, before all else they want to be amused,—by hook or crook amused.

Unfortunately however, their poets and composers also wish to amuse themselves betimes. In Paris the word is: Make a hit, and thenceforth be a made man with dividends and credit. In reason, should one take it ill of those who at last have won this grand success, if they bethink them also of amusements? Do you know what it means, to win this success? It means to have consumed the best forces, the fairest years of an artist's life in want, in care, in torture, toil, in suffering and hunger. You know these people only after they have conquered; but can you figure to yourselves the physical exhaustion with which they reached that triumph in the end? In truth, with a grain of humanity, one cannot grudge them rest when they are at the goal; and for the Parisians, rest means—Amusement. When this grand success, whose struggles have consumed their youth and blanched their cheeks, is reached at last, hey presto! everything puts on another face; the artist turns into a capitalist, the stoic an epicurean.

Take Dumas and Auber; what trade do they ply now? —They are bankers, frequent the Bourse, and bore themselves to death at their own plays and operas. The one keeps mistresses, the other horses. If they're in need of money, they take the practised scissors of their talent, and snip a piece or opera from the gilt-edged security of their renown, just as any other capitalist cuts off his darling coupons; they send it to the theatre, instead of the bank, and amuse themselves.

The bright particular star of this firmament is decidedly the mighty *Scribe*. I really ought not to speak of him but in inspired verse, or at the least with a hymn like that to the divine Rubini. This hymn would have to begin somewhat thus: "To Thee, high God of pen and paper, creative Genius without a peer, Autocrat of all the theatres of Paris, Man of the exhaustless rents, Ideal of productive force in weekly numbers, to thee resound my reverent lay!"

But as I should have to repeat the phrase a score of times, to enumerate a host of inomissible appellatives, I spare the hymn for fear of wearying my readers. Nevertheless I crave permission to express in prose at least my awe and admiration of the mighty man.

You all know who Scribe is: his Collected Works have appeared; no one, therefore, can any longer doubt his being a great poet. But he is more: he is the epitome of the art of Amusing, and has gained the most astounding credit for the establishment over which he presides with exemplary diligence. His establishment is the whole mass of the Parisian theatres. In this household he receives all Paris every night, and has the knack of entertaining all as each desires: the gorgeous dame and rampant lion he welcomes to his salon—the Grand Opéra; for the intriguing diplomat he unlocks his library—the Théâtre Français; the little music-room—the Opéra Comique—he opens to the pretentious bourgeoisie; the conversation-chamber—of the Vaudeville—to the chatty tradesman; eh! affably does he conduct the grisette and the gamin past his private study—to the Gymnase and the Ambigu Comique. See! what a spacious mansion; and, most surprising thing of all, you'll find him everywhere, everywhere entertaining, everywhere up to his eyes in amusing!

It is amazing! You're losing your heads?—Nay, see how cool, how clear the great man keeps his own! With kindly dignity he hastens from one to the other; asks what they lack, with the best waiter in a restaurant; serves smartly and promptly, and pockets modestly the little tip assured him in the swingeing tantièmes.

Despite this easy, taking grace in the man's demeanour, would you not expect him to be utterly fatigued next day, after the exertions of such a social evening?—Go visit him at ten o'clock in the morning, and you'll be astonished.—You behold him in a most elegant silk dressing-gown, at a cup of chocolate. He certainly requires the light refreshment; this very instant has he left his desk, where for two whole hours he has been flogging his hippogryph through that romantic wonderland which smiles upon you from the great poet's works. But think you he is really resting, with that chocolate? Look round, and you'll observe that every corner of the charming room, each chair, divan and sofa, is filled by a Parisian author or composer. With every one of these gentlemen he is engaged in weighty business, such as would not brook a moment's interruption in the case of other people; with every one of them he is hatching the plot for a drama, an opera, a comedy or vaudeville; with every one of them he is devising a brand-new intrigue. With this, he is knitting an inextricable knot; with that, on the point of unravelling the most ingenious confusion; with one he is just calculating the effect of some hair-bristling situation in a new opera; with another he has come to terms a second ago about a double wedding. Moreover he is busied at the same time with a pile of well-turned *billets* to this and that client, polishing off this or that applicant by word of mouth, and paying five-hundred francs for a puppy. But amid it all he also gathers matter for his coming pieces, studies with a fleeting smile the characters of strangers just announced or done with, sets them in a frame, and in fifteen minutes makes a play of which no one as yet knows a word.—I rather fancy I myself one day became a subject for him in this fashion, and shall be much surprised if we don't presently see a piece in which my plaintive wonder at the costly purchase of the puppy becomes the pivot of a telling situation.

Now that you have seen him, you can form some sort of notion what Scribe is! When he dies, a perfect marvel of routine will die with him, for no one else could follow in his footsteps. His art will cease, like the Napoleonic sway: thousands combined would not have wit to seize each separate thread the despot holds together in one hand.

Indisputably, Scribe has gone great lengths: he is the prime condition of all fortune, fame, success, all honour, all receipts—particularly for composers. Whoe'er should write an opera without his aid, would rush upon a certain doom; and if any man has gone so far astray as to set music to the book of other authors, as a rule he at least endeavours to rectify his error by humbly praying Scribe to put his name above the others, and be so obliging as to accept half the *droits d'auteurs* in recompense. He usually does it.

Without Scribe no opera, no play—no genuine Amusement. And do you imagine that he draws no profit from it? Oh, he is the blessedest of mortals! He takes payment for successes won by others; and though everybody is convinced that the music of *Robert*, for instance, is worth more than the text, yet everybody knows that Scribe draws more from this opera than Meyerbeer.

But let us not pry into the dark corners of this great palace of delight. Let us not lift the veil of many a wondrous mystery the gods so graciously enshroud in sparkling bliss! — One glance into the garden of the Tuileries or any concert-room, and every sad suspicion will be put to flight. We nowhere stumble there on misery or kill-joys; nothing but well-dressed, well-to-do people: for you must know that, both here and there, to dowdy and distressful folk admittance is forbidden. And quite right too, for Parisian joys and elegant toilettes are one thing and the same; and where this harmony is marred, there necessarily crop up contrast, conflict, and lastly revolution. To obviate such ills and keep the world of elegance as much and as exclusively together as possible, to smother it with pleasures and thus bind it ever faster to the amusing consuetude of the Established, is therefore a chief maxim of the present government. In this sense Louis Philippe has thought necessary to arrange by a secret edict for as many concerts, matinées and soirées, as there are hours in the day. Before I arrived at discovery of this most high and hidden cause by a process of induction, I could find nothing to account for so monstrous a phenomenon; for the result of all this entertainment is most fatiguing to the public.

You shall hear what a Paris concert consists in: there's no need of a programme, for you always get the selfsame things in the selfsame order. Only you must remember that, broadly speaking, these concerts divide themselves into three orders of merit, dependent on the status of the singers who take part therein. Let us begin with the lowest, or third class:—

These are generally got up by those unfortunate creatures who come to Paris with the intention of conquering it, but content themselves as a rule with an *au cinquième* in the Faubourg St Denis or St Martin. For the most part they are pianoforte-players, young people from twelve to forty-four years old who have applied themselves with diligence to learning up the Paris decalogue, and concentrated all the energy of years upon their concert. The singers at these concerts are generally "second prizes" of the Conservatoire, scarce worth the naming, and Herr Boulanger, a drawing-room tenor scarce worth considering. The songs are "*Robert, mon âme!*" and romances by Demoiselle Puget;* the audience has free tickets, is unassuming, and amuses itself.

In the second class we rank the concerts given by the standing army of teachers. These teachers are the daily virtuosi of the pianoforte, of incipient culture; they compose those Fantaisies brillantes, Mosaïques and Airs variés, which follow in the wake of each new opera. They are usually spirituel, and give good lessons. Here one hears Mme Nau and the Dorus-Gras, very much worth naming, Dupont and Alizard, quite worth considering. They sing "*Robert, mon âme!*" and romances by Demoiselle Puget. The audience consists of young-lady pupils and their relatives, has paid for its tickets, instructs and amuses itself.

The first rank is taken by the concerts of virtuosi of renown; their arrival is usually announced in the musical journals; they are called Celebrities, and act accordingly. They play now on the pianoforte, now on the violin, and as a rule are received in state. At their concerts one hears the Dorus-Gras and the Garcia-Viardot,† most excellent! Masset and Roger, magnificent! The audience has made a *queue*, goes into raptures and amuses itself.

As, however, there are always things too lofty for classification, so there are concerts here which stand above even the first rank. These are customarily described by the papers as "*les plus beaux et les plus brillants de l'année*," and are given either for some noble end, or by the proprietor of one of the musical journals.‡ In these is heaped up all that Paris has of attractive and entrancing; and, to

* Loïsa Puget, born 1810, composer of countless little bourgeois and religious songs and romances.—Tr.

† In Paris, nearly twenty years later, Mme Garcia-Viardot became Wagner's first "Isolde," at a private performance accompanied on the pianoforte. Roger was also then concerned with him, in the beginnings of the translation of the *Tannhäuser* text.—Tr.

‡ It will be remembered that Wagner's *Columbus* overture was given at one of the concerts (Feb. 4, 1841) of Maurice Schlesinger, proprietor of the *Gazette Musicale*; see also pages 112-113 *infra*.—Tr.

seal them with the *ne plus ultra* of distinction, the whole of the Italians sing as well. There one reels from desire to fruition, and midst satiety of joy one starves for very ennui. There besides "*Robert, mon âme!*" one hears the quite-the-latest arias from Rossini's *Donna del Lago*; one prodigy hustles the other from the carpeted platform, one virtuoso tears the fiddle or piano from the other; the storm of applause which sped the parting guest rolls over into that which welcomes the latest arrival; "all men become brothers," till at last one can hear neither singing nor playing. Further, we must not forget that the elegance of the audience at these concerts is at its culminating point; for when the Italians sing, velvet and satin are the most ordinary of wear, patchouli and portugal the vulgarest of perfumes. In the journals next day these distinguished assemblies are dubbed in an access of rapture "more aristocratic than aristocratic," and Russian Princesses play in them the leading rôle.

You see in what a sphere the Virtuoso lives; to be sure, even here the world of singers takes front place, but none the less the sphere belongs by actual title to the virtuosi. They shine at the head of the advertisements, as givers of the concert, and the feast itself is called after them. As a rule the Paris virtuoso wears his hair long, and cultivates a careful beard; this is of great importance, both tokens serving to distinguish him from the singer, who generally affects a fantastic cockneydom in dress.

Of the utmost significance is the working apparition of the virtuoso in the salons of the upper world, for commonly he is the only professional there. In general the salon-singers consist of dilettants—or more correctly, dilettantesses, of whom there is a shoal, since to every dame it seems so easy to dilettate in song. They mostly sing romances by Demoiselle Puget; they betray a strong bias toward zealotry, however, for they adore to sing religious pieces such as little Ave Marias, or *à la Vierge*—downright—in two to three, or preferably in one, part choruses. In fact the salon often thus becomes a praying-hall; and this fervour is mostly so deep and sincere, that it makes one rigidly abstain from earthly pleasures such as tea or light refreshments. Whoever, therefore, enters such a room with worldly thoughts or crude desires, usually finds himself compelled to practise dreary self-denial; everything forces him to none but pleasures of a higher sphere. Indeed this pious chant effects a quite transfiguring impression, since it makes itself heard as a rule when the hubbub is at its very highest; when the crush of guests has tied itself into the most hopeless knot, when the heat is at the level of the Lybian desert's, there suddenly goes up this fervent orison, addressed to the Virgin by unseen dilettanti; for, beyond the first few rows, no mortal present can espy them for the suffocating throng. Habitually the effect is indescribable, when those dulcet one or two-voiced chords float up in soft contrition o'er the heads of manhood praying in an agony of death; many will then break loose from the knot, and resolve in the street to become better men. Those left behind, more hardened sinners, require yet other revelations, and therefore doggedly await a romance of Demoiselle Puget's; when this has been delivered, again a large detachment will withdraw into itself, and out of doors. To the rest the virtuoso ministers.

I, too, need rest: I can no more!—Who, not a Parisian born, could longer bear this load of pleasure and amusement? For believe me, I have still kept back a deal from you; I haven't spoken of this and that, which belong to the Parisian's enjoyment as bread to your housekeeping. But everything has its bounds, and a man who has no country-seat wherein to rest off the pleasures of a Paris Summer, must necessarily abstain from a large slice thereof, such as balls, Dlle. Rachel, the Bois de Boulogne, and so on. A single Civil-list ball is enough to ruin for life a poor foreigner of modest powers of enjoyment; would you have me tell you, then, of the Opera balls with their suggestive quadrilles and galops of Hell? Only a Frenchman can report on these, for a Frenchman alone is capable of enjoying things we simply marvel at.

Surely everyone who has followed my logical chain with sufficient acumen, will admit the justice of my main contention, that the Parisians really need no Carnival. Did I not assume that this Carnival is about to be invested with some mystic-religious meaning, and did I not hold that any approach to religion would be very beneficial to the character of the French, I should—considering that I stand very well with Louis Philippe, and he often allows me a candid expression of my opinions—I should beg the King, in all seriousness, to chase the dying Carnival from off the streets for good.—As said and shewn, there is no dearth of other Amusements; and he who has his country-seat behind him, may sip them to his heart's content. So provide yourselves with country-seats, should you be thinking of coming to Paris!

V.

PARISIAN FATALITIES FOR THE GERMAN.*

TO ask the shop-fronts of the Palais Royal, with their blaze of gas, of silks, of gold and silver; ask the Garden of the Tuileries, with its elegant and well-kept alleys; ask the Champs Elysées, with their resplendent carriages and powdered coachmen; ask the Boulevards, with their teeming brew of luxury and diligence; ask the boxes at the theatres, with their maddening toilets and mystic coiffures; ask the Opera-balls, with their witching grisettes in velvet bodices, their costly *Femmes entretenues* in exclusive dominos of black satin;—and finally, if it be summer-time, ask the private country-houses, parks, gardens, hermitages, and the thousand lordly rural joys to which the Parisian yields himself in charming innocence,—ask all these things if they exist for weariness of spirit.—How they will protest, and laugh such a question to scorn! Yet there is a whole race of men these glorious things can only fill with deadliest ennui; this race consists of the resident Germans.

'Tis true enough: all things considered, it is most ennuyant to be a German in Paris. To be a German at home is splendid, where one has soul (*Gemüth*), Jean Paul, and Bavarian beer; where one can quarrel over the philosophy of Hegel or the waltzes of Strauss; where one can read in the fashion-journals about Paris murders and absurdly low-priced *Gros de Naples*; where, lastly, one can hear or sing a good old song, and eke a new, about our

* See footnote to page 70.—Tr.

Father Rhine.* We get nothing of all this in Paris; and yet there live a host of Germans here. How terrible must be their ennui!

On the other hand, I almost think the German is the only thing that can weary the true Parisian. For why: folk take the German as a rule for honest, and trust him readily; which is bad for him. Since men have trust in him, they necessarily believe him stupid; and a fool, according to their meaning, is the bugbear of the Parisians. But whoever is unable to enter into those piquant chicaneries, those ingenious sinuosities of their marvellous talent for intrigue, they must perforce deem stupid. And by God! they can do no otherwise; for he who cannot manage here to hit the mark, or is weak enough to die of hunger, must—according to Parisian notions—have no understanding.

You may judge, then, what a parlous attribute is honesty, in Paris; and how sorry a figure he must cut, who is burdened with it of or against his will. By weight of this single virtue the German finds himself shut out from all that makes Paris both brilliant and enviable: fortune, riches, fame and pleasure, are not for him; his companions are the ragged beggars, his haunts the muddy streets. At most the grocer pays a tribute to this virtue; he brings it into reckoning, and gives a little credit; but not too much, for he knows that the unlucky owner of this virtue will never reach a state where he can liquidate a heavy bill.

This is the heart of the evil: the Parisian doesn't believe in the honesty of the rich; so every honest man he straightway counts as poor. But Poverty is the greatest crime in Paris; and as people here consider every German poor, in a certain sense he ranks at once as stupid and bad, i.e. criminal.

* The *Bayreuther Taschen-Kalender* for 1892, in its reprint of this article, informs us that about this time (1841) Becker's song: "Sie sollen ihn nicht haben, den freien deutschen Rhein," to which Wagner subsequently refers in his *Capitulation* (Vol. V. 20), had attained to very great celebrity.—Tr.

It is an awful curse, this curse that rests upon our countrymen. Be as rich as one may in one's own estimation, without the most crying of proofs to the contrary one will be relentlessly treated as poor. To this day I have never succeeded in convincing the Parisians of my affluence, although I draw about two-hundred gulden every year [£20]; an income which in a German Residenz would be amply sufficient to gather a troop of trencher-mates around me. But so flourishing a state of finances counts for nothing here, and I find that people are gradually ceasing to take me for an Englishman.

Thereby hangs a tale, and a good tale too. The Parisians, as all the world knows, are vastly polite; to them it is an impossibility to say anything disagreeable to people, saving when their purse is touched. Wherefore as a German and a stupid, bad—i.e. an honest, poor—man have become one and the same thing in their conception, they believe they cannot treat us with greater delicacy than by pretending to take us for Englishmen. True, that the French hate the English; but this hatred, as everyone knows, is merely political and applies to the nation in bulk. Each several Frenchman is mortally fond of each several Englishman, and loads him with every conceivable mark of respect; for in his eyes all Englishmen are rich, however poor they often may be in their own. What greater flattery, then, can a Frenchman pay us, than by asking: "*Pardon, monsieur, vous êtes Anglais?*"

As it is certain that Germans unnumbered have suffered by this evil habit of the French, I cannot refrain from admitting that it has caused myself a deal of trouble.

My unlucky star would have it that I should tread the soil of France for the first time at Boulogne-sur-mer.* I had come from England, indeed from London, the city of costly experiences, and breathed again as I touched the land of francs, i.e. of twenty-sous pieces,

* The author himself, in fact, stayed there for four weeks in August and September 1839, on his way from London to Paris.—Tr.

leaving well behind me the dreadful land of pounds and shillings; for I had reckoned that I could live at least twice as cheaply in France, arguing from the relative numbers of sous and pence, of which latter there only went twelve to the handsomest shilling, whereas the least presentable of francs yet holds its twenty sous. I thus had made out that, especially with the subdivision into centimes, whereof it is notorious that a hundred go to the franc, I should be able to lay by a goodly portion of my annual income; upon which circumstance I then—in fact, during the passage on the steamboat—based all kinds of pleasant prospects and, in particular, plans. I had even gone the length of reckoning that I soon should be able to set about buying one of those castles in southern France, close by the Pyrenees, of which Prince Pückler has told us such cheap and agreeable things: for instance, that in such a castle one can live, in fullest keeping with one's rank, on no more than 2000 fr. a year. I fancied Prince Pückler had even a little exaggerated this sum, from a princely perspective, and that by aid of my centime-system I could certainly reduce it to a fourth of the amount, which would completely accord with my revenue. —— O gruesome habits of the French, how have ye nullified my splendid plans!

Arrived at the hotel, I at once was asked: "*Pardon, monsieur, vous êtes Anglais*?"—The voyage on the steamer and the intoxicating Pyrenean-castle plans had so benumbed my brain, that for the moment I really could not quite remember what country's child I was; it never occurred to me that I was a German, and as in my long absence from home I had had no definite tidings whether my birthplace still belonged to Saxony, or already to Prussia, I deemed it shortest to end my inward confusion about my nationality by a hasty "*Oui*!"

Unhappy voyage on the steamer, that had filled me with such intoxicating plans for the purchase of a Pückler-Pyrenean castle! Wretched plans, that plunged me into such confusion when the Boulogne hotel-keeper asked about my nationality! Ruinous uncertainty as to the colours of my native city, that prompted my unpatriotic lie! Fatal lie! O ghastly "*Oui*!"—All my smiling future, based so firmly on the soundness of my centime-system, have ye overthrown!

Replying on French cheapness, I had stayed two days in the hotel; an excellent garçon had served me with especial reverence and attention. I had not been wrong, when I ascribed this notably obsequious service to the respect the creature cherished for my quality of Englishman; of this I was positive when I observed his sudden change of manner after overhearing one of my frequent monologues. I naturally had held it in my mother-tongue, and the garçon, a native of Geneva, did not hesitate to recognise me at once for a German. What of respect and reverence he withdrew from me after this discovery, the good man quite made up by a surprising familiarity and equalisation. He became my brother; sat down to table whenever he brought up my coffee; helped himself to the sugar, as he saw that I was taking none; and when I asked him to fetch some tobacco, told me how to find the shop to buy it for myself.—Unfortunately, however, this change of estimate on discovery of my true nationality had not come equally to pass in the cloudy mind of mine host. He seemed to have punctiliously stuck to my "*Oui*!" when he made up the reckoning for his hapless hospitality. To oblige me, he had written out this bill in English; certain inexplicably large figures upon it made me think there was some mistake, and that they were intended for another person, presumably a genuine Briton. But the host soon helped me out of doubt, and confirmed me in the true belief. The items were correct,—the Pyrenean castle of Prince Pückler was lost for ever. My paradise also was lost,—my beautiful conviction of the soundness of my centime system done to death. With sad resignation I noticed on this bill the same, nay, even higher prices than those of London; and their appearance was much more terrifying, since they were reckoned in francs, of which it notoriously takes more to a pound than of shillings, and whose figures even for an equal value present a far more dreadful show.

Since that time I have carefully avoided answering the constant question, "*Pardon, monsieur, vous êtes Anglais?*" by a vacant "*Oui!*"—in fact I have accustomed myself to add to the most emphatic "*Non!*" a trenchant "*Allemand!*" Whatever was possible, I have gained from this practice, but I have had to abandon all claims to attentive regard. If under my true national colours I ask for a lodging, I am sent without further ado to the fifth-floor high, and it always takes quite a chapter of explanations to induce the concierge to shew me a room on the fourth, not to mention the third. The garçon at the restaurant, whom I informed of my Germanity, prudently warns me off all dearer dishes, and unbidden brings me Sauerkraut or such-like delicacies, as better suited to a German's taste.

The thing, however, has its good side too. Through his name for neediness the German is lifted above all temptation to sin against his inborn morals:—it is clean impossible for him to have a maîtresse. What that means in Paris, ask anyone who has been there! To have a maîtresse is indispensable for every man, whatever circle he may move in, who wishes to pass as a somebody. The mechanic when he returns from his work, the counter-jumper when he leaves the shop, the student when he comes back from lectures, meets his maîtresse like the gentleman of highest station; for so it is ordained, and a mechanic, clerk or student, who did not comply with this rule, would never count for anything.

This excellent custom is naturally repugnant to the German, and he may thank his stars that in this respect he is never exposed to the smallest disturbance. However great the muster of the fairer sex, however eager for shelter, and however changeable they be in their engagements, it would never occur to a grisette to offer herself for a temporary alliance with a German. Still more seldom would a German push his audacity and want of principle so far, as to court the grace of such a damsel; for too often would he have to blush for shame upon seeing himself in the looking-glass, a thing impossible to avoid in Paris for reason of the mass of mirrors. The Germans therefore leave the commerce of fair dames to their fellow aliens, the Britons, who take high honours in the game, for not one of them is a day in Paris without striking up a sweet, albeit fleeting friendship with at least an opera-dancer.

But on account of this little circumstance the German stands completely severed from Paris society; to all Parisian joys he stays a stranger. For him no ball, no Chaumière, no Prado and no Tivoli,—for him no country pleasures, no town recreations. The Parisians troop about in pairs, a manikin and a womanikin: as hermit glum the German slinks between the merry ranks, looks timidly upon their touching dances, and vows himself to un-free-willed abstention.

It could not well be otherwise; for in the wildest flights of imagination I have never yet been able to picture to myself a German dancing the Cancan. I have made every possible attempt to bring the fictive spectacle before my mental eye,—I have summoned the most frivolous forms, with the most expressive physiognomies I ever met in Germany,— I have indued them with a ten-years' familiarity with Parisian manners,—but never have I succeeded in figuring one of these conjured individualities as shining in that graceful dance. 'Tis a mystery whose rites no German understands, a riddle whose solution shuns the German mind. True, I remember having seen the efforts of one of my countrymen, a madcap youngster, to share in this dance; the poor fellow seemed to be stepping a minuet, and came to grief for very shame.

All the higher, however, do the Parisiennes rate the German's qualifications for the state of actual wedlock. There are ranks in which domestic virtues are much desired, where people think more of lawful marriage-bonds than fleeting unions. In these ranks the man is valued highest who stays at home, looks after bolts and bars, goes to the cellar, strikes lucifers, takes the baby-in-arms for the Sunday walk, and hooks his spouse's gown. As much conjugal fidelity as possible, is a wished-for virtue in such a man, but mildness, affection and honesty are the chief desiderata. Of these the last-named is the most important, for on exclusive account of this virtue are Germans married here, and that by the widows of *marchands de vin*, tobacconists and estaminet-keepers.

These widows—of whom be it said, in passing, there are very many—have generally brought the late lamented a small fortune as dowry; as a rule, both sides have carefully laid out this capital: it therefore is quite natural that, after death of the beloved partner, the survivoress (for seldom does the man survive a first wife, unless he has beaten her to death in a fit of ill-temper, which does occur from time to time), that the survivoress, I repeat, should take very good care not to "bring" again the brought and increased dowry, but rather to increase it more, wherever possible. Henceforth the widow fights for her exclusive property, her hearth and halidom, and it never enters her head to share it again with another.

Yet the situation has its difficulties. The lady is vigorous enough; she looks after the books and correspondence with unflagging zeal, keeps the cash with an unparalleled eye to business, and thrones majestically upon her stool behind the counter. However, she badly needs a male creature for taking down and putting up the shutters, going to the cellar, filling bottle and glass; in a word, for the duties of a Garçon. But there are easily-imagined disadvantages in hiring an ordinary garçon,—who trusts the honesty of such a being? And then, how many other things stay still undone, which no garçon upon earth is fit for! Who is to attend to the children; who go to market; who promenade with the lady on Sunday afternoons at four; who shew her little kindnesses in general? For, among her other admirable qualities, the widow is full of feeling.—All these things did the late lamented. Only from a husband can they be asked. A husband must therefore be taken again.

But the widow's prime concern is to keep her property exclusively to herself; and where shall she find a man to take up all the countless duties of a wedded husband without insisting on an equal share of everything? A Frenchman would never submit to it; and if he did, it would only be to cheat the good lady in spite of all her watchfulness.

So the widow finds herself compelled to lay aside her national prejudices; she knows that there flows no modester and more honourable blood in the veins of any nation, than in those of the German: therefore she does not hesitate to make one of our countrymen happy for life. In him she finds all she needs, with the additional advantage that this husband costs her next to nothing and affords her much amusement by the thousand *doubles ententes* with which, though not particularly witty, he naïvely adorns his daily speech.

This wedded lot is the final outcome of the anguished and sorely disappointed hopes of many a German in Paris; it is the haven into which he steers his storm-leaked ship, pathetically renouncing further ventures. The vow he registers before the mayor, is the vow of abstinence wherewith religious souls once bade farewell to the world after many a vehement struggle with contrary life, and gave themselves to the healing shelter of peaceful cloister-walls. —Thus a still community has arisen in Paris, whose Brothers, tranquilly removed from all the turmoil of tempestuous strife, live in strict obedience to their order's rules. Their heads, it is true, are not "shorn," but often roundly "washed" instead by their spouses; from the vow of chastity—towards their wives—they are absolved, but other pleasures are sternly forbidden them. They are pledged to the upbringing of youth, the refreshment of sucklings — please understand, by feeding-bottles, — the maintenance of cleanliness in swaddling-matters, and total abstinence from the fingering of silver or copper coin.

Their food consists of a *pot au feu* in the morning; in the evening—out of special regard for their nationality—of a plate of sauerkraut, for ill luck will have it that the French believe we Germans live on nothing else.

From this order none emerges, saving through the death of his better half. As the latter is generally well on in years at the time the vow is registered, it would commonly be expected that the youthful victims of German honesty would outlive their ruthless gaolers; but these matrons are possessed of enormous vitality, and the renunciant never sees the world again.

Who can guess what remarkable individuals may be found here and there in this order? May it not be that we have already received a glass of eau-de-vie at the hands of the most accomplished student of the Hegelian philosophy? That a poet of five-act dramas in verse has sold us two-sous worth of snuff? That we have drunk a stoup of Strassburg beer drawn by the most inspired contrapuntist of the school of Kirnberger?—The imagination is palsied by the wealth of possibilities that here present themselves. Who can conceive all the sacrifices which those hapless have made, to keep life in their bodies? Who imagine the renunciations it has cost them, to be received into that order?

I have followed the brief struggle for existence of one German in Paris;—like everything here, it went full speed, and ended in less than half a year. He was a young man whom God knows what sad chance had driven to Paris. His attainments were quite beyond the common, for he was physician, jurist, writer, poet and scholar; he understood Goethe's *Faust* from the Prologue in Heaven to the Chorus Mysticus, could write prescriptions and lead actions-at-law with any man; moreover he could copy music, and prove you that man has no soul. Relying on these enormous acquirements, he naturally thought it easy to make a distinguished career in Paris even without a sou in his pocket, especially when he took count of the warlike preparations afoot in France last autumn, which undoubtedly must call *one* of his faculties into action. He was full of faith when he visited me first, though he confessed that Guizot's peaceful policy was playing him a scurvy trick.*

Eight days after that visit I received a letter from the hospital of the Hôtel Dieu :—my accomplished countryman had fallen ill and taken toll of the hospitable charity of the Parisians. In this most excellent institution I found him busy acquiring a knowledge of the French language by aid of a grammar : his courage was somewhat damped,—nevertheless he had a thousand plans in his head, directed for the moment to providing against future hunger. Among others he spoke of correcting proofs, of colouring woodcuts, of covering matchboxes, but with great predilection of chorus-singing at the Grand Opéra ; for my gifted fellow-countryman knew also how to sing. I promised to do my best towards the realising of his plans, and supplied him with snuff.

Soon afterwards I had another letter from him, but this time from the hospital of Pitié ; I visited him there too, and had the opportunity of noticing that this infirmary is far more scantily furnished, and less cleanly kept, than the Hôtel Dieu. I couldn't quite make out why my intelligent compatriot had effected this change of hospice, but my mind was set at ease upon finding him in fairly good health. I learnt that nothing had come of the opera-singing, the matchbox-covering, the colouring, or the correcting ; on the other hand, he was elaborating a proof that the soul consists of carbonic acid and galvanism, and hoped for immediate redemption from evil.

Then came the 15th December, the day of bringing home Napoleon's ashes. All the world knows that on that day God gave the Parisians an unparalleled degree of cold ; for four hours had I frozen on the terrace of the Place des Invalides, and was envying my sheltered fellow-countryman, whom I believed to be under the warm blankets of

* According to the *Taschen-Kalender* "in 1840 it seemed as if Louis Philippe would allow himself to be incited by Thiers to an attack upon Germany ; but the Guizot Ministry smoothed things down again."—Tr.

the Pitié. The unhappy man, however, had not been able to resist the chronicler's temptation—for he wrote history too—to take personal stock of the interment of the Imperial remains. Well as this was, since he might otherwise have been betrayed into denying the fact of that interment as lightly as the existence of the soul,—yet the poor creature's clothing was quite unsuited to the bleakness of that memorable day; obviously it had been tailored in one of the bygone summers of its owner's blither life, and obstinately declined to yield sufficient covering to the somewhat massive figure of my else so careful friend. So piteous a spectacle did he present, that it pierced my very heart and soul. Some counsel must be taken for his most pressing needs;—I was able to find employment for one of his humblest faculties; the philosopher, jurist, medicine-man and historian—must copy music.

However, this channel soon dried up, as I unfortunately didn't know an overwhelming number of people with music to copy. Other ways must be tried. After I had lost sight of my soul-denier for some few days he unexpectedly came into my room, and told me that he had every prospect of a sort of book-keeper's post in a factory at Beauvais; a substantial salary would enable him to save a little capital ere long, which would place him in the position to devote a spell of leisure to the main purpose of his life, namely the explanation of Goethe's *Faust* to the French, whilst he would have ample opportunity of gaining the requisite insight into the French language through his contact with the factory-hands.

When he came to bid farewell to me a short time after, I congratulated him and wished him good luck. But on my asking if he would be back in Paris soon, he explained that it would be a matter of some difficulty, as he thought of going to Australia for the present. Nothing had come of Beauvais, but in his capacity of physician he believed he had secured a berth as doctor to an emigrant ship from London to Australia, and was expecting the passage-money to London that very day. This time we had a most affecting parting, for a journey to Australia is no joke. I soon had to discover that my withers had been wrung in vain, however, since the passage-money did not arrive.

My unfortunate countryman was now at his wits' end what to do. He had nothing left to live on, and I couldn't conceive how he got his food. I had observed that it took an astonishing amount of victuals to satisfy the demands of his extraordinarily powerful constitution; in fact this circumstance had already warped his else so clear and upright judgment, when he declared that the dietary of the Paris hospitals was calculated for the ruin of patients, as the weak did not get food enough to regain their strength, and the strong were necessarily reduced to weakness.

At last I ascertained that two well-to-do ladies of the millinery profession, attracted in the first place by an interest in his not uncomely figure, had devoted to him a certain sympathy; on the part of one of these dames it took the form of furnishing victuals and drink, on that of the other, of lending him twenty-sous pieces. I don't quite know whether the fickleness of these compassionate ladies, or my well-behaved compatriot's sense of degradation, was to blame for this relation's also coming to a speedy end; thus much is certain—one day I found him victim to a struggle of an altogether different sort. He disclosed to me that the widow of an estaminet-keeper in a side-street off the Rue St Antoine had cast betrothful eyes upon his aptness for a model husband. As he explained to me, his straits had already forced him into negotiations with this lady as to the conditions on which to base a conjugal alliance desired by her. She had promised him board and lodging in keeping with his station, together with all other rights and titles of a wedded husband, excepting any claim upon her property; in return it would be his duty to devote himself exclusively to household details, and this was the knotty point to which my high-soaring countryman would never and never agree. He had consented to take over the duties of the husband of an estaminet-proprietress from noon to night, but stipulated for unconditional freedom in the morning hours to work at his explanation of *Faust* and his proof of the non-existence of the soul. Thereon the lady had repeatedly declared that the morning hours were the most lucrative for the estaminet, and he therefore must always serve the pot-au-feu and leave *Faust* and the soul unproven.—The struggle between the pangs of want and the consciousness of a higher earthly mission was hard —but noble; the breast of my soul-denying countryman swelled full, and with a melancholy sigh he determined to abjure the matrimonial shelter at the corner of the Rue St Antoine.

To make amends, a fine opening soon presented itself to him, namely the post of overseer in a madhouse; beyond the advantages of board and pay, it was most important and desirable for his scientific demonstrations. God only knows what objections the lunatics may have had to him,—but here too, in the long run, he had to stand back. Once more he cast a glance on the estaminet-widow, but decided rather to colour bonbon-mottoes, or publish a German journal. The one plan met as many difficulties as the other, and the marriage fight commenced afresh in his plagued but self-disowning soul. However, this strife he definitely ended when the most favourable prospect shewed itself of getting a situation as tutor to the children of a famous English scholar. This Englishman, besides his riches and his children, had the property of being a historical-researcher; my well-informed compatriot, as we already know, was also an adept in history; so that nothing could be more suited to him, than this engagement. Truly, fortune seemed to smile upon him; the Briton recognised the value of the candidate's enormous stock of qualities,—and the affair was settled.

For awhile I saw my enviable countryman no more. As I knew that the Englishman had intended to travel, nothing was more natural than to assume that his private tutor was accompanying him. One day I visited the

Jardin des Plantes, and was contemplating the young bears who had but shortly seen the light of day, when close beside me I heard the intolerable bellowing of a boy about four years old :—I turned round,—who can depict my astonishment at seeing the badly-brought-up child in the arms of my well-clad Faust-explainer, and at his side a worthy dame with a huge knitting-bag and a tiny girl ! After the first shock, my friend greeted me with an embarrassed smile, and invited me to call on him in his wife's estaminet at the corner of the Rue St Antoine.— — — Poor France, who now shall explain thee Goethe's *Faust*? Erring mortals, who now shall prove you the non-existence of your souls ? He who could have done both with such surprising clearness, in verse and prose, will spend his life in serving pot-au-feu and drawing Strassburg beer !— —

This story certainly has matter enough to fill at least ten years of life, in a German Residenz ; here, as already stated, it passed in less than six Parisian months. Nay, it would have spun itself off in still briefer time, had my richly-gifted friend employed more vehemence in the solution of his problem, had he stooped to ruse or means forbidden, in a word, had it seemed good to him to try the Parisian system of intrigue and hocus-pocus. 'Tis past belief, how futile in Paris are the most ingenious of those tricks by which a German often helps himself at home to years of credit and repute ; here they become mere child's-play, against the immense perfection of the tactics of the *chevalier d'industrie*. To my regret I remember having met another fellow-countryman, who—apparently less because he thought it good, than because he held it necessary—embarked on the unfortunate attempt to assist himself by daring swindles and tranquil circumventions of the laws of Paris. I believe he has reaped the experience, that the lawless Parisians have a law against everything, including German strokes of genius. This countryman stayed an uncommonly short while in Paris.

In effect, Invention seems to be quite the most fruitless gift of poor German devils, for getting on in Paris; far better suited is the gift of Music. For that the Germans have acquired such credit, that no Frenchman can possibly conceive a German who doesn't understand it. When a difficulty arises in any social gathering about a pianist to accompany a romance by Demoiselle Puget, and folk learn that a German is present, at once they conclude that their trouble is over; for why was this German begot by his father and born of his mother, if not to play the pianoforte? Should it happen that in his study of the Hegelian philosophy a German has really forgotten to unearth and cultivate his musical talent, so that he is obliged to reject the appeal of a Parisienne for accompaniment in a Pugetian romance, the lady had best make haste and cross herself; for to her that German is a ghost, a phantom, an unholy thing. But if the German understands music and can play the piano, he has prospects and claims to a quite brilliant career; for he may become virtuoso, teacher, and God knows what, only not a Minister as Spontini with us. What is far more, however,—he may become the bridegroom of a banker's daughter; for even in the upper circles there is shewn a certain bent to German marriages, especially when the match results from art-enthusiasm, which none knows better how to kindle, than the German sitting on the music-stool. But here the musician's vista closes; more than a banker's son-in-law he never can hope to become, at least through what he is and performs:—if he attains to even dizzier heights along this path, for instance if he becomes a leading composer at the Grand Opéra, like Meyerbeer, he will have done it in virtue of his bankership; for in Paris a banker can do anything, even compose operas and get them produced.

Thus it may be argued that the rank of Banker is the most consummate qualification of a German in Paris. Yet the German bankers, of whom there are a good many here, no longer count as Germans; they stand high above all nationality, and therefore above all national prejudices; they belong to the Universe and the Paris Bourse. Let these bankers, then, be furnished with never so many government-securities and dividends, the French prejudice for considering the German poor remains the same; for it would never occur to anybody to acknowledge the German nationality of one of these bankers. At the very least the Parisians observe the distinction that, when talking of a German banker, they say "*Ce monsieur est banquier, je crois allemand*," but of a German author, "*Il est allemand, je crois homme de lettres.*" Rothschild in their eyes is more a universal-Jew; even his German name they hardly ever mention, and usually call him "No. 15, Rue Lafitte."

Moreover the bankers' own first care, after they have brought their business to a certain pitch, is to doff their German nationality; they take pains to be more French than the Frenchmen, and indeed are the only men who succeed in copying French customs to a T. Their greatest success is with Parisian egoism, their smallest with refined French manners; I am told of German bankers here who have fits of rudeness equal to any police-official's in the Fatherland. Usually they are covered with confusion, when addressed in their mother-tongue; a chaste flash of shame then makes their eyes gleam, and reddens charmingly their yellow cheeks; for every German banker, however corpulent, preserves a heavy eye and pallid cheek in daily life, and when speaking French. They are dearly loved for it by the Parisians,—and do good business.

The most excellent, the truest Germans are the poor; in Paris they learn to prize their mother-tongue afresh, and forget the while to master French. Their oft enfeebled sense of patriotism here gains new strength, and, however much they shun return to home, they pine of true home-sickness. They require a whole year, to get accustomed to Parisian ways; until then they stumble over every gamin, and against each picture-stall. They soon learn to steer clear of the gamins, to adore and reverence the picture-stalls. Whole hours will they often pass before the latter, for here they make their study of Paris and first acquire real knowledge of its habitants. At these stalls they con the open secrets of Parisian life; for hardly a day goes by, but they behold fresh pictures and character-sketches disclosing to them the political and social meaning of the capital. When two Germans meet, it is only natural that they should tell each other their latest experiences; these experiences, however, often reduce themselves to an account of what they have learnt at those picture-stalls. They will relate how they saw two children come up to a picture representing Adam and Eve, and one child asked which was the man and which the woman in the painting, whereon the other answered: "No one can say, for they haven't any clothes on." *—They will further relate how they saw a grocer return from his time in the National Guard, to find his wife just hiding her lover away; the grocer draws his sabre, to mow his rival down,—but the lady throws herself upon him with the cry: "Wretch, would you kill the father of your children?"—Such experiences are daily to be reaped before these picture-stalls; the German pockets them, and is convinced he has witnessed the living occurrence.—

These needy Germans generally have plenty of talent and phantasy, and above all, are faithful friends; for my part, I here first learnt what friendship is. They also form a still community in Paris, and observe the vow of abstinence; they are chaste, and scrupulous obeyers of the law. At times, however, they harbour plans for conquering Paris, and daring wishes spring not seldom in their hearts. But who could stay impassive, when he has paid four francs at the box-office, and bought the right to occupy a crimson-velveted fauteuil in the Opéra parterre? In front he sees the supplest and most elegant of dancers in the world, stretching yearning feet towards their lovers in the box of

* This little anecdote of 1841, probably from the *Charivari*, is later made the subject of a note to page 199 of *Opera and Drama* (Vol. II. of this series); it is a little odd to find it recurring last year (1898) in a so-called comic London paper which professes a horror of what it terms "whiskered chestnuts."—Tr.

the Jockey-club; on either hand above him he beholds most graceful ladies, with blinding necks and paralysing toilets, who rain the most intoxicating perfumes on his gas-accustomed nose; behind him he may gaze upon a mysticly-illumined box, which bears the awe-inspiring initials *L. P.* (Louis Philippe), sometimes mistaken for the monogram of the Opera-director, Léon Pillet. All this combines to an ensemble often positively dangerous to the vows of the poor German brotherhood in Paris. True, it would never occur to a member to break them,—what brother should possess the needful force or fortune?—but impious wishes are sometimes hard to smother down.

Such wishes generally lead to the most desperate ennui; then the arts of Liszt * and Chopin, the tones of Duprez and the Dorus-Gras, nay, even Rubini's immortal trills, are seldom able to dispel a tedium they far more frequently increase.

What a mercy then, when Spring appears and gives one a pretext for fleeing from Paris with its unspeakable temptations and stupefying din. For nothing then is left for a German to do in Paris, save at most to go and see the giraffes, or wait for some new revolution. Of course there are a thousand other things to engage the Parisians, even in summer-time; but, after a winter passed in hard abstentions, the German yearns for the tranquil joys of country-life.

Yet how to find country round Paris?—This city has a circumference of forty German miles at least;—everywhere villas of bankers, and houses full of ministers and plutocrats.

* It is well known that Wagner was never an admirer of what he calls *Virtuosenthum*, and at this period Liszt's fame as a virtuoso was at its zenith; we therefore need not be surprised that from the solitary meeting of the two predestined friends, in Paris, our author should have derived an unfavourable impression (see Vol. I. p. 386). That meeting appears to have taken place between March 24 and April 6, 1841; whilst this article must have been written subsequently to April 29, the date of Wagner's removal to Meudon. Not till three years had elapsed, did Liszt and Wagner meet again; this time at Dresden, where the foundation-stone of their lasting friendship may be said to have been prepared.—Tr.

So it was with real delight that, two leagues from Paris, I discovered a lone old-fashioned house. How I breathed again! for, to have no neighbours is a rare piece of fortune one learns in Paris first to prize. Upon hiring a room in this building I was enraptured by the circumstance, as I gathered from the endless mass of pictures in its owner's chamber, that my host was a painter. However awful these pictures, they filled me with a comforting assurance of the silence of their author's trade,—for pictures, so long as one hasn't to see them, are non-disturbing things.

I was amused by the original cut of my landlord, a man about eighty years old with the vigour of forty. He told me he had passed a great part of his life at the court of Versailles, and therefore was a Legitimist, above all since the July-Revolution had robbed him of a pension of 1000 fr. I confirmed him in his faith, and gave him my reasons for considering Legitimism a first-rate thing. This pleased him immensely; but the more did he deplore my indifference in Legitimistic matters, when I chanced, in absent-mindedness, to wound his feelings;—he was telling me that he distinctly remembered the funeral of the wife of Louis XV., whereon I gauchely asked him whether he referred to the Pompadour or the Dubarry.

Nevertheless we remained firm friends the whole first day. My only upset was a discovery which I made upon looking out of my window into the garden at back of the house: in its middle there flaunted a washing-tub, which my Legitimist had filled with water in the morning, left to warm in the sun, and entered before dinner in highly illegitimate undress.

More disturbing than this sad discovery, however, was what the worthy minion of the Dubarry gave me to hear in the evening. I had not seen all his rooms, and thus was unaware of the substantial assemblage of musical instruments he kept in one of them. Besides his painting and legitimism, the fiend had devoted himself to the invention of implements of sound, which he tested every night and morning, one after the other. My sufferings under this terrible habit of my landlord's will be conceived, when I state that till this day my each attempt to guide his dreadful talent for invention into other and more silent paths has proved completely fruitless.

It is impossible to withdraw into solitude, away from the evidences of Parisian culture, without making a goodish journey. Lucky the banker, who can afford such journeys! Lucky the born Parisian, who needs them not! But woe to the Paris-residential German who isn't a banker. He will be swallowed past all rescue in this sea of pleasureless pleasures, can he not succeed in becoming a banker.

To you, ye 30,000 of the German nation now in Paris, may redemption be granted!

VI.

LETTERS FROM PARIS, 1841.*

I.

Paris, February 23, 1841.

YOU have asked me for news from Paris: me, a poor German musician, for news from a city of endlessness, glitter and dirt. For long I was puzzled, hardly knowing upon what terrain to cast myself, to answer your wish most superbly. I wavered between planting myself in the Tuileries and thence entertaining you with some brilliant actions-of-State, or dreaming myself into the sanctuary of the Institute and thence conveying you some choice eavesdroppings anent the noble and the useful arts. But, to tell you the truth, with all these pretty stories I should only have been duping you; for I have convinced myself that German emigrants to Paris, save in a few extremely rare and special cases, never get so far as to be able to pass a valid judgment, from their own observation and with full conviction, on those loftier exclusive circles of Paris notable-society. I will not say that a German would lack the address to move in those circles as far as needed; only, they form a world so wholly foreign to the

* Of these Letters from Paris, the first eight appeared in the Correspondence columns of the Dresden *Abend-Zeitung* on the following dates:—No. 1, March 19, 20 and 22; No. 2, May 24-28; No. 3, June 14-17; No. 4, August 2-4; No. 5, October 1-2; No. 6, December 4-8; No. 7, December 25, 1841; No. 8, January 10-11, 1842. The last in the series, No. 9, appeared in the *Neue Zeitschrift für Musik* of February 22, 1842. So far as I am aware, only No. 1 has been reprinted in the full original German text, namely in Joseph Kürschner's *Richard Wagner-Jahrbuch* for 1886 (the only year of issue of that "annual").—Tr.

German way of life, that the first entry on it makes us ill at ease, and robs us as a rule of wish and courage to penetrate it farther. However engaging and amiable the exterior of these Frenchmen, you may take it from me that they are more reserved in their inmost being, especially toward foreigners, than even the inwardly and outwardly rugged English. We consequently are reduced to what one calls Publicity in general. This consists in a visit to the Chambers, to the cafés with their journals, and finally —ah! how my breath comes back!—the Theatre.—The Chambers, cafés and their journals, I may conveniently leave to the political papers; but to you I turn, ye countless theatres, and gladly would I also turn to you, ye concert-halls, were there but any of you, in a stricter sense, in Paris!

What a mercy that Music exists in the world, and above all in Paris! What should we numberless Germans who have become musicians, not tailors or watchmakers,—what should we do in Paris without it? 'Tis a glorious bond, with power to chain us to this else so alien world, and at like time give us a faint taste for Paris public life.—Once more, blest be Music! and blest the happy dispensation that made the Paris world unanimously adopt it into its amusements! Here lies the means of perfectly explaining Paris to the German mind, and in virtue of it we may wager that we understand Paris from the flageolet-notes of Duprez to the actual flageolet of the Balls in the Rue St Honoré. What lies beyond, or utters itself through other organs, pray leave on one side, my brave fellow-countrymen! for it ever will remain as dark and enigmatic to you as the drear, incomprehensible calculations of the *mont de piété*.*

I propose because of this, the next free week, to write a history of Parisian music with all sorts of interweavings, such as the completion of the *hôtel de ville*, the fortifications, and other matters of the kind that soon will all fall under

* The State-pawnbroker's shops. It is scarcely necessary to underline the personal application.—Tr.

Music. For I foresee that we soon shall have all such undertakings musically accompanied, much in the same way as the re-interment of the remains of the July victims, or the home-bringing of the *cendres de Napoléon*,—which, by the by, are now most scrupulously called *le corps de l'empereur* since the day when people learnt that the hero had been found in tolerably good preservation; wherefore, also, the elegant "charge" of Dantan's,* representing Thiers with a casket containing Napoleon's ashes under his arm, has suddenly vanished.—Thus much is certain: a proposal has already been broached to instal a mighty orchestra in the Chamber of Deputies, with the object partly of enhancing such speeches as those of Marshal Soult† by a recitative accompaniment, and partly of idealising the noisy interruptions of the deputies by making them delicate and charming. Without delicacy, nothing can be rightly done in Paris; and music, in the Parisian sense, is the daintiest herb for those charming sauces with which everything here, even sorrow and misfortune, is swallowed down at last. —However, that history of Parisian Music and its bearing on modern affairs will occupy much time, and as I am not quite sure whether to write it in verse or in prose, I will confine myself for the present to relating you just this and that from the surface of our art-world.

To begin with, a death-announcement! The Paris Grand Opéra is at its last gasp! It is awaiting salvation from the German Messiah—from *Meyerbeer*; if he delays its rescue much longer, the death-agony will soon set in. The trouble is this:—Auber has turned prematurely old, and Halévy has not stirred himself for three long years; but Meyerbeer, who only plays his hand in the fame-game here with high

* These "*charges*" were caricatures in plaster of Paris, for which the sculptor Dantan junior (1800-69) had acquired a European reputation. Two marble busts by him, the one of Grisi, the other of Malibran, dated respectively 1837 and 1839, were recently exhibited in the vestibule of Covent Garden Opera-house.—Tr.

† Prof. Kürschner tells us that on the 29th Oct. 1840, after Thiers' resignation, Marshal Soult for the third time accepted the Presidency of the Cabinet, and for the second time the Portfolio of War.—Tr.

and deliberate stakes, has his reasons for not allowing his newest work,* on which all hopes are set, to appear just yet. So the Opéra is in travail, and long has been forced to seek its weal in Mediocrities. The public, on the other hand, has the whim to bestow its approval on nothing but Superiorities; and I must admit that, on this point, it earns my full respect. Brilliant reputations and dazzling names may be good enough to impose on directors and entrepreneurs, but the public declines to be blinded. And thus it comes, that none but true Superiorities can keep themselves afloat; thus comes it, that one has *Robert* and the *Huguenots* appearing again and again, when the Mediocrities have been compelled to withdraw. With *Robert le diable* in particular things wear a wondrous, almost an uncanny look; and were I Herr Donizetti, Herr Rualtz, or any other of those unfortunates "who have already found their ruin in a like attempt," I should hate this Robert as a Devil proven. For this opera is an unerring barometer of the success, or rather, failure of those authors' works; if a new opera has made no mark, after the first few performances "*Robert le diable*" goes up again; so that one may be sure, when one sees this work on the posters once more, that the new opera has come to grief. Robert is immortal! Despite the often scandalous performances; despite even Duprez having done his worst at last to murder the notes and buffoon the acting of the title-rôle; despite the dresses and dances having faded and dulled under the huge fatigue of two-hundred-and-thirty representations,—despite all this, I say,—*Robert* continues to share with the *Huguenots* the pride of being the only operas with a really brisk demand. One can easily imagine, then, how eagerly the present Director of the Opéra, Herr Léon Pillet, awaits the master's newest work, which promises a sure and great success. Meanwhile the public and quite especially himself, the Director, make up with the *Favorite*.

This *Favorite*, as you probably know, is an opera by Donizetti, and maintains a fairly good success. Through

* *L'Africaine*, eventually held back till after the composer's death.—Tr.

this opera I have made an interesting discovery, which I now will impart to you. It is, that Paris lies midway between Germany and Italy. The German composer who writes for Paris, sees himself compelled to throw off a good share of his seriousness and rigour; whereas the Italian maëstro instinctively feels spurred to grow more earnest and sedate, to lock up his fal-dals, and shew himself in his better nature. I refrain from conclusions, which in any case would fall out favourably for Paris, and simply add that the *Favorite* affords immediate proof of the second part of my assertion. In this music of Donizetti's, besides the acknowledged merits of the Italian school, there reign that higher seemliness and well-bred dignity which one misses in the countless other works of this inexhaustible maëstro.

For us German patriots, however, this same *Favorite* has had a fatal influence. The Director and public had previously decided that the Grand Opéra required a first singeress, and both parties had cast expectant eyes on Fräulein *Löwe.* But Mme Stoltz, who sings that Favorite, has given Herr Léon Pillet distinctly to understand that *she* herself is the first singeress in the world, and therefore the person in question;—in fact, she seems to have proved it to him so conclusively that he now has not a moment's doubt, and, to avoid the misfortune of having two first singeresses in the world, he has decided *not* to engage Frl. Löwe.—We Germans have thus been played a pretty trick, whilst Frl. Löwe is placed in a sorry fix. She comes hither, rejecting the most tempting offers to chain her again to Berlin, sings once with great success at a public concert, and in consequence of that success she learns next day that the doors are shut to her in future.*—For the rest, the matter almost led to a disaster: —Herr Moritz Schlesinger, to wit, our principal music-

* Sophie Löwe (1815-66) had been engaged at Berlin since 1837 at a salary of nearly £1000 a year. In 1848 she married Prince Friedrich von Liechtenstein, and retired from the stage. The concert referred to here, and in the next paragraph, was that mentioned in my note to page 83 *antea.*—Tr.

publisher and a zealous patron of Fräulein Löwe, in his capacity of mediator between the two parties found himself so provoked by an offensive remark of Herr Léon Pillet's, that he appealed to his trusty sword and challenged the offender to a duel. Messieurs Halévy and Jules Janin, the seconds of Herr Schlesinger, endeavoured to arrange the affair, and submitted an *amende honorable* to Herr Pillet for his signature; but as this gentleman declined, the day of combat stood already fixed. Upon that day itself, however, the Director at last thought fit to sign the honourable amend; and so a dire mishap has been escaped, which would have affected even *me*, since I am bound to both the gentlemen by iron bonds of industry and ambition.* An Opera-director and a Music-publisher,—what indispensable people for a struggling composer!—Joking apart,—the affair is annoying, especially for Frl. Löwe; who, by the way, is called in the journals here first Loëwe, then Looëwe, and finally Loeuve. At the concert of the *Gazette Musicale*, in which she made her first and last appearance, she celebrated—as already said—a signal triumph. She sang the "Adelaide" and an Italian aria, as though to give a glimpse between the German and Italian methods of what she would do in the French. It was generally and admiringly recognised that, in addition to enormous throat-dexterity, she has the peculiar advantage of a melodious voice; which unfortunately is not the case with the established virtuose here, the Dorus-Gras, Quint-Damoreau † and Persiani.

The concert in which Fräulein Löwe sang, was characteristic enough. The programme was occupied almost exclusively by Germans, among whom my Insignificance also had the honour to figure. One journal protested in fact, albeit in a whisper, against its *parfum allemand*;

* The draft plan for the *Flying Dutchman* had not as yet been definitely rejected, or rather, extorted by Pillet for another composer.—Tr.

† According to Prof. Jos. Kürschner (*Wagner-Jahrbuch*), from whom the substance of most of the notes to this first Letter is borrowed, the lady's name should have been printed as "Damoreau-Cinti" (1801-63). It was for her that Meyerbeer wrote the part of "Isabelle" in *Robert le diable*.—Tr.

H

nevertheless the French appear to be gradually accustoming themselves to having to pronounce more German names than French, especially in matters musical. Not without a certain opposition is this taking place, however, and the little private school of the Opéra Comique—with its numberless atomic Thomases, Clapissons, Monpous, &c.*—explosively gnashes its wee quadrille milk-teeth; but it won't help these gentry in the slightest, and if they don't soon bestir themselves to leave their tinyness, they'll one day find themselves drummed out from this terrain as well. This terrain of Light Opera is truly run to woeful seed. This theatre, which once was the chosen home of the national French school, has dragged for some years through a tangle of tactless vapidities, like a stream, all mighty in its starting waters, that shamefully loses itself at last in sand and sludge. It would take me too far afield, to cite the many causes of the downfall of this popular institute, to follow their workings one by one. Suffice it to say that nowhere has lethargy more plainly been felt after a period of lustre, than in the life of the Opéra Comique after the brilliant epoch when Boieldieu, Auber and Herold gave such brotherly voice to their countrymen's character.

For a series of years, beyond question, Halévy has been the most talented chief of the newest French school. Unfortunately, he came too soon by the idea of aping his predecessor, Auber, i.e. of writing with the greatest and most easy-going nonchalance; he had forgotten, alas! that he really had not marched so far as his model, who truly could say that he had made a brand-new manner for himself and now might venture to indulge

* Of these composers the first-named, of course, is (or has been) well-known to operagoers through his *Mignonne* and *Hamlet*; but at that time he had done little more than Comic work. Antonin Louis Clapisson (born 1808) made some name by his songs, but had little success with any opera save his earliest, *La Figurante* (1838). Hippolyte Monpou, a composer of the same class as Clapisson, was born in 1804 and died in August 1841. In my preface to Vol. VII. the names of all three appear, as represented by productions at the Opéra Comique in 1840-41.—Tr.

his humours. And thus it came that Halévy, the gifted creator of *La Juive*, produced a string of worthless works, which, to the honour of the public, moreover failed. His *Drapier* was the last of those operas, and from that time forward he seems to have seen the error of his ways, and pulled himself together in all seriousness for a brilliant revenge. This he at anyrate has lately achieved with his *Guitarrero*, a work worthy of the best period and the best masters; that surprisingly beautiful opera has had an unqualified success, and perhaps may mark a new and brilliant epoch in the history of the Opéra Comique. For it is noteworthy that a successful work, such as this, never appears alone, but is always followed by its like, called forth by emulation; without which stimulus those manikins, as named above, are too lax and lazy to exert themselves in earnest.

As I have said a word about the Opéra Comique, it will be only fair to add at least half a one about the Théâtre Italien. How my heart rejoices when I think of you, ye happy, thrice, nay, four-times blest Italians! If I were Louis Philippe, I should say: Were I not Louis Philippe, I would choose to be Rubini or Lablache! For my part, I would far rather be one of these beings than King of the French. What a life of joy, what an existence full of pleasant things! Laurels and banknotes are the ever-lasting lot of these un-aging demigods. They come from the most delicate of dinners; for their digestion, and the three-hundredth time, they sing the *Cenerentola*: before them a public swimming in perfume, satin, velvet and enthusiasm; for going home they set upon their heads, not sordid hats, but the charmingest of laurel-wreaths; they go to bed and dream of dividends,—is that not magnificent, or who could wish a better fate? And to crown it all, their sempiternal life! For, to tell the truth, I can never clearly figure to myself these people dying, or even losing their power of song. "Rubini, Lablache &c.," so runs the song, if I mistake not, since a hundred years, and so will run for at least as many years again. One thing is certain, that we ourselves shall not survive it.—Nevertheless even *they* must have a care to freshen up a bit, for there are weak moments in the life of the Paris public in which it suddenly imagines that it has seen somewhat too much *Cenerentola*. The consequences of such fits of depression are, as a rule, that the crowd grows smaller, and the eternal tenants of the boxes, in their perfumes and satins, look pettishly around them for the missing black-cloth ground-work of the parterre, which really is so indispensable as foil to the glimmer of their toilets. On ill-whimmed nights like these the immortal heroes put their heads together with that of the easily-mortal Director, and decide on some expedient for avoiding such-like doleful evenings. And so it happens that for once in a way a new opera is newly studied, or an old one newly cast,—nay, in extreme cases one goes the length of playing a trump, to draw the eyes of all Paris to the Odéon again. One can but see such a stroke of genius in the very latest, which has only just come to my ears as the freshest of news, and you therefore shall have without delay:—Frl. Löwe, who, as I told you above, has had the doors of the Opéra slammed in her face, will make her début at the *Italiens*. Thus our German fellow-countrywoman will not quit Paris without a sounding satisfaction. The news is still too new, for me to furnish you with further details; but even in its brevity it is interesting and important.—

To close my report with something really cheering, I announce to you a great talent and a great success, acknowledged aloud and unanimously lauded by the Paris public as a musical event. I speak of Vieuxtemps and his first appearance here. This in every respect extraordinary artist arrived a short while back, triumphantly preceded by a considerable renown. He made his first appearance at the first Conservatoire-concert of the year, and played in a Grand Concerto of his latest composition.* Alike his

* His opus 10, in E major, given January 10, 1841. Wagner had already made the young artist's acquaintance at Riga in 1838, when Vieuxtemps was touring with François Servais.—Tr.

execution and his composition had the most immense success, before the most critical audience in Paris; in my opinion this success and this composition, taken in conjunction, form a musical event of the first magnitude. So one man has dared at last to vault the endless rut of plaudit-seeking virtuosi with their horribly dishonouring *airs variés*, and restore his art to that pristine dignity from which it had been so shamefully debased! So one man has dared to place himself before the jaded ears of the crowd with a noble, sterling piece of music, purely and chastely conceived, performed with life and freshness,—a composition for which he claims the exclusive attention of his audience, and to which he manifestly welds his art of virtuoso with a single eye to lifting his work to an ideal understanding! Not only is it that this noble aim is in itself remarkable, nay, altogether admirable; but to attain that aim so thoroughly, to be in possession of such rich powers of mind and mechanism as to succeed in the most striking fashion,—this constitutes a phenomenon which cannot be too highly rated! And this rare artist—incredible as it may seem—has only just completed his one-and-twentieth year! O all ye virtuosi with your fantaisies, your variations and *polacca guerriera*s, bow low before this stripling, and strive to emulate him; else, I forewarn you, in less than five years ye will all be dead and buried!

Herewith I pray you let me close, for I know nothing worthier or finer to report; unless it were about the *Bœuf gras* who has been dragging his weight through the streets of Paris since yesterday, and, as I am told, is to dance on the Pont Neuf to-day to a quadrille of Musard's composed expressly for the purpose.—You see, even here comes Music tripping down my pen; I assure you, one cannot get away from her in Paris. Wherefore you may congratulate yourself on having turned for news to a musician; for you may take my word that Paris, as it is to-day, and as alone it can display itself to a German soul, can become quite clear and comprehensible to none but a musician.

You shall soon hear more, with, and perhaps also without music, from

Yours

RICHARD WAGNER.

2.

April 6, 1841.

There are dismal days in the life of the Parisian public—days clad in sorrow, big with fate,—days when it bitterly feels the truth of that painful doctrine of the fleetingness of beauty, the changefulness of the amusing. On such days I'm sorry for the Paris public, and unobserved I often weep a pitying tear; for who could but weep when witnessing the heart-break of such days? These days are certain evenings that follow the first days of Spring; they are necessary and unavoidable, for they are founded on the nature of things, conditioned by the laws of all existence.

Such a day came lately, when the Italians gave their last performance; they sang *I Puritani*, and took leave of the lofty world of Paris. No tearing of a lover from the arms of his beloved could be more sorrowful, no parting of father and daughter, of mother and son, more pathetic and tender, than when the Italian Opera tears itself from the convulsive embraces of Paris society. When I beheld this grief, my heart was softened, and in profound fellow-feeling I flung a daring question in the face of Fate: I asked—*Why* this speeding? *Why* this parting?—Then my eye, turned sadly upwards, met that of *Shakespeare* (for he too is among the distinguished poets whose portraits grace the ceiling of the Odéon); he frowned on me, as if he had just written his "Lear," and said: "Presumptuous Saxon, thinkest thou we English want no amusement too?"—I took the hint, and sighed in silence. But it was impossible for my heart to do aught but break, when I was forced again to hear and witness what went on. Mingling sobs with doleful cheers, the whole assembly begged mementoes of the leave-takers. Locks it was not possible for them to give, for, despite his enormous growth of hair, Rubini himself must have gone home bald, had he tried to content each petitioner; so an expedient was found, and the heavenliest arias and duets in the world were sung with such expression, such a glow, that the grief grew greater every moment. Men plucked their beards in handfuls, while ladies tore their most expensive dresses;—the one half fainted, the other threw bouquets.— — How it ended, I know not; too deeply moved, I left my box. In the corridors I saw chasseurs and attendants with satin mantles and burnouses on their arms; good souls!—even they were weeping!—

If this evening's impression resembled the intoxicating sorrow of the parting of Romeo and Juliet in Bellini's opera, where one knows not whether to huzza for very pain or wail for very rapture, another evening at the Théâtre Français spread a gentler, more sentimental hue. It was the night when Madame Mars bade her definitely last farewell. Though one had got accustomed to the leave-takings of Mme Mars; though one had long familiarised oneself with the thought that the respected lady might really one day bid her last adieu; ay, though there were many persons who cherished the belief that she long ago had played for the last time,—yet her final edict made an uncommonly acute impression. The French took stock of themselves on this evening, grew serious and introspective, and cast a searching glance upon their past. They could not clearly call before their soul the life and doings of the Mars, without thinking back to the Restoration, the Empire, the Consulate, the Revolution; nay, some got as far as the times of the Fronde, and fancied they had even then been living, even then had seen the Mars performing comedy. So, when the public took its leave of her, it believed it was parting with a notable slice of its own past history; and when the Frenchman falls a-thinking on his past, he generally becomes as staid and sober as a German. There is no one who can work on such a mood, like Madame Mars; so that you may imagine the impression she produced this evening, of all others. It was grand, deep, sentimental, melancholy, affecting and—resigned.

The intentions of Mme Rachel, also, have spread no little consternation; for her "last appearances," too, had been repeatedly announced. Some believed she was in such an advanced stage of consumption, that she no longer dared to work at Racine's "transfiguration"; others saw the affair in its true light,—it was an engagement-dispute, about 5000 fr. of future pension more or less. The lady has given in,—Racine lives again, whilst Victor Hugo will shortly die. Questions of engagement and management, like this, are habitually of great moment to the enormous Paris public, and rouse its interest in no small degree; to one large section a change of Directorate, for instance, is of just the same importance as a change of Ministry to the rest. As a matter of fact, the two things mostly coincide.

The Directors of the Royal Theatres—i.e. those which receive a regular subsidy, such as the Théâtre Français, the Royal Academy of Music [Grand Opéra], the Italian Opera, the Opéra Comique, and the Vaudeville—are appointed by the Government, to carry on the business of their theatre upon their own account, subject to certain statutes. Such a director naturally has a good berth, and its bestowal offers Ministers a decent opportunity of rewarding faithful services. The services that can be rendered to a Ministry here, consist almost exclusively in those of the Press. If a journalist has for some time served the cause of any noted personage of State through thick and thin, and that personage gets into the Ministry, the journalist has a reasonable claim upon his gratitude. Then the word is: "Choose yourself a favour!"—and the customary reply runs: "Give me the Grand Opéra!"—for everyone thinks the Grand Opéra the best-paying post in the State. Unfortunately there is only this one Grand Opéra, but quite a number of deserving journalists, especially in view of the constant change of Ministers. Yet only one man at a time can be Director of the Opera,—

so how is the existing tenant to be ousted? At a pinch we have recourse to money; one has his appointment bought from him; for another a brand-new, ideal, a never-dreamt-of post—such as "Inspector of the Royal Theatres"—is created; and the deserving journalist becomes Director of the Grand Opéra. Such arrangements take place almost every six months, that is to say, as often as a new Ministry succeeds to the helm. The time of rulership thus being short, you can imagine the diligence with which these gentlemen pursue their opportunity. Generally speaking, they are worthy paterfamiliases, and retire into private life after a hasty year of office; unless, indeed, they are made Ambassadors, and brought at last into the Government itself.—Such cases are by no means rare, and not long since it happened that an outgoing Director of the Opera, Herr Véron, was entrusted with an important mission to London. It must have been delightful to observe the horror of the English, when they found themselves obliged to engage in diplomatic business with an Opera-director; they cannot but have expected that the man would appear in fleshings, with feathers on his head.

How things stand with the progress of Art, in these circumstances, may easily be conceived. Each Director finds it his first duty to treat the art-institute confided to him as a machine, a sort of steam-press for minting money as fast as possible. The treasury is the main affair; next come the singers; upon their heels the costumes, dancers (as a rule they understand these best) and, bringing up the rear, the composers and poets. The latter don't give the Director many sleepless nights; their choice is light, for there are only three or four of them who enjoy the privilege of writing for the Grand Opéra, for example. He peacefully takes what they offer him, and orders scenery and costumes; then he invests in bonds, and tries to keep the current Ministry on foot.

Should his composers not have brought him wares enough, or have sold him rubbish in spite of his astuteness, then the director will overhaul his ancient score-bag and give whatever he draws out. In this fashion it sometimes happens that quite firstrate things are brought to light, and to a providential dip into that lucky bag we apparently owe the recent revival of "Don Juan," among other matters. With this "Don Juan" of ours I had a strange experience. I had a longing to hear it once again, particularly as I was curious to see if the French performance would please me better than that of the Italians, from which I had always come away with the idea that these inconceivably famous singers had sung and played incomparably badly.

To tell the truth, I can't quite remember what the singers, dancers and machinists of the French Grand Opéra did with our "Don Juan"; they sang, acted, danced, machined and sceneried with such enthusiasm, that at last I fell asleep amid it all. In my sleep I had a dream, and in my dream I saw the two accurst Black Knights. The history of the two Black Knights, however, I necessarily must relate to you before my dream can be intelligible.—In a townlet not far from my birthplace I once saw a representation by a licensed strolling company. Just as the play was about to begin I heard a babel on the stage, and soon picked out an anguished cry, apparently that of the manager: "The hermit! The hermit! Where's the hermit?" As the impatience of the audience assumed a more and more boisterous tone, that cry soon took a more comminative character, as: "Where the devil's the hermit? The scoundrel has got to begin! Find me the cursed hermit!"—An answer could be distinguished: "He's swilling in the tavern." Then, after a most unrepeatable oath, I heard the order given at last in hasty resignation: "The black knights!"—The curtain went up: from opposite sides two black-clad knights came proudly on; with blood-curdling shouts of "Ha! This shalt thou pay me!" they savagely rushed on one another, and hit out right and left in the most merciless manner. Finally the hermit appeared, and the black knights marched off. But as often as the players were missing; as often as a scene stuck fast; as often as the leading lady was behindhand with her change of dress: in short, as often as the rushing stream of action halted,—so often did the abandoned black knights appear, and fall on one another with the cry: "Ha! This shalt thou pay me!"

I have met those Black Knights very often since, especially where the pleasures of Art were in hand, and I confess to being seized with deadly terror whenever I see them arrive, at times quite unexpectedly.

In that dream which I dreamt at the Paris Grand Opéra, when (wonderful to say) I fell asleep over "Don Juan," those two Black Knights appeared to me again. Their combat was lifelike, and every moment more embittered; this time they seemed to have really sworn to kill each other, and I was rejoicing in my inner heart that at last I should be rid of this pair of fiends for ever. Yet neither of them budged an inch, and neither yielded; neither of them would die, though their strife became so savage that the deafening blows and ghastly noise awoke me, and I started to my feet.—The audience was cheering; the overture to "Guillaume Tell" was just ended.

See what a trade the Black Knights practise even here! The singer of the part of "Don Juan" had sung himself hoarse; the overture and an act of "William Tell" must stop the gap.*

My dream had exhausted me, and I went home.—

In the Chamber of Deputies (I mean the Opéra Comique as distinguished from the Grand Opéra, which latter is sufficiently characterised now by honourable spokesmen like Mozart, Weber, Spontini etc., as the House of Peers) —in Light Opera then—things have been pretty lively for

* This actually occurred on March 31, 1841, at a "reprise" of *Don Juan*, when Barroilhet had to throw up his part with two acts yet to follow; the overture and trio from *Guillaume Tell* replaced them (see *Gaz. Mus.* for April 4). But what would Wagner have said to our Covent Garden management's deliberately announcing the first and second acts of *Figaro* to be followed by *Cavalleria Rusticana*, and that in a season (1898) so largely devoted to his own works?—Tr.

some while past. Of Halévy's "Guitarrero" I told you last time, and it only remains for me to confirm its success. This opera has once more verified my opinion of the nature and attitude of modern French composers. They all have issued from the school of the Opéra Comique; thence have they drawn their fluency and briskness, their bent to chanson-patterned melodies, their snap (*Keckheit*) in handling the ensemble. Their music is chiefly conversation, for the most part witty conversation, combining the merits of the Mannerly with those of the Popular. It has really been a mere enlargement of frame, by no means an abandonment of terrain, when the French pushed on into the realm of grand Tragic Opera.* Upon that basis of their own had they developed, formed and fortified their powers; and now they boldly threw themselves upon Grand Drama, with the same energy as their tenderest dandies threw themselves on the barricades of Paris. This shews the most characteristically with *Auber*: his home has always been the Opéra Comique; there he assembled his forces, to fight a good fight, and win a great victory like the "Muette de Portici" [*Masaniello*]. Halévy, however, forms a decided exception; for as yet there is nothing to prove that he has reversed the French schooling for others too. *His* creative impulse, at anyrate, made a start with Grand Opera; his whole nature and the powerful blend of his blood set him directly on the larger field, and helped him win his fight at once there. Unfortunately, he had matured too quickly: it looked as if he had never had a past; and, as it were to live back into one, he now stepped into the cradle of French music. In truth, he found himself ill at ease in Comic Opera; to seem light and elegant, he thought needful to grow flat and superficial; he turned volatile on principle. Alas! he bore this volatileness back into his old terrain; in "Guido and Ginevra" his struggle between levity and solidness is quite repellent.

* For many of the ideas in this paragraph compare *Opera and Drama*, Vol. II. p. 54, also the article on Auber in Vol. V.—Tr.

In more recent times Halévy appears to be really on the road to the usual course of French development; his forces have concentrated more on Comic Opera: his "Guitarrero" is a proof that he means right and feels at home. Who knows if, like Auber, he isn't even now preparing his main attack from the side of the Opéra Comique? Of his just-completed grand opera for the Académie, "The Knight of Malta,"* I hear great things.

Auber too, to whom opera-composing has become as much of a habit as lathering to a barber, has let his voice be heard once more at the Opéra Comique. But the great master often stops at lathering now, and sometimes at bare soap-sudding; his fine keen razor, bright though its blade, one feels but seldom; when he does apply it, one finds out now and again that he hasn't remarked a notch in its edge, and, without his knowing, it scrapes one horribly. Thus the public often quits the barber's shop with its beard unshorn, and is left with nothing but to wipe off the soapsuds, however sweet-smelling, if it would not wait till they fly away of themselves—which happens, as a rule, before one reaches home.—

For all that, the "Crown-diamonds" (the title of Auber's new opera) are not unimportant; once or twice the Black Knights frightened me here as well, but their fight was never very desperate, and the right man generally appeared in good time. The whole way through, one sees that a master wrote this opera, and a brilliant technique is nowhere to be denied.

The texts of the new comic operas are mostly Portuguese. Scribe is at present over head and ears in love with the land of Dona Maria. As a fact, Portugal is convenient beyond all measure; it lies a tidy stretch from Paris, no omnibus plies that road, and an author therefore has little fear that one will track his geographic solecisms. In Portugal Scribe may chop and change as he likes, and nobody will disbelieve him, since we must take him for very well-travelled in that country, as he tells us stories

* Eventually called *La Reine de Chypre*; see later, also Vol. VII.—Tr.

and describes localities which no one else had ever heard of. Who, forsooth, should know all the subterranean caves where coiners hide—particularly in Portugal—and young unmarried Queens repair to get paste diamonds, so that they may pledge, if not actually sell the real ones in times of impecuniosity?—In effect we here must yield the pas to Scribe, and meekly let him lead us by the hand; otherwise there's instant danger of barking our shins against awkward corners.—You see how important it is for a theatre-poet to make early acquaintance with the most recondite nooks of foreign lands, and especially to go in search of hidden treasures; for only in such wise could Scribe have succeeded in stumbling on so productive a vein of gold as that which now replenishes his chests and strong-rooms. Long live Portugal!—

The subjects from the days of Louis XV., the Pompadour and the Dubarry, which so long and exclusively held the boards and particularly the wardrobe of the Opéra Comique, are now completely out of fashion. Scribe has well pondered the question: What is the upshot of all these costly wenches with their hoops and powdered hair? They have all the extravagant outlay; but it is he that has to pay the bill in the long run, to avoid a revolution. True, there remain the satin gowns and golden tresses; yet—God knows how soon satin gets shabby, and tresses, if they are not quite genuine, turn black or rusty: and who is going to buy them of him then?—Indeed, Scribe was obliged to look round for something solid; and as there isn't much of that in Paris, he could light on nothing better than Portuguese Queens, especially when he stoutly backs them up with Bankers, as in the "Guitarrero."

Bankers!—A weighty chapter!—and as it comes so very pat, I can't refrain from paying it a passing mark of homage.

So:—

Liszt has lately given a concert. He was the sole performer,—no one else either played or sang; the tickets cost 20 fr. each; he had no expenses, took 10,000 fr., and is shortly to give another. What assurance! what infallibility!—I mean in the speculation; for his playing is always so sure and infallible, that it no longer is worth the pains to speak about it. The Black Knights began,—I mean the Overture to "Wilhelm Tell" of Schiller, set to the piano by Rossini and played by Liszt; they were followed by many other wondrous things. Alas! I understand naught of all these things,* and therefore can only give you an amateur's account. But stay! you will relieve me of even that: you in Dresden, also, not long since heard the wonder-man. So I have no need to tell you who and what he is,—which suits me very well, as I really should not know how to do it. That day I came by such a terrible headache, such painful twitchings of the nerves, that I had to go home and put myself to bed.

Just opposite me lives Henri Vieuxtemps; he had seen me arrive home ill, and, humanitarian that he is, he came across with his fiddle, sat down by my bed, and played me something *gratis*. I fell into a lovely sleep; delicious dreams came over me; I heard the voice of Goethe singing:

"Schwindet, Ihr dunkeln	Crumble, ye gloomy
Wölbungen droben!	Vaultings above there!
Reizender schaue	Rob no more blindly
Freundlich der blaue	Hearts of the kindly
Æther herein!"	Heaven's blue light!

I saw those fields, those meadows, I drank of those wells and breathed those odours; my gaze pierced the clearest æther, and in broad daylight I saw in heaven's heart that godlike star which drenched my soul like the blessing-freighted eye of Mozart. All grew bright and happy; when I awoke, the player still was standing calmly by me, as though he had just fulfilled a work of mercy. I thanked him, and we spoke of it no more.

Eternal dreamer that I am! From the Bankers I have unwittingly dropped among the Musicians. Propensity! I've no talent for speculation, and my life-long no prudent thing will come of me. For a Correspondent I'm least fitted of all, and I heartily pity your sufferings. The

* See note to page 105, also Vol. VII. p. xv.—Tr.

only reparation for "my unbusinesslike bent towards woolgathering," would be at least to collect my wits and tell you something sensible of Vieuxtemps. But the secret of our friendship is out, and though I had reason not to conceal my gratitude for that lucky cure, many people might think I was praising the fiddler from motives of coterie, or because he had furnished me a household remedy for headaches. And—however tranquilly I tried to speak—I could but *more* than praise him: I should have to glorify him, raise him to the skies. But if Herr Ole Bull were to read this, perhaps he too would want to be raised to the skies by me; and, as I have given myself away by the tale of my cure, I should run the risk of *his* coming to my bedside too, some day, and playing his "*Polacca guerriera.*" Such annoyances one must try to avoid: wherefore I am silent about Vieuxtemps; and the more readily as he has no need at all of my praises, since a hundred Frenchmen's quills have lately made it quite impossible to say anything fresh or more exhaustive of him. With the swiftness of lightning has he made his epoch; and this epoch will be of such high worth, such lasting weight, that it will drive ennobling paths in each domain of art. He now has gone to England; to every quarter of the globe he'll go, and slay all Black Knights like a venging demigod.

Already one can plainly trace the influence ordained for Vieuxtemps' epoch; and firstly, as goes without saying, at the seat of true and genuine music, the concerts of the Conservatoire. It was here that Vieuxtemps' appearance was first acclaimed, and here the very next successor was made to learn *whither* to turn, if he would keep his footing. This was the once so able and distinguished violinist, Ernst; he, too, had a hearing at the Conservatoire, and though there was nothing to be said against his virtuosity, the same public that had just heard Vieuxtemps' concerto could not receive Ernst's concertino otherwise than unfavourably, nor spare the formerly popular artist a bitter lesson.

Let anyone who appears in these Conservatoire-concerts

be on his guard! We Germans are far too apt to form a superficial estimate of the standard to which they are kept. The audience at these concerts consists of the keenest and most squeamish knowers and lovers of music, who, however middling their previous education, perforce attain expertness through a constant hearing of the most masterly performances of the soundest compositions.—The orchestra, notably as regards its strings, is ideal. Plume ourselves as much as we choose on *understanding* the works of Mozart and Beethoven more inwardly than other nations, they yet are *performed* the most perfectly by the French,—at least, by the band of the Conservatoire. To hear Beethoven's Last Symphony here, is to admit that one here first learns to understand many parts of it! Especially in the first movement of this giant work, I remember that I here first gained full understanding of certain passages and melismi; at performances in Germany they had always seemed unclear to me, or insignificant, whereas they here affected me so deeply as to throw an entirely fresh light on the mighty intentions of the lofty master.

However, should there still be points in the rendering of Beethoven's works that have escaped the Conservatoire orchestra, all doubts will soon be swept away; for He is here, Beethoven's man in the flesh—*Schindler*, the intimate Schindler. He has left his home; the voice of the Lord has driven him forth to preach to all the Heathen, for yet is no light in the world, yet are we groping in darkness, and know not the high evangel bequeathed us by the master!—I needs must speak with unction, for the man of whom I talk is full thereof, and further bears a striking likeness to some Apostle whose face I can't just call to mind. He has a brave appearance, mild manners and beaming eyes, wears a brown coat, and ordinarily Beethoven's portrait.

Schindler must have singled out Paris for the first stage of his mission with a view to prove his courage and steadfastness by casting himself at once into the very hot-bed of the heathen. Indeed it will be a hard test, since the godless Parisians refuse to believe in him at all, and, what is worse, make merry over him. If he could only laugh, things perhaps might go better; but since he isn't even equal to laughing at the most ridiculous thing of all, to wit himself, I am afraid he will come to grief in Paris. One might prophesy that his benevolent character will harden in time, so that he will end by thinking the world not worth the being enlightened. In every respect this would be a pity, especially for those mild and pliant qualities of his, of which he gave the world a most obliging specimen only the other day. It was thus: in his book on Beethoven he had thought fit to pronounce a portentous anathema on a brochure published by *Anders* in Paris for the benefit of the fund for a monument to be erected to Beethoven, which pamphlet contained a French version of the "Notices" of Ries and Wegeler upon the life of the great master. Anders,* a pupil of Forkel's and one of the most thorough-paced and erudite of music-bibliographers, was exasperated at this strange outburst of insolence on part of the else so kindly man; for the latter had brought an accusation most wounding to any conscientious writer, namely, that he had disfigured those Notices with arbitrary additions and inventions for the French, and shamelessly had painted Beethoven *al fresco* as a wild man of the woods. When the Man of Beethoven reached Paris, he was so agreeable as to invite Anders to a conference, with the object of radically proving to him the truth of his assertion. The conference took place; it was a dreary day, and Schindler in a surprisingly mild mood. After Anders had demonstrated to him line by line that he had not allowed himself the smallest material addition to the original Notices, the beaming eyes of the Man of

* As stated in my preface to Vol. VII. on the authority of C. F. Glasenapp, at the time of writing this letter Wagner was himself engaged with Anders in the preparation of a Life of Beethoven; the project, however, fell through.—Tr.

Beethoven ran over, and in an excess of tameness he seized Anders by the hand, assuring him with deep emotion that, *had he known* him, he certainly would never have permitted himself that little jest; moreover, he solemnly promised him a *brilliant satisfaction* in the second edition of his book.— —

I have cited this instance to shew how great is the docility of the glorious Schindler, and how strongly developed the bump of his astounding logic. It therefore pains me to see him bootlessly squandering his eminent elucidative powers on the incorrigible Parisians. May his good angel waft him soon from hence!—

I observe, honoured Sir, that I again have chattered much, but without touching on many a weighty point whose discussion is more imperative than anything else in the world. I therefore must refer you once more to a future communication. Till then I crave your favour,

RICHARD WAGNER.

3.

May 5, 1841.

It is becoming clear to me that I must employ main force, to speak of *Berlioz*, for the thing will not arrange itself through opportunity. This very circumstance, that in discussing the everyday events of the Paris world of pleasure—or if you will, of Art—I have not had occasion to touch on the gifted musician, to me seems characteristic enough; it further affords me a good introduction to my estimate of Berlioz, who in any case has the right to demand a quite particularly lengthy page in my Reports from Paris.

Berlioz is no incidental composer, and so I could not light upon him incidentally. He stands in no connection, and has nothing to do with those pompous, exclusive art-institutes of Paris; after his first appearance, alike the Opéra and the Conservatoire shut their doors against him with affrighted haste. People have compelled Berlioz to be and stay a marked exception to the long, great rule; and this he is and stays both outwardly and inwardly. Whoever would hear his music, must go direct to Berlioz, for nowhere else will he meet it, not even where one meets Mozart and Musard cheek by jowl. One hears Berlioz' compositions only in the concerts he himself gives once or twice a year; these remain his sole domain: here he has his works played by an orchestra trained expressly by himself, and before a public he has conquered in a ten-years-long campaign. But nowhere else can one hear a note of his, unless it be upon the streets or in the Dome, whither he is summoned from time to time to a politico-musical function of State. This isolation of Berlioz', however, not only extends to his outward standing, but also forms the mainspring of his inner development: however much a Frenchman, however great the sympathy of his nature and aims with those of his compatriots,—yet he stands alone. He sees no one in front of him, on whom to rely; no one beside him, on whom he might lean. From our Germany the spirit of Beethoven blew across to him, and there certainly have been hours when Berlioz wished to be a German; it was in such hours his genius spurred him on to write as our great master wrote, to utter the selfsame thing he felt was spoken in his works. But so soon as he seized the pen the natural pulsing of his own French blood set in again, of that same blood which surged in Auber's veins when he wrote the last volcanic act of his *Muette*,—— happy Auber, he knew no Symphonies of Beethoven! But Berlioz knew them, and, what is more, he understood them,—they had inspired him, inflamed his brain,—and yet he was reminded that French blood ran within his veins. Then he felt that he could not become as Beethoven, but neither could he write as Auber. He became Berlioz and wrote his "*Symphonie fantastique*," a work Beethoven would have smiled at, just as Auber smiles in fact, but which was able to send Paganini into ecstasies and gain for its author a party that will hear no music in the world save Berlioz' "Symphonie fantastique." Who listens to this symphony played here in Paris, by Berlioz' orchestra with himself at its head, can but believe he is hearing a wonder never met before. A titanic inner force of phantasy drives a swarm of passions as out from a crater; what we behold, are colossal clouds of smoke, parted and modelled into fleeting shapes by lightnings and tongues of fire. Everything is gigantic, daring, but infinitely painful. Beauty of form is nowhere to be found, nowhere the reposeful majesty of a stream to whose sure motion we might trust ourselves in hope. The first movement of Beethoven's C-minor Symphony would have been to me a simple charity, after the *Symphonie fantastique.*

I have said that the French tendency is predominant even in Berlioz; in fact, were this not the case, or were there any possibility of his weaning himself therefrom, in him we perhaps might have a worthy disciple of Beethoven, in the good German sense. That tendency, however, makes it impossible for him directly to approach the genius of Beethoven. It is the tendency outwards, to search for points of correspondence in extremes (*das Aufsuchen der gemeinschaftlichen Anklänge in den Extremitäten*). Whereas in social life the German loves to withdraw into himself, to probe within him for the genuine wellspring of his productive force, on the contrary we see the Frenchman hunting for that spring in the uttermost outcrops of Society. The Frenchman, whose first thought is for entertaining, seeks the perfection of his art in the refinement, the intellectualising of this entertainment; but he never loses sight of the immediate goal, namely that it shall be pleasing and attractive to the greatest possible number of hearers. Effect, the instantaneous reaction, thus is and stays with him the main affair: if he entirely lacks the inner power of Beholding (*innere Anschauungskraft*), he is content with the attainment of this goal alone;—if he is gifted with true creative force, however, he certainly avails himself of this Effect, but merely as first and weightiest means of publishing his inner intuition.—

Now what a conflict must arise in an artist-soul like Berlioz', when on the one hand a strenuous force of intuition bids him draw from the deepest, most mysterious fount of the world of ideas, while on the other the demands and qualities of his fellow-countrymen, whose sympathies he shares, ay, his own constructive bent itself, all urge him to make the outward elements of his creation his chief concern! He feels that he has something quite out of the ordinary, something infinite, to utter; that Auber's speech is far too small for it; yet it must sound fairly like that speech, to gain admittance to his public's ear. And so he falls into that wild and whirling modern idiom with which he stuns and charms the gapers, but scares away all those who would have easily understood his intentions from within outwards, yet decline the pains of finding their way in from without.

Another evil is, that it seems as if Berlioz were pleased with his isolation and sought to entrench himself therein. He has no friend deemed worthy to be asked for counsel, none he would permit to draw his notice to this or that sin against form in his works. In this regard I was filled with regret by a hearing of his symphony on "Romeo and Juliet." Amid the most brilliant inventions, this work is heaped with such a mass of trash and solecisms that I could not repress the wish that Berlioz had shewn this composition, before performance, to some such man as Cherubini, who, without doing its originality the slightest harm, would certainly have had the wit to rid it of a quantity of disfigurements. But, with his excessive sensitiveness, even his most intimate friend would never dare a similar proposal; whereas he grips his audience to such a point, that they account him a phenomenon beyond compare and past all criticising. Wherefore Berlioz will always remain imperfect, and maybe shine as nothing but a transient marvel.

And that's a pity! If Berlioz would only make himself master of the many excellences which have issued from the brilliant latest period of modern French music; if he could abandon that isolation which he maintains with so much pride of spirit, to take his stand on any stronghold of the musical present or past, he would undoubtedly acquire so mighty an influence over the musical future of France that his fame must be undying. For Berlioz not only possesses creative power and originality of invention, but is graced by a virtue as foreign to his composing fellow-countrymen as to us Germans is the vice of coquetry. This virtue is, that he doesn't write for money; and whoever knows Paris, and the ways and doings of Parisian composers, knows how to rate that virtue in this country. Berlioz is the remorseless foe of everything low, beggarly, and rank of the gutter,—he has sworn to strangle the first organ-grinder who shall dare to play his melodies. Terrible as is the oath, I haven't the smallest anxiety about the life of any of these street-virtuosi, for I am convinced that no one would more thoroughly look down on Berlioz' music than the members of their widespread guild.—Yet no one can deny in Berlioz a talent for entirely popular composition: popular, that is, in the most ideal sense. When I heard his Symphony for the re-interment of the July-victims,* I felt sure that every gamin in a blue blouse and red cap must understand it to the very bottom; though I should call such understanding more a national than a popular, for it certainly is a long cry from the *Postillon de Lonjumeau* to this July-symphony. In truth I am half inclined to rank this composition above all the rest of Berlioz' works; it is noble and great, from the first note to the last;—all morbid excitation is kept at bay by a lofty patriotic fervour, which rises from lament to high apotheosis. When I further take into account the service done by Berlioz in his altogether noble treatment of the military 'wind,' the only instruments at his disposal here, as regards this symphony at least I must withdraw

* The re-interment took place on July 28, 1840, Berlioz' music being played in the procession; the "Symphonie Funèbre" was repeated at Berlioz' own concert in the Salle Vivienne on August 6, 1840, also at a festival concert in the Opera-house on November 1; see *Gazette Musicale* of that year.—Tr.

my previous remarks about the future of Berlioz' compositions,—with joy I must acknowledge my conviction that this July-symphony will live and kindle, so long as there shall live a nation which calls itself the French.— —

I observe that I have completely fulfilled my duty of writing a word upon Berlioz, especially in the matter of length and breadth. It therefore will now be proper, and of advantage to my correspondence, for me to pass to topics of the day.

In the very first I get back to Berlioz; for I have to tell you of the concert given by Liszt for Beethoven's memorial, and conducted by Berlioz. Wonderful! **Liszt—Berlioz—** and in the middle, at the head, or at the tail (whichever you please), **Beethoven!** One might dilate, and write a Berliozian symphony upon this curious threefold theme! One might put questions to the power which makes, and has made, all that is and was,—one might ask — — — We will not ask,—but marvel at the wisdom and bounty of Providence, which created a Beethoven!—Liszt and Berlioz are brothers and friends; both know and honour Beethoven, both brace their forces at the wonder-fountain of his wealth, and realise that they could do no better thing than give a concert for his monument. Yet there is a small distinction to be drawn between them; above all, *this*, that Liszt gains money with no expense, whilst Berlioz has expenses and gains nothing. But this time, having replenished his coffers by two golden concerts, Liszt gave exclusive thought to *gloire*; he played for poor mathematical geniuses and Beethoven's memorial. Ah! how many would gladly give concerts for Beethoven! Liszt could do it, and at like time prove the paradox, that it is splendid to be a famous man. But *what* would and could Liszt not be, were he no famous man, or rather, had not people made him famous! He could and would be a free artist, a little god, instead of being the slave of the most fatuous of publics, the public of the virtuoso. This public asks from him, at all costs, wonders and foolish tricks; he gives it what it wants, lets himself be carried away at its hands,—and plays, in a concert for Beethoven's monument, a fantasia on Robert the Devil! This, however, was against his will. The programme consisted of nothing but Beethoven's compositions; nevertheless the fatal public demanded with a voice of thunder Liszt's *tour-de-force par excellence*, that Fantaisie. For the gifted man there was no escape, but with chagrined words: "*Je suis le serviteur du public; cela va sans dire*!" he sat down again at the piano, and played the favourite piece with crashing brilliancy. Thus is each crime avenged on earth! Some day in Heaven Liszt will have to perform that fantasia on the devil before the assembled public of the angels. Mayhap it will be for the very last time!

Among Berlioz' most eminent qualities must be reckoned his ability as conductor; he proved it afresh at the concert aforesaid. There is much talk of his soon obtaining the post of Chef-d'orchestre to the Grand Opéra, and Habeneck's taking Cherubini's place at the Conservatoire. The only obstacle is Cherubini's life; everybody is waiting for his death, apparently to follow it with concerts for his memorial, since he has already been so badly forgotten in his lifetime.

Would you believe that the composer of the "Water-carrier" lives here in Paris, yet in none of the thousand places where people make music can one hear a note of that opera? I am uncommonly fond of everything new, devoted to the Mode as no man, and nurse the firm conviction that its rule is just as necessary as powerful:—but when fashion goes the length of a man like Cherubini being clean forgotten, I feel disposed to return to the old dress-coat in which I was confirmed, the coat I wore when first I heard the "Water-carrier."

However, old operas are given us now and then. With real delight I remember "Joconde,"* played last winter at the Opéra Comique; my heart was full, though the house was very empty; that evening I couldn't conceive why Herr Clapisson composes operas, for one really doesn't need

* By N. Isouard, first performed in 1814.—Tr.

them while one has "Joconde." But the needs of man, especially of Theatre-directors, are passing strange; these gentry often get pieces made, and operas composed for them, foreknowing that they will be worthless, that they are bound to fail, that no one will listen to them,—and yet they pay 20,000 fr. for them! God knows what they want them for! This was about the case, the other day, with an opera by Herr Thomas, "*le comte Carmagnola.*" It had only two acts, was absurdly wearisome, made an amazing failure,—yet the Director of the Grand Opéra had paid the sum above-named for it,—apparently as compensation for the *droits d'auteur*, which surely can't amount to much with an operatic failure. You see how one makes one's fortune here!

It just occurs to me that I have told you nothing as yet about the *Heinefetter* (Kathinka),* though this delightful acquisition merits notice, above all in a German letter. This charming singer, who, as you will have heard, made her début in the *Juive*, continues to establish herself more and more firmly in public favour. She may boast of having achieved a veritable triumph at that début, for not only was she *not* supported by the Opera-director, but that gentleman positively turned the engine of his Claque *against* the débutante. Certain complications had impressed it on the Director that such a manœuvre was necessary; what saved the Heinefetter in his despite, was in the first place her own fine talent, in the second the very circumstance of the Director's intentions being a little too manifest. The whole house took her part, and it was refreshing to see how the lions of the boxes routed the knights of the chandelier—as one calls the members of that charitable institution of the Claque—by perfect tempests of applause.—The position of the Heinefetter is assured, and the diligence and modesty which she combines with her talent admit the confident assumption that in her the Opéra has gained one of its greatest ornaments.

Things have not gone quite so happily with Fräulein

* See note to page 77 *antea*.—Tr.

Löwe. I have already told you of her first success, as well as the result of that success upon an engagement at the Grand Opéra. At like time I informed you that Frl. Löwe was engaged for the Italian Opera; that report I now confirm, but must add that it was merely for the London season,* so that the German vocalist has arrived at no appearance on a Paris stage. She thus has been confined to concert singing, and I am sorry to say that her later appearances have by no means had the same success as her first in the concert of the *Gazette Musicale*. Certainly, her general choice of pieces has been most unfavourable. If the first time one passed over the fact of her singing the "Adelaïde," a composition not unreservedly suited to her voice, at last one was astounded at her singing almost nothing else. In vain she tried an aria of *Graun's*, or the like, to relieve the monotony of this procedure: the unlucky aria but added to her failure; the Frenchmen found these yard-long, out-of-date roulades by far too foolish, and, good Christian though I am, I confess that laughter seized myself. What could you expect of the Parisians, then, who believe in nothing, not even in Graun?† It is possible and desirable that Frl. Löwe may repair her somewhat damaged fame at the Italian Opera in London; however, a victory will be no light matter for her, even there; for, all things considered, one must allow that the Grisi, too, is something, and not so easily put in the shade.

But let us not anticipate events in London; my right of Correspondence does not extend as far as there. I must keep to Paris; and here, alas! there will soon be

* In *Grove's Dictionary of Music and Musicians* we read that "she appeared at Covent Garden, May 13, '41, in Bellini's *Straniera*, but her success was only temporary . . . She had been puffed as a new Grisi, there being an idea that Grisi had lost her voice."—Tr.

† Carl Heinrich Graun (1701-59) was born at Wahrenbrück, near Dresden, and educated at the famous Kreuzschule, whither Wagner himself went a century later. In Germany his *Te Deum* and his *Tod Jesu* are celebrated; the latter work has been annually performed in Passion-week since 1755 in the Cathedral of Berlin. See *Grove's Dictionary*.—Tr.

nothing of importance for my pen. Summer is coming, and with it Actions-of-State and Revolutions,—a bad chapter, from which a German musician must hold aloof. Nevertheless my Correspondence shall have a dazzling politico-historic close. What could be more historic, more political, or more dazzling, than the baptism of the Comte de Paris and the fireworks allied therewith? Yet again—not to fall out of line with Music!—what could be more brilliant than the *Concert monstre* which is to be given a few days hence in the gallery of the Louvre in presence of Louis Philippe, during which—as I have been informed in strictest confidence—he will abdicate the throne under cover of an aria of Auber's? It will be an exciting scene, and, as I particularly require repose at present, I shall therefore have to decline the pressing invitation sent me—no doubt—with a view to the concert's proper puffing in the *Abend-Zeitung*. So I shall leave your Political Correspondent to report on that concert, and confine myself to the baptism and fireworks. With estimable courtesy the ancient Notre Dame received the little man (you know the baptisee is getting on for three years old) and listened admiringly to the speech which (as I am assured by one of the immediate bystanders) the young Count delivered at the font. At night the selfsame Notre Dame blazed forth in Roman candles, rockets and crackers*—not religious ones, however, nor yet political. For convenience' sake it had been erected not far from the Tuileries, cunningly contrived of card-board, wood, and powder. Down to the smallest stone, each pillar, every ornament of the sublime stone-mother was counterfeited; all the world huzzahed and leapt for joy—for myself, I seemed to see the bell-ringer aloft. The people pressed and crowded; I praised the foresight of the Government in ordering a special set-piece to be fired at the Barrière du Trône, to keep the rowdy dwellers of that suburb at a tidy distance.

You see, I am becoming political; so let me stop. A

* "Schwärmern" means also, and more generally, "fanatics."—Tr.

further sally into the field of baptisms and fireworks must inevitably end in by-ways from which, perhaps, I could find an exit only through the approaching concert in the Louvre. As this Concert Monstre, however, with its five-hundred musicians, is quite beyond my powers, my only safety lies in committing myself to your hands in all haste and obedience, as

Yours most sincerely,

RICHARD WAGNER.

4.

July 6, 1841.

They have not been able to slay it, our dear, our glorious **Freischütz**! They have done to it the worst the beautiful Parisian laws demand; they have provided it with ennui, and left it all its "want of logic"; in fact—to put it briefly *this* time—they have played all the pranks which I lately reported in full to the readers of the *Abendzeitung*:* *yet they have been unable to kill it*! They give it again and again; the house becomes more and more crowded; the public grows warmer and warmer, and cries "*bis*!" at every decent opportunity. At first I could not quite decide as to whether to give the credit to the Paris public or the Freischütz; I was even beginning to think that the performance must have become more satisfactory. But no, it was not so: everybody dreamed, whined, and shivered as before,—the same abominations with the Wolf's-gulch, the same unselfish joviality of Caspar's. At last my mind was made, and I can now assure my fellow-countrymen that once again the Freischütz merits more laudation than the Paris public.

Nevertheless it speaks volumes for the power of endurance and marvellous elasticity of this public, that, after the terrible *dégoût* which the first performance must have cost it, it should have had the heart to re-assemble on the

* See Vol. VII. pp. 183 et seq.—Tr.

crimson-velvet benches of the Opéra, prepared to hear the Freischütz once more from beginning to end. In such circumstances the work itself was bound to make its way at last: * for all the tedious trappings, it was bound at last to step before them in its native freshness, youth and sheen.—Yet stay! I am going too fast:—in its *native* freshness, youth and sheen, it certainly could not present itself; what we Germans love so fondly in it, never and never could speak to the hearts of the Parisians,—'tis past all possibility; the Paris code forbids. On the other hand, the French seize points of beauty which almost escape ourselves in a performance of the Freischütz, or at least which we accept with the contented calm of habit. I am speaking of the purely-musical beauties of the Freischütz, of the many wonderful effects that strike the French as something altogether new to get from means so unpretentious, and they therefore appreciate with unassumed enthusiasm. You cannot imagine the rapture with which the Paris public receives the beautiful B-major section of the last Finale, notwithstanding that the whole protracted close, with its eminently worthy Hermit, to them is an atrocity. The few bars where all the solo-voices combine, in this section, here produce so enthralling an impression that, to the honour of the Parisians, I must say I never yet have heard even the most ravishing cadenza of Rubini's demanded *da capo* with a like enthusiasm, in spite of Berlioz having implored the public in the *Journal des Débats* to keep silence after this section, so as not to drown the passage where the Hermit makes such a lovely modulation to C-major. My God! what do the French care for a hermit, even when he modulates into C-major?—

In this happy turn of the tide for the Freischütz here, against all expectation, there can be no doubt that the immense renown of the German masterwork has had the

* Referring to the first month after the Paris production, in a private letter dated Jan. 18, 1842 (*Letters to Uhlig &c.*), Wagner says: "The fourth to the ninth performances were those that enlisted the sympathy of the public here; *after* these, they became *villainous*."—Tr.

strongest share. Woe to the Freischütz, had it been the product of an unknown composer, and put on the boards in Paris for the first time *so*! Both it and its creator would have been lost beyond rescue, and no musical-biographic lexicon in the world would ever have recorded the author's name. The Charivari would have reported the event in the same terms as the reception of Berlioz' *Benvenuto Cellini*: "the audience slept, and woke hissing." An epigram—and buried for all eternity!—But here the case was different; moreover the public must at least have arrived at a dim idea of the Freischütz' mystic splendour, for it to have been so possessed by a production which had quite disgusted it, that it finally conceived the inexplicable longing to hear the Freischütz again on the morrow. More than that, as already said, was not required,—the "Freischütz" itself was bound to do the rest. *It has done it*; one goes in crowds, one claps and cheers, *O glorious Freischütz*! People are even talking of *generosity* to the heirs of the German master. We shall see!—*

But we have also had a German *ballet*; it plays, or rather dances in Silesia, not far from Breslau, and a *German poet*, Heinrich Heine, suggested the idea. It is founded on the legend of the *Willi's*, those brides who have died with unfulfilled love-longings, and climb out of their graves at midnight to dance men to death. What peculiarly pleased the French in this fantastic saga, was its high adaptability for Ballet; indeed, what opportunities for the most indicible pirouettes, the most supersensual entrechats, does this weird craving of the *Willi's* not afford? And the adaptor did right to give the dance-murder a shade of plausibility by laying his scene in the circuit of Breslau, instead of in Paris; for only on the assumption that they are Germans, or in fact Silesians, could the French explain these victims of the dance-craze. Any onlooker at a Paris masked-ball has ample occasion to convince himself that it is a physical impossibility to

* From the letter cited in the preceding footnote it appears that nothing came of this, despite our author's own exertions.—Tr.

dance a Frenchman to death. The character, the habits and propensities of the French make many things downright unthinkable to them, especially in the domain of poetry, so that the authors of operas and ballets are often obliged to seek their wonders from abroad; whereby they gain not only the chance of a thousand curious situations, but the extra advantage of counting on the public's unconditional faith. Provided the foreign wonder—now astoundingly in fashion—is imported under an outlandish name, there is nothing more to be said: against a "*Franc-tireur*" the French would have raised all kinds of objections, whereas upon "Le Freischutz" they are quite agreed; to them it means, and will mean, a Bohemian village. "Les Willis," then, to them are perfectly in order; why on earth should they dispute about them? *They* find male beings they can dance to death; so one believes there really are such irregular and inadequately-constituted sons of Adam, little as one can form a mental picture of them. "What strange folk they must be in Silesia, Thuringia, and the adjoining countries!"—We Germans need no "Willi's";—one single Ball at the Paris Grand Opéra is sufficient to deliver us into the arms of Dancing Death.—

For the rest, this ballet is much like all the others; one dances well, one has lovely scenery and costumes, one makes spruce music. The latter, in the present instance, has been made by Herr *Adam*, the same who created the "Postilion" and the "Confectioner." This creator has worked himself out with quite shameful velocity; he has composed himself to death in almost as brief a time as the Willi's victim danced there. With *his* case the French are familiar; wellnigh every month they see a composer succumb to his music, and are always ready to help carry him to his grave. Now and then they learn that the deceased is still doing business with his music in Germany; so that we need not be surprised, if they take that country for the land of ghosts and goblins.

Herr Adam, however, is still spooking around in Paris;

each month one is on the point of having clean forgotten him, when he announces himself once again. With the "Willi's," too, he merely put in an appearance before starting on a journey; for he is always starting to-morrow or the next day for Petersburg, Berlin or Constantinople, to dash off a little ballet for a trifle of 100,000 fr. Uncanny spook!—

Quite recently a learned young Alsatian artist, Herr *Kastner* by name, made his début at the Opéra Comique. Hitherto known—at least in Paris—almost purely as a clever theorist, he sought an opportunity of shewing himself as dramatic composer; an opportunity not so exceedingly hard to find, in view of his unusually favourable family-connections. In the abominable state of arrangements at the Paris theatres, however, he was fairly forced to accept the first textbook put into his hands by the directorate. As to any free choice, any agreement with a poet, such a thing was not to be thought of, if only for the reason that there is no choice, and no poet, in Paris; moreover the Directors are so accustomed to looking merely at the business aspect, that they never would comprehend what one meant by choice or poetic agreement, were it possible to meet with both. Well, Herr Kastner was given so wretched and worthless a book that he evidently knew not what to make of it, and so he wrote a string of fugues; at least, the public avers that it heard nothing but fugues from beginning to end of the "*Maschera*." This didn't at all suit the easy-going frequenters of the Opéra Comique; they protested that it was against the terms of their subscription, and that they had never undertaken to hear Händel. To my mind this score contained many fine things, only I think that Herr Kastner should be recommended to abstain in future from dramatic music, and devote himself to a genre more fitted to the somewhat passionless severity of his musical gifts. In this tranquil staidness he is a notable exception among the hordes of composers who people Paris just now.

At the same theatre a bonny little novelty, "the Two

Thieves" with music by Herr Girard, conductor of the Opéra Comique orchestra, was given a short while since. In this opera one steals a number of diamonds and a gold watch, with much elegance and ingenuity. The trifle is important enough, you see, especially as the stealing was done with such truth to life that the whole audience involuntarily fumbled for its diamonds and watch; I was the exception.—

But what are these trifles, against the dire calamity that now has befallen Paris!—Not the dead season, not the departure of every political notability, not the puns of Herr Sauzet, not the untold price of beef and veal, not the horrible deficit in the Exchequer, not the terrible taxes for the fortifications, not the outlook on an instant revolution,—none of all these! Quite another cataclysm it is, that empties the fashionable quarters at a blow, turns the Faubourg du Roule and the Faubourg St Germain into hamlets, lets the grass grow on the pavements of the Chaussée d'Antin, and makes their hôtels dwellings for the bat and screech-owl! Those dazzling hôtels—ah! how I pity them! Their velveted and perfumed erst inhabitants —how I mourn with them!—for **Rubini** will never come back. With wreathed smiles and soft endearments will the lofty being pay a blessed visit to his friends in fiery Spain and frosty, not to say freezing Russia, then pass through Berlin to his forefathers in Italy. But for all that, as said, he never will come back to Paris. The dejection is universal:—the cobbler throws away his awl, the tailor his needle, the dressmaker breaks up her shapes, the perfumer gives his extracts to the winds of heaven; to Lyon no more orders go for silks, to Lille one writes no more for ribbons. For alas! the tender guests of the Italian Opera will now wear garments made of hair, and no more silken; in place of ribbons, they will bind a hempen cord around their waist; instead of perfumes they'll strew ashes on their head, and in lieu of satin shoes be shod with toilsome sandals,—for *Rubini*, RUBINI for whom all these were worn,—**Rubini** comes not back.—I fail to understand Louis Philippe; there *must* be a revolution somewhere! Had he not power enough to keep Rubini?

Tout s'en va!—The case is desperate.— —

In Germany too—so I read—one has sad reports from Paris. People are filling their columns with a painful affair which occurred here to the poet *Heinrich Heine.* It appears that they are uncommonly delighted with the incident, and consider they have every right to be; for they pretty plainly express their conviction that Heine richly deserves the treatment just dealt him.—

I must say, we Germans are a generous folk! In our midst we see arise a talent whose like is rare in Germany; we rejoice at its fresh and crisp unfolding,—we cry it "triumph" and "vivat" as it wakes our younger generation from an utter lethargy and offers up the fulness of its powers to break a path and point the unborn forces of our Literature towards a new, unknown, but necessary goal. Whoso among our younger men takes up a pen, he seeks to copy *Heine*, well or ill, unconsciously or consciously; for never has so sudden, so lightning-swift, so unawaited a phenomenon pursued its path so irresistibly, as this of Heine's. Yet not enough, that we quietly looked on while our police were hunting this splendid talent from its native soil; that we indolently overlook the fact that its spreading roots are torn from that earth which alone could give them nurture; that we thereafter remark with a sleepy yawn, that friend Heine has unlearnt in Paris his "Reisebilder"-writing; that our indifference ends by taking all heart out of him and forcing him to cease to be German, though he never can become Parisian; —not enough, that we cut the ground from under his feet so far that nothing remains for his teeming wit, but to exert itself on the Ridiculous one leaves it unawares;— not enough, that we look *callously* and pettily at the maiming of a talent which, with happier tending, would have rivalled the greatest names in our literature:—no! we clap our hands for very *joy* when this Heine at last receives a treatment such as we practise at home on our penny-a-liners! And in Germany one does it with so rabid a greed of scandal, that one hasn't even time to ascertain the facts of a sad affair which one is so glad to regard as a merited chastisement. The unathorised reporter in the *Leipziger Allgemeine Zeitung*—as I can vouch for—has taken his whole account of the scene from the statements of the assailant; a precipitance he tries in vain to justify by reading Heine a moral lesson as charming as appropriate.* To no one has it occurred, to hear Heine's own account of an affair which took place without a single competent witness. I therefore appeal to my countrymen's sense of justice, and ask if it be not disgraceful, ruthlessly to condemn one party on the unsupported statement of the other?

At the present moment Heine is at a watering-place in the Pyrenees, lying sick unto death. If in truth he had not the courage to avenge a shameful insult put upon him, we must *deplore* the fact; but none of us has the right to *revile* him for it, except it be our army-officers and the corps (*Landsmannschaften*) of our universities, with neither of whom has Heine aught to do. Thus much is certain: the French would have known better, not only how to keep their poet, but also to behave themselves in similar circumstances, despite their owning wags enough to draw the matter for a passing jest from such a scandal. *Defamed* their poet, they would never have; especially without hearing his side of the tale. I have no reason to be passionately fond of the French; but here I take them as a pattern.

RICHARD WAGNER.

* The reference is to an unsigned article "from Paris, June 17," appearing in the *Allg. Ztg.* for June 23, 1841. The statement was to the effect that one of the persons mentioned by Heine in his book, *H. Heine über Ludwig Börne*, had given its author what we should call a "horse-whipping" in the streets of Paris on the 14th of that month, and that Heine, to put it practically, had run away. The "moral lesson" was phrased pretty strongly by the reporter.—Tr.

5.

September 8, 1841.

No one doubts but that Summer times are times superb. To cast off all the studs, cravats, waistcoats and swallow-tails—the hateful burden of a civic Winter; to lie down in the woods and dream a thousand lovely things,—that's something to make life worth living,—who will dispute it?—But ah! these dreadful summer times in Paris! Dust and heat, stench and hubbub, houses—seven stories high, and streets — seven feet across; bad wine — flat water; river-baths swarming with a thousand dirty gamins, —and to crown it all, the satanically tight-fitting clothes into which one is squeezed by diabolic Paris tailors! As compensation for these sufferings, bad stage-performances, at the Palais Royal no *Dejazet*, at the Variétés no *Audry*; —no *Bouffe* at the Gymnase—no *Rachel* at the Français; no *Duprez*, no Dorus at the Opéra! If even the Parisian feels depressed by such a state of things, how much worse it is for a Correspondent! Happy the political reporter! From the perplexity into which he is plunged by the hush and absence of all diplomatic action he is extricated by the lucky circumstance that the Paris journals, no matter the pinch, are obliged to come out every day. The mintings of the anguish of their hearts he may take in peace and circulate as sterling coin; for, under cover of a few authorities, he knows that everyone in Germany will credit him. But as for art and fine things like it, one would have to do a little minting on one's own account, to take in others,—and that has its attendant hardships, particularly without imagination, a thing the German loses as a rule in Paris. However, as it would appear incredible to you, if I told you that absolutely nothing of note had happened in Paris since my last report, I will at least endeavour to avoid the charge of palming off a negative lie, and therefore will not hide away my scanty spoil of mournful verities.

Of the famous illumination of the Champs Elysées for

the July fête you surely will have heard and read enough, —how could any political reporter let slip such an unquestionable truism? Of the grand display of waterworks at Versailles the whole world also knows,—so that I am dispensed from all necessity of entering on the specialities of the Paris public Summer; for, beyond the illuminations and the waterworks, to my knowledge nothing whatever has happened in the streets this year—no Revolution, no Berliozian Symphony. The little earthquake appears to have existed nowhere but in the letters addressed by dwellers in the Rue and Faubourg Montmartre to Herr Arago. People will have it that this division of the inhabitants of Paris is very exalted, and actively inclined to a lugubrious cast of romance; as ground of which idiosyncrasy one names an ardent reading of the works of Paul de Kock and the "Journal des Débats." I cannot bring myself to believe that this is the real cause.—

The chief theatre of this quarter is the Théâtre des Variétés. It has stayed quite unmolested by the earthquake, yet continues to exalt its public's heads. The pieces performed here are mostly of a very extravagant kind, and no theatre-poet has brought this mad farrago farther than Dumersan,* the author of "Canaille." His latest piece is called "Un tas de bêtises." This charming title in itself prepared one for all sorts of fooleries; for in "a heap of nonsense" every man is sure to find a morsel for himself. As a fact, we all were struck by the peculiar nature of this piece: it was completely bare of actual plot,—to say nothing of Intrigue; instead, there moved a host of allegoric figures on the stage. Not a novelty of the day, not a half-and-half remarkability in the field of public life, but was personified. The famous Artesian Well played one chief rôle: it was ushered-in by two Chinese who, slumbering on their native soil,

* Dumersan, a very prolific playwright, commenced a translation of Wagner's *Liebesverbot* into French for the Théâtre de la Renaissance towards the end of 1839; but the whole thing came to naught, owing to one of the periodic bankruptcies of that establishment, as previously stated.—Tr.

had been gathered by the penetrative bore-spoon and sucked-up through the bowels of the earth into the heart of Paris; on the way they had been nipped by a sudden frost, which gave them so violent a shaking that they had reason to suppose the recent earthquake was due to it alone. Herr Arago is said to set but little by this explanation. But the maddest of all was, the piece had no ending. I'm not quite sure what allegoric figure was strutting on the stage, when in the parterre, and eke the boxes, things suddenly began to stir: there, too, were actors given rôles, and from roof to floor, from seats to ceiling, they fell a-questioning and wrangling with each other; with the natural result that the attention of the audience was distracted from the stage to the confederates among, below, and high above them. As this nig-nag was drawing to a close, we turned our eyes back to the stage—the curtain had fallen unnoticed. This piece was hissed off the boards.

With the Grand Opéra things are going very sadly; its performances are beginning to annoy even the Claque; the head claqueur is said to have demanded an enormous advance, without which he can't get his men to stick to their guns. It's all these evil, evil Summer times! In the summer a Paris first-singer thinks it beneath his dignity to sing at all; the second singers deem it not worth while to sing in tune. Under such conditions one gets performances like the last of the "Huguenots": nothing flatter or more exasperating can well be conceived.—In general, the difference between earlier and later performances at the Paris Opera is characteristic. With operas of great success, as these same Huguenots or the "Juive," the first twenty representations are usually superb;—a gust of enthusiasm inspires the whole,—everyone outstrips himself,—even the faulty chorus does capitally:—but thereafter 'tis as if a line were drawn; everyone thinks he has done enough, and I pity the stranger who comes to Paris with the idea of hearing one of those vaunted opera-performances, and finds a thing he cannot imagine ever having won applause. Then the most amazing, almost intentional carelessness and indifference are the rule; and nowhere outside the Paris operahouse has one seen the conductor's odious violin-bow fulfil its mournful function with such a swish and rattle.

Somewhat more briskness prevails at the Opéra Comique. Before you can turn your wrist they give you novelties, and one-act operas spring like mushrooms from the earth.* A short while since, the son of glorious Boieldieu made another trial with an opera of this type: he had clothed himself with the first and second acts of the "Dame Blanche"; they were the wings in power whereof he thought to soar on high. . . Ah? what a burdening heirloom is a father's famous name!

But even at the Comic Opera are tragical events:—quite recently a text of Scribe's brought one composer to the brink of the grave, and thrust another in. Think on't!—an opera-text made by Scribe in two days!—What a colossus Scribe's genius must be!— —The facts are worth noting. There exists a composer named *Clapisson*; to him Heaven's favour meted out a Scribian textbook. In accordance with a beautiful custom of the Paris Directors, Clapisson had to pledge himself to deliver the finished score by a certain hard-set day, or pay a fine of 20,000 fr. He gazed in wonder at the textbook, pondered things unheard, and conceived no less a notion than that of composing original music; then he fell into gloomy brooding on some comic scene or other, and became ill. The Director stepped to the bedside of the haggard, wasted man, and saved him from a certain death by taking the fateful text away. Clapisson sprang to his feet, composed two quadrilles and a romance, and became *well* as a fish in the water.—But there existed another composer, and he was called Monpou; on him fell the mantle. Monpou had made some daring flights to Biblic regions, composed a "chaste Susannah"; there was the very man for the job. In valiant mood he took up Clapisson's engage-

* See my preface to Vol. VII.—Tr.

ments, and began to set Scribe's text to music. Yet the more he composed, the more he, too, was seized with a passion for original music,—he thought and thought,—no inspiration came. The wretch decided on a taste of ardent spirits,—he tasted,—pondered, and—fell sick! But to *him* came no Director,—the terrible text remained in his hands, —the contract weighed him down,—and he succumbed,—he died! Is this not a moving story? If this sort of thing is to continue, Scribe will soon have murdered all the younger French composers;—he is said to have handed-in eight full-blown operatic texts since then,—who's going to compose them?—

At last the lethal text has been given to *Halévy*. It was the best way out of the difficulty; for whoever has seen Halévy's thickset frame, his sturdy fist, will guess that Scribe's text cannot hurt him. We soon shall have the new opera, and learn where the mischief sat.

Further, we shall soon get a hearing of Halévy's last grand-opera, "the Knight of Malta." People say that Mme. Stoltz has fourteen numbers to sing in it, and therefore advise the composer to insist on a skilled physician being in constant attendance upon the stage.

Much else is being prepared for. Herr Adam is instrumenting *Grétry's* "Richard Cœur-de-lion"; he himself declares that it is merely a matter of a little brass, in which the good Grétry was deficient, yet without which no true "lion-hearted" can be conceived. He has undertaken this friendly addition; presently we shall hear the work at the Opéra Comique.

Presently, also, the Italians will return; the Salle Ventadour is being dressed for them with gold, with silk and velvet;—presently they will sing, and—presently, therefore, you shall have preciser news of all the wonders now making ready and soon to come to pass.

RICHARD WAGNER.

6.

November 5, 1841.

Should you wish, respected Sir, mere news about the Autumn in and round Paris, I could have placed myself at your command some time ago; I would have told you of fearsome soughing and howling of the most autumnal and most obstinate of all the winds, which for three full moons has stormed throughout the Paris country,—of merrily flickering chimney-fires, of mournfully fluttering leaves of trees, of sturdily streaming floods of rain—so that you should recall the best of Hoffmann's fairy-tales. All this has arrived here with such astounding prematureness, that there even are people who declare the dreary autumn-time commenced quite six months since. But no one asks a Paris Correspondent for reports on *Nature*; his business is to speak of *Art*. Now, as art-junketings invariably come in with autumn here, it was only natural that such outspoken weather-signs should have set me hunting long ago for art; but anew I found how much Parisian Art departs from Nature:—no piping wind, no floods of rain, no frost, no yellowed leaves, can persuade the Parisians that it's Autumn and the time for Art; to bring them this belief it takes Italians, *i.e.* the Italian Opera, and that through the material evidence of its return to Paris. For its first performance the first autumnal dresses are got ready, mantles and furs here make their début, and *henceforth* are not lain aside, though the author and ordainer of all weather-matters should please to let the hottest sunshine stream upon autumnal Paris. News of this *Art* autumn, then, I have to give you;—so learn!—*it has begun*, for the Italian Opera has opened.

Ah! into what a house of mourning methought I had fallen, when on that opening night I passed into the dazzlingly restored Salle Ventadour! Gloss, gloss, everywhere gloss;* and yet this gloomy mourning spread

* "Glanz, Glanz, überall Glanz!"—compare "Wahn, Wahn, überall Wahn" in *Die Meistersinger*.—Tr.

above the gloss!—O glossy misery! O miserable gloss!—RUBINI— —voice forsakes me, to tell you of him whom it never forsook!— —Indeed I had foreseen that some day we should really lose him; how often had this god-like man sung so *piano* that one positively couldn't hear him! Were only this ethereal body too (so thought I then) to melt beneath the untold glow of this expression, then, as already from our ears, he finally must vanish also from our eyes. I was right,—the man in truth exists no more! O that all singers would take a lesson from it! Squander ye not your utmost strength on *pianissimo*, O never melt too much away in tender glow,—ye see to what a tragic end that man has come whose portly shade now flits from land to land, with barely 100,000 francs of interest to consume!—

The immediate consequence of Rubini's terrible demise was this: one was forced to open the Italian Opera *without* him. The effect of this defect was easy to foretell: ice-cold, death-stillness.—But the Director wasn't content with that: he took thought for a replacer. A replacer of *Rubini!!* And yet, it must be! All the tenors of Italy were bidden; to each went out the question: Wilt thou replace Rubini? —How great was their respect for Rubini, one may judge by the fact that after many an invitation there at last announced himself one *primo uomo*, who thought he might dare the dread replacement on the following terms. The letter of this shrewd aspirant ran somewhat thus:—"As it is to be foreseen that I shall be as little in a position as any tenor in the world to equal Rubini, and as I therefore may expect great hardships from the Paris public—the probability of even being hissed off the boards, and such-like —, I can expose myself to all these disagreeables only in consideration of my courage being rewarded by an income of 100,000 fr., with a carriage thrown into the bargain."

The Director—God knows for what reason!—declined this advantageous offer, and hit on another means of replacing Rubini. The filling of the monstrous gap is to be compassed by *three* individuals. *Mario,** a tenor Count, who had previously indulged the caprice of singing nothing but French, is placed at the head of this replacement-triumvirate; he takes over the tender, inaudible rôles of his peerless predecessor—an office he promises to fulfil to perfection. A Signor *Mirate* takes over the melting glow: attention was paid to this gentleman's owning a powerful frame. A signor of some other name has let himself be loaded with Rubini's raging rôles: he will probably come to an actual appearance as little as did Rubini's rage; for this was so purely ideal, that one may assume that it never existed at all. With this arrangement the repertoire is of uncommon difficulty. In most of his rôles Rubini was at the same time tender, glowing, and ideally raging:—is one to let all three replacers act at once? Oh, how difficult! For Rubini had the charming habit of singing two bars quite unhearably, but the third with awful violence. Are the unhearable and the violent to stand together on the boards to sing? That certainly would spoil dramatic unity and truth; and these were things Rubini set such passionate store by. The solution of this problem is still in abeyance.

So far as tenor-matters go, the Grand Opéra is luckier. For long one had heard tell of a cooper's man from Rouen, who had come to Paris with a glorious tenor-voice to wait upon the dwellers in this good city. The kind directorate of the Grand Opéra took him under its wing, got him taught and weaned of his barrel-manners, and after eighteen months of cultivation has let him make his début as Arnold in Rossini's "Tell." *Poultier*, as he calls himself, has fulfilled every hope; his voice is fine and flexible, and he himself possesses feeling and dramatic talent. He is particularly affected by the Liberal Press; it terms him a Man of the People, in contrast to the artists of the upper

* According to *Grove's Dictionary* Mario made his début at the Grand Opéra on Nov. 30, 1838, and in 1840 he left it for the Italian Opera of Paris, having meanwhile made his London début on June 6, 1839. As Wagner was writing on the spot, however, the date (1841) given by him is the more likely to be correct as regards the *Paris* Italian Opera.—Tr.

world, whose fame is nurtured on the impure air of salons. When the workmen of the Grand Opéra congratulated him on his success, Poultier shook hands with them and styled himself their equal: that pleased every whit as much as the melting accents of his voice.

Herr Castil Blaze is said to have just discovered a similar tenor prodigy in the south of France. His man is a clerk, with whom, immediately after the discovery, he struck a bargain whereby the individual is to be educated for two whole years at C. Blaze's expense; the anticipated profits of the next ten years, however, the discovered is to share with the discoverer. Nothing new!—

At the Opéra Comique things are going with a hum: old and new live side by side in beauteous concord. Grétry's "Richard Cœur de Lion," which I announced to you last time, has made its appearance, mailed in Herr Adam's brass. This opera has won the public's ear afresh; it will have the best receipts of the winter, a thing which at last has decided the Director—a wary man who, for that matter, understands nothing—to take the hint I lately gave him in the *Abend-Zeitung*. You will remember, honoured Sir, the sorrow I expressed that in Paris, where *Cherubini* still lives and moves, his "Water-carrier" should not have come to hearing for so many years. You may judge, then, what credit your paper must enjoy in Paris itself, since Herr Cerfbeer could do no else than pay prompt attention to its chiding words:—Cherubini's "Water-carrier" is announced for this very winter. Herr Cerfbeer is unboundedly obliging!

As this occasion brings me back to Cherubini, I can't help giving you a little portrait of him. 'Tis sad to say, but Cherubini's influence on the musical evolution of the present epoch may almost be called completely null; still sadder is it to hear that this misfortune—as one necessarily must denote the withholding of his undoubtedly salutary influence—is due, less to a pardonable weakness in his character, than to its hardness. People aver that he often has slammed the door in the face of young persons of talent who sought his tutelage and advocacy.* A curious thing, in this regard, was lately said by Alexander Bouché, a red-hot musical enthusiast of the older order: "*J'admire Cherubini, mais je le déteste; cet homme n'a fait que des chefs d'œuvre, jamais il n'a fait une bonne action.*" It would be distressing if one had to attribute to this hostile mood of Cherubini's that seclusion from the music-world of nowadays in which this extraordinary master has found himself for many a year.

The new, which the Opéra Comique gives amid the excellent old, is heartily bad. The defunct Herr Adam has announced himself once more with a three-act opera, and his three-act opera is called "*la main de fer.*" The text of this "Iron Hand" is by Scribe and Leuven, or by Leuven out and out; for we may hope that Scribe had no hand in it, but merely lent his costly name. This opera is really of weight; permit me therefore to devote it a few special lines of analysis, though I do not ask you to print them in large type.† So:—

"*La main de fer*"—in German: "*die eiserne Hand.*"

Once on a time there lived in the land of Hanover an Elector-prince who had slain his brother; a coup de main, in fact, that had enabled him to become Elector of Hanover. This man had made a law and followed it with conscientious strictness, the law, to wit, to hang or behead whomsoever he pleased: this wise decree he called the "iron hand," and his subjects, ever mindful of the gracious mercies of their prince, called him himself "the Iron Hand." This pleased the man Leuven uncommonly, when he heard of it in Paris, and he resolved to turn it into a comic opera-text for his dear friend Adam, who had hitherto composed a few Postilions, Pastrycooks and Brewers, but never yet an Iron Hand. To make the proposed work comic,

* In 1825 Franz Liszt, then a marvellous boy of fourteen, was refused admission to the Paris Conservatoire, of which Cherubini was Principal.—Tr.

† All this "Correspondence" is printed small in the *Abendzeitung*, whereas the articles on *Der Freischütz* and *La Reine de Chypre*, the "Pilgrimage" and "End" are given leading type.—Tr.

however, he could not possibly let the gruesome "iron hand" go striking all the time; nay, if one came to think of it, the Iron Hand was really not at all well suited for personal manœuvre in a merry opera *à la Fidèle Berger*. So the man Leuven hit on a clever means of keeping the abominable Elector quite out of sight, and creating instead a Princess who had allowed a nephew of the "Iron Hand" to wake too hasty mother-feelings in her—which necessarily must lead to splendid complications. To give these complications no objectionable twang, however, the Leuven man resolved to make this Princess and the cause of her motherly afflictions non-visible as well. In spite of this expedient, whereby all rocks of coarse offence were happily avoided, the tender conscience of Leuven (as we will call the man henceforth, for short) could find no rest before he made this invisible Princess desire the hallowing of her hasty love-bond; this hallowing, or so to say espousal, was to be effected by a Hermit who had already won her confidence through his bold defiance of the dreadful "Iron Hand" on some occasion—in a thrilling scene, of course. The proposed espousal through the Hermit was merely to form the brilliant climax of the comic opera. But Leuven, who is never at a loss for second thoughts, remembered at the nick of time that the Opéra Comique had never had to do with Hermits; wherefore he decided that this important person, too, should stay unseen. Thus was the whole thing settled, when Leuven suddenly discovered that he hadn't a single visible character left in all his opera; this evil must be set to rights, and no mistake, for Leuven saw that otherwise the materialistic Parisians wouldn't believe a word of his opera. So he borrowed the best characters from the "Postilion," the "Pastrycook," and "Brewer"; made one of them the confidant, another the confidante, a third the Hermit's pupil; and *so* the thing was straightened out. As earlier of the Paris Police, these persons *here* all went in terror of the "Iron Hand": fright, confusion—winding up with a happy release of the "Iron Hand"—and the loveliest comic-opera text was finished, without afflicting the minds of the audience with the smallest realistic horrors.—

But as every story here is wont to issue from two different mythic cycles, there is yet another saga for the origin of the "Iron Hand." According to this, the much-named Leuven had just finished one of those texts of his, which, like all before it, had its subject in a Parisian complication such as Herr Adam is so wonderful at composing; to give this text a special sanctity, Leuven found good to beg *Scribe's* name as collaborator. As Scribe is most obliging, he didn't reject the petition, but saw at a glance that the book might be made far more interesting if the visible Paris police were turned for once into an invisible German bloodhound. It instantly occurred to him that he once had heard of a knight with an iron hand,—Hanover, with its wretched state of things political came also to his mind:—the knight is left out, but one lets the unseen iron hand go striking away at Hanover:—"Thus, my dear Leuven, you not only have a most excellent title, but, of course, the half of the droits d'auteur. *Bon jour*!"—

Add to this Adam's ghostly music, Sir, and you know what will fill Vienna with untold raptures within the next four weeks; at least, Herr Adam is far from not pretending to that future for his latest work.— —

As I am so thoroughly in the vein for things dramatic, I cannot possibly pass by the so-called *second Théâtre-français* just founded in the Odéon. The Italians, who had occupied this house for two whole winters after the burning of their former quarters, have removed to the Salle Ventadour, as you know already: the latter house had hitherto been doomed to ruin all its tenants; the German Opera, which pitched there once upon a time, can tell you about that; so can the last Director, Herr Antenor Joly, who drenched this hall for three years with the sweat of his brow under the load of a Théâtre de la Renaissance. Only the Italians, relying on their invincible power of attraction, could dare the perils of this fated house; yet it almost seems that even *they* are to come beneath its malign spell, for up to now their performances here have been dull and coldly received; which, by the way, may find its reason in the everlasting sameness of their repertoire—a repertoire which knows no escape from a see-saw between *Cenerentola* and *Puritani*.

To return to the newly-founded Second Théâtre-Français at the Odéon, I must premise that it is that same well-seasoned Director of the defunct Renaissance-theatre, to whom the benevolent Ministry have entrusted this new undertaking by way of recompense. Alas! keen-scented folk already say that neither can this charitable enterprise survive for long: the house is to give both plays and operas, an order which has never yet been carried out successfully in Paris. Meanwhile one gives nothing but plays; the opera remains to be found. The new pieces with which this theatre opened, are "*L'actionnaire*" by Dumersan, the playwright of the Variétés;—then a grand drama, "*Matthieu Luc*," a satanic piece with an obligato Louis XI., by a young poet called Delanoue,—and finally "*Un jeune homme*," a modern-moral duel-piece by Doucet. With great delight one saw between these novelties "*Les fourberies de Scapin*," by Molière; there are people who even declare it was best of the bunch.

The luckiest are a few of the older accredited Boulevard-theatres, and among them in particular the Théâtre de la Gaieté. By its name one would expect nothing but mirth from this theatre, pretty much as from the Ambigu Comique: —but one would very soon find himself mistaken, when he saw the horrors that are staged at both these houses. Were these often nonsensical pieces but badly played, or their mounting mean and paltry, despite the ill augury of their posters one might hope to laugh in keeping with the house's title. But such is not the case. These pieces are played in a masterly fashion, and put on the boards most effectively. More especially does the little Gaieté distinguish itself in this respect: the immense successes of "*Le massacre des innocents*" and "*La grâce de Dieu*" are known enough, and now a new piece has appeared there, which is bound to have as great success. It is called "*Les pontons*," its last two acts being founded on that species of galleys in which the Spaniards let their French prisoners languish during the Napoleonic wars. The picture of these pontoons with their human sacrifices is heart-rending, and the effect of the final scene quite sets one's hair on end. The hero of the piece, a Frenchman, has undermined one of these pontoons, on whose upper deck we see the insolent Spaniards holding orgy; at a signal the mine explodes, the water comes in from below, the boat spins round and round, and sinks to the bottom,—the Spaniards drown and the French are saved, according to the liberator's plan.—All this was represented at the little Boulevard theatre with such a subtlety of realism, that no one could refrain from shouting a Hurrah! combined of horror and delight.

The same kind of thing goes on each night at the Cirque Olympique, where you now may see Murat's biography from beginning to end. There you have battles and skirmishes, colours and horses, enough to tire your eyes out.

When one sees how these minor theatres are outbidding each other in clatter and glitter, one may guess why the first-class houses, and especially the Théâtre Français, will have almost nothing at all to do with that sort of thing. On the contrary, the Théâtre Français seems to pride itself on shining solely by the substance of its representations, putting all outward attraction as much aside as possible. This tendence has come more and more to the fore since the representations have drawn farther and farther back into the realm of so-called Classic Tragedy and Comedy. Of late one gets almost nothing at the Théâtre Français but pieces by Corneille, Racine and Molière; Scribe's lighter comedy, and here and there a drama by Dumas or Hugo, afford the only variation. Everybody knows that the reason is mainly to be sought in the idiosyncrasy of *Rachel's* talent; whether the taste will die out with this artist's eventual retirement, or still will persist, yet remains to be seen. Thus much is certain: a possible retirement of this lady is prognosticated for an early date by people with political noses; the mist which has afforded them this scent is of extremely mystic nature, losing itself in those wondrous regions whither strayed that Princess from the "Iron Hand," as I wrote you above—at like time informing you that her creator had endued her with the need of seeking a hermit's blessing on a bond that woke the troubles of maternity too early in her. For it is anticipated that, in case she should set any store by Christian uses, Dlle. Rachel may feel impelled to seek a similar hallowing; whilst all kinds of circumstances bound up therewith allow one to presume that in this and kindred matters the Racinian Tragedy must suffer a grievous blow. Oh, these uncompassionate Prime Ministers!

To my sorrow I perceive that I am on the verge of defiling the threads of my Correspondence, in themselves somewhat loose, with a stray piece of scandal. Preserve me God from such a thing! Yet it at least will shew you that there are scandals-of-State in Paris as well; a discovery of a certain weight to anyone who thinks himself at first quite unregarded in this odiously big city, but sees the prospect thereby opening-out of his being some-day raised, himself, into the subject of a scandal.* And verily 'tis no small feat, to reach that point!

I observe that in to-day's communication I have not overstepped the circle of the Theatre (in Paris a very considerable one); so, as I am just about to bring it to a close, I won't diverge into another field, particularly as there wouldn't be much to gather there, since almost all the art-sensations which constitute the Paris Season are exclusively confined at present to the theatres. But, seeing we have Autumn here till nearly the end of December, I can safely promise you a continuation of my *autumn* notes without fear of running short of news; for a month like

* The "some day" was a matter of just twenty years—with the production of *Tannhäuser* at the Grand Opéra.—Tr.

this never passes in Paris without supplying Correspondents of my kidney with an ample store. The "Maltese Knight" of Halévy still delays its appearance; everybody is much excited about it; you therefore may rely on my giving you a prompt and circumstantial account of the production, so soon as it comes off.

In conclusion, a joke from the "Charivari." At the recent wedding of Jules Janin Herr Chateaubriand was among the guests; the bridegroom begged him for his blessing, which he refused with the words: "*All that I have blessed, has fallen.*"—Now the "Charivari" tells us that no sooner had these words been heard, than from all the ends of France, from every town, from every village, one cry went up to the far-famed writer: "*Chateaubriand, we implore thee, bless the governmental system! O bless the Ministry!*" — — — So, honoured Sir, if I am finally to wish you something extra good, in the name of the "Charivari" it can only be Chateaubriand's *curse.*

RICHARD WAGNER.

7.

December 1, 1841.

In continuation of my Autumn report I must first devote a few words to Delaroche's last great painting, which was exhibited yesterday, though only to professors and his pupils. Through one of these pupils, the talented painter Kietz of Dresden (at present engaged on Delaroche's portrait), I myself was allowed, in advance of the public, a sight of the master's last creation, and will profit by this lucky circumstance to tell you at once as much about it as lies in my power.

Delaroche's task was to furnish a mural painting for a semicircular chamber in the École des Beaux Arts, expressly constructed for the award of prizes; it was to fill the whole half-circle, having for subject the distribution-of-prizes itself. To its execution Delaroche has given four years of unremitting labour, and whoever looks on his creation will be seized by the conviction that the artist had no less in mind than to make it the starting-point of a new epoch in the history of French painting. Without doubt you soon will receive more detailed and expert opinions on this masterwork; allow me therefore to describe to you at least its subject.

In the middle of the great half-circle Delaroche has placed the heroes of Greek plastic art, the painter Apelles, the sculptor Phidias, and the architect Ictinus, as judges; they are awarding the prizes, which are distributed by a maiden in the picture's foreground who appears to be casting laurel-wreaths right out of its frame. Below the three judges rises a low flight of steps, against whose balustrade lean four magnificent female figures, representing Greek, Roman, Medieval art, and art reborn by the great Italian masters. This central group is flanked on either side by a peristyle of Ionic columns, bounded by the open sky; its whole space is occupied by an assemblage of the greatest artists from the time of the Renaissance to the close of the Seventeenth Century, the sculptors being marshalled on the left, the architects on the right pavement of the peristyle, while the painters are placed at either end of the half-circle, in the open landscape. The representatives of various schools are grouped according to their mental kinship, and engaged in a lively discussion of matters of art. The great group of painters on the left depicts the more sensuous artistic line, its principal figures being Titian and Rubens; here brilliance and glow of colour prevail in the costumes, and an almost heedless gaiety pervades the whole. The group on the opposite side expresses the ideal, the high-poetic tendency in painting: Raphael and Leonardo da Vinci are here the leading types.

What most appealed to me, was the delightful, the thoroughly artistic ease displayed in the grouping of these four-and-seventy figures, mostly portraits, from the most diverse ages, in the most unlike of costumes, and with rigid adherence to the character of every individual. The point of the contrasted dress of wellnigh five whole centuries, is that on which the experts more especially praise Delaroche's mastery; for you might fancy that a gathering of men, one of whom wears the long and sumptuous garment of the Venetian, another the short cloak and doublet of the Netherlander, and yet another the strict monastic cowl, would easily incur the piebald semblance of a masquerade. Delaroche, however, with the greatest faithfulness to details, has been able to give the whole so spiritual a life that one does not take the least offence at seeing artists from remotest centuries in friendly converse with each other.

One rare distinction of this work is the full daylight in which it is painted. In the room for which this masterpiece was planned, and executed on the spot, the brightest sunshine enters from above, and the figures' lights and shades are therefore so arranged as to give the exact effect of living persons. We thus are rid at once of all those thousand arts of lighting, high lights, shadows and chiaroscuro, which ordinary painters use for their effects; and the whole is stamped with a severe and noble character, albeit softened by the air of intellectual cheerfulness.

Right heartily I wish you a reporter of riper and more authoritative judgment than mine can naturally be, one who shall know how to give you a lucid idea of all the splendours of this masterwork. For I should only plague you with the painful vagueness of a little-practised friend of art, were I to try to analyse the countless beauties which aroused the master's pupils, assembled before the giant painting, to such a pitch that they almost stifled Delaroche with their enthusiasm when he came into the room at last;—he himself was so moved, that he had a hard fight with his tears while addressing his scholars in a touching and heartfelt little speech, which he concluded by urging them to courage and perseverance.—From to-day the hall is open to the public, so that you probably will soon receive from a better hand than mine a reasoned and precise account of this masterpiece of French art.

In conclusion I have to inform you that the day before yesterday Scribe's long-awaited comedy "*Une Chaîne*" was played for the first time at the Théâtre Français. Up to the present I have been unable to get near a ticket, and whoever has seen the human sea that floods the approaches to the theatre from four o'clock each day, after a success like that achieved by this new piece, may reasonably despair of finding a seat with German comfort before the next two weeks are out. Thus much I can tell you, however: the success appears to be complete, particularly when I compare the verdicts in the different journals, all of which are in Scribe's favour with the exception of that of J. Janin, who has been extremely exercised of late by the question of Morals—somewhat drolly for him, the smirking little manikin. Are *morals* to become as consuming a passion with the French, as *logic* has been till to-day? The game might suitably begin with Janin, since he has just got married; but how if the whole of France were to follow his example, and get married too? Oh, what a loss it would be!

Please make shift with these hasty lines to-day. Autumn isn't at an end as yet; before it is, you shall certainly receive the promised budget from

Yours most faithfully,

RICHARD WAGNER.

8.

December 23, 1841.

I must really put my best foot forward, if I am to keep my promise of concluding my Autumn report from Paris before the commencement of winter. With all my might I was awaiting the first performance of Halévy's "Maltese Knight"; for I knew that I should need some right good novelty, to give my present batch of news the needful, indispensable splendour. Now this "Maltese Knight" has put in no appearance at all, but in his stead the "Queen of Cyprus" by the same Halévy; yet, despite the fact that this opera contains extremely little, as good as nothing, of Maltese knights, we all are convinced that it is one and the same work, merely pre-announced under a provisional title. And thereby hangs a tale:—composers and poets have learnt to their cost that premature acquaintance with the title of their works gives waggish heads not only opportunity, but also matter, for parodying them into the ridiculous before they have been even performed. A well-known case is that of Meyerbeer's "Huguenots," which, owing to the somewhat long delay in its appearance, was *travestied* at a Boulevard theatre before its serious self convulsed the public from the boards of the Grand Opéra. The maddest joke, however, was that indulged-in by the "Charivari" anent a tragedy, "*La délivrance de la Suède*," whose production at the Théâtre Français had long been announced: this journal gave out that by dint of showers of gold and banknotes it had obtained sight of the manuscript, and held important to acquaint its readers that the subject was altogether different from what would have been guessed from the piece's title; for its meaning was not "the liberation of Sweden," but "the delivery of Mme. Schwede." The plot, it said, was much as follows:—

In Germany there lived a certain inn-keeper, whose name was *Schwede*;* his wife, a buxom dame, was therefore called in general *die Schwede*. Now this Frau Schwede, after years of wedded happiness, hadn't presented her husband with a child—whereat her spouse was sore distressed; all the more rejoiced was he, when his wife at last announced that she felt justified in holding out most brilliant and indisputable prospects of perpetuation of the Schwede lineage. You may imagine the touching pictures of connubial bliss set flowing from the poet's pen by this occasion! But the tragic principle fails not to come to

* "Schwede" in the German vernacular means "an honest fellow."—Tr.

work: Frau Schwede very soon displays the most disturbing cravings; now she longs for a melon, then for a pheasant, anon for lobster, again for God knows what. You may conceive the troubles of the honest Schwede, obliged to run now here, now there, to still the cravings of his wife! It costs no end of money, and causes terrible distress. Who's to take care of the inn? Everything goes topsy-turvy. But finally there comes the epoch of delivery; this forms the utmost-tragical catastrophe, given by the "Charivari" with a wealth of detail which it pretends to borrow from the manuscript itself: a mighty scene in many stanzas.— — Fearing a similar fate, Herr Saint-Georges, librettist of "*La Reine de Chypre*," may have purposely kept back the proper title of his poem: in which case he is liable for the contingent bankruptcy of about a hundred German stage-directors; for we may be certain that, relying on the long-known title "The Maltese Knight," they have laid in nothing but costumes for knights of Malta, which, save for one that plays a very short and minor rôle, can now be made no use of.

After all this talk of the new opera's title, I must inform you that I cannot possibly unload my mind about *itself* in these hasty lines: the work and its attendant circumstances embarrass me with so much matter for discussion, that I deem better to reserve it for a special article. Let it suffice for to-day to tell you that Halévy's opera was really given yesterday, the 22nd of this month, and won a marked success; further, that both text and music are far superior to "Guido and Ginevra," and therefore it is generally supposed that Halévy has ground down all the dents in his renown, with this latest opera, and taken a brilliant revenge. A more exhaustive report I promise you, as said, in a separate article.*

On the other hand, I think I owe you fuller news of Scribe's new five-act comedy, "*Une Chaîne*." At last I have been able to get a decent place in the Théâtre

* See Vol. VII.—Tr.

Français, to enjoy this much-praised comedy in peace and comfort. In truth, a good seat and a certain aristocratic *aisance* are indispensable in this handsome, truly decorous theatre, if one is to enter fully into the spirit of what its poets and performers set before its pampered audience. How sad must those tortured wretches feel who, squeezed into some dismal corner of the parterre, or crammed into one of the dizzy cages of this house, behold in front of them—and often at their elbow—that affluent spectacle which rolls the whole refinement of its comfort before their eyes! Must it not be plain to these poor people, that those gentlemen and ladies on the stage are not addressing them at all, not playing for the likes of them? And especially with a play like Scribe's "Fetters," where everything moves with that unforced, pliant grace so characteristic of French Comedy, making it the first and only one in our modern world! Indeed, when I lately saw this piece performed by the actors of the Théâtre Français, it became clear to me why we Germans have no Comedy worth the name, and why the French will always have to help us out. 'Tis the whole thing: Paris, its salons, its countesses, boulevards, lawyers, doctors, grisettes, maîtresses, journals, cafés—in short, just *Paris*, that makes these comedies; Scribe and his friends are really nothing more than clerks, amanuenses of that great, that million-headed playwright. That Scribe, however, is the cleverest and best-equipped among these journeymen, is proved afresh by his latest play. If you look with German curiosity into the matter of this piece, you cannot but be astounded at its seeming staleness: a young man on the eve of his marriage tries to break the love-bonds chaining him to a lady of high station, to whom, moreover, he owes his fortune; on the point of being sprung asunder, these fetters draw closer once more, till they are loosed at last by resignation. This is the extremely simple subject—but see what *Paris*, with all its specialities adduced above, has done through Scribe's pen to form a comedy that keeps us constantly on the alert, charms, kindles, entertains, and —makes us laugh! It's extraordinary! If in his "*Verre d'eau*" Scribe had historical figures, which lent his piece an interest entirely of themselves, he here has dispensed with any such expedient, thus making his task considerably harder, in my opinion, and setting his talent in a still more meritorious light through its happy achievement. But this is a modern-*Parisian* comedy, in the fullest sense of the term, and accordingly of great importance; for Paris, once and for all, is a very large slice of the world, and whoso would study the latter will not do ill to learn his Paris. I recommend this piece to you,* and only wish it may be given in Germany with the same spirit, and particularly the great refinement, displayed by the actors of the Théâtre Français. I am convinced that our German actors possess the faculty of making even that advantage of the French their own, for our character is manysidedness—only, I wish they would copy the Frenchmen's *diligence*; for I am persuaded that, next to their great talent, the actors of the Théâtre Français owe the fine perfection of their *ensemble* mainly to their exceptional diligence. And verily a piece like this "*Chaîne*" of Scribe's both merits and requires it, for a smooth performance is just as much the base of its existence as Paris itself, the world-city.—

One would think I had become a stage-manager;—I am far less that, than your very faithful servant,

RICHARD WAGNER.

(*With the above the Correspondence in the* Abendzeitung *ends; but a further letter of Wagner's appeared in Schumann's* Neue Zeitschrift für Musik *of Feb.* 22, 1842, *above the cypher* "*H. V.*"—*Tr.*)

* Councillor Winkler, editor of the *Abendzeitung*, had commissioned Wagner to pick up new Parisian pieces for adaptation in Germany.—Tr.

9.

Halévy's *Reine de Chypre* is not bad; some of it beautiful, much of it trivial—as a whole, without special importance. The accusation of noisiness is unjust; in the fourth act it is in place (above all, for our epoch), in the remainder a striving for simplicity is notable, particularly in the instrumentation.—Do not forget: Halévy has no private means. He has assured me that, were he well-to-do, he would write no more for the theatre, but only symphonies, oratorios, and so forth; at the Opéra he is made a slave to the interests of the Director and singers, and compelled to write poor stuff with open eyes.—He is frank and honest; no sly, deliberate *filou* like M.*—

The run on the Opéra Comique is no fee to simplicity, but purely to fashion. You may take this on my word of honour. Just think! *Richard Cœur-de-lion* has been instrumented and revised by Adam (!!). As for noise, it consequently is much the same as with *Zampa* etc. Then the singers. They sing "*O Richard, o mon roi*" with the same *entrain*, the same admired tomfooleries, as *Fra Diavolo*; they modernise from crown to sole; that pleases—and after all, Grétry did write charming music. *Voilà tout!*

We Germans cherish dire illusions about the generous taste of this public, its seeming justice, and so on. But Paris is large; why should there not be 200 human beings in it, who have acquired a taste for Beethoven's symphonies at the Conservatoire? The real opera-public, however, understands nothing but *cancan*. Spare me a translation of that word.—For heaven's sake, look at B. . . † The man is so ruined by France, or rather by Paris, that one can no longer conceive what he would have done with his talent in Germany. I have loved him since he owns a thousand things which stamp him for an artist; but would that he had become a whole Jack-pudding! in his halfness he is nothing. He lately

* For which read Meyerbeer.—Tr.

† Berlioz.—Tr.

gave a concert that systematically drove the audience out of its skin. Whoever had not wholly left his skin through boredom and *dégoût*, was obliged to at the end of his apotheosis in the July-Symphony—for very joy: that's the remarkable feature; in this last movement there are things which nothing could surpass for grandeur and sublimity.—For all that, B. stands quite alone in Paris.—Parisian taste is at its lowest ebb: think back to the times of Boieldieu, of the *Dame blanche*, of Auber's *Maçon*, *Muette* etc., and compare what is produced to-day—Adam etc. At the Opéra Comique it is dreadful; the very worst of Auber's gewgaws make out the standing system of these young composers, Thomas, Clapisson etc. In everything prevails a hideous falling-off.

For the decay of the charming French style at the Opéra Comique *the Italians are chiefly blamable*: they are unconditionally deified and copied. The delightful couplets of days gone by either have become a worthless, wholly unmelodious jingle in $\frac{3}{8}$ time, or imitate the Italian *sentimental manner* (!). But this Italian *sentiment* is a grave misfortune; it leads even honest folk astray: they stake everything on the singer's execution, and the composer at last becomes an audience, with nothing to do but applaud his singers, forgetful if what they sing he wrote.—There you have the story of the *Stabat mater*; it is given every week at the Italian Opera: since the Italians sing it, it must be good—'tis the *fashion*. To put it briefly: here nothing pays but *virtuosity*; here Liszt plays just as much the rôle of a buffoon, as Duprez upon the stage. Everything that looms above the Paris horizon—let it be never so firstrate—becomes bad and mountebankish.—I hear that M[endelssohn] has been invited to compose an opera for Paris: if he is so insane as to accept, he's to be pitied. To my way of thinking, he is not even in the position to succeed with an opera in Germany; he's much too intellectual, and totally wanting in *passion*: how could that answer in Paris?—If he had only seen the *Freischutz*!—How lucky it would be for us, to bid a last farewell to Paris!—It has had a great epoch, which certainly has influenced us for good. But that's over now, and we must give up our faith in Paris.—Presumably I shall not need to warn much longer.

Dessauer was lately commissioned to write recitatives for *Fidelio*: he has fulfilled his task with tact and artistic conscience. This sort of thing astounds the French.—

H. V.

Paris, February 5, 1842.

VII.

HALÉVY AND "LA REINE DE CHYPRE."

(*From the* Gazette Musicale *of Feb.* 27, *March* 13, *April* 24 *and May* 1, 1842; *a companion article to that appearing in Vol. VII. of the present series.—Tr.*)

TO make a good opera, it not only needs a good poet and a good composer, but also a sympathetic accord between the talent of the one and that of the other. If both were equally enthusiastic for the same idea, so much the better; but to obtain a perfect work, it would be necessary that this idea should come at like time to the musician and the writer.* We are aware that that is a case almost unheard of: nevertheless it would not be impossible for our hypothesis to be realised. Let one imagine, for example, that the poet and the composer are friends from childhood; that they have arrived at that stage in life when the divine and generous ardour wherewith great minds aspire to drink in every joy and suffering of all created beings has not as yet been chilled by the contaminating breath of our civilisation; that they are standing beside the sea, with avid eyes devouring the immensity of its waters, or before a ruined city, their thoughts transporting them to the shadowy depths of the past. Of a sudden some marvellous tradition conjures up before them figures vague, indefinite, but beautiful and enchanting: ravishing melodies, quite novel inspirations besiege their brain, like dreams and poetic forebodings; then a name is uttered, a name

* See "Opera and Drama," Part III. caps. iv and vii,—written 1850-51. —Tr.

from tradition or history, and with that name a full-fledged drama has occurred to them. 'Tis the poet who uttered it; for to him belongs the faculty of giving clear and definite form to what reveals itself to his fancy. But what weaves the charm of the ineffable around the poetic conception, what reconciles reality with the ideal,—the task of seizing that belongs to the musician. The work elaborated by the talents of them both, in hours of calm reflection, might be justly called a perfect opera.

Unfortunately this mode of production is altogether ideal; at least, we must assume that its results never come to the ear of the public. In any case it has nothing in common with Artistic Industry. The latter it is, in our present day, that serves as mediatrix between poet and composer; and perhaps we ought to thank her. For without this wonderful institution of the "droits d'auteurs" things would probably go in France as they go in Germany, where poets and musicians keep a dogged isolation from each other; whereas those "droits d'auteurs," a remarkably fine thing in themselves, have led to more than one happy and fruitful alliance of talents. It is these "droits," if I mistake not, that suddenly converted M. Scribe to a taste for musical inspirations, and determined him to write libretti which for long will serve as models.* Yet these same rights have prompted other celebrated poets to write opera-texts for all they are worth, the Directors of our art-establishments never daring to set up difficulties when it concerns the products of a famous author; so that composers are obliged to content themselves with whatever one deigns to offer them, and the result of this forced alliance is nothing but mediocre works appearing under the ægis of an illustrious name.

* Wagner himself in 1836 had sent Scribe the draft of an opera founded on König's "Die hohe Braut," with the request that Scribe should versify it for him, and get it produced in Paris as soon as the young man had composed it. Nothing came of this project; but in his Dresden period Richard Wagner prepared the text of this work for his friend Johann Kittl to set to music, and it was produced with great success at Prague in February 1848 under the title "Bianca und Giuseppe, oder die Franzosen vor Nizza."—Tr.

So far the thing is clear enough: it is perfectly natural that works conceived without enthusiasm, and elaborated in a spirit of blind routine, cannot kindle the public. What surprises us, and what we must regard as a veritable stroke of luck for art, is that from time to time this method of procedure gives birth to creations which delight the parterre, and moreover stand the scrutiny of a rigorous criticism. Admitting that the composer remains the same, that his productive force knows no enfeeblement, it is none the less true that the care to maintain his renown of great artist would not suffice to rouse in him that wondrous exaltation which gives its flight to talent; for that there needs a spark divine to fall all burning on the artist's brain, to steep him in a kindly flame that circulates within his veins like generous wine, and dews his eyes with tears of inspiration cloaking from his sight all common, vulgar things, to let him see but the Ideal in all its purity. Ambition alone, however soaring, will never strike that spark divine; and he is truly to be pitied, the poor artist who after many a triumph, after manifesting his creative power, finds himself plunged in some arid stage-intrigue, to hunt all breathless for a gust of inspiration, as the traveller scours the desert for a well of living water.

Whatever envy one may bear those happy mortals who, heaped with honours and radiant with glory, alone among thousands of composers have the right to speak through the most brilliant organs to the premier audience in the world,—ye who aspire to a kindred fame would never seek the honour of their place, could ye see them on some fresh and lovely forenoon resigning themselves with martyred air to the fabrication of a duet whose subject is the theft of a watch or the offering of a cup of tea. So, be not jealous of these gentlemen, if it pleases God at times to summon a true poet and cast into his heart that spark which shall incend the musician in turn! Without any after-thought of grudge or envy, congratulate Halévy that his good genius sent him texts like those of the Juive and the Reine de Chypre; for this favour, after all, is but the strictest justice. In effect, Halévy has twice been completely fortunate, and one can but admire the manner in which he has profited of this double favour to create two monuments that will mark the history of musical art. Certainly Halévy's talent lacks neither grace nor freshness; nevertheless, through the predominance of passionate gravity in his character, it was upon our Grand Lyric stage that he was destined to develop all his force and volume. And it is worthy of remark, that in this respect the talent of Halévy essentially differs from that of Auber and the generality of French composers, whose veritable home is decidedly the Opéra Comique.

This national institution, where the various modifications, the curious changes in French character and taste have come to light with greatest clearness and in the most popular manner, has at all times been the true domain of French composers. Here Auber had the fullest scope for revealing the fecundity, the flexibility of his talent; his music, at once elegant and popular, fluent and precise, graceful and bold, bending with marvellous facility to every turn of his caprice, had all the qualities to win and dominate the public's taste. He mastered vocal music with a keen vivacity, multiplied its rhythms to infinity, and gave the ensemble-pieces an entrain, a characteristic briskness scarcely known before his time. The Opéra Comique is decidedly the true domain of Auber's talent, the field where he could venture, yet not quit his basis. After having practised and developed his talents at the Opéra Comique, at last he delivered a grand battle, whose risks he faced with as much courage and bravery as those light-hearted fops of Paris displayed in the famous days of July. The price of victory was no less a one than the colossal success of La Muette.*

With Halévy it has been quite otherwise. The vigour of his constitution, the concentrated energy that marks his nature, ensured him in advance a place on our first

* *La Muette de Portici*, produced in 1828; known in Italy and England as *Masaniello*.—Tr.

lyric stage. According to usage, he made his début at the Opéra Comique; but it was only at the Grand Opéra that he revealed the whole depth and compass of his talent. Though in compositions of an inferior rank he perfectly succeeded in relaxing the springs of his natural energy and giving it those airs of graceful elegance which flatter and delight the senses without affording us profounder joys, without moving our soul very strongly, I do not hesitate to say that the essential characteristic of Halévy's inspiration is before all else the pathos of high Lyric Tragedy. Nothing could have been better suited to the type of his talent, than the subject of La Juive. One might almost say that a sort of fatality led the artist's footsteps to this "book," predestined to incite him to employment of his every force. It is in La Juive that Halévy's true vocation manifested itself in a manner irrefragable, and by proofs the most striking and multiple: that vocation is, to write music such as issues from the inmost and most puissant depths of human nature. It is terrifying, and makes one dizzy, to gaze into the awful caverns of the human heart. For the poet it is impossible to render in words all that passes at the bottom of this stanchless fount, which responds in turn to the breath of God and of the Devil; he may speak to you of hate, of love, of fanaticism and frenzy; he will set before your eyes the outward acts engendered on the surface of those depths: but never can he take you down into them, unveil them to your look. It is reserved for Music alone, to reveal the primal elements of this marvellous nature; in her mysterious charm our soul is shewn this great, unutterable secret. And the musician who exerts his art in this direction, alone can boast of mastering all its resources. Among the most brilliant and vaunted masters cited by the history of musical art, there are very few who on this side could prove their title of Musician. Among the composers whose names are household words in every mouth, how many there are who ignore, and always will ignore, that beneath those splendid and seductive trappings, which alone they have been granted to perceive, there lurks a depth, a wealth immense as the creation! On the meagre roll of true musicians, in this sense, we must place Halévy.

As said, it is in La Juive that Halévy disclosed his vocation for lyric tragedy. In attempting to characterise his music, our first duty was to sound its depths: there lies his point of departure; from thence he took his view of musical art. I am not talking of a fugitive passion, inflaming the blood, to die down at once: I speak of that faculty of strong emotion, incisive and profound, quickening and convulsing the moral world of every age. 'Tis it that constitutes the magic element in this score of La Juive, the source whence spring alike the fanaticism of Eléazar—that rage so fierce and sombre, yet sending forth at times such blinding flames—and the dolorous love that consumes the heart of Rachel. In fine, it is this principle that gives life to each figure appearing in this terrible drama, and thus it is that the author has known to preserve æsthetic unity amid the most violent contrasts, and avoided all effects too brusque or likely to offend.

The external music of La Juive, if so I may express myself, is in thorough keeping with the primary and intimate conception: the common, the trivial, from it are banished. Albeit all is calculated from the point of view of the whole, its author none the less devotes himself to fashioning the tiniest details of the work with indefatigable care. The various sections of the scenic scheme are knit and welded to each other; and in this respect Halévy differs markedly and advantageously from the majority of opera-makers of our era, some of whom believe they can never take sufficient pains to separate, to isolate each scene—what am I saying?—each phrase from that which goes before or after, undoubtedly with the not very honourable object of drawing the attention of the audience to convenient passages where it may signify its satisfaction by applause: whereas Halévy keeps throughout the knowledge of his dignity as dramatic composer. Moreover the fecundity of his talent is evinced by a great variety of dramatic rhythms, particularly to be remarked in the orchestral accompaniment, whose motion is always characteristic. But what strikes us as above all worthy admiration, is that Halévy has succeeded in stamping on his score the seal of the epoch at which the action passes. To solve this problem, it was no question of consulting antiquarian documents, to drag out archæologic grossnesses anent the manners of that day, affording no artistic interest; the question was, to lend the music the perfume of the epoch, and reproduce the men and women of the Middle Ages in all their individuality. In that the author of La Juive has perfectly succeeded. Without doubt one could not point to such and such passage as more especially denoting this intention of the author's; there he has shewn himself true artist: but for my part I avow that never have I heard dramatic music which transferred me so completely to a given reach of history.

How did Halévy arrive at this effect? That is a mystery whose key must be sought in his mode of production. One might rank him in what is called the Historic school, were it not that the constituent elements of this composer's mode concur with the Romantic; for as soon as we are carried away from ourselves, from our sensations and impressions of the hour, from the habitual sphere where our existence passes, and transported to an unknown region, yet with full retention of all our faculties,—from that moment we are under the spell of what folk call Romantic poetry.

We have thus arrived at the spot where the road along which Halévy marches, parts company with that pursued by Auber. The composers of this latter path bear the stamp of nationality to the point of becoming monotonous. It is indisputable that the essentially French character of Auber's music ensured him in a very little while a firm position, and an independent, upon the field of comic opera; on the other hand it is evident that when it became a question of conceiving and writing lyric tragedies this national idiosyncrasy, so sharply marked, prevented him from rising to that standpoint where national interest is effaced and one sympathises only with the purely human. Of course I am speaking here of nationality in the most restricted sense. To conform, to identify oneself with national modes and habits, is the sole condition by which the poet or composer in the genre of comic opera can be sure of acting strongly on the masses. The poet will employ the adages, maxims, plays on words etc., that are current in the nation for which he writes; the composer will seize the rhythms and melodic turns encountered in its popular airs, or even invent fresh turns and rhythms in keeping with the national taste and character. The more pronounced the nationality of these airs, the greater will be their favour; and no one has succeeded better in this genre, than Auber. It is precisely this, that fettered the composer's talent in Lyric Tragedy; and albeit in the Muette he pursued and emphasised this exclusive direction with superior skill, it nevertheless is cause that this master, unequalled on his own field, has succeeded far less with his other grand operas.*

I allude to the dramatic type of melody. Apart from cases where the first concern is to bring certain national idiosyncrasies into relief, this melody should have a general and independent character; for only then is it possible for the musician to give his pictures a colouring whose elements are drawn from elsewhere than his epoch and the world in which he lives: when melody expresses purely human sentiments, it must not bear the traces of a French, Italian, or any other local origin. These sharp-cut national nuances distort the melody's dramatic truth, and sometimes destroy it entirely. Another disadvantage is the lack of variety; however apt and skilful the employment of these nuances, their essential features always end

* It is worthy of note that the author's whole present estimate of Auber is endorsed in the special article which he wrote on that composer's death in 1871.—Tr.

by reappearing every instant: the ease with which they are recognised, ensures them the popular favour, but it effaces dramatic illusion.

Speaking generally, in Auber's manner one observes a marked tendency to underline the rhythmic construction of the periods. It is impossible to deny that his music thereby profits much in clearness, one of the essential qualities of dramatic music—which ought to act upon us instantaneously. As to this, no one has been happier than Auber, for he has succeeded more than once in co-ordinating the most complicated and passionate situations in a fashion to make them understood at a glance. I need do no more than cite Lestocq, one of his choicest and most solid productions. In this opera the musical cut of the ensemble-pieces involuntarily recalls the Figaro of Mozart, especially in what concerns the finish of the melodic tissue. But the moment these clear-cut contours of the rhythm, this balance and four-squareness of the melody are not in harmony with the dramatic situation, they end by fatiguing; and further, if this brilliant monotony in the melodic design does not respond to the general expression of a tragic sentiment, it will sometimes happen that these splendid and glittering melodies have the air of being superimposed like a crystal cage on the musical [?—dramatic] situation which they, as it were, enclose.

This method is of great assistance to the composer whenever he has to write ballet-music. The marvellous perfection with which he treats that genre, will give a clear idea of what I mean by the squaring of rhythm and melody beloved of Auber. That obligatory cut of airs-de-danse, with its eight-bar periods returning periodically, their cadences on the dominant or relative minor,—that air-de-danse cut, I repeat, with Auber has become a second nature; 'tis it, decidedly, that impedes his giving to his conceptions that character of generality so indispensable to the composer who writes tragic airs, that is to say, who expresses in sounds the feelings of the human heart, feelings ever the same and yet of so prodigious a variety.

After going to such a length of detail on the subject of Auber and his manner, it will be the easier for me to convey in a few words the difference that exists between this composer and the author of La Juive and La Reine de Chypre. Abruptly breaking with the system of Auber, Halévy boldly sprang out of the rut of conventional turns and rhythms, to enter the career of free, unlimited creation, recognising no other law than that of truth. Indeed it needed a very resolute confidence in his own strength and the resources of his talent, for a musician thus voluntarily to desert the beaten track, which could but lead him sooner and more surely to popularity; it needed high courage and dauntless faith in the power of truth; and to succeed in this adventurous attempt, it needed all the concentrated energy of Halévy's talent. The happy issue of that resolution proves anew the inexhaustible variety of Music, and will form an important chapter in the history of Art. True, this proof could never have been so decisive, and Halévy would not have been able to accomplish his task with such success in general, had experience not matured his talent, and had he not proceeded to the composition of his work with calm and reasoned perspicacity. Had he chosen to reject all constant forms as flat and insufficient; if, prompted by a passionate self-will, he had insisted on creating an absolutely new system and imposing it upon the public with the imperious pride of the inventor, it is certain that, however great his talent, he would have come to grief with his inventions, his very talent would have become inexcusable to the public, and lost its dramatic value. But had Halévy need of such a system? Were there not before him and beside him lovely things, things grand and true, so that his piercing eye could easily pick out the route he had to follow? That route he found, nor did he ever lose that feeling for beauty of Form which in itself is one of the essential properties of talent. Without this, without this care for finish and firmness of detail, how could he have avoided doing violence to the heart and head of the hearer when painting feelings so profound, passions so lurid and terrible?

So we come to this: that truth does no less injury to itself in hiding beneath seductive and conventional trappings, than in proudly asserting itself with an exaggerated estimate of its often mistaken value.

March 13th.—To resume my subject at the change of direction which may be observed in Halévy's talent dating from La Juive, I have to say that this composer has renounced the stereotyped style of modern French opera, yet without disdaining its characteristic qualities. It was only by proceeding thus, that he could escape the danger of drifting aimlessly without a style at all. Nor was it blindfold instinct, but reflection, that conducted him.

This style consists in the attempt to externalise with the greatest possible clearness and precision what passes within us, under forms in keeping with the spirit of the age. Now, in measure as the artist subjects himself to the impressions of his epoch, and obliterates himself before it, it is obvious that his style must lose in both independence and value; on the contrary, the better he knows how to express his individual intuition, the more will the style itself be elevated and ennobled. The master who has full consciousness of his intuition, alone can stamp his epoch's style with a powerful and lasting impress. From another side, the artist who knows all the importance of style, alone can fully reveal his ideas and impressions. Thus open to us two false roads to which an epoch may commit itself: either its composers may rid themselves of any style at all, or the style may so vulgarise itself that it becomes a mannerism. Where both these aberrations are evinced, we may be sure that the decay of musical art is imminent.

Almost all contemporary young composers have strayed into one or other of these roads, and without doubt it is the laxity and indolence wherewith most of them have turned to mannerism that accounts for their never having felt the influence of the brilliant energy wherewith Halévy has sped the style of French Grand Opera along a novel path. This is a phenomenon of most afflicting import, and I think it my duty to inquire into its causes with the fullest freedom; an inquiry all the more necessary, as I do not remember this circumstance having yet been paid the notice it deserves.

It cannot be denied that since the time when Auber's talent reached its height of popularity, French music—to which he had given a new impetus, as powerful as auspicious—has steadily declined from day to day. To touch at once the lowest depth of decadence and degeneration, it only needs to adduce the wretched products that fill the repertory of the Opéra Comique conjointly with the masterpieces of French genius. It is scarcely credible that such a natural institute, where even the youngest among us have had occasion to greet the happy advent of works of the first order, should seem condemned to bring to light from month to month a file of pitiful rhapsodies (with very few exceptions) which the most enervated taste could never find supportable.* As their principal characteristic is the most absolute vacuity, a total want of force and inspiration, it is the more surprising that these compositions are far less the work of superannuated masters, than of young people on whom depends the musical future of France. Don't talk about Auber's exhaustion! † Beyond doubt this illustrious master has arrived at the extreme limit of his artistic career, where creative force should stop because it cannot renovate itself, where the artist should confine his efforts to maintaining himself at the point he has reached, and preserving his glory intact. Granted that this is the most perilous position for an artist, seeing that

* One has only to consult the *Gazette Musicale*, to learn the incredible number of still-born works produced at the Opéra Comique during the 2½ years of Wagner's stay in Paris.—Tr.

† At this date Auber was sixty years old.—Tr.

it verges toward decline, whilst persistent entrenchment behind an unalterable system must inevitably tend to monotony and restrict the composer's sphere of action; yet we have to recognise that no one knows as Auber to give life and grace to the forms by him invented, to mould, to polish and to round them with such admirable sureness and perfection. Once and for all, it is precisely the consideration that these forms were invented by himself, that inspires us with the most profound esteem for his fine talent; and we gladly grant him the exclusive use of forms familiar to him by just title. But, far as we are from branding Auber as the corruptor of musical taste, it cannot be denied that the style created by him, as pointed out above, appears to have ruined our younger composers for ever. It seems as if they had understood nothing of his manner except its mechanical processes, and that these are all they found to imitate. As for the wit, the grace, the freshness, which enchant you in the master's products, you will not find a shadow of them in his copyists.

Now that we know what to think of the cotemporaries or successors of Auber—whichever you like to call them—, and have ascertained their feebleness and impotence, we may easily explain why none of them has dared the path so gloriously driven by Halévy in La Juive, 'spite all the volleys of applause that have saluted this important work. We have already said it: the distinctive feature in Halévy's talent is its intensity of thought, its concentrated energy. These qualities and the exuberant wealth of forms wherein they manifest, forms at once independent and worked out with the greatest care,—all this quite crushed that race of pygmies, to whom Music appears to have revealed herself in no form save that of $\frac{6}{8}$ time, of couplets and quadrilles. If, then, they have never recognised that their safety lay in boldly throwing themselves into this new career, we shall find the reason in the profound artistic demoralisation into which they fell from the first day of their entry upon the career of art; for, with a little verve, a little elasticity, they would have leapt into the footsteps of the author of La Juive.

But if Halévy has not had a potent action on the artists who surround him, let him turn his gaze on Germany. The Germans, who so readily give up their stages to the foreigner, had taken to appreciating the voluptuous music of Rossini down to its minutest details; they next became enthusiastic for the ravishing melodies of the Muette de Portici, and would hear nothing from the boards except French music, which thenceforth dethroned the Italian. To be sure, it entered the head of no German composer to choose a model from among the French or the Italians, to write according to the style of Auber or Rossini. In their honest lack of prejudice they welcomed what was brought them from abroad, and enjoyed it with true gratitude: but the foreigner's work was appreciated merely as such, and stayed foreign to them; it never fastened on their mode of thought, of feeling or producing. The music of Auber, precisely because it bore so strong an imprint of the national, could electrify the German public, but not awake that perfect sympathy we cherish for a product to which we yield our soul and faculties without reserve. Here lies the explanation of the somewhat curious fact that next to nothing but French music has been heard of late at German theatres, yet without a single composer having manifested the desire to familiarise himself with the style and brilliant resources of this school, although by following that course he might have hoped to meet the momentary cravings of the public.

On the contrary, Halévy's Juive * has made a strong and twofold impression in Germany: not only did its representation evince that power which moves and fascinates the soul, but it woke those sympathies, both inner and outer, which betoken kinship. It was with an amazement full of pleasure, and greatly to its edification, that Germany discovered in this creation—which otherwise has all the qualities that distinguish the French school—the most striking and splendid traces of the genius of Beethoven, and in some sort the quintessence of the German school.

* First produced in Paris 1835.—Tr.

But even had this relationship not shewn itself at once so patently, the diversity, the universality of Halévy's style, in fine what we have tried to characterise above, would have sufficed to give the Juive a high importance in the eyes of the German musician. For it was precisely the qualities inherent in Auber's manner—qualities often brilliant, but restricted to a very narrow sphere—that deterred the Germans from all copying of that composer; whereas the greater freedom of Halévy's style, the passionate energy revealed in his music, appeal most keenly to their musical faculties. This sympathetic tie has shewn them how they may appear again in the province of Musical Drama—which they seemed to have completely abandoned—without renouncing their individuality, without offending the national genius, or effacing its character by imitation of a foreign mode.

Things ripen slowly in Germany, and fashion exercises there but little influence on artistic products. Nevertheless in more than one work published recently it already is recognisable that a new era is dawning for the dramatic music of our neighbours. When the time shall have come, we will shew in what degree the influence exerted by Halévy has contributed thereto. For the present we must limit ourselves to the assertion that this influence will be more perceptible than that which emanates from the modern coryphæi of the actual German school itself; among whom Mendelssohn-Bartholdy is undoubtedly the most conspicuous, for in him the veritable German nature declares itself most characteristically. The type of intellect, of imagination, in fact the whole interior life revealed in his instrumental compositions, so finished in their smallest details; the pious quietude that breathes from his religious works,—all this is profoundly German, but does not suffice for writing dramatic music: nay, this peaceful and abstemious piety is diametrically opposed to the inspiration demanded by Drama. To write an opera, the composer needs passions strong and deep, and further must possess the faculty of painting them vigorously and with breadth of stroke.

Now, that is just what is lacking in Mendelssohn-Bartholdy: moreover, when this eminent composer has made an attempt in Drama, he has remained beneath his level. It is not from this side, therefore, that we can hope to see a fertile, energetic power arise to vivify dramatic music once again in Germany. The impulse given by Halévy, coming from a talent which, though foreign, has an intimate affinity with the German spirit, will have results far more decisive. And whoever can appreciate the solidness, the dignity of German music, to him the influence exerted on one of its most important branches by the author of La Juive will not seem one of his smallest titles to glory.

The more reason for regretting that our younger French composers have not found strength to follow in the footsteps of this author. And what is still more deplorable, is that they have had the cowardice to undergo the influence of fashionable Italian composers. I say cowardice, because it seems to me in fact a culpable and shameful weakness to renounce the good one finds in one's own country for sake of aping foreign mediocrities, and without another motive than to profit by an easy means of catching the fugitive favour of the unreasoning mass. Whilst Italian maëstri devote their time to serious labours ere appearing before the Paris public, in order to acquire the grander faculties which distinguish the French school; whilst they diligently apply themselves (as Donizetti, to his great honour, has recently proved in the "Favorite" *) to conforming to the requirements of this school, to giving more finish and distinction to their forms, to drawing their characters with more precision and exactitude, and above all to ridding themselves of those monotonous accessaries which have served a thousand times already, those trivial and stereotyped expedients whose sterile abundance marks the manner of the Italian composers of our epoch; whilst these maëstri, I say, spend all their pains on tempering

* Produced at the Grand Opéra, Dec. 2, 1840; Wagner himself was employed in the following year to make arrangements from this work for various instruments.—Tr.

and ennobling their talent out of respect for the stage where they wish to appear,—the adepts of this venerated school prefer to garner what those others cast aside with shame and scorn.

Were it merely a matter of tickling the ears of the public by the voices of such and such admired songsters—never mind what they sing, but simply how they sing it,—it would be a sufficiently good calculation, on part of these gentry, to employ the easiest method in the world (that is to say, the Italian manner) to satisfy the wishes of an audience so little exacting. True, that in this calculation the end which every genuine artist aims at, namely the ennoblement and elevation of the mind by pleasure, would count for nothing. But experience proves that it would be a crying injustice to the public of the two Parisian opera-houses, to attribute to it a taste so unenlightened and so easy to content. The verdicts of the parterre of the Grand Opéra are a law to the musical world, and the crowd that throngs to the performances of Richard Cœur-de-Lion * would give the lie direct to any such assertion. Beyond doubt there are people, and even men of brains and taste, who are proud to tell you that Rossini is the greatest musical genius of our time. Yes, many circumstances combine to prove that Rossini is a man of genius, especially when one takes account of the enormous influence he has exerted on his epoch; but one had best keep silence, and not exalt the greatness of this man of genius beyond due measure. There are the good and the bad genius: both issue from the source of all that is divine and vital, but their mission is not the same. . . .†

* Grétry's *Richard Cœur-de-Lion* was produced in 1784; the revival, here referred to by Wagner, took place Sept. 27, 1841, at the Opéra Comique. —Tr.

† These dots, existing in the French, are eloquent of a little story told by Wagner in his "Auber" article of 1871, for which see Vol. V. pp. 37-38. Unfortunately, together with the original German MS., the omitted passage has passed into the omnivorous and secretive jaws of the private autograph-collector; but the context would rather imply that it was Halévy who in 1842 was pitted against Rossini.—Tr.

To return to the public of the two lyric theatres of the French capital, I believe we may justly pronounce it the most enlightened and impartial public in the world, having no bias save for that which is good. It may shew too much indulgence for the aberrations of our young composers, but there is nothing to prove that it ever seriously encouraged or compelled them. The feebleness and impotence of these gentlemen would be the more inexplicable, and the future of Music in France of yet more gloomy hue, were it true that the playbills acquaint us with the names of the only artists in France to whom Heaven has committed the maintenance of the honour of the French school. We have every reason, however, for believing that the playbills acquaint us with but the sorry pick of would-be composers whom a fortuitous concourse of weird circumstances has placed in evidence; whereas the true élite, in both the capital and France itself, struggles obscurely with hunger and want, and consumes its strength in fruitless efforts to reach the doors of those great caravansaries of art. These doors will some day open to true talents, and then let all who have at heart the interests of the great and sterling Musical Drama, adopt Halévy for their model.

April 24th.—It is in La Reine de Chypre that the novel method of Halévy has shewn its greatest brilliance and success. With the first lines of this article I had occasion to propound the conditions which govern the production of a good opera, in my opinion, when pointing out the obstacles that stand in the way of their perfect fulfilment at like time by the poet and the composer. Whenever these conditions are realised, it is an event of high importance for the artistic world.

In this case every circumstance combined to bring about the creation of a work distinguished, even to the eyes of strictest criticism, by all the qualities that constitute a good opera according to our attempted definition. We do not propose to examine the libretto of the Reine de Chypre in detail; to be in the position to form an exacter estimate of the score, however, it first is needful to denote that aspect of the poem which was bound to give it moment in the eyes of the composer.

Before all, I would have you observe that the poet has had the singular good fortune to give the constituent elements of his action a colour such as the musician would wish for. If I have rightly grasped the poetic trend of the libretto, the drama is founded on a conflict between human passions and Nature.* From the first we are struck by the contrast between egoistical Venice, with its terrible Council of Ten, and that charming island which the ancients vowed to Venus. From the sad and sombre city we are borne to the enchanted groves of Cyprus; but scarcely has their balmy air consoled us for the trouble that oppressed us, when in the envoy of the Council of Ten, that cold-blooded assassin, we are horrified to meet the destructive principle once again. In the thick of this deadly conflict stands the noble nature of Man, trusting to the twin stars that guide him here below, of Love and Faith, courageously fighting the infernal power, and albeit sacrificed yet conqueror; that is how we apprehend this admirable Lusignan. What a magnificent and poetical subject! What enthusiasm it must have kindled in the mind of a composer who has so high an idea, as Halévy, of the dignity of his art! Let us now review the means by which he has succeeded in communicating this enthusiasm to ourselves.

In its outward form Halévy's opera is composed of two distinct parts, determined by the scene of action.

* It must be remembered that this part of the article for the *Gaz. Mus.* was written at least two, if not three months after the German article for the *Abendzeitung*, which had been composed under the immediate influence of the first performance of *La Reine de Chypre*. In the meantime Wagner would appear to have read into his impressions of the text a pretty large dose of his own idealism, owing to that more complete acquaintance with the *music* imposed by the necessity of studying it for the purpose of "arrangements."—Tr.

Now, the characteristic difference of place has never been of more importance than in this drama, where it gives a peculiar stamp alike to the action and to the forms under which it manifests itself. If you lend but half an ear to Halévy's accents, you will understand how one may express this local difference by means of sound: in this respect he has surpassed the poet.—The curtain rises. We are at Venice, in the midst of palaces and canals: nor trees, nor verdant fields are shewn our eyes, or even left to our imagining. Yet a flower there thrives in this environment: 'tis the love of Gérard and Catarina. Fresh and pure as the evening breeze, from afar there glides to us the simple, joyous air of Gérard, the herald of his advent to the sweetheart who awaits him. Here we have a tender, naïve buoyancy, and withal a stoutness of heart, that initiate us into the young man's character. To win our sympathy for the pair of lovers in advance, the composer has put the whole enchantment of his art into the duet in which they breathe the feelings that possess them. Behind these radiant strains of happiness, however, we see the dusky background whereon are limned these two charming figures, as against a lowering cloud, imparting to them a strangely melancholy interest. For nobleness and grace combined, nothing equals the magnificent melody of the latter part of this duet. The conception of this theme alone would suffice to prove what I said above on the subject of dramatic melody, as understood by Halévy. With all its gracious tenderness, and notwithstanding that it is perfectly clear and seizable at once, this melody is quite exempt from mannerism, from all those hackneyed turns to which contemporary authors who make for popularity at any price are wont to trim this kind of motive; its notes are disposed in such a manner that no one could name its land of origin, whether French, Italian, or what not; it is independent, free, dramatic in the full acceptance of the term.

This graceful love-scene, awaking sentiments so sweet,

is consecrated, so to speak, by the ensuing trio between the young couple and Catarina's father. It seems as if both poet and composer had wished to make us forget that we are at Venice, by painting in such glowing tints a happiness which cannot often have been met with in the palaces of that stern and proud Venetian aristocracy. The prayer: "O vous, divine Providence!" is a hymn of gratitude ascending to heaven from the hearts of happy mortals. The appearance of Mocénigo lays bare to us the poet's aim; he could not have produced a more potent effect, than by making the harbinger of evil arrive at the very moment when our hearts are yielded to the peace in which the earlier scenes have plunged us. That effect the composer has admirably rendered by the simplest of means, without all quirk or affectation. The whole scene is from the hand of a master, as also its sequel between Mocénigo and Andréa. Here a great difficulty presented itself: it was no question of expressing a storm of passions, but of depicting the reserve, the cold and calculating calm, of masked ambition. The sombre and terrific aspect of this ruthless agent of a despotic oligarchy, this Mocénigo who brings distress into the midst of so much happiness, could not be more skilfully characterised than as we find it in this scene. One knows not which to admire most, the simplicity of the means employed by the composer, or the unerring tact that prompted their choice. What proves the author to have proceeded here with full deliberation, is the extremely moderate use which he makes of the orchestra: he has prudently renounced all garish flash of instruments, yet orchestrated with an incontestable superiority; in fact, it was only by such sobriety that he could hope to preserve the dramatic character of this situation. The passage where the orchestra so aptly marks the tortuous policy of the Council of Ten—a phrase repeated in light echoes at various places in the score, and notable for a certain void in the harmony*—is admirably contrasted

* Perhaps the parent of the Tarnhelm and Potion motives in the *Ring des Nibelungen*.—Tr.

with the moving theme of Andréa: "Eh quoi! vouloir qu' ainsi je brise," completing the characteristic picture presented by this scene. The Finale of the first act, where every passion rages like a tempest, is one of those chefs-d'œuvre where the talent of Halévy unfolds itself in all its puissance. That grandiose energy wherewith the composer habitually expresses violent emotions is concentrated here upon a magnificent air for the basses: in the first notes the anger of Gérard's partisans is drawn with force and haughtiness; thenceforth the rhythm gains more and more in speed, and admirably strikes the climax of ascending passion. From a purely musical point of view, moreover, this Finale offers quite a mass of novel features.

The commencement of the second act, which shews us the romantic side of Venice, is one of the most original conceptions that have ever left Halévy's pen. The musical introduction, with its incessant monotonous pizzicato of the 'celli and its dreamy harmonies for the 'wind,' unites with the chorus of Gondoliers to form a whole that takes us with resistless charm. The chorus of Gondoliers is a piece of music where nature is caught in the act: here we have a grand and naïve simpleness, of magical effect. Those barcaroles with their modern rhythms and piquant harmony that abound in our operas whenever the scene is laid in Italy, what are they beside this natural piece where for the first time the primitive character of those vigorous sons of the Chioggia who earn their bread by plying the canals of Venice is revealed in all its truth?—The succeeding scene has much dramatic animation. The slumbrous melancholy to which the grief of Catarina has succumbed, is rendered with a touching charm in the Adagio; the vocal part exhales a languor that laps our hearts in salutary rest. But her sorrow reawakes with added force: Catarina seeks from Heaven its consolations. When she finds the lines from her lover, her heart recovers hope; her joy, her gratitude, the keen anxiety wherewith she waits his coming, could not be rendered with more truth and energy. In our opinion the composer has been particularly fortunate with his principal motive for the Allegro. The appearance of Mocénigo, the fiend whose business it is ever and everywhere to dash the happiness of the two lovers, again conduces to the best effect; the terrible words he utters are perfectly characterised by the alto and 'cello accompaniment. The arrival of Mocénigo prepares the way for a scene between Gérard and Catarina, one of the most striking ever given to the stage. I may specially note the captivating grace of the air for Gérard, upon his entry: "Arbitre de ma vie," as also the motive in which Catarina breathes forth her grief after Gérard has told her he casts her off, a grief restrained but none the less intense; in the mouth of the unfortunate girl the composer places notes so sweet and suavely touching, that they break our heart, and produce far more effect than could be obtained by discordant cries and shrieks.

May 1st.—What a marvellous change we find at the beginning of the third act! It is here that occurs that transference of locality of which I spoke above, assigning it such great importance. From this moment the breath of a new inspiration informs the music; what it paints is beauty, happiness, and Nature in her lavish wealth: the contrast with the first act is complete. The joyous chorus of the Cypriot lords, "Buvons à Chypre," sets us in a new sphere at one blow: this chorus teems with vibrant melody; from one end to the other it bubbles with gaiety and careless mirth. The song of the Venetians does not lag behind in charm, but at like time breathes a jealous mockery and pride. The opposing characters of the Venetians and Cypriots are excellently blended in what follows, and the frivolity common to them both is perfectly denoted in the gaming chorus. The couplets of Mocénigo: "Tout n'est dans ce bas monde," are of incomparable beauty and welded to the ensemble without either affectation or any interruption of its rhythm; there is nothing trivial or common about them: their expression of graceful levity, not to the exclusion of nobility, makes of these couplets a model for their genre. The sensuousness, the mad desire of pleasure, which form the distinctive character of all this picture, attain their culmination in the dancing chorus that completes it. One sees that the composer meant to surpass himself here by lavishing his talent's full melodic store: the delirium of revelry could not have been rendered in colours more intoxicating.

By a transition most marked in contrast, we arrive at the grand duet between Lusignan and Gérard which concludes the act. How entirely this number differs from all that have preceded it! Enthusiastic chivalry and virile nobleness are painted in this piece, one of the most important in the score; for it is from this point that the tragic interest is given a definite direction. The pathetic romance: "Triste, exilé sur la terre étrangère," so thoroughly in harmony with the means of the two singers, is a precious pearl in the rich tiara of this score. All that emotion has of most profound, all that chivalric courage has of most manly and exalted, are blent here in one single melody, with a matchless art whose simpleness of means but heightens its merit.—In general, one cannot praise Halévy too much for the firmness with which he resists all temptations to trap applause by blindly trusting to the singer's talent, as the custom is with so many of his colleagues. On the contrary, he insists that even the most renowned of virtuosi shall obey the lofty inspirations of his Muse; and this he obtains by the simplicity and truth he knows so well to stamp on his dramatic melody.

With the fourth act an extraordinary magnificence and splendour is deployed before our eyes. In La Juive we have seen how Halévy can lend theatric pomp a dignified and characteristic import; in La Reine de Chypre his aim is different. In the first of these operas the scenic pomp receives from the musical accompaniment a strain of religious fanaticism appropriate to the Middle Ages; in the second, on the contrary, it reflects the joyous transports of a people that beholds in its young Queen a pledge of peace and happiness. The shimmer of the sea, the southern richness of the landscape, all contribute to the brilliance of the fête. It is in this sense, as it seems to me, that one must explain the song of the sailors when the vessel nears the shore. But it is the prayer, "Divine Providence," that gives the picture its finishing touch of individuality. This prayer is a number of inestimable worth: from the first bars sung by the tenor, one involuntarily recalls those pious processions we sometimes see advancing through the fields with cross and banner. The serenity allied here with religious fervour forms a striking contrast to the sombre melodies intoned by monks and prelates in the procession of the Council of Constance.—The air of Gérard, which succeeds the march, is powerful in effect: each bar is stamped with a dramatic impress that touches us profoundly; the various sentiments, that agitate his heart in turn, are rendered perfectly; a continuous flow of melody pervades the piece. One of its finest motives is that of the last Allegro, "Sur le bord de l'abîme": it would have been easy to miss the right melodic colour for this passage, because of the extreme emotion here revealed; the composer is the more worthy admiration for having set the voice in harmony with the impassioned soul.—The swift and energetic motion of the Finale, the art with which the most diverse feelings are blended in the principal motive, again attest the superiority of Halévy's treatment of ensembles.

But what shall I say of the fifth act, where poet and musician seem to have outvied each other in attaining the most marvellous effects of their art? It would be impossible to find a more touching picture, a more nobly pathetic. The air sung by Catarina beside the deathbed of the King, the accents he addresses to his wife, spring from the inmost fountains of the human heart; no words could describe the truly heart-rending grief depicted here. —The duet between Gérard and Catarina commences with an excellent introduction, and maintains the same high level to its close; its principal motive, "Malgré la foi suprème," is full of truth and expression: the climax of this motive is forcibly worked out, and will always have a very great effect.—However, the most sublime number in all the score is the quartet, "En cet instant suprême." Here, more than anywhere else, Halévy's talent shews itself in all its individuality; the grandiose is allied with the terrible, and an elegiac melancholy appears to spread a funeral veil above this solemn scene—a scene arranged moreover with that clearness, that simplicity, which mark great masters.

To cast one parting glance on the whole Reine de Chypre, to carefully sum up its salient qualities:—we find its author still advancing on the road he struck-out in La Juive, for he pays more and more attention to simplifying his means. This tendence in a composer whose exuberant powers might rather have led him to doubt the efficacy of the means in use already, is of great significance: it proves afresh that none save people who abuse those means, will find them insufficient; that the artist should seek his riches in the creative puissance of his soul. It is indeed a fine sight to see how Halévy, while purposely and palpably delimiting his means, has succeeded in obtaining so great a variety of effects; to say nothing of his having thereby made his ends more clear and intelligible. For the rest, the method employed by Halévy, and its indubitable influence on contemporary art, are too important to be merely touched in passing. We therefore reserve to ourselves the right of returning to this subject at some other time, and treating it with all the study it deserves.

RICHARD WAGNER.

VIII.

JOTTINGS ON THE NINTH SYMPHONY.*

BEETHOVEN'S Ninth Symphony.—A rare feast is shortly to be offered all admirers of the wondrous master, *Beethoven*, if such a word as "feast" be not almost too sensual to designate the sublime effect of his last work of the kind, the Ninth Symphony with closing chorus on Schiller's "Ode to Joy," when worthily performed and nobly apprehended. The Kapelle's choice of *this* work for their so-called Palm-Sunday Concert of the present year, seems meant to prove to what a height this excellent and ample band of artists can reach; for, just as this Symphony is indisputably the crown of Beethoven's genius, as undeniably it constitutes the very hardest task for the executants. In view of the lofty spirit that has always dwelt in these grand Palm-Sunday performances, however, we may be perfectly certain that that task will find complete fulfilment.—So, at last the larger public of Dresden may hope to see this most pregnant and gigantic work set open to it; the work of a master whose other Symphonies already have attained a noble popularity, while it has hitherto remained enshrouded in a mystic riddle. Yet its solution surely needs no more than a wholly fitting opportunity, a strong and hearty feeling for the noblest and sublimest type of art, which nowhere has revealed itself with more convincing

* These are the "anonymous jottings" referred-to on page 243 of Vol. VII. They appeared in the *Dresdener Anzeiger* of Tuesday, March 24 and 31, and Thursday, April 2, 1846; the Palm-Sunday concert, at which the Ninth Symphony was performed under Wagner, occurring on April 5. Glasenapp has reprinted the German originals in the second volume of his "Life" (3rd ed.) from copies kindly furnished him by Dr Hugo Dinger.—Tr.

eloquence than in this last Symphony of Beethoven's; for all his earlier creations of the kind appear to us as sketches and preliminary drafts whereby the master gained the power to soar to the conception of *this* work. O hear and marvel!

March 31.—Would it not be well, if at least an attempt were made to bring the *Last Symphony of Beethoven*, to whose performance in a few days' time we are looking forward, somewhat nearer to the understanding of the general public? We are thinking of the extraordinary misunderstandings and preposterous interpretations to which this work has been so variously exposed, that we fear, not so much that the public may not attend the coming performance in sufficient numbers (since that is guaranteed by the rumoured eccentricity of this last great creation of the master's, whom some people assert to have written this Symphony in a state of semi-madness!)—as that a not insignificant portion thereof will be plunged into confusion by a first and only hearing of this tone-poem, and thus go wanting of a genuine enjoyment. More frequent opportunity of listening to such works, would certainly be the fittest means of spreading an understanding thereof; but unfortunately that favour is mostly bestowed on works whose wellnigh over-obvious easiness of comprehension does not need it at all!

April 2.—There once lived a man who was impelled to express whatever he thought and felt in the language of Tone, as bequeathed him by great masters. To speak in this tongue was his innermost need, *to hear it* his sole happiness on earth; for he otherwise was poor in goods and joy, and people vexed him sadly, however good and loving was his heart to all men. But his only happiness was reft from him,—he fell deaf, and no longer might hear his own, his glorious language! Ah! he then came near to wishing speech itself were also robbed him: his good spirit held him back;—he continued to express in tones what he *now* had to feel as well. His feelings, however, had turned to something marvellous and unaccustomed;—what other people thought of him, could but be foreign and indifferent to him: he now had only to take counsel with his inner soul, to dive into the deepest depths of the source of all passion and yearning. What a wondrous world he now became at home in! There might he see and—hear; for there it needs no physical ear, to apprehend: creation and delight are one.—But that world, alas! was the world of *loneliness*: how can a childlike-loving heart belong to it for aye? The poor man turns his eye towards the world surrounding him,—to Nature, in whose sweet ecstasies he once had revelled, to Men, to whom he yet feels so akin. A tremendous longing seizes, thrusts, and drives him to belong to Earth again, to taste its thrills and joys once more.* —When you meet the poor man, who cries to you so longingly, will you pass him on the other side if you find you do not understand his speech at once, if it sounds so strange, so unaccustomed, that you ask yourselves: What would the man? O take him to you, clasp him to your heart, in wonder listen to the marvels of his tongue, in whose new wealth you soon will greet sublimities and grandeurs never heard of,—for this man is **Beethoven**, and the tongue in which he speaks to you the tones of his **Last Symphony**, where the wonder-worker shaped all the sorrows, joys and yearnings of his life to an *artwork* such as never was!

* The poem of *Lohengrin* had been completed only about four months previously.—Tr.

IX.

ARTIST AND CRITIC.*

THE artist should address the public through his artistic doings only, which ought to be the witness to his capability: this principle is right enough, and, in our opinion, should never be transgressed even in reply to open criticism. If the artist can operate direct, can bring his aim to unmistakable presentment through the organs lent to him by Nature, he should abide unconditionally by that maxim. But if he can operate only indirect, and that through means over which he has not absolute control; and if moreover his artistic aim is diligently flouted by the critics,—then a strict adherence to that principle must place him in a sorry plight. If an artist is brought into such a plight by a critic whose judgment he, in common with the general public, has many and good grounds to neglect, assuredly the general judgment will not suffer by his behaving pretty much as I myself have behaved to the musical reporter of the local *Abendzeitung*,† of whose attacks and calumnies I have taken no notice whatever. But if he meets a man like the latest reviewer of the operatic performances at the Royal Court-theatre, Herr C. B. in the *Dresdener Tageblatt*, by whose verdict some store might be set; and should he see—as, if I am to preserve the slightest self-respect, I am bound to see in this gentleman's recent pronouncements on my

* "Künstler und Kritiker, mit Bezug auf einem besonderen Fall"—reprinted in the *Musikalisches Wochenblatt* of June 19 to July 17, 1890, through the instrumentality of Dr Hugo Dinger—originally appeared in the *Dresdener Anzeiger* of August 14, 1846, in reply to two articles by the critic Carl Banck in the *Dresdener Tageblatt* of July 13 *et seq.*—Tr.

† Julius Schladebach.—Tr.

conducting of Mozart's *Figaro*—that God-knows-what personal incompatibility has saddled him with yet another captious adversary for the whole term of the latter's reportership, then his wish to defend himself for once may possibly be pardoned, especially when the one-sidedness of local criticism (as practised by its mere handful of representatives in Dresden toward myself) offers no reasonable prospect of anybody else's intervention on his behalf. Wherefore if I am overstepping the strict line that should divide the executant artist from the critic, may I be judged in the light of a man challenged forth without cease, who plainly feels within himself the strength for combat, yet of whom convention asks the sacrifice of leaving himself undefended. If I now am acting imprudently, let the reader reflect that by the time an artist-nature is completely broken-in to outward prudence, that nature itself must already have lost its force; while I still am young and hearty, may he therefore overlook this hastiness, if such it be.

I should not care to say much about the actual causes of the disgrace in which I stand with the majority of the little band of Dresden critics. For the most part they are clear as day, and so naturally grounded on annoyance at the various distinctions, especially the honourable appointment, conferred on one who was entirely unknown not such a long time back, that the public has no need of being nudged to see the source of many an animosity outpoured upon myself. Though I willingly assume this motive to have the smallest weight with Herr C. B., it is impossible to leave it altogether out of count, since it affords the only conceivable explanation of the overbearing tone in which that gentleman expresses himself in my regard, whereas he observes a certain respectful moderation in all his references to other persons. Finally, to my way of thinking it is just that—let us be honest!—very envied appointment to so honourable an institute as the Royal Kapelle, that makes it my duty not to leave unanswered such charges as Herr C. B. has fastened on me; for I feel it most incumbent to throw light on several things in its regard which, even were a public champion to stand up for me, could be cleared by no one more explicitly than by myself.

To come to the point. In the first place Herr C. B.'s outburst and its motive are doubly tainted, in my eyes, by his aiming it at the performance of a Mozart opera; involuntarily I recall the fact that among musicians with whom I do not mix it has been asserted, Heaven knows why, that I disdain Mozart,—an absurdity against which I should be ashamed even to protest. If anybody bears a grudge against me, however, it is to his great advantage to trot out such impertinences; for there is no surer way of damaging a youngish musician in the mind of the public, than by saying that he disdains Mozart. Now, if there is one thing that annoys me in connection with the works of Mozart, it is the sciolism and presumption of so many musicians, each of whom lays claim to the only right conception of the spirit and essence of Mozart's music. Nevertheless, were I ever permitted for once in a way to get up a Mozartian opera with singers who had never sung in it before, perhaps even with an orchestra that had never played it; further, if our orthodox adherents of the letter were to allow me to assume that many a weighty indication had been omitted from the graven score, for instance of *Don Juan*, either by the carelessness of the corrector, or even through a defect in the manuscript copy,—and were that copy Mozart's own (for he certainly did not denote the rendering in his scores so punctiliously as he dictated it at his rehearsals by word of mouth); in short, could it be freely granted me to express my mature artistic conviction and scholarly enthusiasm for Mozart by the spirit of such a representation of one of his masterworks, I then would accord Herr C. B. the right to judge, or even to condemn, my conducting of a Mozartian opera. So long as all this cannot be granted, may Herr C. B. reflect in future cases, similar to the recent one of *Figaro*, what a standpoint is assigned me when my official duty places me at head of a performance whose spirit is entirely foreign to me, since I have been able to do as good as nothing to prepare it.

On an earlier occasion Herr C. B. himself discussed with knowledge and acumen the manifold faults in our modern stage-system, and admirably proved how present ills make truly finished performances such infrequent events in the repertoire; but he at like time committed the grave injustice of charging all these faults to one sole theatre, and that the Royal Court-theatre of this city. A wider survey would necessarily have taught him to put the fact foremost that this state of affairs prevails on every stage in Germany without exception, and the root of this general ill lies so deeply implicated in the nature of our whole German historic development, that no candid observer could think of making one single Management responsible for evils which only in the happiest event could be removed without striking at the root-evil of all the German theatres, with which this one but exists in combination. The consequences of these evils, as regards our own Court-theatre as well, Herr C. B. has stated for the most part quite correctly, and I haven't the smallest objection to applying his words to what concerns myself.

With the insight he thus has won, let him figure to himself my own position when called to place myself at the head of the orchestra, to conduct an opera, and in particular an opera of Mozart's.—I myself have not got up* these operas, nor, that is to say radically, has my immediate predecessor. No: they are committed to me in a certain traditional guise, to which I have to try and accommodate myself—in some respects against my own conviction—in order to steer the performance through as smoothly as possible under the conditions. Into what a painful conflict my artistic feeling, my personal views and convictions must be brought with the endeavour to maintain

* "Einstudirt," a word for which I know of no English equivalent, as it means a thorough *course* of practising; to replace it by a simple "rehearsed" would convey an entirely erroneous meaning here.—Tr.

the existing tradition, may be imagined by anybody who has had the smallest experience of such a task; how little the occasional resultant inequalities and slips should be ascribed to the conductor's wrong intention or downright misconstruction, only he can overlook who has no knowledge of the matter, but in its stead ill-will.

Though I believe I now have cleared myself of any stricter responsibility for the general spirit of the last performance of *Figaro*, Herr C. B.'s further reproaches demand a special confutation. Herr C. B. is much mistaken if he feels called to counsel me to learn from older musicians * the true traditions of the tempi in Mozart's operas. With particular reference to *Figaro* I have gathered most authentic intimations, especially from the late Director of the Prague Conservatoire, Dionys Weber (an exclusive admirer of Mozart); as eye-and-ear-witness of the first production of *Figaro* and its antecedent rehearsals by Mozart himself, this gentleman informed me how the master could never get the overture, for instance, played fast enough to please him, and how, to maintain its unflagging swing, he constantly urged on the pace wherever consistent with the nature of the theme. But even had I not this testimony, an irresistible inner feeling would compel me to adopt a similar course, however often Herr C. B. might protest against it; for I take leave to assert that anyone who does not feel this keen necessity at once in the first theme, e.g., with the advent of the passages for the wind in the four bars before the first forte, can have no particularly keen feeling at all, and should take his musical enjoyments with the metronome henceforward. With music so full of life and so varied of character in almost every longer section, as that of Mozart, could there possibly be a more pernicious stipulation than that this manifold expression should never gain the slightest support from a modifying of the tempo? If through higher artistic development of his own productive powers the conductor has acquired that keenness of feeling, and with it that

* Implicitly Reissiger.—Tr.

nobler warmth, which enables him to take into his mind the products of a master-genius with clear perception of the clear necessity of their every fraction; and if he has the indefinable gift of imparting to the executants that delicacy of feeling and that finer warmth—then, with wholly adequate forces to lead, there must come about a performance whose style, even though differences of opinion may legitimately arise in respect of details, would yet be the most consummate: and we may safely assume that the author of the work himself would give the palm to this class of rendering above all others, since every creative artist knows from personal experience how killing is the letter to his work, how vivifying the spirit. Far be it from me, however, to assume this kind of responsibility for the occasional unevennesses in the last representation of *Figaro*: on the contrary, I have disclaimed such a thing in advance. Rather, with Herr C. B.'s permission, I will cite a few examples to shew how they arose. Not only my natural feeling, but also tradition derived from the source above-mentioned, determine me to read the tempo of the so-called Letter-duet between Susanne and the Countess as an actual Allegretto, in accordance with its title: involuntarily I therefore started with what I am convinced is the proper tempo, light and tripping; but the singers, tempted by the cantabile, like most of our German lady-singers, had accustomed themselves to delivering this piece more or less in the fashion of a sentimental love-duet; so that I saw myself obliged to yield to their somewhat slower tempo, and that with the very natural object of not upsetting the performance by an untimely insistence on my reading, albeit the more correct. A similar thing occurred with the duet of Susanne and Marzelline in the first act, which is generally so over-driven (on the authority of the engraved score, which accidentally contains an Alla-breve mark in this place, though omitting it as a rule in the fastest Allegros) that the exquisite grace of this number, its mockery and politely-veiled taunts, can but assume the character of a vulgar squabble;—here again, beyond doubt, my reading fell into a wellnigh inevitable conflict with the present custom,—and similarly may Herr C. B. account for most of the cases which offended him in this way. I have already declared that the spirit of kindred performances most certainly does not delight me; on the contrary, it perhaps affects me still more painfully than Herr C. B. himself: but the reasons, why I nevertheless cannot escape such representations, lie too remote from the subject of this discussion for me to engage in their exhaustive recital.

Herr C. B., however, not merely gives his verdict on my conducting of *Figaro*, but polishes me off with a general statement that I never can take a tempo right or stick to it, and a passing remark on the indefiniteness of the outward tokens of my beat. As regards the latter, I may calmly reply that so long as the Kapelle is not hindered by my style of beat from such achievements as the performances of *Gluck's Armida and Beethoven's Last Symphony*, no one, and quite certainly not Herr C. B., is justified in taking offence at it; for, if he only meant to be just and impartial, he would have to admit that those achievements of the Royal Kapelle have never yet been surpassed by itself. Consequently I might have replied to Herr C. B.'s bare three-line censure of my conducting ability by a still briefer rejoinder; relying on the public evidences just adduced, I needed but to ask *what proofs has he afforded that he understands what he is speaking of?* But, in answering his curt dismissal at greater length than needful on my own behalf, I wish to heap coals of fire upon his head by shewing him that I respect him more than his abandonment of all respect for me and my position entitles him to claim.

Though it is more than time to end, I cannot refrain from returning, in the interest of the institute itself, to the general reproaches and accusations directed by Herr C. B.—as to many an essential, with indisputable understanding—against our Operatic repertoire; charges which I have already described as unjust because addressed to the Royal Court-theatre of this city in particular, whereas they apply with far more justice to the German Theatre as a whole. I resume this point in order to assure Herr C. B. that he is much mistaken if he believes that his essay tells anything new to the General-Direction, and to inform him that after a special scrutiny of the German stage-system, and unceasing efforts to remedy the evils recognised, our General-Direction has quite recently become convinced to its sorrow that no one-sided action can avail, but the only cure would lie in an equally energetic endeavour on the part of every German Management. Even this conviction has not been so much as felt as yet by the most and the larger of the other theatres of Germany; whilst if one compares the appreciation of nobler and more solid fare continually displayed in the arrangement of our repertoire with what is done for Opera in Berlin, for instance, under far more favourable conditions, it cannot be denied that the Dresden Opera is the very one that signalises itself to-day the most encouragingly for true art. Long before Herr C. B. divulged to it his plan, however, the General-Direction has fully understood in what way alone it is possible to classify the items of a repertoire so as to prevent all mixture of conflicting styles; above all (and especially since unavoidable considerations have made it necessary to perform each night before the public of a not immoderately large capital) it knows that this can only be effected through the establishment of a company strong enough to be evenly distributed among the different varieties of Opera; yet its repeated efforts to acquire the necessary complement of practised artists but bring it sad experience of the cheerless state of theatres elsewhere, and (with this utter hopelessness of obtaining the needful support from a supposed reserve of strength at other German theatres) it sees itself assigned the task of heading an attempt to remedy the fundamental ills inherent in the German stage-system at large. Anyone may perceive what an exceptional task is this, and almost beyond the powers of *one* sole theatre ; yet plans are already at hand, which, called forth by the untiring energy of the General-Direction, set about with intelligence, and carried through to the best of ability, promise, fortune favouring, to afford the only possible cure in the future. No reasonable being, however, would expect to see such comprehensive projects brought to full maturity in half a year. That without a radical improvement in the basis of the German Opera-house,—the first step toward which, in my opinion, would consist in the acquisition of a troupe of singers equipped by speciality of talent for distribution among the *several classes* of Opera required by our extensive repertoire, and in such a way that each of these classes should be *equally well* represented,—that without such an organised foundation, I repeat, it is impossible to displace those present evils which Herr C. B. has denounced, is recognised by everyone who also sees *that these very defects make it impossible to follow out a plan such as Herr C. B. proposes for our operatic repertoire, and of whose impracticability the General-Direction must have long ago convinced itself.* Until we can arrive at that more perfect state, already aimed at with full consciousness, may the stern critic of the musical doings of the Royal Court-theatre be patiently grateful for the good, eh! excellent, that yet is offered him in such untoward circumstances, and offered oftener and more significantly than by any other German theatre,—a statement which Herr C. B. himself does not seem minded to dispute, and we might prove by facts if need were. Let none take it ill of a party, however, if—in proportion to his recognition of the imperfectness of affairs in which he is interested, and at like time to his consciousness of the zeal wherewith he tries to remedy it so far as he is permitted—he openly expresses his disgust (as I here have felt compelled to do) at the pretensions of a set of know-alls, especially when they lack that closer knowledge of the matter which can only come to the profession, and even that impartiality without which the shrewdest utterance must stay of no effect and tainted with an air of sophistry.

That this standpoint is adopted nowadays by almost every critic, particularly as touching institutions like the Theatre, is undeniable, alas! and in his catalogue of evils that obstruct a bettering of the Theatre Herr C. B. has clean forgotten *the mischief done by incompetent and one-sided criticism.*

Before all things, a critic who has never acquired the requisite knowledge by practical experience (as almost invariably is the case) might be asked not to bother his head with the guidance of an art-institute when he sees it officered by people whose most natural and wellnigh personal interest it must be to speed it to the utmost; for his more or less uncalled-for interference in things which he could only understand if they were brought to his knowledge in all their bearings, and not one-sidedly as usual, can but become a nuisance to those who necessarily must understand their business better than he. If he would fulfil a really important function, let him form the intellectual bond between the public and the artistic object, and represent the public's wishes and objections clearly and distinctly, above all with unbounded impartiality, not as a single unit, but as the filtered voice of the community. If he would accordingly avoid the minutiæ of performance, and cease to tax the player or other executant with this or that particular fault, he would restore to those expressly appointed to superintend the artistic doings of the company a right they are almost totally deprived of through the present state of Criticism. For, with all this harassing and sermonising of the players, the conductor or regisseur at last must fear to muddle them entirely when he too, as in duty bound, has to pass his own opinion—often at variance with the critic's. Whilst if things are further complicated by the reporter's personality, here favourably disposed and there unfavourably, the mischief reaches such a pitch that the necessary agreement between the right and proper officer and the performers is rendered all but impossible. Thus we arrive at the deplorable plight, that the salutary and becoming influence which the conductor or regisseur both might and should have on the spirit and substance of the performers' work is altogether lost, whereas the cruder and more arbitrary influence of everyday Reporting, venal more or less (albeit not always in the most materialistic sense), thrusts more and more 'twixt persons whose artistic and official status should bring them nearest to each other, and naturally introduces coldness and mistrust in their reciprocal relations.

In circumstances so constant and general, what service Criticism has rendered, and particularly theatric criticism as practised now, is simply nil; what harm it has done, is pretty evident from this exposure—in which, however, certain grave and hideous blots have been left untouched, for fear of sinking to the personal. Wherefore, if these Sir Critics did but know what the intelligent think of their praise, and almost everybody of their blame, they wouldn't deem it worth their while to practise either, at least in this accustomed way; to them a paltry profit from the one, a meagre satisfaction of temper by the other, would scarcely seem sufficient recompense for the almost universal odium in which every reporter must stand with both public and artists, provided he hasn't the rare faculty of keeping himself entirely impartial and remote from all personality: for only at that price could one overlook his want of experience from time to time.

As to Herr C. B. himself, if he can lay his hand upon his heart and declare that no personal intercourse or special relation with this or that man ever affects his judgment, or even moves him here to suppress his blame, there give it prominence,—if openly and honestly he can attest that he has no personal feeling against me for this or that reason, were it but an omission, and consequently that his supercilious tone towards me bears not a breath of animosity,—then I certainly have not another word to speak with him. To the public, however, I leave it to judge between us two.

Dresden, August 11, 1846.

RICHARD WAGNER.

X.

GREETING FROM SAXONY TO THE VIENNESE.*

NOW is my heart from care set free,
  No longer need I sorrow ;
Since rescued whole is Germany,
  With joy I greet the morrow.
What evil of ourselves we thought,
  It now has turned to good ;
Who once to shame our honour brought,
  Them have ye well withstood.

From France resounded Freedom's cry ;
  In answer have we spoken.
The bonds that knit our slavery,
  Those bonds we now have broken.
The tempest no man could escape,
  And whom it struck, he fell ;
The foes who Freedom's fame would rape,
  Full soon they heard their knell.

His lead our praise we may accord ;
  All honour to the Frenchman !
That in our hand lay Freedom's sword,
  We owe to that first henchman.

* According to Glasenapp, who prints the German of the above in an appendix to vol. ii. of his *Das Leben Richard Wagner's*, these verses originally appeared in the *Allgemeine Österreichische Zeitung* of June 1, 1848, above Wagner's full signature. Within little more than two months there had been three insurrections in Vienna, and at this time the city was temporarily governed by a Committee of Safety composed of citizens and students. At Frankfort the German National Assembly had just been convened.—Tr.

Thereon to shew the German way,
  Our victory to crown,
How could we think our cry to stay
  Till hostile cries died down?

All hushed are the aristocrats,
  Tho' erst their voice was harder!
Yet secretly their palm now pats
  The lords of stoup and larder.
The bloated lords of wine and meat,
  They money have and land;
For gaolers, soldiers, will they treat,
  That all may tranquil stand.

"Oh! Freedom is a fine affair,"
  You'll hear them all conceding,
"We, too, can price it to a hair;
  But better is good feeding."
Their stomachs, spoilt beyond a cure,
  They writhe in sore distress,
And squeal: They never could endure
  The public's daily mess.

Thro' all the land you hear the shout,
  From every nook and hollow:
"Alas! our thraldom's vanished out!
  What have we now to swallow!"
Who with the money-bags once hid,
  Come forth without a fear,
And those whose fetters we undid
  Prick up an eager ear.

The bookworms creep from out their hole
  To prove, if you will trust 'em,
That Freedom still must pay its dole
  To Wont and ancient Custom:

"The German Folk might suffer harm
From what does others good;
A little bondage—no alarm!—
Beseems the German mood."

They talk behind, they talk before,
Bid men not be too bold here;
Say quiet fits the burgher more,
And valour more the soldier:
"You see how bad this is for trade;
Much mischief has it brought.
The son gets what his father made,—
What then, if he made nought?"

Accursed traps are all they set us!
And into them we run?
The day whose dawn had scarcely met us,
Already pales its sun?
The moment for decision bides,
The answer's in our power:
How far the German's courage strides?
And shall we do, or cower?

XI.

ON E. DEVRIENT'S "HISTORY OF GERMAN ACTING."*

AFTER the Viennese populace had revolted last March, beyond the Jesuits, police-spies and many others, it drummed out the Ballet and Italian Opera. The Directors of theatres had at like time to learn that the flabby, sickly viands of their repertory no longer agreed with the public, that the time for theatrical offal was over, and other allurements must be offered the young people with the resolute, courageous mien. Wherever a sound piece breathing truth and freedom was to be had, it was brought upon the boards; the farce had to doff its ribaldry and join with gusto in the new hymn of Freedom, while the Jesuitic vice was scourged, the buoyant death-defiance of the cheery Vienna heroes celebrated: everywhere was made good what a spirit-slaying Censorship had mutilated.

To these observations we might add many another, as that, in consequence of "March," the Intendant of the Berlin Royal Playhouse was moved by cat-calls to give good classic pieces; but these will suffice to shew that our Theatre is really of State interest, that weal and woe of the State are mirrored in inevitable reflex from the Theatre. And how should it be otherwise? Beyond it we have but the Church, to act directly on a larger

* The above review was sent by Richard Wagner with a letter of enclosure dated Jan. 8, 1849, to the Augsburg *Allgemeine Zeitung*; it was not "accepted," but remained in the possession of an autograph-collector on that paper's staff until it was printed in 1877, and thereafter, by Ludwig Nohl—see Glasenapp's *Leben R. W.'s* II. 297, also Vol. VII. p. 330 of the present series.—Tr.

public; but if the incomparable effects of religious fervour can less and less be brought into the calculations of our modern State-economy, and if we reflect, on the other hand, how the impression produced on all the senses by the warm immediate life of the artistic vehicles of theatric representation is able to remain at all times fresh and living, because it ever refreshes and rejuvenates itself from the actual life of the present,—it now might seem high time to pay exceptional attention to the Theatre. It is to be hoped that the free State, so soon as it shall have come a little to its senses, will recognise a duty toward itself in assuring to itself the uncommon efficacity of the Theatre for attaining the noblest and freest object, the object of the State itself; this it will reach by so supporting the Theatre that it shall be made independent of every consideration other than that of invigorating and ennobling the taste and manners of the people. This aim must be the only one assigned it. Freely and self-sufficiently must it be able to pursue this single end; every influence beyond that of the artistic intelligence of those appointed, and the uncorrupted moral feeling of the whole community, must be held aloof from it.

If we thus have rightly seized the duty of the State towards the Theatre, and if we are not mistaken in considering the present moment of our political evolution the very one for drawing the State's attention to its task, then, for complete enlightenment on this important point we can recommend nothing more urgently to all who agree with us, than the above-named book of Eduard Devrient's, of which the third volume has just appeared.

As it is never the mere connoisseur, standing outside the object of discussion, who can feel and say the truest thing about it; but only he who practises an art, is also in the position to comprehend it: so we may fitly pass by all the clever things that poets and æsthetes have said about the art of Acting, after the statements and disclosures here made to us by an eminent actor himself. The feeling of profound dissatisfaction aroused in him by the present state of our Theatre appears to have led our artist consistently on, from an inquiry into its proximate causes, to the deepest core of his art; his enthusiasm waxes with his knowledge of the high vocation of that art, and through his reaped conviction that the noblest independence must constitute its essence. Plainly to prove, that the Player's art has developed of its own incentive; that it obeys no other conditions than those of its own essence, without suffering for it; that it is a product of the Folk and its spirit, in a degree beyond all other arts; and that its firm adherence to the folk-spirit, particularly in the German nation, is the root of all its weal and woe,—this could but come the surest to the author on the path of history; and in the work before us it has prospered in the most convincing fashion.

He shews us how the art of Acting, with the Germans, has clung directly to the character and temper of the Folk much longer and more durably than with any other European culture-nation; that the eventual attempts of Literature to gain possession of it, after obstinate resistance, have only been successful since our Literature began to strike a hearty friendship with the essence of Play-acting, and to refresh itself thereat; and that, if we have not yet reached the level of the French and English, (apart from other outward causes) this is to be attributed to the fact of our as yet having had no Shakespeare or Molière arise among us, i.e. as yet no actual player who united in himself, as these, alike the highest powers of poetic creation. We see how our greatest poets who turned with active love towards the Drama, Goethe and Schiller, yet abode too much by the absolute-literary standpoint, outside the art of Acting, to gain a decisively beneficial influence over it; and that a period like our own must end by completely undermining its welfare, since it has made the Theatre dependent on all sides upon considerations and demands which have nothing but its outmost shell in common with the essence of the Player's art.

With the noblest ardour, the sense of highest moral right,

our author—as champion of his glorious, but so forsaken art, and in full consciousness of the dignity of a status still so misconstrued by society—now approaches the State with the well-founded challenge: To recognise its highest interest in the Theatre, and provide that it shall beneficially and freely exercise its high vocation as a worthy member of the constitution. What noble mind, nay, what mind at all intelligent, could refrain from wishing him a blessing on his efforts?

XII.

THEATRE-REFORM.*

THE proposals recently published by Eduard Devrient for a reform of the Theatre inevitably encounter three varieties of antagonist: (1) the present *Theatre-directors*, whose mostly ignorant procedure has brought the Theatre to a pass now generally considered more than critical; (2) those individual *Virtuosi* who have drawn their special profit from this state of things; and (3) the so-called *Theatre-lovers* who have found contentment in that state of things through personal contact with the first two classes. Judging by his signature (*Scenophilus*, in German "Stage-friend,") the author of the article upon this subject in the Spener'sche Zeitung, so benevolently reproduced in the Dresdener Anzeiger of the day before yesterday, appears to belong to the third class; just possibly he may be numbered in the first, scarcely conceivably in the second, as in that case we should have expected from him a more favourable estimate of an art pursued by himself, however wantonly.

This "stage-friend" winds up with a confession of faith in the "high vocation" of the histrionic art, after having thrown contemptuous doubt on the actor's ability to preside

* In his *R. Wagner, sein Leben u. seine Werke* W. Tappert reprints this article from the *Dresdener Anzeiger* of January 16, 1849. Though it is signed with a pseudonym, Tappert's proofs of its authorship are incontestable, as he quotes from a letter of Wagner's to a Berlin friend dated Jan. 15, 1849: "I beg you to get the enclosed contribution (written by myself) to the Dresdener Anzeiger reprinted in some wide-read Berlin political paper, for reasons which will be apparent to you from the article itself, on 'Theatre-reform'"; Tappert has also seen in Dresden a copy with a marginal note in Uhlig's hand, assigning it to Wagner.—Tr.

over his own art, and denied to the whole profession the possibility of an orderly organisation for the representing of its interests. This art of Acting, which is to be brought up to a "high vocation," would consequently be the only art that is not to belong to the liberal arts, inasmuch as its doings are to be conducted, not by artists of this art itself, but by rank outsiders; thus, for all its vaunted "high vocation," an art that would be exercised by artists who didn't understand their art, and accordingly should be directed by people who didn't exercise it and *therefore*, apparently, were the only ones to understand it. This certainly sounds a little obscure, though it seems to be our "stage-friend's" notion of the matter: let us therefore try to clear it up.

If the Actor is thus incapable of leading the day's-work of the art of Acting, who then is the proper person for the post?—The *Playwright*? According to Eduard Devrient's plan he already is associated with the management, as representative of the interests of Literature (and reasonably, he can only be *associated*, for he cannot be set *over* the art of Acting, as his part is that of Poetry, not Playing); just so the Musical Director is made a sharer in the management, according to that plan. Wherefore, as we could not possibly think of putting the Ballet-master or Machinist at the head of affairs, we should have to turn our gaze towards the teeming host of "connoisseurs": under this splendid name is gathered almost everything that has received its breath from God; as to the worth of its knowledge, you may go ask poets, painters, musicians and so forth, what has been their daily experience thereof! But have we ever seen an art-struck Major of Hussars appointed to the control of an academy of Painting? No,—and our "stage-friend" seems to go the length of admitting that the Orchestra should be conducted by a musician, not a lawyer. Merely a company of Actors is to be conducted by a learned lord-in-waiting, a skilful banker, or perhaps a clever journalist?

As a fact, it is people of this sort, who have been entrusted with the command of theatres hitherto; and we have to thank their management for such a confusion of ideas as to the essence and object of the art of acting, that any unprofessional outsider now imagines he can estimate the "practical" issues of the matter, and treat the views of professional experts as "unpractical" twaddle. Your "praxis," ye Stage-friends, has brought great ill into artistic fellowships, so great that ye think yourselves justified in denying them the capability of looking after their own affairs! Through your finicking rules and regulations, ye precious "practicals," ye have brought things to such a pitch that these companies now scarcely know that they are banded for a *common* end of art, that one thing alone can lead them to their goal, the *feeling of community*. Ye have hounded one against the other, rained favours on the incompetent who flattered you, rejected the inspired who contravened your "practice." Thus have ye undermined all fellowship: sullen, only careful for his own benefit and others' harm, the unit has severed himself from the whole, forgotten that he can serve the higher ends of his art in naught but combination with his comrades; and thus the state of things was bound to arrive, at last, that makes you smile contemptuously at the "unpracticalness" of proposals which simply aim at re-establishing that spirit of community yourselves have shattered. Yet see! we feel ourselves by so much loftier than your cleverness, that we feel in our hearts the crying need of reviving that common spirit of artistic fellowship among ourselves by suitable arrangements.

So rest assured, ye "practical," that none knows better than the artistic fellowship itself, *who* is fit to lead its joint performance: none knows better than the actor, whether this or that regisseur understands his business, none better than the bandsmen whether their conductor is equal to his task or not; and therefore none knows better than *they*, whom to choose out of a list of candidates: each time they will choose *that man* who has their confidence, and the man of their confidence they obey as zealously and successfully as they lazily submit themselves without success to a man imposed upon them by an act of alien favour *against* the company's trust. For this last event ye have "*commands*" in readiness; but what ye thus effect towards the prospering of an *art-establishment* is shewn by the results of the action of our theatres to-day: a mournful, weary slippety-sloppety, makeshift fatuity, strain with no object, fatigue without wage. This is about the complexion of your "*practice*"!

This glimpse into the undeniable plight of things theatric seems to have clean escaped our Berlin "Scenophilus" when reading Eduard Devrient's reform scheme, though it there is offered plain enough; otherwise he needs must have recognised the logical necessity of the remedial measures there proposed. We therefore can only conclude that "*Scenophilus*" should be translated this time, not high-Germanly as "stage-friend," but low-Germanly as "theatre-lout"; unless we have inadvertently stumbled on the living God-be-with-us—that is to say, the Upper-court-theatre-intendant of Berlin himself.

Our money will go no farther*; so we must close our contribution, although we had a few things more to tell Herren Hande and Spener. But we beg the charitable transplanter of that article from the Berlin paper into the Dresden Anzeiger to have the kindness to see that a migration of this rejoinder to Berlin is brought about with like success.

J. P.—F. R.
Actor out of engagement.

* See footnote to Vol. VII., p. 243; the names at the end of the sentence are those of the proprietors of the "Spener'sche Zeitung."—Tr.

To Dr Hugo Dinger, author of an as yet unfinished work on "Richard Wagner's geistige Entwickelung" (referred to on page vii. of my preface to Vol I.), we owe the discovery and German reprint of the two succeeding articles from Roeckel's short-lived Volksblätter. *As to the second, almost all Wagnerian authorities are now agreed that it is from the master's pen, and Glasenapp has followed Dr Dinger's example by reproducing it in an appendix to the second volume of the new edition of his Life of Wagner. As to the first article an equally unanimous opinion has not yet been expressed, but to my mind there is ample internal evidence to justify the article's assignment to Richard Wagner, especially when taken in conjunction with that Vaterlandsverein Speech which figures in Vol. IV. of the present series.*

These articles originally appeared in the issues of the Volksblätter *for February 10 and April 8, 1849, respectively, the German titles being "Der Mensch und die bestehende Gesellschaft" and "Die Revolution."*

Dr Dinger has also reprinted a few brief extracts from two or three other articles in the Volksblätter *which he inclines to believe had Wagner for their author; but as that journal is practically inaccessible, at anyrate to myself, I am not in a position to verify his hypothesis in their case.*

TRANSLATOR'S NOTE.

XIII.

MAN AND ESTABLISHED SOCIETY.

IN the previous number* it was shewn how Established Society, recognising its greatest enemy in the increasing education of the people, has taken stand against it, yet without being able to stay thereby the threatening danger. *In the year 1848 Man's fight against Established Society began.* Let it not deceive us, that in most countries this war has not as yet been openly declared, that the two largest German States, for instance, outwardly present us with nothing but the old comedy of a struggle for supremacy between the various *sections* of Society. These latest struggles of a privileged Nobility in Prussia and Austria, this last upflickering of Royal Prerogative, fed on a brute force that daily melts away before the light of knowledge (*Aüfklärung*), are nothing further than the death-throes of a body from which the soul, its life, has flown already, nothing beyond the last mists of night set scudding by the rising sun. Not with the unconscious writhings of a corpse in agony of death, not with that rearguard of darkness, is the conflict of our age, even though the timid take affright at the convulsive shrieks, the eye of the dull cannot pierce the dense haze; for we know that the *fiercest* bout is that with death—we know that when morning-mists weigh heaviest on us, an all the brighter day ensues.

The battle of *Man* against existing *Society* has begun. Those struggles of the stragglers from a bygone age which

* Dr Dinger informs us that the "previous number" had contained a leading article on "Our Society," in all probability by August Roeckel himself, taking for text a rumoured saying of Thiers: "There are only two ways of saving society: 1. A general War, or 2. Suppression of the Folk-schools."—Tr.

we see in Austria, Prussia, and to some extent in the rest of Germany, cannot deceive us; they merely serve to clear the field for that last, sublimest fight. Already it has openly commenced in France; England is preparing for it; and soon, full soon, will it spread to Germany. We are living in it, and have to fight it out. In vain should we attempt to shun it, to hide till the flood pass by; it seizes us, however secure our place of refuge, and all of us, the prince in his palace, the pauper in his hut, we all must join in this mighty battle, for we all are *men* and subject to the *time's* decree.

Unworthy were it of reason-dowered Man, to give himself resistless, like the beasts, to the will of the waves. His task, his duty bids him do with *consciousness* what the age demands of him. As thinking men, our earnest aim must therefore be to attain this consciousness, this knowledge of what *we* have to do; and we shall attain it if we take the pains to find the cause, the reason, and accordingly the *true significance* of the movement in whose midst we live.

We have said: the battle of *Man* against existing *Society* has begun. Now, this is only true if it be proved that our existing *Society* is an assault on *Man*, that the ordering of *established Society* runs counter to the *destiny*, the *right* of Man. Whether and how far this is the case, we shall discover if we take *man's destiny and right* and ascertain how far *established society* is qualified to lead man to his destiny, to assure to him his right.

Man's **destiny** *is: through the ever higher perfecting of his mental, moral, and corporeal faculties, to attain an ever higher, purer happiness.*

Man's **right** *is: through the ever higher perfecting of his mental, moral and corporeal faculties, to arrive at the enjoyment of a constantly increasing, purer happiness.*

So that, from man's *Destiny* proceeds his *Right*; destiny and right are *one*; and the *right* of Man is simple, to fulfil his *destiny*.

Now, if we look for the force wherewith a man is armed to guard his Right, fulfil his Destiny, we find it altogether lacking. Where is man's force, to perfect his own self in spirit, mind and body? Where is man's force, to teach himself what he does not know? Where is man's force, to distinguish Good from Evil, to practise good, to flee from evil, since of himself he knows not what is good, what evil? And how shall man create from out himself a greater strength of body than he owns?—We see that man is of himself unable to attain his destiny, that in himself he has no strength to unfold the innate germ that marks him from the beasts. That force which we miss in *man*, however, we find in endless fulness in the *aggregate of men.* What remains denied to all forever, so long as they are *isolated*, they reach when they *combine.* In the **unification** of men we find the force we vainly seek-for in the **units.** Whereas the spirit of the *isolated* stays buried ever in the deepest night, in *combination* it is woken, roused, unfurled to ever ampler strength. Whereas the *isolated* is without morality, since he can discern neither good nor evil, from the *union* of men there springs morality; they learn to recognise Evil in what harms, Good in what profits, and their morality increases with the clearer consciousness wherewith they shun the evil, exercise the good. Whereas the strength, the skill of the *isolated* remains stationary in its weakness, because his needs are always the same, in *combination* men's strength increases ad infinitum with their needs. The more extended, more intimate the *union*, the more amply unfolds the spirit, purer becomes the morality, more many-sided wax the needs, and with them grows the strength of men to satisfy them.

Thus we perceive that only in *union* can men find the force to lead them toward their destiny; but only where the *force* exists, can the *destiny* be also; therefore it will be more correct to say:—

It is the destiny of **Mankind**, *through the ever higher perfecting of its mental, moral and corporeal forces, to attain an ever higher, purer happiness.*

The *individual* is but a *fraction* of the *whole*; *isolated,* he is *nothing*; only as part of the whole, does he find his mission, right, his happiness.

Men's combination we call *Society*.

We have seen that *Society* is nothing accidental, arbitrary, voluntary; we have seen that without Society man is no longer man, no more distinguishable from the beasts: we accordingly see that Society is the necessary condition of our *manhood*.

Men therefore are not only **entitled**, but **bound** *to require Society to* **lead them to ever higher, purer happiness through perfecting their mental, moral and corporeal faculties.**

How does our Established Society fulfil this task of hers?

To *Chance* she leaves the intellectual perfecting of certain of her members, while *forcibly* debarring the majority from any higher evolution; to **Chance** she leaves it, whether the few shall morally improve themselves, whereas she everywhere engenders and protects both vice and crime. To Chance she commits the training and growth of our bodily forces, the while her efforts are directed to restricting our needs, and thus to lessening our capacity for satisfying them. To *Chance* our standing Society abandons *all*, our spiritual, our moral and corporeal progress; 'tis *Chance* decides if we shall near our destiny, attain our right, be happy.

Our Established Society is without knowledge, without consciousness of her task; she fulfils it not.

The fight of **Man** against **existing Society** *has begun*. This fight, it is the holiest, the sublimest ever fought, for 'tis the war of *consciousness* with *chance*, of *mind* with *mindlessness*, *morality* with *evil*, of *strength* against *weakness*: *'tis the fight for our destiny*, *our right*, *our happiness*.

The Existing has a mighty empire over man. Our Established Society has a terrible power over us, for it has deliberately arrested the growth of our strength. The strength for this holy war can come to us from nothing save perception of the *worthlessness* of our Society. When we have clearly *recognised* how our existing Society disowns its task, how violently and often craftily it withholds us from our mission, our right, our happiness, we shall have won the *force* to fight, to conquer it.

Wherefore our first, our weightiest task is this: to search and ever more distinctly grasp the essence and the agency of our Society, on every side; *once it is* **recognised**, *it also is* **doomed**!

XIV.

THE REVOLUTION.

IF we peer across its lands and peoples, we find throughout the whole of Europe the effervescence of a mighty movement, whose first vibrations have already reached us, whose full weight threatens soon to crash upon us. Europe seems to us a huge volcano, from whose inside an ever-waxing fearsome roar resounds, from out whose crater columns of black smoke ascend to heaven big with storm, and mantle all the earth with darkness, while here and there a lava-stream, a fiery harbinger, breaks through the hard-set crust and bears destruction to the vale below.

A supernatural force seems clutching at our quarter of the globe, intent on lifting it from its old rut and hurling it to pathways new.

Ay, we behold it, the old world is crumbling, a *new* will rise therefrom; for the lofty goddess **Revolution** comes rustling on the wings of storm, her stately head ringed round with lightnings, a sword in her right hand, a torch in her left, her eye so stern, so punitive, so cold; and yet what warmth of purest love, what wealth of happiness streams forth toward him who dares to look with steadfast gaze into that eye! Rustling she comes, the e'er-rejuvenating mother of mankind; destroying and fulfilling, she fares across the earth; before her soughs the storm, and shakes so fiercely at man's handiwork that vasty clouds of dust eclipse the sky, and where her mighty foot steps falls in ruins what an idle whim had built for æons, and the hem of her robe sweeps its last remains away. But in her wake there opens out a ne'er-dreamt paradise of happiness, illumed by kindly sunbeams; and where her foot had trodden down, spring fragrant flowers from the soil, and jubilant songs of freed mankind fill full the air scarce silent from the din of battle.

Now turn and look below, around you. There you see one, the mightiest prince, with halting heart and catching breath, yet seeking to assume a tranquil, cool demeanour, to shut his eyes and those of others to what he clearly sees to be inevitable. There see another, his leathern face all ploughed by vices, exerting all those petty sharper's arts that have brought him in so many a titlet, so many an order's crosslet; you see him with his diplomatic smile and air of mystery among the teeth-nipped lordlings, the ladylings all snatching at their smelling-salts, whom he tries to reassure by half-official information that highest personages have deigned to pay attention to this strange phenomenon, that couriers have been sent already to various parts with Cabinet-orders, that the advice of that wise government-artist Metternich is even on the road from London, that the right authorities have had instructions all around, and accordingly the interesting surprise is in preparation for high-born society, at the next Court-ball, of taking a peep at this horrid vagrant Revolution—of course in an iron cage and fetters.—There see a third man, speculating on the approach of the apparition, running off to the Bourse, minutely reckoning the rise and fall of bondlets, higgling and haggling, alert to catch the least per-centlet, till all his plunder scatters to the winds. There, behind the dusty office-desk, you see one of those warped and rusted wheels of our present State-machine, scratching away with its stump of a quill, and doing its unceasing best to add fresh lumber to a paper world. Between these files of documents and contracts the hearts of live humanity are pressed like gathered leaves, and fall to powder in these modern torture-rooms. Here rules a strenuous activity, for the web outspun across the continent is torn in many a corner, and the startled spiders are busy knitting up fresh threads to rectify the holes. Here not a ray of light breaks in, here reign eternal night and darkness; and into night and darkness will the whole dissolve.—But listen! from that side there sounds shrill warlike music, swords flash and bayonets, heavy guns clatter past, and serried ranks of troops unroll their length. The valiant host of heroes has set out for its brush with Revolution. The General bids march to right and left, here stations infantry, there cavalry, and wisely parcels out his bristling columns and his dread artillery; and Revolution comes apace, her head high in the clouds,—they see her not, but wait for the foe; and she stands already in their midst,—they see her not, still waiting for the foe; and she has seized them in her mighty whirlwind, has scattered the ranks, dispersed the force which craft had stolen,—but the General, he sits there, absorbed in his map, and calculating from which side the foe may be expected, and what his strength, and when he will arrive!—Stay! there you see a troubled face: an upright, thrifty burgher it belongs to. He has toiled and moiled his whole life long, has honestly cared for the weal of all, so far as lay within his power; no shame, no wrong attaches to the mite his useful diligence has earned, to keep *himself* in feeble age, to give *his sons* a footing in this joyless life. He feels indeed the advent of the storm, he knows full well that no force can withstand it; yet his heart is sad when he looks back upon his life of hardships, whose only fruit is destined to destruction. We cannot gird at him, if timidly he grapples to his hoard, if futilely he puts forth all his blindfold strength 'gainst the invader. Unhappy man! uplift thine eyes, look up to where a thousand thousands gather on the hills in joyous expectation of the dawn! Regard them, they are all thy brothers, sisters, the troops of those poor wights who hitherto knew *naught* of life but *suffering*, have been but strangers on this earth of Joy; they all are waiting for that Revolution which affrights thee, their redemptrix from this world of sorrow, creatrix of a new world blessing *all*! See there, there stream the legions from the factories; they've made and fashioned lordly stuffs,—themselves and children, they are naked, frozen, hungry; for not to *them* belongs the fruit of all their labour, but to the rich and mighty one who calls men and the earth his *own*. See, there they troop, from fields and farmyards; they've tilled the earth and turned it to a smiling garden, and fruits in plenty, enough for all who live, have paid their pains,—yet poor are they, and naked, starving; for not to them, or others who are needy, belongs earth's blessing, but solely to the rich and mighty one who calls men and the earth his *own*. They all, the hundred-thousands, millions, are camped upon the hills and gaze into the distance, where thickening clouds proclaim the advent of emancipating Revolution; they all, to whom nothing is left to grieve for, from whom men rob the sons to train them into sturdy gaolers of their fathers, whose daughters walk the city's streets with burden of their shame, an offering to the baser lusts of rich and mighty; they all, with the sallow, careworn faces, the limbs devoured by frost and hunger, they all who have *never* known joy, encamp there on the heights and strain their eyes in blissful expectation of her coming, and listen in rapt silence to the rustle of the rising storm, which fills their ears with Revolution's greeting: I am the e'er-rejuvenating, ever-fashioning Life; where *I* am not, is Death! I am the dream, the balm, the hope of sufferers! I bring to nothing what exists, and whither I turn there wells fresh life from the dead rock. I come to you, to break all fetters that oppress you, to redeem you from the arms of Death and pour young Life through all your veins. Whatever stands, must fall:* such is the everlasting law of Nature, such the condition of Life; and I, the eternal destroyer, fulfil the law and fashion ever-youthful life. From its root up will I destroy the order of things in which ye live, for it is sprung from sin, its flower is misery and its fruit is crime; but the harvest is ripe, and *I* am the reaper. I will destroy

* Cf. "Alles, was ist, endet"; Erda in *Rheingold*.—Tr.

each phantom (*Wahn*) that has rule o'er men. I will destroy the dominion of one over many, of the dead o'er the living, of matter over spirit; I will break the power of the mighty, of law, of property. Be *his own* will the lord of man, his *own* desire his only law, his strength his whole possession, *for the only Holiness is the* **free man,** *and naught higher there is than* **he.** Annulled be the fancy that gives One power over millions, makes millions subject to the will of one, the doctrine that One has power to bless all others. Like may not rule over like; like has no higher potence than its equal: *and as ye all are equal, I will destroy all rulership of one over other.*

Annulled be the fancy that gives Death power over Life, the Past o'er the Future. The law of the dead is *their own* law; it shares their lot, and dies with them; it shall not govern Life. *Life is law unto itself.* And since the Law is for the living, not the dead, and *ye* are living, with none conceivable above you, *ye yourselves are the law, your own free will the sole and highest law, and I will destroy all dominion of Death over Life.*

Annulled be the fancy that makes man bondslave to his handiwork, to property. Man's highest good is his fashioning force, the fount whence springs all happiness forever; and not in the *created,* in the *act of creation itself,* in the *exercise of your powers* lies your true highest enjoyment. Man's work is lifeless; the living shall not bind itself to what is lifeless, not make itself a thrall to that. So away with the bugbear that restrains enjoyment, that hems free force, that sets up Property outside of Man, and makes him thrall to his own work.

Look hence, ye wretched ones, upon those blessed fields ye now flit through as thralls, as aliens. *Free* shall ye wander there, free from the yoke of the living, free from the chains of the dead. What Nature made, what men have tilled and turned into a fruitful garden, belongs to *men,* the *needy,* and none shall come and say: "To *me* alone belongs all this; ye others are but guests I tolerate so long as I may please and they shall yield me tribute, guests I drive forth when so inclined. To *me* belongs what Nature made, what Man has wrought, and the living needs." Away with that lie; *to Need alone, belongs what satisfies it*, and such is offered in abundance by Nature and your own strong arm. See there the houses in the cities, and all that gives delight to men, which ye must journey past as strangers; Man's mind and strength have made it, and therefore it belongs to *men*, the *living*, and *one* man shall not come and say: "To *me* belongeth all that toiling men have made. I alone have a right to it, and the others shall enjoy but what I please and they pay toll for." Destroyed be this lie, with the others; for what the strength of men hath made, belongs to mankind for its unrestricted use, as everything besides on earth.

I will destroy the existing order of things, which parts this one mankind into hostile nations, into powerful and weak, privileged and outcast, rich and poor; for it makes *unhappy* men of all. I will destroy the order of things that turns millions to slaves of a few, and these few to slaves of their own might, own riches. I will destroy this order of things, that cuts enjoyment off from labour, makes labour a load (*Last*), enjoyment a vice (*Laster*,) makes *one* man wretched through want, *another* through overflow. I will destroy this order of things, which wastes man's powers in service of dead matter, which keeps the half of humankind in inactivity or useless toil, binds hundreds of thousands to devote their vigorous youth—in busy idleness as soldiers, placemen, speculators and money-spinners—to the maintenance of these depraved conditions, whilst the other half must shore the whole disgraceful edifice at cost of over-taxing all their strength and sacrificing every taste of life. Down to its memory will I destroy each trace of this mad state of things, compact of violence, lies, care, hypocrisy, want, sorrow, suffering, tears, trickery and crime, with seldom a breath of even impure air to quicken it, and all but never a ray of pure joy. Destroyed be all that weighs on you and makes you suffer, and from the ruins of this ancient world let rise a *new*, instinct with happiness undreamt! Nor hate, nor envy, grudge nor enmity, be henceforth found among you; as *brothers* shall ye all who live know one another, and free, free in willing, *free* in doing, *free* in enjoying, shall ye attest the worth of life. So up, ye peoples of the earth! Up, ye mourners, ye oppressed, ye poor! And up, ye others, ye who strive in vain to cloak the inner desolation of your hearts by idle show of might and riches! Up, in miscellany follow my steps; for no distinction can I make 'twixt those who follow me. *Two* peoples, only, are there from henceforth: the one, that follows me, the other, that withstands me. The one I lead to happiness; over the other grinds my path: for I am *Revolution*, I am the ever-fashioning Life, I am the only God, to whom each creature testifies, who spans and gives both life and happiness to all that is!

And lo! the legions on the hills, voiceless they fall to their knees and listen in mute transport; and as the sunbaked soil drinks up the cooling drops of rain, so their sorrow-parching hearts drink in the accents of the rustling storm, and new life courses through their veins. Nearer and nearer rolls the storm, on its wings Revolution; wide open now the quickened hearts of those awaked to life, and victrix Revolution pours into their brains, their bones, their flesh, and fills them through and through. In godlike ecstasy they leap from the ground; the poor, the hungering, the bowed by misery, are they no longer; proudly they raise themselves erect, inspiration shines from their ennobled faces, a radiant light streams from their eyes, and with the heaven-shaking cry *I am a Man!* the millions, the embodied Revolution, the God become Man, rush down to the valleys and plains, and proclaim to all the world the new gospel of Happiness.

XV.

INVITATION TO THE PRODUCTION OF "TRISTAN" IN MUNICH.*

Honoured Friend!

YOU still are the only editor of a major political paper on whose support I can count when I have to appear before the public in any way. For me it is a real good fortune that we are bound by ties of older friendship; otherwise I should not know what means to adopt to inform the more serious friends of my art, strewn here and there, that they actually will soon be offered the opportunity of witnessing a representation of my "Tristan und Isolde." Therefore, while heartily beseeching your utmost circulation of this notice, please allow me at like time the small satisfaction of acquainting you with the peculiar significance I attach to the forthcoming performance of my work. Perhaps by briefly relating to you the history of its former hitches I shall be furnishing a not inconsiderable contribution to our modern Art-history in general.

In the summer of 1857 I decided to break off the musical setting of my Nibelungen-work and undertake a shorter labour, which I meant to bring me into contact with the Theatre once more. "Tristan und Isolde" was begun that very year, though its completion was delayed by all manner of interruptions until the summer of 1859. As I still was shut from all the countries of the German Bund, yet could not think of a first performance without my personal co-operation, I had it in mind to arrange with

* An open letter to Friedrich Uhl, Editor of the *Wiener Botschafter*, 1865, reprinted in the *Bayreuther Blätter* for June 1890. Uhl had already published Wagner's article on "The Vienna Opera-house" in his journal for 1863; see Vol. III.—Tr.

some director for a German-operatic season in the summer months at Strassburg. Upon my asking the advice of the Director of the Grand-ducal theatre at Carlsruhe, Dr Eduard Devrient, he explained the great difficulties of such an undertaking, and counselled me to wait and see if the generous intervention of the Grand Duke of Baden would succeed in obtaining me leave to go to Carlsruhe for the period of my work's rehearsal, in which event every requisite for a good performance would be gladly placed at my disposal. Unfortunately the steps taken for that purpose in Dresden by my illustrious patron remained without the desired result: in view of the great and unusual difficulties of the task proposed, and the necessity of a proper understanding with the singers chosen for my work, so soon as my personal presence at Carlsruhe was proved impossible we had to renounce all further attempts to solve it. Had I been summoned to Carlsruhe at that time, I should have found there the very singers for the title-rôles of "Tristan" whom, after six years' interval and with full freedom of choice, I have discovered to be the only fitting ones in all the numerous personnel of German opera-houses. I allude to that admirable wedded pair of artists, the Schnorrs of Carolsfeld, who have since become my intimate friends.

You will smile with amaze when you hear what a circuit it needed, to arrive at what then lay close beside me, only barred by the above considerations.

To attain the possibility of a first performance of "Tristan und Isolde" under my personal guidance, I removed in the autumn of 1859 to—Paris. My plan was to call a model German-operatic company to Paris for May and June 1860; the Italian Opera-house, always vacant at that time of year, was to be hired for it. As I found the majority of my friends and acquaintances among the artists quite ready to accept my invitation in general, my principal care was the material aspect of the undertaking. A business-manager, in the person of one of the proprietors of the Italian Opera-house, was easy to find; harder was it to procure the financial guarantee of a capitalist. The requisite courage must be instilled into a certain rich well-wisher, the friend of one of my Parisian friends: at my own risk I gave three grand concerts in the Italian Opera-house, at which I had fragments of my music executed by a large orchestra—needless to say, in Paris, at great expense. The undeniably potent impression of these concerts on the public had one sole object in my eyes, to win the confidence of that wealthy gentleman whose support we hoped-for in my contemplated opera-enterprise. Unluckily, that elderly gentleman was prevented from attending the concerts at all: the calculations of my friends were wrecked. Whilst it turned out that the German singers to be invited by me could not all assemble at one time, because of the difference in their leaves-of-absence, and the very sacrifices and exertions occasioned me by these three concerts scared me off from further ventures of the sort, on another side my appearance in Paris developed a very surprising result. The Emperor of the French gave his command for the production of my "Tannhäuser" at the Grand Opéra.—You know pretty well into what new and strange perplexities I was plunged by this affair, which caused some little noise in Europe; it cost me a profoundly harassing year of my life. Whereas I really should not have known what to do with a big success, had it even been possible, in the throes of the most appalling failure I felt as though freed from a terrible incubus which had checked me on my own true road; and, since Paris at least had helped me to re-admission into Germany, that road led straight to Carlsruhe, to pursue at last the consummation of a first performance of my "Tristan" there.

It now was May [1861]. At once assured of the gracious auspices of the most Serene Grand-ducal pair, on the other hand I had to deplore the absence of the artistic pair, the Schnorrs, who had left to take a permanent engagement in —Dresden. In accordance with the wishes of my noble patron, I was now to seek out for myself the artists to be summoned to Carlsruhe for a model representation of my work. A visit to Dresden was not permitted me as yet:

I hurried to Vienna, to take stock of the forces there. With me, dear Uhl, you attended the fine performance of my "Lohengrin"—to me a first one—and can appreciate my feeling that everything which I witnessed on that intoxicating night of May gave suddenly a new direction to my life. To obtain leave for the excellent singers of the Imperial Opera to come to Carlsruhe for a performance of my "Tristan," was forthwith shewn to be impossible. On the other hand I had no desire to meet the offer of the supreme control of the Imperial theatre, to bring "Tristan" to a speedy performance in Vienna under my personal superintendence, with any serious objections.—You know where lay my chief hesitation: of the favourite singer Ander, whose recent death has filled us all with heartfelt sorrow, it would have been too much to expect the uncommonly arduous task involved in the principal rôle of "Tristan." However, as all the other rôles could be admirably cast, I might consent to effect the alterations, cuts and adaptations needful to bring his task within the power of this singer too. In the autumn of 1861 the rehearsals were to begin.—You will remember that a tedious affection of the throat debarred Ander from any serious exertion for all that winter; another singer was not to be procured just then,—neither Tichatscheck nor Schnorr, both in Dresden, could come away. The affair had to be postponed for a year.—In the summer of 1862 I was already despairing of the possibilty of the work being taken up again in Vienna, when to my surprise the management informed me that Herr Ander felt completely restored to health and ready to resume the study of "Tristan und Isolde."

That summer I made acquaintance with the admirable, and to me most sympathetic qualities of the excellent Schnorr von Carolsfeld, a genuine vocal and dramatic musician; he and his wife, formerly Fräulein Garrigues, admired as a true and noble artist at Carlsruhe, had already learnt the leading rôles of my work out of pure inclination, and with such great love and inner understanding that when they came to visit me on the Rhine, where I was staying for a while, we were able to have complete musical performances of "Tristan" in my room, to Bülow's inimitable accompaniment on the pianoforte. This happened in my chamber, though at no theatre could I be offered a like possibility. In Dresden too—where there were all the requisites for a production of my work—I now might set foot once again; but when I went there for a few days in the autumn of that year, I saw at once, from the peculiar bearing of the General-Direction of the Royal Court-theatre, that there was not the remotest idea of any concernment with me or my work there. What hopes I might base on the directorates of other large theatres in Germany I further learnt when, on my road through Berlin a short while after, I announced myself for a visit to the General-Intendant of the Royal Prussian Court-theatre—and that gentleman simply forbade it.

In such circumstances I had to direct my hopes, however dwindled, to Vienna anew. Here, since the first delays with "Tristan," the musical press had made it its special delight to prove that my work was altogether inexecutable: No singers could either take my notes or hold them. This theme became the text for everything reported, written or said about me, throughout all Germany. A French singer, Madame Viardot 'tis true, one day expressed her surprise to me at the bare possibility of such assertions as that a note couldn't be taken, and so forth: Are the musicians in Germany not musical, then? I really didn't know what to answer, especially to an artist who once had sung a whole act of Isolde at sight and with great expression. Nor in truth was it at all so bad with my German singers: in Vienna they gave me the great joy at last of hearing the whole opera sung at the pianoforte without a fault, and really movingly, under the direction and owing to the uncommonly intelligent zeal and industry of my valued friend Kapellmeister Esser. How they could later have come to say that they had never been able to learn their parts

—for so I've been told—to me remains a riddle over whose solution I will not break my head: perhaps it was out of politeness to our famous Viennese and other musical critics, who were amazingly anxious to have my work considered unperformable, and whom a performance notwithstanding would have positively outraged; but perhaps what was told me, itself is untrue; everything is possible, for in the German Press of nowadays things are not always quite Christian-like. Enough! At Moscow in March 1863 I received a communication from the management of the Imperial Opera to the effect that I needn't hurry back to Vienna for the full rehearsals of "Tristan," appointed for about that date, as illnesses had made the performance impossible before the stage-vacation. That vacation passed, and—not a word more was said about "Tristan." I believe the opinion prevailed in the company that, with the best of will, Ander would be unable to "last out" his part, to say nothing of repeating it often. In such untoward circumstances the management couldn't possibly consider "the opera" a gain to the "repertoire." This, and much besides, I found so entirely in the nature of things, that at last I gave up bothering about the various stories borne to me. Candidly: I had had enough of it, and dismissed the subject from my mind.

So my "Tristan und Isolde" had become a by-word. Here and there I was friendlily treated: people lauded "Tannhäuser" and "Lohengrin"; for the rest, I appeared to be done for.

Fate, however, had decided otherwise.—No plan conceived till then, even if successfully executed, would have altogether solved the question bound-up with the performance of this work;—to compass that solution, as clearly as the circumstances of the present day make possible, was yet reserved for me. When everyone forsook me, a warm and noble heart beat all the higher for my art-ideal; it cried to the rejected artist, "What thou desir'st, I will!" And this time the will was creative; 'twas the will of—a *King*.

The wondrous beauty of the stimulant and nutrient force which entered my life a year ago, and has usurped my utmost earnestness with sweet compulsion, I can only reveal to my friends through the deed of its dictating. Such a deed I announce to you to-day. And what kind of art it is, that is here to be manifested, you may judge when I relate to you the manner in which "Tristan" is to be presented to my friends.

The performances of "Tristan und Isolde," three whereof are promised for certain, will be altogether model and exceptional. In the first place, the impersonators of the two uncommonly difficult principal rôles have been expressly summoned to Munich, in the persons of my own dear friends, Ludwig and Malwina Schnorr v. Carolsfeld; they are accompanied by my dear old comrade in artistic arms, Anton Mitterwurzer, as "Kurwenal" faithful and true as steel. So far as circumstance at all permits, the casting of the other parts has been arranged in the most generous and adequate fashion; all concerned are devoted to me. To be relieved of every disturbing influence from a daily round of stage-work, the cosy Royal Residenz-theater has been made over to my exclusive use: here everything is studiously provided for the needs of a thorough, clear and intimately-intelligible representation according to my wish. Here we have the splendid Royal Court-orchestra, Franz Lachner's exemplary creation, for almost daily rehearsals, whose frequency gives us full leisure to attain the height of artistic refinement and correctness in the rendering. To make it easier for me to supervise the general ensemble, my dear friend Hans von Bülow has been associated with me in the control of the orchestra — — the very man who once achieved the impossible by making a playable pianoforte-arrangement of this score, though to this day no one knows how he did it. With him, who has such an intimate acquaintance with this enigma to many musicians that he knows each tiniest particle by heart, and has imbibed my intentions down to their faintest nuance,—with this second self by my side, I can enter into every detail of the musical and dramatic portrayal with that tranquillity which nothing but affectionate companionship with truly friendly artists can ever bring about. Beautiful scenery and fine characteristic costumes have been cared for with a zeal as though it were not a mere stage-performance, but a monumental exhibition.

Thus transported from the desert of our theatrical market-driving to the fresh oasis of an artist's studio, we are preparing the work for a dramatic performance which, purely as such, must needs be epoch-making to all who shall attend it.

These performances—perhaps only three in number for the present, as announced—are to be regarded as feasts to which I am allowed to bid the friends of my art from far and near: they will consequently be removed from the ordinary character of theatrical representations, and quit the usual circle of relations between the Theatre and Public of our day. My august protector wills that these significant performances shall not be offered to habitual curiosity, but solely to more serious interest in my art; I am therefore empowered to issue invitations far and wide, wherever my art has won men's hearts.

They will take place about the second half of May,* and, so far as can be predetermined, the exact dates will be advertised in good time through the widest-read papers. We assume that whoever doesn't mind a journey to Munich expressly for this purpose, is drawn by no mere surface aim, but thereby testifies his earnest interest in the success of an attempt to solve a high and important artistic problem; and everyone who applies to the Royal Intendance of the Court-and-National Theatre at Munich in the sense implied, may be certain of finding a seat

* In the event they occurred on the 10th, 13th and 19th of June, and the 1st of July—the *last* for several years.—Tr.

reserved for him on the date which he selects.—Alike to foreign, as to native friends of my art, an invitation will be issued in identical terms and to the same effect.

As for any taunt that such measures seem intended to secure a mere audience of friends, to please whom it would need no such mighty great art, we shall quietly reply that it is not a question this time of pleasing or displeasing, that wonderful modern stage game of hazard, but simply of Whether artistic tasks such as I have set in this work are to be solved at all? In what way they are to be solved? and Whether it is worth the while to solve them? And here I must remark that the last question doesn't mean the discovering whether this kind of performance will bring in much money (the current sense of pleasing or displeasing at the theatre), but simply whether first-rate performances of works of this sort can at all produce the expected effect on the cultured human mind: that is to say, the chief concern is with purely artistic problems, and therefore those alone are to be begged to share in their solution who really are prepared and qualified by a serious interest in the cause itself. Should this problem be solved, then the question will widen, and it will also be seen in what mode we are striving to give to and prepare the people proper for a share in the highest and deepest things of Art as well, even though we do not believe that we can view the regular public of the theatre-goers directly in that light just yet.

So, my dear Uhl, if you think I've been telling you of no quite unimportant art-event, and that it would repay the trouble to do something toward circulating the above announcement, I entreat you to use your journalistic connections in whatever way you deem best for the purpose. I am modest enough to be aware that, with my invitation, I am addressing myself to few; but I also know that these few are surprisingly scattered. To them, the scattered, I fain would send forth my appeal; for even should the art-work fall below their expectations, what calls them in the first rank to a rare forgathering is in any case so rare, so fair and glorious a Deed, that it demands attention far and wide.

Let our motto be: *Hail to the Noble Author of that Deed!*—

With the heartiest greetings I remain
Ever yours sincerely

Munich, 18 April, 1865. RICHARD WAGNER.

POSTHUMOUS.

I.

"Die Sarazenin."

(1841-1843.)

Of the Posthumous publications, No. I., "Die Sarazenin," *was first sketched by Wagner in Paris 1841, as related on pages 313-15 of Volume I. In 1843 the idea was resumed, and "the scenic draft completed" as an operatic text, for Frau Schröder-Devrient (see p. 321* ibid.*). Again it was abandoned, in fact, the draft itself mislaid; so that the Bayreuth master was unable to include it in his* Gesammelte Schriften, *as he had intended. A somewhat imperfect copy of the manuscript, however, was found among the papers of Domkapellmeister Greith, of Munich, just five years after Wagner's death; Greith's widow gave it to Herr Heinrich Porges, who in turn transferred it to the Wahnfried archives; and thus it came to be printed for the first time in the* Bayreuther Blätter *of January 1889, from which I have borrowed the above particulars.*

TRANSLATOR'S NOTE.

"THE SARACEN WOMAN.'

OPERA IN FIVE ACTS.

DRAMATIS PERSONÆ.

Fatima, soprano.
Manfred, tenor.
Lancia, bass.
Nureddin, tenor.
Burello, bass.
Ali, bass.
Feretrio, bass.
Chorus of Saracen nobles and warriors.

FIRST ACT.

Manfred's castle at Capua. A fête is being held in a hall of oriental splendour, opening on a garden. Manfred lies indolently stretched on cushions. Galvani Lancia sits beside him; knights and lords are ranged in groups; noble pages hand wine and refreshments; Saracen dancing-girls execute an elaborate national dance. Applause rewards the dancers; Manfred asks for change of entertainment. Someone proposes a task for the singers. Lancia begs Manfred to display his mastery in the art of song.

Manfred.

What shall I sing you?
Of fame, of lofty deeds?
(half aside) Woe's me! the time of deeds is over!—
Of love? Of pleasure?

O that they but had power to still this heart! O all that earth contains of joys, could I conjure you to besiege my breast, that I might dream the world holds naught desirable beyond you!

The Saracen (appears; she is veiled, but presently throws back her veil):

Be answer'd, Manfred!
What thou desir'st I'll shew thee.

All are amazed at the stranger's beauty.

Manfred. Who art thou?
Saracen. A simple singer.
Manf. I ne'er have seen thee at my court.
Sar. My foot first treads the land-of-eve to-day.
Manf. Who sends thee to me?
Sar. Great Kaiser Friedrich,
Thy father sends me!

Manfred is horror-struck; all present, profoundly stirred, turn their eyes in great excitement toward the woman, who takes advantage of the pause to seize a lute and boldly advance to Manfred, thus beginning:

Sar. Tho' ye in land-of-evening call the greatest Kaiser dead, I bring you living tidings of him from the land of morn: ne'er dies he there, for ever lives his august memory. A thousand songs keep green his fame; would ye hear one of them, so listen!

When, led by him, the might of Christendom invaded Palestine to win the Cross ye venerate, what were your swords, your deadly arms, were't not for him alone, who gained you peace? Treason was woven round him by the Templar rout; for sordid gold had they resolved to sell him to the Sultan, ay, had sworn it: Zelima, fairest of the faithful, she foiled the traitors' plan. Him had she seen, the great Kaiser, and loved him; and on the Sultan she prevailed to waive the treachery; with noble heart he warned the Emperor himself what menaced him. And so no longer would he be the Sultan's foe: they swore eternal friendship, and lordly songs soon sang the love of Friedrich and Zelima. Christian and Mussulman embraced: for he, the great Kaiser, was neither Mussulman nor Christian; a god was he, and reverenced as god he lives still in the morning-land.

Burello has appeared.

Burello. An thou hast heard enough of singing, Manfred, to me now lend a gracious ear.

Manfred (who had listened to the song as if entranced, now rises vexedly). What brings thee here, to mar the pleasance of my court?

Bur. Who e'er could move thee from thy glut of pleasures, while thou canst feed on others' goods unscathed? Manfred, Prince of Tarentum, liegeman of the Pope our master, how long dost think to keep my chattels from me?

Manf. Of what wouldst thou remind me?

Bur. Of my right! The things that our liege-lord assigned me, from thee I claim them, and am resolved to wait no longer for thy whim to give me up my property.—

Lancia. Divin'st thou, Manfred, what time has come for thee?

Manf. Burello, hear! Tho' the mischances of my house have humbled me so low that alien hands presume to grant my property to men like thee, yet know a Hohenstaufe never brooks affront. Tho' for the peace of the Apulian realm I recognise an over-chief to whom no lordly kingdom such is due, yet heaven-high o'er thee I stand, and first demand thou bare thy head before me.

Burello (derisively uncovering). Your pardon, I misjudged your majesty! Ye counts, ye lords and knights, ye see the woman-dummy there imagines it at least is Kaiser. Shall we indulge its humour?

A number of those present support Burello's mockery.

Lancia (together with others).

— — — — — —

Burello, shameless wight, know'st not the mighty Kaiser's son?

Bur. Good, Lancia, that thou ask'st it! What wager'st thou, this is no bastard?

Manf. (beside himself, rushes at Burello, and deals him a blow). Take that for bastard!

Burello, foaming with rage, clutches at his sword; his friends hold him back.

Ensemble.

Burello and his followers. Ha! direly shalt thou pay for this; the deed remember! To ruin has it doomed thee. The Ghibellines' last blood shall flow to shame and horror!

Manfred and his followers. Shameless one, hence! Be thankful thou escap'st so lightly. Go hence and cry to all the Folk what took thee when thou mock'dst a Kaiser's son!

Both parties separate in great commotion; the dancers had left the stage before. The Saracen woman alone remains.

Sar. Praised be the power of my song, that kindled him to action. Allah! O give me strength the lofty work to finish!

Nureddin enters hastily, and goes toward Manfred's chamber.

Sar. Nureddin!

Nureddin. That voice!

Sar. 'Tis I, Nureddin.

Nureddin (with utmost passion). Fatima, Fatima! Where am I? Allah! Who's borne me o'er the sea to distant palm-groves? Who breathes me this sweet kiss from fairest home? Fatima! O Fatima! Is't thou in truth?

Fatima. Be not amazed! I promised thou shouldst see me once again, when forth I sped thee from our home to fight the Kaiser's fight in land-of-evening. The boon I promised thee when 'neath the palms we lay, a pair of children, it shall be thine!

Nur. Fatima, ah! what had I to bear for thee! How many years afar from thee, from my dear home, had I to pass in savage wars! Bound was I held by thy command; among the valiant, of the most loyal was I one; but ah! the flower of my soul was fading: yearning for thee, for my dear home, devoured my heart. But now—O say it! —now my loyalty I've proved, thou com'st to tender me the boon; now fare we to our lovely fatherland?

Fatima. The boon? First be it fought! In shame I find the mighty Kaiser's house. My coming was to lend you fire. Nureddin, in thy zeal I lay my people's welfare. 'Tis time. Say, lives my uncle Ali, to whom I sent thee?

Nur. He dwells with the Lucerians, where Friedrich made our second home.

Fatima. Up! haste to him! Great doings are afoot. Win thou our brethren for the Kaiser's son!

Nureddin. And thou?

Fatima. Soon am I there myself. Pray ye to Allah! He must dispose.

Nureddin. And then?

Fatima. Across the sea to home!

Nureddin leaves her, drunk with joy; Fatima also departs.

Finale.

Lancia (rushes on, calling the Saracen watch). Where is the Prince? Manfred! Manfred!

Manfred (hurrying from his room). What ails?

Lan. Manfred, I bring bad tidings. Burello!— —

Manf. What boots the varlet?

Lan. He left in anger, and has gathered round him all his friends; thou knowest them, the cursed Welfs.—

Manf. And know too my Ghibellines!

Knights and Nobles (Manfred's friends, appear). Manfred, be on thy guard! The number of thy foes increases.

Lan. They're mustered in the palace of the Legate.

Manfred. The Legate?

Lan. Thou know'st, Burello is the Pope's own kinsman.

(More Knights come hurrying in.)

Manfred, thy life's at stake. The Legate comes.

Manfred. I here await him.

Voices. Way for the Legate!

The Legate (appearing with his retinue). Manfred, Prince of Tarentum, a heavy accusation hath been brought against thee. We cite thee to our lord's tribunal. Appear'st thou not without delay, his ban is on thee! (Departs.)

Manfred. Who am I? Ha! What fate befalls me?

Lancia. What wilt thou do?

Some of the Knights. Appear before the judgment-seat.

Lan. If thou appear'st, thou courtest ruin.

Others. Nay, nay! Conciliate the Pope.

The Saracen (steps between them). Never! Manfred, abid'st thou here, thou'rt lost. Flee hence, and trust the God of the Ghibellines! The Kaiser calls. To him! His spirit will protect thee.

Manf. To me! who's true to me. Forth into night and peril! The die is cast. Whoe'er would ruin me shall find me, weapons in my hand.

Night has fallen ; a storm is gathering.

Lan. We cleave to thee ; but secret be our flight! Ye all, disperse, to meet unnoticed past the gates! There shall our further plans be told you.

The Knights. Manfred, rely on us! We're true to thee in want and death. Treason avaunt!

Lan. What password shall we give each other?

Saracen. Let Kaiser Friedrich be the password!

All (in enthusiasm). "Kaiser Friedrich!"

They scatter in different directions ; Manfred seeks to detain the Saracen ; she motions him to flight, and rushes off.

SECOND ACT.

Wild mountainous country. Between high rocks a hospice, a humble dwelling, occupying one side of the background. It is night : a violent storm. From the hospice sounds the "Nona" of the monks. Several of them appear : they are waiting for the monks who have been sent out to rescue pilgrims lost on dangerous paths.

From a gully Manfred and his followers mount one by one, laboriously struggling with the hardships of the way ; a Brother from the hospice guides them ; as they approach the hospice, they are greeted by the Prior.

Manfred.

Praised be God, who led us to a friendly roof in such a wilderness!

Prior. And who art thou, a-wandering with so many knights in this waste place?

A Brother (advancing). Manfred it is, the God-accurst!

Others. He's under ban.

All. Back, cursed man! Thy feet ne'er cross this threshold.

The Brethren swiftly close the door. Loud peals of thunder.

Manfred's companions. The dastards! Burst the door!

Manf. Desist! No sacrilege! What though the Church's curse is on me, the world shall know I ne'er profaned her.

Lancia. Thou grantest us no rest, no cease from toils I never thought to suffer? Untrodden paths we climb through torrent-courses; amid a thousand perils we avoid each house, each castle, for that we know not friend from foe. Come tell us, whither wouldst thou flee?

Manf. Are ye weary, friends, so rest you here. Look ye, the storm's abating. God witness, should things go according to my wish, the hardships of this flight shall be repaid you richly.

Behold me, whom ye saw knee-deep in luxury, whom often ye have blamed as weakling: thus I defy discomfort, frost, fatigue.

A fire has been made; all camp around it, cover themselves with their mantles, and lie down to sleep. From the hospice the prayer of the monks is heard again.—Manfred alone remains. He watches the knot of sleepers, then turns his eyes away and falls into deep thought:

And was't not *she* who drove me to decision? How honourless, how poor, how lowly stood I there! Lost was my name, extinct the glory of my high descent; scarce durst I even hope for action:—then she appeared before mine eyes, and breathed upon my soul the wondrous perfume of far distant days of fame. Who is she? What magic brought her to my path? Ever I seem to see her, in daring circuit o'er the mountain's wildest pass. Mine ear oft tells me her sweet voice is sounding forth my name athwart the bleak ravines. Is it the guardian spirit of my fathers, that summons me to knightly deeds? O soothing spell, to thee I yield myself. From chill reality I vault, sweet dreams, into your kingdom!

— — — — — —

Tired out, he falls to sleep. The storm has passed away entirely; the moon has broken through the clouds: the mountain's crest is crossed by the ghostlike apparition of an army, at its head Kaiser Friedrich II. surrounded by his heroes. The figure of the Kaiser halts a moment, and beckons to Manfred, who makes an answering movement in his sleep.

When the vision has passed, the name of Manfred sounds, in the Saracen's voice; she herself appears on a jutting crag in the foreground. Once more she calls:

The Saracen. Manfred!

Manfred (awakes, and staggers to his feet). Thou call'st me? Then my thought was true; thou art not of this world of ours!

Sar. Thou errest, Manfred. Of this world I am, but sent to lead thee on to happiness and greatness.

Manf. Again I ask, *who* sent thee?

Sar. My sender *he* thou lately saw'st in dream.

Manf. Enchantress, all my senses swoon! Who art thou, ah! who art thou?

Sar. Allah hath given me the word, to lead thee on to action. Manfred! give ear to what I tell thee:—let this night be the last that witnesses the Hohenstaufen's shame! Soon as the sun dyes red anew these mountain-tops, let dawn the morning of thy fame! Thine be the Hohenstaufen's realm, and to thy name let Christendom pay heed, for the great Kaiser called thee his dearest son: his eyes thou'st closed—let thine now open, that all the world may know thee and behold the Kaiser!

Manf. Ha! Inspiration such as but a god can wake, thou breath'st into my soul! In my veins pulses Hohenstaufen blood! Once more, thou heavenly being, who art thou, how may I call thee?

Sar. If magic I appear to thee, believe in it and venture not to foul it! Manfred, when this same sun has sunk again, that makes the moonlight now to pale, before Luceria's gates shalt thou be stationed; within its walls I wait thee.

Manf. I fathom now. Where should I find more loyal souls than in Luceria, where erst my father gave the Saracens a second home, expelled from Sicily? Well may I count on them; no stauncher fighters are there for the Kaiser's cause, than these devoted sons of Araby.

Sar. Confide in them, and in thy weal! Upon no better couldst thou count. Manfred, farewell! In Luceria we meet again.

Manf. Thus distant wouldst thou part from me—in parting giv'st me not thy hand?

Sar. Manfred, farewell! In Luceria thou grasp'st my hand.

Manf. Nay, nay! Descend'st thou not to me—these rocks I climb—thy hand thou must extend me—

(He is about to climb the crag.)

Sar. Back, Manfred! Profane not the hour of election!

Manf. To save my brain from reeling, name thyself! Say but, who art thou? What share hast in my lot?

The Saracen answers with the refrain of her song from act i.

"They swore eternal friendship each to each,
and lordly songs still praise the love
of Friedrich and Zelima" *etc.*

Manfred, listening with averted face, does not observe that Fatima has quitted the crag and vanished while singing. Her song dies away in the distance.

Manfred (looks up and starts, at seeing Fatima no longer). So this, too, was a dream.

The sun begins to tint the peaks with deepest purple. In the hospice the bell is rung for morning-prayer.

Lancia and the Knights awake.

Manfred (suddenly breaking from his stupor into the highest enthusiasm).

Up! Up, ye friends!
Awake and greet the day that once more makes
the Hohenstaufen kingdom subject unto me!
Up, Lancia! Up, ye fellows of my shame!
To Luceria, to our friends! Mark well this day!
Henceforth we conquer to ourselves the kingdom of Apulia.

Lancia and the Knights. Ha! Whence this lofty mood?
What god has now inspired him?
Manfred, our blessings on the day

that makes of thee a hero!
Lead us! The wide world we defy.
At thy side victory or death!

As they make ready to depart, the curtain falls.

THIRD ACT.

Luceria. A street, bounded at the back by the principal gate. The buildings, originally erected in the medieval Italian style, have been gradually transformed by the Saracen inhabitants into an Arabian aspect. In the right background projects the façade of a mosque; on the left the ruins of a Christian church. The stage is filled by the Arabian populace, warriors, greybeards, women, children, arranged in characteristic groups. The guard at the gates, and on the walls, is being changed and reinforced. Great animation prevails in all the groups. The approach of Ramadan is under celebration.

Ali and Nureddin step forward.

Nureddin. As yet thou hast not seen her?

Ali. Not a glimpse.

Nur. Strange! Now here, now there, I fancy I behold her. Ah! if yearning had consumed me ever since I sped from home, it now has robbed me of my last remains of strength since I so wondrously set eyes on her again, to part from her so speedily once more.

Ali. Thou dreamer, Nureddin! When wilt thou e'er learn reason? Say, what do we lack here? Allah reward the great Kaiser's hospitality! Have we not all that we could wish?

Nur. Ha! Thou remind'st me of my pledge. O Fatima, O wouldst appear, to give us further counsel! How are we hindered in the good work, since Burello has to-day been made our master.

Ali. That man's the clergy's servant.

Nureddin. And Manfred's bitterest foe.

The dialogue between Ali and Nureddin has been carried-on in the extreme right foreground. On the left, before the ruins of the Christian church, a throng has gathered round a veiled woman, who, standing high upon the broken masonry, now addresses the assembly :—

The veiled Fatima. Arabia's children, know that I am come to warn you of disaster; threatened is the home great Kaiser Friedrich here bequeathed you.

Nureddin. Fatima! Fatima!

Fatima. Know that the Christian's spiritual chief, with whom the sovereignty of so fair a country ill accords, presumes to claim by force the lordship of this city, which countless loyal services have made your own.

Ali and Nureddin have joined the throng.

Ali. Is't Fatima, my sister's child?

Fatima (continuing). So say, my brothers, sisters! Say who is your lord!

All. The Kaiser, the Kaiser alone!

Fatima. Yet the Kaiser is dead. Dead is his son, the king Konrad. Who then is your lord? Manfred it is, the Kaiser's best-loved son.

All. Manfred, Manfred's our Kaiser!

Fatima. And suffer ye that men should make Burello, Manfred's enemy, your lord?

All. Never!

Fatima. So hold yourselves prepared, this very night to greet the Kaiser's son. Till then keep peace, let no one gain suspicion. Joy be with you; to you I promise glorious days, the days when Christian brother is to Mussulman.

Ensemble.

The Folk (bursting into enthusiasm).

Allah, Allah, bless the prophetess!
Give heart to us, and courage!
In fight and battle give us victory!

Ali repeats the Folk's words.

Nureddin. O wondrous being, prophetess, God's envoy! Dare I make bold to call myself thy lover?

Fatima, having disappeared among the people, now comes forward unveiled, close by Nureddin :—

Fatima. 'Tis I, Nureddin, loved one! Soon I am thine!

Nureddin (beside himself). Fatima, O Fatima!

Ali. Know'st thine old uncle?

Fatima. Have thanks for your unbounded troth!
Yours am I, never more to part.

(Brief Ensemble.)

Voices. Way for the Commander!

Fatima (hurriedly to the Folk). Softly, betray you not!

Burello (appears with armed Christians). For whom these cheers, this hubbub that resounded to the castle?

Ali. It is our custom thus to greet the feast of Ramadan, which comes again to-morrow; we think then of the olden times, the Prophet's times, the happy times for Araby. Ye know them not—but so tradition runs with us.

Burello. Ye know what I demand of you: close-guarded be this town as if the foe were at its gates; no one may out or in; so hither with the city's keys!

Ali draws the key from the gate. Armed men from Burello's train examine if the gate be duly locked. Meanwhile:—

Burello. No trustier could be sent, to check the miscreant's flight; long as I live, he ne'er shall cross the threshold of this town; in squalor let him perish, who put on me such foul affront!

Fatima, Nureddin and Chorus.

Eh, brood revenge, sir scoundrel! Dark as the night within thy breast, so brightly shall the sun of Manfred shine upon this city!

Ali brings the keys, and gives them to Burello.

Burello. Once more receive your orders. Each post upon the walls be strictly guarded; who shews himself remiss, his head is forfeit. Who watches at this gate?

Ali. I vouch for that; with me Nureddin.

Burello. Ye know what fate awaits you for neglect. Disperse, ye others! Let none disturb the peace!

(Exit with his retinue.)

From the top of the mosque on the right, the call to evening-prayer is heard as the sun goes down: "Allah is great" etc. All fall to their knees, and prostrate themselves in prayer upon the ground. The sun has set by the time they rise and depart in different directions; Fatima alone remains, in a praying attitude; she has pressed her hands to her eyes, and weeps convulsively.

Nureddin (perceiving it, springs to her side). Fatima, thou weep'st? For whom these tears?

Fatima (rising, buries her face on his breast). O Nureddin, be brave, that soon we may return to home.

Nureddin (agitated). Our home? Shall I e'er see it more? Allah! Hast spared to me thy grace?

Fatima. Shall I e'er see it more?

Nur. O Fatima, in truth I see that Allah hath inspired thee; yet fear thou not to solve this riddle: Why settest thou thy life upon a deed whose goal is foreign to thee?

Fatima. Manfred I must see Kaiser! Nureddin my husband!

Ali. Come Nureddin, to our posts! Thou know'st for whom we guard them.

Fatima (suddenly aflame again). For Manfred!

Nureddin (troubled and brooding). "For Manfred!"

(He slowly moves towards the gate.)

Ali. Fatima, wilt keep our watch with us? Say, canst still sing as sweetly as of yore, thou know'st how glad I'd listen.

Fatima (rejoining them). Thus will I keep you waking. I'll sing to you the palm-tree song.

(She sits down on the ground between Ali and Nureddin, and sings an Arabian folk-song with the refrain: "O dearest, sweetest palm-tree!")

"O dearest, sweetest palm-tree,
Thou my love's shelter!
For thee I yearn,
That I may find my love again" etc.

(Nureddin falls into a trance.)

Ali. O Revery, thy song keeps not awake. Hear, children, what I sing you!

(He sings a vigorous Arabian song, while Fatima reclines against his breast and watches Nureddin with keen emotion.)

"My horse, my horse, my mettled horse
Comes prancing through the desert,

As to my love I hasten.
Hei! how it bounds and leaps for joy!
So leaps my little maid for glee
When she her dearest sees" *etc.*

During a pause in his song the voice of Nureddin is heard, softly singing in his sleep the refrain of Fatima's song: "O dearest, sweetest palm-tree, thou my love's shelter" *etc.*

Ali. Ah! how the poor young man's in love!

Loud knocking at the gate. Fatima springs up.

Ali. Who's there?

Manfred's voice (without). Entry for Manfred!

Ali. Manfred! Manfred!

Fatima (exultantly shouting down the street). The Kaiser's son is here! Luceria, up! Your gates throw open!

From all sides the populace pours in, crying: "Up! Up! The gate!"

Ali. Open there; the key!

All. The key! Haste to Burello!

Fatima. Nay, burst the door!

All. Burst the door!

The door is swiftly broken in with pikes and hatchets. Manfred and Lancia, with mounted followers, dash through the gate.

Folk. Hail Manfred! Hail the Kaiser's son! Allah! Allah give thee greatness!

Burello (entering in alarm, with soldiers).
This uproar! Ha! What must I see?
Manfred in Luceria! Treason! Treason!

Ali and Chorus. The traitor thou! Down on thy knees!

Bur. Manfred, account for this!

Manf. I—account? In the realm of my father!

All. Burello, down in the dust!
To thy knees before the Kaiser's son!

Burello. Never!

(He is forced to his knees.)

Manf. How now, Burello? Must Arabia's sons compel thee to such homage?

Know then! From this day forth Apulia's realm belongs

to its king's house again. I take possession, and will govern it by right and might.

Say! Is my race so hateful to thee? Who was it, raised thee to so high estate? Speak! Hast thou so forgot the wealth of boons wherewith my father Friedrich heaped thee? See if I am not worthy to be called his son; the lenience of his grace shall be my mentor: Burello, rise! The lands thou claimedst, they are thine; and more, as *Count of A.* — -- be my friend!

(Burello rises in confusion, and does homage to Manfred.)

The Chorus (lauds Manfred's indulgence).

Who worthier to be our Kaiser? *etc., etc.*

Manf. (espies the Saracen). Thou livest? Art no dream! Sublimest witch, now reachest me thy hand?

Fatima extends her hand to him; he kisses it passionately.

Ensemble.

Manf. To thee I owe it, that my star now shines anew, *etc.*

Fatima. See, how the Kaiser's star begins to shine, *etc.*

Nureddin's dawning jealousy: Burello's hidden thirst for vengeance. (Day breaks: the Muezzin calls to morning-prayer. The Saracens kneel down.)

Manfred. Up, my brothers! Like lightning let us end the troubles of this land! To arms! Apulia is ours! Through your fidelity I conquer.

Enthusiastic final chorus.

FOURTH ACT.

Palace at Capua, as in act i.

Burello (alone).

He's victor, then! Like a rushing flood his fortune has o'erwhelmed Apulia. No stand against him! Manfred is lord. Yet is it so unheard a thing, that a native should rule in fair Italy? Was the sweet fragrance of our valleys merely meant to fawn on rude barbarians from the North? Were our women clothed with grace but to sate the appetite of these invaders? Our women — — Ha! Manfred, that it is which gives me strength thy death to compass. My own wife's shame is known to me.

Betrayed am I! With honours, wealth and favour has he heaped me. To think that I myself must help him to his braggart fame! This soaring stem of Hohenstaufen, with branches erst spread dominant o'er all the world, too suddenly it seemed to rot. Captivity; a hurtling death! Konradin, a mere child, the only scion beyond the Alps,—what stock had we to take of him, in times when e'en a man like Friedrich must go under?—And yet —this Manfred, whom we plunged so deep in shame that none still deemed him worth reviling,—this Manfred is to be our King? No, no! And by what right? How dare he bid for it, while Konradin still lives? That child shall be our rescue—that child be King—and that means, we shall have no ruler. I but await the trusty friends I sent by stealth to Swabia, to offer my allegiance to the child Konradin.

Feretrio (enters). Art thou alone?

Bur. Feretrio! Back already? Whence comest thou?

Fer. I had no need to cross the Alps; at Sienna, from the Legate, I heard the hidden news that sets the Church a-trembling: "Konradin is dead!"

Bur. Hold to! What sayest thou?

Fer. 'Tis true, but to this day the greatest secret. Thou easily mayst guess how well 'tis guarded.

Bur. Ha! That man's luck!
Quick! But a few days more the news keep secret; the time we'll use for Manfred's fall. Haste! meet me in my house anon!

Exit Feretrio.—After a little deliberation, Burello is about to depart on the other side. Fatima has overheard the preceding scene; she calls to Burello:

Fatima. Burello, look to thy head!
Thou know'st the penalty for treason.

Bur. (half stunned by her presence). My evil spirit!
'Twas she who sang him the insidious song
That made him conqueror of a kingdom.—
I know thee—in Luceria I saw thee—
Wanton, best hold thyself in heed!
Woe's thee, if thou shalt cross my path anew!
(Goes off, raging.)

Fatima. Scoundrel, depart! Allah hath granted me to sound thy baseness. Mine eye keeps watch and ward o'er Manfred. Now clearly do I see—my goal is near—soon may I be once more a woman.

Manfred (enters). Can I believe my fortune? At last! At last alone I meet thee. Thou wilt not, shalt not flee away!

Fatima. Back, Manfred! Never mayst thou hold me.

Manf. O stay, thou marvel! For thy approach I thirst, for thy dear presence! Ever before mine eyes art thou; in flight, in bloody combat, where death's blast was hottest on me, there sped thy lofty vision to my side,—as God's own angel hast thou scared away each peril. Now here, now there, thy glance inflamed me, and kindled wondrous courage in my breast. But ah! I cannot clasp thee to me! Extend my hand—and thou hast vanish'd:—yet sworn have I that I must hold thee, press thee to this heart, e'en tho' I bid farewell to happiness for aye!

Fatima. Insensate, back! Thy fortune am I while I flee thee; but horror and despair to thee, shouldst thou e'er hold me.—Manfred be King!

Manf. Arch-temptress, what dost dare conjure me? O sweet one, hear me! This kingdom I have conquer'd through the wonder-strength thou breath'dst into me, I give it to my father's heir. Might, honour, crowns can I forgo, not thee! I ask no longer, who thou art,—this one thing only do I crave—be no more marvel,—to me be woman! With thee I'll fare where'er thou wilt: thither, to that far land whereof thou sang'st, where yet my father liveth.

Fatima (aside). Allah! Have pity on me!

Manfred has fallen at Fatima's feet. Burello and Nureddin appear at the back.

Burello. Thy eye on her! I've said enough.

Nureddin. Horrible!

Fatima (aloud to Manfred). Unworthy one! Am I to call thee last of all the Hohenstaufen? Betrayer of thy name, thine honour! Look hence, to what awaits thee still! Thou'st scarce begun; wouldst end already?

Son of Kaiser Friedrich! Thine be the realm of Christendom; and let a humble Saracen depart for home in peace!

Manf. I'll not release thee.

Fatima. Who shall prevent my following my husband?

Manf. Thy husband?

Fatima. The truest of thy soldiers, Nureddin, I wed this day.

Manf. Distraction! Nureddin——

Fatima. The loved of my youth, he won me through a thousand hardships borne for me.

Nureddin (beside himself, falls at Fatima's feet). Fatima! Angel of Paradise!

Burello (advancing slowly). And yet thou art betrayed!

Quartet; Ensemble.

Fatima.

O Nureddin, thou darling of my soul! The time of trial's past for thee. Thine am I now—a woman may I be to thee, tender and full of love as thy dear heart could wish.—

Nureddin.

O how my soul forgets all toils I've borne for thee! As breaks the sun through leaden clouds, thy lealty cleaves my heart, and thousand tears of joy and penitence I weep to thee.

Manfred.

Hence, at one breath, the fairest blossom of my soul!

A veil of mystery enshrouds my head: through it am I to look on fortune,—and I, unhappy, cannot seize it!

Burello.

Ha! work of vengeance, steal thou back into my soul! Thro' mask of hypocrites I look, where treason lies in ambush; treason, as — — — — wrought: treason, as I have ne'er avenged!

Fatima (makes a deep obeisance to Manfred, with Nureddin). Once more shall I see thee, to greet thee King!

(Both depart.)

Manfred has turned away and sunk upon a couch, as if stupefied. Burello watches him, and clutches at a dagger, when the cry is heard from the terrace leading to the garden:

"Hail Manfred!"

Lancia enters, with a numerous gathering of Counts and Lords.

All. Hail to thee, glorious scion of the proudest Kaiser-house!
We greet thee, daring victor, hero of our age!
Hail, Manfred, hail!

Lancia. Manfred, hear me, thro' mouth of whom Apulia speaks to thee! This fair dominion thy great father raised to be the jewel of the world, it lay of late in ruins and a prey to scandalous corruption: by strength and courage hast thou conquered it apace, and lifted it to union; wherefore the princes of this land have joined their vows to honour none save him they hold for worthy. So may it please thee to assume the crown we proffer thee!

All. Hail Manfred, our King!

Burello. The madmen! I foresaw it!

Manf. Away with your crown! 'Tis none of mine; I'll not be King!

Lan. Say, what means this? Manfred, compose thyself!

Manf. (aside). Ah! durst I tell you *what* has robbed my heart of pride! (Aloud.) Ye nobles, think on what ye do! If fortune has so amply favour'd my emprise, 'twas but to save the realm for him to whom by right divine it falleth.

Feretrio. Ye princes, truth he speaks. To whom belongs the crown indeed, save Konradin, King Konrad's son?

Some Nobles. A child shall never be our King.

Bur. For thy own good I warn thee, Manfred: be deaf to their entreaties,—for evil must it bring to thee when comes the lawful heir!

Lan. Who here is heir? Look thou, Burello, how poor is now thy friendship! The Hohenstaufen house had lost this land; Konradin's rights had lapsed long since: thus Manfred, conquering this realm, has no old right revived,—a new right has he won him!

All. Hail our King Manfred!

Manf. Not so! A truce to words! King will I never be. The fortune that so boldly becks, I'll none of it.—

Arabian wedding-music is heard,—from the garden ascends a procession, with Fatima and Nureddin as bride and bridegroom.

Lan. The Saracen!—Bid her approach! She, who so oft has turned the scale, shall now determine.

The procession reaches the front of the stage; Nureddin and Fatima prostrate themselves before Manfred.

Manf. Heavens! How can I bear it?

Fatima (rising). Hail, Manfred! Plighted was my troth to give my hand as wife to this the faithfulest of lovers, so soon as I durst greet thee King.

Behold me wedded!

And Manfred, thou—art King.

Manf. Never! If thou must greet this kingdom's King, so hie to Germany; for there lives Konradin.

Fatima. 'Tis false, and wear the crown thou must, for rightly it belongs to thee now Konradin is dead.

(Great sensation.)

All. Is't possible? Who brought the news? Who is thy witness?

Fatima. From Germany the Legate had the tidings at Sienna, as those two there can witness.

Lancia. Burello? Speak! Feretrio?

All. Traitors, betrayers!

Hail Manfred, King of fair Apulia!

Manfred. It must be, then! Who longer could withstand the fate she holds within her hands?—King will I be.

Ensemble. Cheers and greetings of the populace and nobles, alternating with the wedding-music for the Saracen:

To the coronation! The coronation!

The curtain falls.

FIFTH ACT.

The orchestra plays a pompous prelude, gradually diminishing in force; as the curtain rises, this is continued softly by a band behind the scene, till it dies away in the distance.

The stage represents the harbour and gulf of Naples: among the ships is a Saracen vessel, under sail for departure.

Fatima (ascending from the harbour).

Thro' all the streets the pageant flaunts:
To coronation fares the King:
All cheer the Kaiser's son.
O Manfred, happy may thou be!
The words I planted in thy breast this night,
When like a vision I appeared to thee,
To fruit may thou fulfil them:
Ne'er cease from thy emprise; thine be the realm of Christendom!
See, blithely waves the flag—
Sweet west-winds breathe around my head:
They bear me to my home,

Whose voice I hear imploring me with yearning, piercing tones: so will I hence, to give the morning back its truest son.

O Nureddin! How shall I e'er repay thy faith?
The flower of thy life to me thou'st sacrificed—

O let me make thee happy;
Myself, my life, to thee I offer — —
For happiness I now abandon—
I feel,—I feel it; ne'er can I be happy.
Once prophetess—henceforth I am thy wife,—
Thy wife—to fade—and wither—for thy weal.

Nureddin comes slowly from the harbour,—he is pale, and lost in dreams.

Nureddin. And if she yet has cheated me?

Fatima. Nureddin, husband! See, our fortune smiles! Yet thou wouldst seem to trust it not? Downcast and sad thou creep'st thy way?

Nur. Canst blame me, if the strength has left my sinews?—To whom have I e'er offered it; for whom has my heart grown sere with longing?—O Fatima, the labour of these years was great!

Fatima. On my breast shalt thou find new life; no toil shall weary thee henceforward; thy day's-work be but love! There 'neath the palm-tree will we lie, to breathe the sweetest scent of blossoms; my songs shall lull thee; the Prophet will I pray to let thee taste the joys of Paradise on earth.

Nur. O sorceress, how sweet thy voice!
When shall we, then, be going?

Fatima. Shipp'd are our goods, and all the treasures richly shed upon us here. Wait but an instant; I'd visit Ali once again: he will not fare with us, for he's contented with this land of evening. So let him stay and send us constant tidings of the weal of Manfred! Soon I return.—

(Goes off.)

Nureddin (brooding). "The weal of Manfred."—Manfred? Manfred!

Cloaked in an inconspicuous mantle, Burello has stood for some time at a street-corner, watching Nureddin. He now accosts him.

Bur. Nureddin, none ever was betrayed as thou.

Nur. (breaking from his reverie with fearful passion). Appalling be my vengeance!

Bur. How is't I find thee so resolved? But yesterday thou waivedst my warning!

Nur. (suddenly calming himself). Who'rt thou, who takest such an interest in me?

Burello. A dupe like thee!

Yet, I deny it not, so great is not this wanton Manfred's crime 'gainst me, as 'gainst thyself:—I never was his friend, and if he brought me to disgrace, I e'er have paid it him with hatred. But thou, I know thee. Thou wast the trustiest that clove to Manfred; the marrow of thy bones hast thou consumed for years to serve him, to protect him,—make him great and glorious—to be the gallant of thy wife.

Nur. The gallant of—my wife!

Burello. Wouldst have the proofs?

Nur. Defend me, Prophet! Proofs?

Bur. Last night—

Nur. Last night—ha! yes, last night—

Bur. Thou tastedst the delights of love?

Nur. Atrocious!—Ha! my memory returns;—she handed me the draught—and I sank down—bemused—unconscious.

Then dreamt I of unholy-sweet delight—at morning, when I woke, she stood before me in the costliest robes, —she smiled—and I——Ha! cursed witch, thou'dst poisoned me!

Bur. With Manfred was she in the night——Not I alone—the guard beheld her.—

Nur. (almost raving). Manfred! Fatima! Manfred!

Blood! Blood! Death! Havoc!

From the distance one hears the sound of bells and the chant:

Salvum fac regem!

Bur. Avenge thyself! His train draws near—this way 'tis coming; advance to him—the King—step up—and hand this scroll to him—but *thou* mayst dare to front him,—for thou art e'en his faithfulest,—shew him this scroll,—and—

Nur. This steel; 'tis worthy of the best believer! Manfred, the price shalt pay me!

(Is about to rush off.)

Fatima appears ; Nureddin falls back, on seeing her.

Fatima. Nureddin, whither away?

Nur. Allah, stand by me!

Fatima. Thy breast heaves wildly—a fearsome fire burns in thine eye,—what wouldst thou?

Ensemble.

Burello.

Ha! my ill star begot this woman! What witchcraft sets she 'gainst my vengeance?

Nureddin.

Her eyes I dare not gaze upon, the shameless wretch who taints my heart: torments of death convulse my breast!

Fatima.

What has befallen? Blackest omens, nameless agony, oppress my soul! The blood congeals within my heart.

Bur. Up, Nureddin! The scroll thou holdest. So laggard art thou in delivering it?

Fatima. Caitiff! I find thee at his side? Now know I, mischief is unchained. Nureddin, what plott'st thou with this varlet?

Nur. My rage! My rage! Allah, forbid it to devour me! Give me but strength to bear to end my vengeance!

Fatima. God's mercy! Ah, most dreadful woe approaches! Nureddin, raise thine eyes, to mine!

Nur. Accursed! Shew the look that sucked the blood from out my veins! Flames dart around me, flames wherewith thou'st seared thy heart. Begone she-devil, sorceress!

Fatima. Madman, hold peace!—Burello, answer!

Bur. Wanton, begone! Dare not to thwart his vengeance!

Nur. Manfred! Manfred!

The music of the coronation-train returning from the cathedral is heard still closer.

Fatima. O horror! All grows clear to me. Nureddin, stay! A miscreant has duped thee. Thou poor betrayed one!

Nur. How so?

Bur. God's truth, betrayed indeed!

Fatima. Hear me! One moment rule thy senses!

Nur. They're poisoned!—Leave me, shameless one!

Bur. Away, away!

Fatima. Stay, stay! My father's spirit, look thou down!—

They struggle. The procession has already reached the stage.—Nureddin brandishes his poniard, about to spring. Burello holds Fatima back; with furious violence she tears herself loose, and seizes Nureddin. In terrible anguish she cries to the guard:

Fatima. Seize him! The King's in danger!

Guards surround the group.

Nureddin. Ha! Traitress!

(Plunges the dagger into Fatima's breast.)

Burello (in utmost alarm, shouts to the crowd). Down with the traitor!

(Strikes Nureddin, who falls down speechless.)

Manfred now appears in the train, which halts at once. He steps forward, and horror-struck regards the group of dying.

Fatima (propping herself against Nureddin). Manfred, behold the trustiest who ever served thee!—

Manfred. Almighty! What has happened?—

Fatima. Beware this lordling; he plots against thy life.

The guards secure Burello.

Fatima. Be happy, Manfred! Pass to happiness across our lifeless bodies—be Kaiser of all Christendom, and think on thy great father!—

Manf. (in unbridled grief). Who art thou?
At last, tell me at last, who art thou?

The orchestra plays soft snatches from the refrain of the ballad in act i.

Fatima (with breaking voice). Friedrich—Zelima—
Manfred—my brother—
The Kaiser's daughter—
I—O my Nureddin!

(Sinks down on Nureddin's body, and dies.)

Manfred (after a violent crisis). And I am King!—

Burello (grimly holding up the scroll which he had given Nureddin). Usurper, Konradin still lives!

Lancia and the Nobles (with sudden resolution)
And still this is our King!

Manfred. From henceforth dead to happiness!

Trumpets sound; the curtain falls.

POSTHUMOUS.

II.

PROSE SKETCH FOR

"Das Liebesmahl der Apostel."

(1843.)

The accompanying prose-sketch of Das Liebesmahl der Apostel *has a singular little history of its own. It is not included in the volume of "Nachgelassene Schriften und Dichtungen von Richard Wagner," published in 1895 (a reprint of the other posthumous publications, which had appeared at various dates since 1883), as its original text was not accessible until the end of 1898, though the manuscript, according to Glasenapp, had made a fugitive appearance at an auction in December 1886. Finally, after having vanished from sight for so long, it was discovered in 1898 at the Royal Library in Berlin, and a copy taken for the* Bayreuther Blätter, *in which journal it was printed for the first time in the number for January of the current year, 1899.*

This prose-sketch, dated "April 21, 1843," occupies one side of a folio sheet of paper, and a small part of the reverse side; the remainder of that reverse side is devoted to the draft of a letter to von Lüttichau, Intendant of the Dresden Court-theatre, concerning certain disputes with Lipinski, the 'first violin.' Together with this folio sheet, however, a quarto sheet of Wagner's manuscript was also discovered at the Berlin Library. That quarto sheet contains the end of the draft letter to von Lüttichau (a fair copy whereof was actually despatched on April 27, 1843), and in addition a brief synopsis of the Liebesmahl—*under its provisional title, "Das Gastmahl der Apostel." Nor is that all: on the reverse side of the quarto sheet occurs a draft report (unused) on a performance of Mendelssohn's* Saint Paul *at Dresden just two months after Wagner had been installed as Kapellmeister to the Saxon Court.*

Omitting the letter to von Lüttichau—which belongs more properly to a biography of the master, than to a collection of his literary works—I reproduce these interesting documents in their apparent order of succession, with the reminder that all three were written in the middle fortnight of April 1843, and the remark that the prose-sketch of "Das Liebesmahl der Apostel" differs in but a few words and rhythms from the finished text of the Liebesmahl *as set to music and performed in the Dresden Frauenkirche on July 7, 1843.*

TRANSLATOR'S NOTE.

LAST Palm - Sunday's concert was signally brilliant, and left a deep impression on its particularly numerous audience. Mendelssohn-Bartholdy had been invited to conduct his oratorio Paulus, and through his readiness in accepting the invitation he afforded us a pleasure of unwonted kind, namely the opportunity of hearing a classical work reproduced under the personal direction of its author. Two public performances, which must be described as thoroughly successful, had already made us acquainted with this masterwork; yet it seemed as if we had not arrived at a right understanding until the immediate personal superintendence of the master filled every one of the executants with a special fervour, inspiring them to such a degree that the merit of the performance almost reached the level of the work itself. The very powerful chorus and orchestra, together with the solo-singers, Wüst, Tichatschek, Dettmer etc., covered themselves with glory in the true sense of the word, and thus shewed us in all perfection a work which is a witness to the highest bloom of art, and fills us with just pride that it should have been fashioned in the age wherein we live. The only thing to be regretted, is that such an oratorio cannot be wholly grafted on our Protestant church-service, as that would be the only way for its true meaning to pass into the hearts of all believers; whereas without this basis, and especially in the concert-room, it comes to us more or less as a mere artwork of serious order, and its real religious efficacy can by no means be so salient as would be the case under similar conditions to those under which Sebastian Bach once gave his oratorios to the congregation. However, even in the concert-room the effect is moving and uplifting.—The Symphony that followed the oratorio (Beethoven's No. 8, in F) was very well performed by the large body of executants; which is the more noticeable, as the execution of this particular symphony by a very numerous orchestra, and under the disadvantages which the building offers to the latter's proper concentration, may be termed a difficult matter. Kapellmeister Reissiger conducted it.

The Guest-meal of the Apostles.

1. Assembling. Mood of dejection.
2. Bad tidings. Threatenings.
3. Prayer.
4. Inspiration. Grand communion of souls and goods.*

Chorus of Disciples.

Supper-chorale in between [written on the margin].

Be greeted, Brethren, in the name of the Lord, who hath gathered us together for the meal that we remember him. Ye who hunger, ye who thirst, come hither; to strengthen you *he* offered up his flesh and blood. Why should we quail and languish, when heavenly nurture such refresheth us?

We are oppressed, the hatred of the mighty threateneth. Heavy with storm, a leaden cloud is low'ring o'er us. We who to-day have gathered here, who knoweth where to-morrow we shall pine in mournful parting? Not long more can we shun the violence of crafty men.

O pluck up heart! See, is the number of the faithful and believers not increasing daily?

* The *Bayr. Bl.* prints this last word as "Guten," i.e. "the good"; but I feel convinced that it should be "Güter"—see the last verse but one in the longer sketch.—Tr.

The more of us, the more we rouse the hatred of the envious! If unity can make us strong, so can it be our ruin.

And should we part?—go wanting of the solace, after each day's toil, to be at Supper but one heart, one soul?

Truly the times press hard on us! Let each man bear the Saviour in his heart; then, what though scattered, shall we be *one* flock.

Apostles. Our greetings to you, loved Brethren! Are ye assembled in the name of Jesus Christ?

[*Disciples.*] We are assembled in the name of Jesus Christ!—For you have we tarried in fear and trembling.

[*Apostles.*] Blessed be all assembled in the name of Jesus Christ!

Ye men, dear Brothers, be ye one in heart and faith, for persecution lifteth up its head; at hand are all the sufferings ye must bear for sake of his high name.

[*Disciples.*] Say, what new danger hath befallen you?

[*Apostles.*] As we were teaching in the Temple, and working miracles through belief in the Lord, we woke the envy of our foes—as ne'er before. When we had sore confounded them, and charged them with the evil deed they wrought on Mary's son—their wrath flamed up, and with fierce threats they bade us never more to teach or even converse in the name of Jesus of Nazareth, under penalty of death. But now are we released, to publish this to all of you.

Prayer.—Almighty Father, Thou who madest all, etc.! Why rise the mighty of this earth against thy heavenly Word? Thou promisedst to shield us from their threatenings; now look Thou down upon the threats wherewith they terrify Thy people! Send us thy holy Spirit, for that we may preach Thy word with gladness.

Voices from above. Be comforted, for I am near you and my Spirit is with you. Go hence and joyfully proclaim the Word that never to eternity shall pass away.—

Disciples. What rushing filleth all the air! What sounds! What voices! And stirreth not the very ground whereon we stand?—Be greeted by us, Spirit of the Lord; thy breath we feel around our heads, and mightily thou fillest all our souls.

Apostles. Ye of faint heart, give ear to what the Spirit biddeth us proclaim! Let men accuse you, with the Word shall ye vanquish them. Ye who but now would part in cowardice, go scatter ye to take each man his path with heart of victory! Is then Jerusalem the world? Look round you! Lo the peoples above measure who await the tidings of the Word! Lo the proud mistress of the world! Lo Rome! There shall the Word have power to prevail throughout the world!—Unite where'er ye meet; in common be your goods! Be glad and joyful, and teach to all the world the Saviour's wonder-works!—

Chorus of Disciples and Apostles.—Who taught to us the Word, the acceptable, now giveth us the courage joyfully and of good cheer to publish it to all the world. Ready are we to journey forth to the whole world, to brave all want and ignominy: to every nation will we preach, that so the praises of the Lord may sound in every tongue; thus willeth God, who offered up his Son for us, who sent to us his holy Spirit! For to him is the power and the glory for ever and ever.—

21st April 1843.

POSTHUMOUS.

III.

"Jesus of Nazareth."

With regard to "Jesus von Nazareth: ein dichterischer Entwurf"—"a poetic draft"—we read in the "Communication to my Friends" (Vol. I. pp. 378-80) that it followed the completion of the poem of "Siegfried's Death," i.e. was written at some date between November 1848 and the early part of 1849—in all probability before Christmas of that winter. The MS. itself, I am informed, bears no date of origin; my authority tells me that it is all contained in one note-book in the order in which it has been printed,—notwithstanding which fact I should be inclined, judging from the phraseology of section II. taken in conjunction with the allusion to the sketch in Wagner's letter to Uhlig of Aug. 9, 1849, to place at least part of that section between "Art and the Revolution" and "The Art-work of the Future." In any case, it can never have been intended to adopt the whole of the voluminous material into a spoken drama.

The work was first published four years after Richard Wagner's death, namely in 1887, with a simple dedication by Herr Siegfried Wagner "to the memory of Heinrich von Stein."

In the matter of brackets (excepting the square ones) and the arrangement of the in-set type—which latter corresponds in this, as in the next group of writings, to marginal notes by the author—I have closely followed that posthumous publication.

TRANSLATOR'S NOTE.

I.

Act I. (Tiberias in Galilee.—A broad roofed space—like a large shed—quite open to the country at the back: at one side it leads to the interior of the house of the publican Levi (Matthew?). Night.—)

Judas Iscariot and *Barabbas* engage in conversation. *Barabbas* contemplates a rising in Judæa against the Roman yoke: the Roman military is unusually weak just now, success quite certain if the people can only be goaded to decisive insurrection: all Jerusalem is full of the Son of David, who has proclaimed himself in Galilee; in him men look for the Messiah. So Barabbas has come to learn for himself what may be expected of Jesus.

Judas informs him of Jesus' mode of life, his healing art, and the great following he has won among the people: he calls himself the Redeemer, but he (Judas) has not yet clearly ascertained how Jesus means to carry out his mission: he, too, heartily wishes that Jesus may seize the reins of the Folk, as King of Judæa freely and openly to bring about the rescue of the chosen people.—The publican Levi, having heard that Jesus is in the neighbourhood of Tiberias, has sent for him to save his little daughter at the point of death; Judas has been sent on before, to announce his coming.—*Judas* knocks at the door,—the *publican* comes forth, lamenting that "his daughter is even now dead."—Loud wailing is heard from the house: women bring out the 12-year maiden on a bier; neighbours assemble. As day breaks, Jesus appears with his dis-

(Barabbas is in league with Mary Magdalene.)

Apostles:
Simon } Bros.
Andrew }
Jacob } Bros.
John }
Philip.
Bartholomew.
Thomas.
Matthew (Levi).
James (son of Alph).
Lebbæus (Thaddæus).
Simon of Cana.
Judas (Iscariot).

Jesus' brothers: James and Joseph.

ciples, and meets the funeral: men call to him: "Master, thou comest too late; the child we now are burying." Jesus examines the child—: "Bury the dead, not the living: she sleepeth."—Awe and amazement: Jesus lays his hands on the child's temples, and then says: "Thy daughter is restored from serious illness: take her into the house, and tend her well." He follows them into the house.—Many people have assembled outside, for curiosity: the tidings spread that Jesus of Nazareth has arrived,—has awaked a corpse;—the disciples withstand the tumult,—many hasten forth to spread the news in the city.—Jesus returns from the house,—the Publican clutches at his garment, and, sobbing and beside himself, falls down at his feet: "Lord, how have I deserved thy grace? My child liveth; thou hast wakened it from death." *Jesus*: "What lived, I have preserved to life: open thou thine heart, that *thee* I may awake from death!" *The Publican*: "What shall I do, Lord, to please thee?" *Jesus*: "Hear my word, and follow it."—The Publican begs Jesus to remain, together with his disciples, and breakfast in his house: Jesus accepts. His disciples acquaint him,—he admonishes them.

A Pharisee enters: he upbraids Jesus for his familiar intercourse with publicans and sinners. Rebuke concerning fasts: Ye may not make the children of the bridechamber to fast, while the bridegroom is with them. But the days will come, when the bridegroom shall be taken away from them, and then shall they fast. (The bridegroom: *life*.) (Upon the Sabbath and the Law.)

(This may take place as result of a rising against Herod, a premature attempt to expel the Greeks.—Mary had incurred the anger of all her compatriots by her commerce

Barabbas catechises Jesus. (Cæsar's-pence.) Undeception of Barabbas. Uproar in the street: an adulteress is dragged on, to be stoned: others ask for her to be set before Jesus: the Pharisee decides on the latter course, to prove Jesus. Mary Magdalene is brought in, the people thronging after her; in wild confusion they tell of the arrogant ways and wickedness of Mary, who had lived in sinful relationship with one of the magnates of Herod's court, to the scandal of the Jews her fellow-countrymen.—(Acquittal: all retire ashamed.—Jesus alone with Mary.—)—(John viii.)

with the Syrian Greeks.)

The meal is prepared:—the Disciples, relatives of the Publican, and persons from the Folk, partake; *Jesus* expounds his doctrine of Love. Beatific impression on all. The Folk crowds the open space and streets to their full. Jesus is informed that his mother and his brothers stand without and cannot reach him; will he send the people away? *Jesus.* "This is my mother, these are my brethren."—

Act II. The Lake of Gennesaret: fishermen's huts lead down to it. Daybreak. *Jesus* sleeping under a tree: *Mary* of Magdala, kneeling at his feet and kissing the hem of his garment, expresses her deep contrition and venerating love for her redeemer.—*Mary* the Mother approaches: the Magdalene turns away in alarm, and throws herself at the feet of the Mother, who questions her: the Magdalene's confession: she has sold all her goods, and given the proceeds to Judas Iscariot, the keeper of the bag for Jesus's community: she implores the Mother to intercede with her son, for she craves to serve the commune as its humblest maid-servant. Mary consoles and dismisses her.

Jesus wakes, and raises himself to a sitting posture beneath the tree. Converse with his mother: she recognises his calling, and submits herself to him: only her anxiety about his life she cannot quite suppress. We learn that Jesus had quickly left Tiberias, as the people wished to make him King. *Jesus* upon his youth, his baptism by John, his sojourn in the wilderness; there did his task grow clear to him, he embraced it not as David's scion, but as son of God. His commencement as physician in Galilee; his goal.—The Mother bows before him, full of humbleness and love. About the Magdalene; Jesus on his state of celibacy. — Jesus' *brothers*—sons of Joseph the carpenter—arrive. They are jealous of Jesus, to whom their mother gives all her love. They challenge him to testify aloud and in Jerusalem, what is his mission, and not to flee before the Folk, who surely would but meet his wishes. Jesus' grief at their misapprehension of his teachings. "Mother, why barest thou these?" etc. (his birth).—

Disciples approach from the fishermen's huts: John leads his aged father to Jesus. Simon (Peter) brings news of the assembling Folk. Jesus to his disciples, on his purpose and impending sacrificial death: they do not understand him, and hope that he will solemnly assume the office of Messiah in Jerusalem. Dispute about precedence. Judas urges Jesus to haste: he talks of Barabbas, who, abandoning Jesus, has hurried to Jerusalem to profit by the favouring moment of the Romans' weakness.—Fresh messengers report the approach of a countless multitude that fain would make him King: *Jesus* bids prepare a boat for himself and the Disciples, to escape the people on the road to Jerusalem. A young man of rank arrives on a mule, with servants: he offers himself to Jesus: the latter interrogates him: the young man boasts of his strict observance of the laws. At the request to sell his whole possessions, and give the money to the commune,—he withdraws ashamed, and mournfully departs with mule and servants. *Judas*: "Lord, bethink thee, he is very rich!" *Jesus*: "Verily I say unto you" etc.; concerning the rich. — Streams of people pour in: — Jesus moves towards the boat, commits the women to the older of the disciples, and embarks with his chosen. While they are hoisting sail, the multitude increases: all cry to Jesus, imploring him to stay: they try to hold the boat fast, but Simon wards them off. Then Jesus bids furl the sails again: his deepest soul is grieved at sight of the unhappy Folk, and he will not leave it unconsoled. He commands the people to dispose themselves upon the shore and listen to him quietly. (Mary Magdalene, Mary the Mother, and other women, distribute bread and wine to the multitude.)

Jesus, standing on board, preaches to the Folk. Comfort and blessing: of the Kingdom of Heaven in Man; his being sent to them as physician, as teacher: his ordinances for his community. On tribulation: the coming strifes: "I am not come" etc. He foreshadows his redeeming death and second advent for the liberating of mankind.—Shouts of the deeply-moved people. At Jesus' order the boat is thrust off.—Farewell. The Folk disperses, to follow him to Jerusalem.

Act III. *Jerusalem*: hall in the House of Judgment.—*Pilate* and *Caiaphas*, followed by rulers and pharisees, appear from a vestibule.—A council has been sitting.—A rebellion instigated by Barabbas has just been quelled with little pains: the impetuous patriot had counted on the general support of the populace, but, filled with the fame of Jesus (as the true Messiah who shall lead the Jews to world-dominion), it has left him in the lurch: so that Barabbas' handful of followers has easily been scattered by the slender Roman forces, he himself been taken prisoner and condemned. *Pilate* is well acquainted with the mutinous temper of the Jewish people: he has written to Egypt and Syria for more troops; until their arrival he sees himself reduced to a skilful manipulation of party-discord to prevent a general rising, against which he has not sufficient strength. He mistrusts Herod, and therefore is alarmed at the news of popular movements in Galilee, which he suspects Herod of having instigated or encouraged in opposition to the Romans. He warns Caiaphas to be watchful, and threatens him with Cæsar's anger: he represents to him how tranquilly the Jews might live under Cæsar, in full possession of their constitution, their faith and usages, whereas the Greek princes at their time of power had grievously molested them and forced them to adopt their customs, and so forth.—He departs with his Roman retinue. *Caiaphas* and the Elders express their fears of fresh disquiet: the whole populace had poured out of the city, to meet the Nazarene. To them this seems the most dangerous demagogue, according to accounts received; the Pharisee from Tiberias bears testimony to his subversive doctrines;—but the people cherish the firm belief that he is the Messiah. His Galilean birth is scoffed at: yet he is said to descend from David, and (as the Scriptures demand) to have been born in Bethlehem. Some hesitate whether to side with them, and so on. *Caiaphas* reproves them: What have they in common with the mob? Do they lack for anything? Have not their laws been left inviolate by the Romans? Have they not the people in the hollow of their hands, through these laws? So long as the Temple and the Law shall stand, *they themselves* are masters of this people, and the tribute to Cæsar they may well put up with, since it is levied on the populace and does not weigh on them. To what purpose, then, a change that could offer us no whit of profit?—Cheers of the Folk without.—Reports of Jesus' entry through the gate.—*Caiaphas*: Let us be on our guard, and compass his ruin, lest he corrupt the people. *The Pharisee* from Tiberias: By open force they would effect nothing against him, but he knows one of his disciples, Judas, who, he hopes, will be able to help them to Jesus.—Let us waylay him, and shew the folk his folly.—(Exeunt.)

Square before the *Grand Steps of the Temple.* The Folk in liveliest motion to and fro. The broad main-stairway and forecourt of the Temple are beset with sellers of all kinds, as at a market.—The people ask and answer of the coming of Jesus, the Messiah, the Son of David, the King of the Jews: music and cheering, nearer and nearer. The Folk spreads carpets and raiment, strews flowers, and so forth.—Jesus' entry: he rides on an ass, his disciples following next: people with palms, dancing girls etc. Jesus dismounts before the steps: he pauses at sight of the market on the stairs and in the portico: denunciation of the profaners of the temple; he tears the bridle from the mule, and drives the sellers from the stairs with stripes, while the others escape from the hall down the side-steps. The Folk acclaims his stern authority.—Pharisees and

Elders approach the stair whereon Jesus stands facing the Folk. "Who is he?"—*Folk*: "Jesus, the anointed of the Lord, the King" etc. They indignantly accost Jesus: "Who hath given him authority here?" etc. Jesus thunders against the Pharisees and the Law, against oppression and injustice.—Agitation of the Pharisees against him, derision: "Give us signs!" (etc.). The Folk begs Jesus to openly proclaim himself Messiah,—Judas urges him secretly.—*Jesus* announces his true mission, his quality as son of God, the redemption of all peoples of the earth through him, not of the Jews alone: his kingdom (as no earthly sovereignty), his sacrifice, his glorification; prophecy (Revel. cap. 18) of the end of Jerusalem and its Temple.—The horrified Folk, harangued and goaded by the Pharisees, falls into the utmost confusion. In the tumult Jesus has vanished, the Disciples (themselves alarmed) seek to calm the Folk; the Pharisees: "You, too, we know!" As daylight wanes, the people gradually disperse in the greatest bewilderment:—the Pharisee from Tiberias leads Judas aside, and engages to meet him that night.—(Mary Magdalene has kept eye and ear on Judas.) Darkness deepening, the square grows emptier and emptier: the Disciples, highly disturbed in mind, go one by one in search of Jesus:—Mary Magdalene informs them that he cannot be far, for she has seen him pass into the temple. They hasten up the steps,—Jesus comes out of the temple and regards the empty square: "Would ye, too, leave me?"—*Peter*: "Lord, we will ne'er forsake thee!" etc. "Where wilt thou that we take the evening meal?"—*Magdalene*: "Lord, grant me to conduct you; a quiet chamber have I found for you."—They follow her.

(The Pharisees wish to arrest Jesus in the Temple; one [? a Priest] restrains them, for the mob cannot be trusted yet: it is merely in doubt, which easily may pass again.)

Act IV.—A room with table prepared for supper.—Jesus has sat down at end of the table, and leant his head upon his hand, in thought. The Disciples stand on the other side in separate groups: they converse in tones of dire anxiety; Judas displays his vexation at Jesus' not having come forward with actual signs and proclaimed his plenary power: he is rebuked; he hopes that Jesus is simply deferring his manifestment of divinity for the hour of utmost peril.—*Magdalene* has timidly drawn near to Jesus, and whispers to him: "Lord, is it thy will, what Judas broodeth?" *Jesus* quietly waves her back with his hand. *Mary* [Magd.] turns aside, and weeps bitterly.—The Disciples, pursuing their talk, face round and look at Jesus. —Mary takes a costly phial from her bosom, approaches Jesus once more, pours its contents on his head, washes his feet, dries, and anoints them, amid sobs and tears.—*Judas*: "What rarest perfume?"—His reproaches of Mary: reprimand by Jesus, who thanks Mary and dismisses her. They sit down to supper: Jesus takes the middle of the table. He prepares the Disciples for the importance of this last meeting. John asks him anxiously and secretly, if danger threatens him?—Episode with Judas.—Judas leaves the table and the room.—Jesus: "Now am I glorified."—Final exposition of the doctrine of Love: of Faith, as the nourishing milk of his doctrine, and Knowledge as the bread of life. Distribution of the Supper. Jesus' one concern is that at least his disciples shall have learnt to understand him thoroughly: this is to happen through his sacrificial death, after which the Holy Ghost shall be sent to them.—(Gosp. John.) Announcement of the future and return.—Peter's boasting: (Jesus' warning against oaths!) Prophecy of Peter's denial of his master.—After supper is over, Jesus begs his disciples to follow him out of the city, to pass the night in open air. They follow him.—Mary enters by a side-door: she breaks into loud lamentation: yet she has understood Jesus and his sublime resolve: she calls herself blessed, to have served him.—Armed Servants of the High Priest, with Judas among them, troop in and ask for the Galilean: —they accuse Judas of having led them astray. Mary de-

("That I may be ever with you, I now must depart from you.")

nies all knowledge whither they have gone. (Judas and Mary—.) The Servants drive Judas forth, to lead them to Jesus or pay with his life: Judas promises to find him. The Magdalene is taken with them, for fear lest she warn Jesus.

The Garden of *Gethsemane* on the Mount of Olives: the brook Kidron flows through it, traversed by a foot-bridge. —Jesus arrives with the Disciples: he begs for solitude awhile,—would the disciples kindly stay behind, and watch against a surprise. He slowly passes over the bridge, and vanishes towards the rising ground at the back.—The Disciples sit down: melancholy, anxiety about their master, —whom (as they now have surely gathered) they soon must lose. Profound and general depression:—they gradually fall asleep.—Jesus comes slowly from the back: he regards the sleepers; inwardly touched, he pardons their weakness, for he hopes, he knows—soon strength and courage will be given them. Suddenly the light of a torch close by falls luridly on Jesus: *Judas* runs up to him: "Master, I long have sought thee," and kisses him: on his heels, the Armed Servants rush on: the Disciples wake in great alarm: Peter draws his sword, and strikes at the knave who is seizing Jesus. The Servants fall on the Disciples. Jesus: "Peter, put up thy sword!" To the armed men: "Are ye come out to take me? Here am I —let those go free!" The Disciples have fled in all directions; only Peter follows Jesus and the Servants who are leading him away, at a distance.

Act V. Square before the Palace of Pilate: the portico of the latter, to which some steps lead up, extends into the middle of the stage. (Night.)—Roman Soldiers encamped round a fire in the court: others guard the entrance to the interior of the palace. Men and women servants pass to and fro: Peter has sat him on the steps outside. He draws nearer, to listen, and asks permission to warm himself at the fire. The soldiers discuss the hardships of their service; so small a force, against a constantly uproarious mob!

Scarcely the rebellion of Barabbas quelled, than the Galilean caused fresh trouble:—however, they now had got them both. The ruck that had come with Jesus, too, would soon be captured: a pest on the lot of them! They should pay for all this drudgery by day and night! Peter asks after Jesus.—"He's inside there, on trial by the Prefect: Caiaphas and the Elders return anon, to hear the verdict." Comments on Jesus' offence; the Soldiers make merry over the whole Jewish nation, with its preposterous customs etc.; when the legions arrived, it was to be hoped a clean sweep would be made of the whole den. "Where are you from, then, friend?" Peter prevaricates. A maid-servant has moved to the fire: "This fellow also is one of the Galileans" etc. Peter denies etc.—As the cock crows, the door of the inner palace is opened, and Jesus brought out by two soldiers. Jesus calls "Peter" ("Simon")—he looks round, is horrified at sight of Jesus, covers his face, and plunges down the steps and out. The Soldiers ask Jesus,—whether this was one of his people?—Jesus is silent.—The Maid: "Of a surety; I knew him." Some of them wish to pursue him: others hold them back, laughing: "Let the coward be! So, these are the heroes you'd rout us Romans with?" They mock Jesus about his kingship:—he keeps silence. *Jesus*: "I say unto you, this man will be a rock" etc. Day has broken: groups of people assemble before the palace: Caiaphas, Priests and Pharisees enter the square, and halt before the steps of the portico: they beg the chief captain to acquaint Pilate with their arrival and summon him forth. "Why don't they go inside to him, themselves?" It is three days before the feast of the Passover, and in this sabbath-time their law forbids their entering the dwelling of an unbeliever. Smiles and astonishment of the Romans, who go within. The Pharisees ply the Folk, direct its sympathies to Barabbas, who at least was no deceiver, and prompt it to ask for him, not Jesus, since *one* man must be freed at Easter-tide. *Pilate* enters the hall by the palace-door: "What seek they at this early hour?" "Sentence on Jesus of Nazareth." Pilate declares that he can find no guilt in him: at first he had suspected him of conspiring with Herod to inflame the mob against the Romans; but he perceives that is not so. Emphatic protests by Caiaphas and the Pharisees: he had sought to elevate himself to Kingship of the Jews, and so forth. Their outcry becomes so violent, that Pilate consents to a fresh trial before all the people: he seats himself on the judgment-stone* against the portico, has Jesus brought before him, and proceeds to try him. Charges and accusations of Caiaphas etc.; questions of Pilate,—answers of Jesus.—When the latter avers that he is son of God,—Caiaphas rends his priestly garments, all the people shout: Crucify him!—Pilate receives a message from his wife, who tells him: He must in no wise condemn Jesus, for a woman (Mary Magdalene might bring the message herself.—Jesus' rebuke to the Magdal:—she craves his forgiveness.) had come in secret to her, and convinced her that this Jesus is an upright man.—Thereupon Pilate announces that he cannot, and will not, condemn Jesus! Moreover, he has to release a prisoner to-day, and chooses Jesus. All cry: Not this man, but Barabbas!—Increasing tumult, menaces: He is no friend to Cæsar! (Barabbas is brought out and delivered to the people. Rejoicing!) Growing solicitude of Pilate. ("Had but the Syrian legions come by now!") —When his attempt to delay the execution has also failed, as the Jews assert that no executions may take place during the next few days, according to their laws—he orders water to be brought, washes his hands before all the people, declares himself guiltless of the murder of an innocent man, and delivers Jesus to the soldiers for crucifixion. Cheers of the populace. He withdraws inside: Jesus is led after him.—John steps from out the crowd, with Jesus' Mother and Mary Magdalene: he seeks to persuade them to follow him thence:—Mary refuses, she means to accompany her son to his death. Jesus' brothers come up to Mary: they are deeply affected. Peter joins them: he is

* "Richtstein"—? execution-block, or stone for standard of measurement?—Tr.

in the most passionate and remorseful grief at his denial of Jesus: he accuses himself to the women, and wishes to expiate his heinous crime by declaring himself the confederate of Jesus and dying with him. Mary restrains him —fierce hordes drag on a beam of wood, for the cross: others bring a hangman, Simon of Cirene, to carry the cross. Jesus is brought into the portico again, wearing a purple mantle and a crown of thorns: Pilate follows him, and has him led forward to the terrace: mocking laughter of the people at Jesus' aspect. *Pilate*: "I here commit to you the man whose death ye sought: his offence I have written in this superscription, the which, in vindication of his death, shall now be fastened to the cross." All: "How runs the superscription?" *Pilate* reads: "This is the King of the Jews." *The Pharisees*: "Not so! He is not King of the Jews,—but gives himself for such. Write: He said I am King of the Jews." *Pilate*, in bitter wrath, "What I have written, I have written!" He turns swiftly round, gives the inscription to the Roman captain, and bids him start at once for the place of crucifixion (exit). The soldiers surround Jesus; he pauses on the steps. With the cry: "Off! Off to the crucifixion!" the crowd has rushed before: only the quieter of the people remain behind,—Jesus looks upon his mother: farewell to her. Peter flings himself at his feet, on the steps, and begs to die with him: "Thou followedst me hither, to deny me; now stay behind, to testify of me. Gather the scattered flock together, and bear them this last word!"—Address to the weeping women of the Folk (Galileans). Last word to the Disciples. Appointments to the Apostolic office.—He is led forth: the two Marys and John follow him. Peter covers his face and sinks down on the steps, overcome. As the square slowly empties, the Disciples gradually assemble, faint-heartedly and from different quarters: the utmost dismay is upon them,—they seek for Peter.—Judas, pale and haggard, staggers forward: he espies and recognises Peter, whom he asks after Jesus: What does he hope of him, now that the hour of utmost peril is at hand?

Peter divines the atrocious deed of Judas, and loads him with the most terrible denunciations. He teaches him to understand the sacrificial death of Jesus, now being suffered: this death is his apotheosis, and not the signs and marvels which Judas had expected of him.—Darkening of the heavens—thunder and lightning.—Judas' despair—the Disciples' loathing of him: Pharisees appear, seeking Judas:—he casts away the money he had had from them, and rushes out as if demented. Earthquake. Tales of horror—women and Folk bewailing:—Priests: The veil of the temple is rent in twain. Interpretation of this event by Peter. *Peter*: "Fear not the terrors of this storm, for we know they are a witness unto Love!"—John and the two Marys return from the crucifixion: "He hath fulfilled." —Peter feels himself inspired with the Holy Spirit: in high enthusiasm he proclaims the fulfilment of Jesus' promise: his words give strength and inspiration to all; he addresses the people,—whoever hears him, presses forward to demand baptism (reception into the community).—The end.—

(Perhaps also, Pilate could receive the news of the approach of his awaited legions. His despair at their having come too late, and threats against Jerusalem.)

II.

Jesus descended from the house of David, out of which the Redeemer of the Jewish nation was awaited: David's own lineage, however, went back to Adam, the immediate offspring of God, from whom spring all men. When Jesus was baptised by John, the people recognised him as the heir of David; but he went into the wilderness, and counselled with himself: Should he abide by his descent from David in the meaning of the Folk? If he succeeded, what else would he be than fellow to those rulers of the world who propped themselves upon the rich and heartless?—And yet, as scion of the oldest race, he might claim supreme dominion of the world, might end the execrable Roman rule of violence: should he succeed, would Man be helped if, merely with a different (perhaps a juster) title, force were exchanged for force? He went still deeper to the founder of his race, to Adam the child of God: might he not gain a superhuman strength, if he felt conscious of that origin from God who stood exalted over Nature? Looking down upon Jerusalem from the pinnacle of the temple, he felt tempted to work a miracle on the sanctuary devoted to his Ur-forefather. But wherein lies the power to work miracles, and whom shall they help, save Man? From Man must come the force to help him, and that is his knowledge of himself before God, who manifests himself in Man. So Jesus brushed aside the House of David: through Adam had he sprung from God, and therefore all men were his brothers: not through an earthly kinghood could he ransom them from misery, but only through fulfilment of the supreme divine vocation he had recognised, in which God changed himself to Man to bring himself to all men's consciousness through this one man who first had recognised Him in himself: the wretchedest, the greatest sufferers, must be his earliest chosen; through them must knowledge pass into the world.—Jesus went to Galilee, where from youth up he had seen the suffering of men.—So long as the Jewish tribal aristocracy believed in the Messiah as their earthly venger upon Rome, they might listen with some personal interest to the Folk's account of Jesus: in this sense did riots (with Barabbas) break out against the Romans. Jesus' entry into Jerusalem coincided with the climax of these movements: but Jesus undeceived not only the infatuated Folk, still more the Aristocracy, through his proclamation in the Temple of his office of Redeemer of Mankind, not of the Jews alone. The people fell away from him,—the aristocracy, which he fain would abolish, persecuted him: the Roman Prefect could easily put down the rising with his handful of men, since it was falling to pieces of itself when the priestly aristocracy delivered up the people's leader—Jesus (till then considered the most dangerous)—for the penalty of death. The abortive riot was finally stamped out by the Prefect through seizure of the ringleaders (with Barabbas): at the trial Pilate recognised Jesus' innocence:—but, since he had to liberate one captive, the Folk consistently reclaimed Barabbas—the man of its party—, whereas it troubled not for Jesus. Pilate—without troops—could not help himself, as he must fear a fresh and greater riot, and so gave way to the Folk. Jesus—as King of the Jews, was therefore mocked in every aspect by the misled people.—

IV. "Ye must believe,—through belief ye attain to knowledge. The learned of this world know, but have no belief: their knowledge is as naught. I know that I am son of God, and therefore that ye all are my brothers: I serve you all, and go for you to sacrificial death: when ye shall know, like me, ye will also do like me. Till then let Faith sustain you."—

I. "John was driven forth from cities to the desert; but me the spirit drives from out the desert into cities (to men)."

IV. "Ye shall not swear"; in Oaths lay the binding law of a world that knew not Love as yet. Let every man be free to act at every moment according to Love and his ability: bound by an oath, I am unfree: if in its fulfilment I do good, that good is robbed of merit (as every bounden virtue) and loses the worth of conviction; but if the oath leads me to evil, then I sin against conviction. The Oath engenders every vice: if it binds me against my profit, I shall seek to circumvent it (as every law is circumvented), and what I should quite rightly do in pursuance of my welfare, through the oath becomes a crime; but if I find my profit in it (without doing harm to another), then I rob myself of the moral satisfaction of doing right at every instant through my own free judgment.

II. IV. "Ye understand me not, for still am I without you: therefore I give to you my flesh and blood to eat and drink, that I may dwell within you."

II. "God is the Father and the Son and the Holy Ghost: for the father begetteth the son throughout all ages, and the son begetteth again the father of the son to all eternity: this is Life and Love, this is the Holy Spirit."

II. "If I protected you from Cæsar, from the King were ye not protected,—if from him, then not from the High Priest,—if from him, not from the rich and mighty,—and protected I you from all these, yet were ye not protected from yourselves if ye knew not the doctrine: wherefore I redeem you by leading you unto the light of the Spirit, for none but yourselves can protect yourselves from all the evil in the world. For that was I sent."

I. III. "I redeem you from Sin by proclaiming to you the everlasting law of the Spirit, which is its being, but not its limitation. The Law, as given you heretofore, was the limitation of your being in the flesh: without that law ye had no sin, but hearkened to the law of Nature: but the Letter was set up over your flesh, and the Law, which taught you to regard the nature of the flesh as sinful, brought you to death; for now ye sinned in doing what, according to the law, ye should not. But I release you from the Law which slew you, inasmuch as I bring unto you the law of the Spirit, which giveth life: henceforward there is no more sin, save that against the spirit; but that can only be incurred through ignorance, and therefore is no sin: yet whoso knoweth the spirit in truth, can sin no longer; for this new law crampeth not, but is itself the fulness of the spirit:—this law is Love, and what ye do in love can nevermore be sinful: in it your flesh is glorified, for Love is the Eternal. Whatever contentment ye long for, ye find in love alone: how could ye then desire aught else, than the law which alone can content your longing? Were the flesh against Love, it were against itself: but it hitherto hath been against the Law, since the Law was at variance with Love: in the Law, accordingly, was Sin; now I slay this law, and thereby root up sin: from sin I thus redeem you, inasmuch as I give you Love: but

God is love, and of love he sent to you his son; whose brothers all men are, and like unto him through love." Every creature loves, and Love is the law of life for all creation; so if Man made a law to shackle love, to reach a goal that lies outside of human nature (—namely, power, dominion—above all: the *protection of property*:), he sinned against the law of his own existence, and therewith slew himself; but in that we acknowledge Love, and vindicate it from the law of the false spirit, we raise ourselves above the brute creation, since we arrive at knowledge of the everlasting law which has been sole power since the ur-beginning; but inasmuch as we know this law, we also practise it, and thus are co-creators with God at every moment, and through the consciousness of that are God himself. Jesus knows and practises God's-love through his teaching of it: in the consciousness of Cause and Effect he accordingly is God and Son of God; but every man is capable of like knowledge and like practice,—and if he attain thereto, he is like unto God and Jesus.

If ye ask why Man set up a law at variance with his nature, we come to the serious error of mankind until the present day; namely, the universal misunderstanding of the principle of Society, which seemed insurable only by making laws to guard Possession, but not the essence of Human Nature in its freedom. As a first law, *Marriage* was entrenched by transferring the law of Love to it: but the law, i.e. the essence of Love, is everlasting: a pair that mutually inclines without compulsion, can do this solely from pure love; and this love, so long as nothing crosses it, can naturally admit no surcease, for it is the full and mutual completion and contentment of the man and woman, which wins in fruitfulness, and in the love devolving on the children, its perpetual motion and renewal. To this complete relationship became attached the concept of Possession: the man belonged to the woman, the woman to the man, the children to the parents, the parents to the children,—love gave duration to this state of Belonging, and continuous Belonging stiffened to the concept of Possession,—

which last developed in especial through the warding-off of violent encroachments from without; who love, belong to one another and none else, above all not to him who is not loved. The Individual's natural rights were consequently extended over those close-knit to him by love: thus ripened the idea of Marriage, its sacredness, its right; and this latter became embodied in the Law. But that Right was bound to turn into a wrong, when it no longer found its basis through and through in love itself; it could but turn into an utter sin, so soon as its sacredness was made to prevail *against* love, and that in two directions: 1° when the marriage was contracted without love, 2° when the parents' right became a scourge upon the children. If a woman was wed by a man for whom she had no love, and he fulfilled the letter of the marriage-law to her, through that law she became his property: the woman's struggle for freedom through love thereby became a sin, actual contentment of her love she could only attain by adultery. Similarly if the children felt themselves blossoming into free expression of their love, and the parents did not exert their natural kinsman's-right over them in the sense of love, that is to say, in the single sense of the free love of their children themselves, then the children must sin against the law by independent satisfaction of their love. In the court of Love it was not they who sinned, but the Law that had blasphemed by transforming the right of love into Possession, thus setting up a dam against love's free eternal movement, inasmuch as it erected one moment of love—namely its duration in a pair made wholly one by love—in place of the eternity of Love itself.—Precisely so was it with the law of Property: in it the love which expresses itself in Man as the bent to satisfaction through the enjoyment of Nature and her products, became hardened into the unit's exclusive right over Nature beyond his capacity for enjoyment: through this right I defend from another the enjoyment with which I already am sated myself, thus seek my satisfaction not in Enjoyment, but in Possession. The sin against property therefore springs from nothing save the law of Property: the man who feels compelled to sin against it by the dictates of Nature, therefore offends only through existence of the law, not in himself.—So Jesus frees our human nature, when he abrogates the law which makes that nature appear sinful to itself through its restrictions,—when he proclaims the divine law of Love, in whose envelopment our whole being is justified.—

IV. Through my death there perisheth the Law, inasmuch as I shew you that Love is greater than the Law.

I. "The commandment saith: Thou shalt not commit adultery! But I say unto you: Ye shall not marry without love. A marriage without love is broken as soon as entered into, and whoso hath wooed without love, already hath broken the wedding. If ye follow my commandment, how can ye ever break it, since it bids you do what your own heart and soul desire?—But where ye marry without love, ye bind yourselves at variance with God's law, and in your wedding ye sin against God; and this sin avengeth itself by your striving next against the law of man, in that ye break the marriage-vow."

Or:—

"It is a good law: Thou shalt not commit adultery, and he who committeth adultery, he sinneth. But I preserve you from this sin, inasmuch as I give you the law of God, which saith: Thou shalt not marry without love."—"Now, he who followeth the law of God, over him the law of Man hath no authority; by it must man's law be put to shame and die, as it erewhile brought men unto shame and slew them."

III. "Where no law is, neither is there sin. Against the law of God ye can only sin through the law of men: but by following God's law ye put the law of men to shame, —and of itself ye follow the law of God, so soon as ye loose yourselves from the law of men, so that ye are free and bound no longer, doing always that which pleaseth you according to God's love, which is in you and only through the law of men forsaketh you.—This also is a good law: Thou shalt

not steal, nor covet another man's goods. Who goeth
against it, sinneth: but I preserve you from that sin,
inasmuch as I teach you: Love thy neighbour as thyself;
which also meaneth: Lay not up for thyself treasures,
II. whereby thou stealest from thy neighbour and makest him
to starve: for when thou hast thy goods safeguarded by
the law of men, thou provokest thy neighbour to sin against
the law. Lay not up the treasures of this world, and heap
not Mammon, for thieves to dig at: neither ask, What
shall we eat, what shall we drink? etc. Do ye according
to the love of God, that is: Shew love unto your neighbours,
and all these things shall be added unto you; for God
hath made the world to your honour and riches, and what
it holdeth is for your enjoyment, each man according to
his need. But where treasures are gathered against human
love, there ye gather too the thieves against whom ye
publish the law: so the Law maketh sinners, and Mammon
maketh thieves. But he who lives according to God's law,
putteth the law of Man to shame, inasmuch as he giveth
occasion for sin neither to himself nor to his neighbour.

"Who heaped up treasures such as thieves can steal, he was the first to break the law, inasmuch as he took from his neighbour what his neighbour had need of. Who then is the thief: he who took from his neighbour what his neighbour had need of, or he who took from the rich man what he needed not? Look ye, so brings the Law offence into the world, and from it ye can redeem yourselves through none but God's commandment: Love one another, —all other law is vain and damnable."

"Sin abideth in the world so long as the Law abideth, and the Law so long as injustice (Wrong): he who liveth in God's love, is upright, and the Law is dead unto him."

I. III.

Ye descend from God: but from God descends no unclean thing. For if the first-fruit be holy, the lump is also holy; and if the root be holy, so also are the branches. Righteous therefore also is man's flesh and blood, and no unrighteousness can be in it: but all offence and sin come through the Law, which is against man; wherefore am I come to redeem you from the Law, without which there is no Sin,—and this I do by teaching you that ye all descend from God and are in him through Love, which is the only law.

II. III. "No longer shall ye think to serve God by going to the Temple, saying prayers, and making sacrifice of things it pains you not to miss: another offering shall ye henceforth bring your whole life through, so long as e'er ye move and breathe: your body shall ye offer daily and hourly, that it may live in the love of God; i.e. in the love of your brethren, that ye now may no more live according to the law, which shielded your unlovingness, but after the commandment which I have brought you: when ye have recognised it in your heart as true, ye shall let your body do according to the heart: this is the sacrifice that liveth forever, holy and well-pleasing unto God—this is Life itself, which is the most reasonable service of God.—

III. Everyone who walketh in Love, is King and Priest over himself, for he is subject unto no man, but to God, who dwelleth in him; but he who walketh without love, is a slave and subject unto every mighty man of earth, for in him dwelleth Sin, and Sin ruleth him."

III. "Your wise men and learned, who have sharpened their understanding to justify the law and the tradition, I bring them to naught by my simple word that sayeth: God is love."

II. Jesus weds not any woman: "The seed of David shall die out with me, that I may leave to you the seed of God." (Cf. I. Corinthians, ix. 25.)

II. IV. "As yet I cannot offer you the strong meat of life, for ye are not able to stomach it: with milk must I feed you, like new-born babes; thus ye cannot yet grasp Knowledge, and I therefore teach you Faith: but Faith, if ye but keep it faithfully in love to me, will lead you on to Knowledge, as milk doth nourish you until that ye are strong enough to eat the bread of life."

(I.) II. "Love is free,—is practised through free will:

it is spiritual, and lieth not in the bonds of Nature, the blood. The Law bound it to the blood, and thus begot Sin of itself.—Love practised brings the highest riches in the world, its opposite the deepest poverty. For all that I can, I have free will: if I practise it in love, I not only do what helpeth myself, but what helpeth many; thereby I multiply the profit of my action even to myself, since many also do what helpeth me at like time. But if I only do of my free will what is to help myself alone, I seek not so much my own profit as the injury of my neighbour, because only that seems profitable to me *alone* whereby a loss is put upon another: my neighbour, not to be the loser, must therefore also seek to help himself by harming me: but these neighbours are many, and nothing but my utmost poverty could make them rich. So, under the Law all strive to harm each other, in that each one seeketh to preserve himself from harm: but no law can bring about the rich and prospering deeds of Love: for Law is restrainment of freedom,—and only then is Love creative, when it is free."

II. "Like as the body hath many and divers members, whereof each hath its peculiar kind and office, yet all the members constitute one body, so are all men members of one God. But God is the father and the son, begetting himself anew forever; in the father was the son, and in the son is the father; as, then, we are members of one body which is God, whose breath is everlasting Love, so do we never die; like as the body, which is God, never dieth, because it is the father and the son, i.e. the constant manifestment of eternal Love itself."

IV. So Death is swallowed up in Love: for the sting of death is Sin, and the strength of sin is the Law. (from which ye are loosed through Love.)

III. IV. "Partakers with God in immortality, are all who know him: but to know God, is to serve him; that is, to love their neighbours as themselves."—

II. Jesus to his brothers (the sons of Joseph and Mary) concerning his antenuptial birth, as to which they question him: "Ye are born of the flesh, but I of love: so I am of God, but ye of the Law."

I. III. "Ye write your laws on stone and parchment, to bind the spirit: I write the law of Love in your hearts, and set the spirit free."

I. "This money beareth Cæsar's token: but whose mark I bear, his slave I am. If ye set your hearts on treasures of gold and silver, ye belong to this world, and must pay tribute to him with whose name and mark your treasures are stamped: but if ye gather treasures of the spirit, and walk in the love of God, ye have to pay tribute to God and Love through works of love which bless and glorify you. Would ye then gather the treasures of love, to have enough for all your life, so cast from you the treasures of the world, wherewith ye cannot still the cravings of one day; wherefore I say unto you: Render to Cæsar the things that are Cæsar's,—and to God the things that are God's!"—

I. "Ye understand not my commandment?—Yet how clear to you was the law which preached damnation and slew you; for through its plainness became ye sinners! Should not rather the commandment be clear, which preacheth the redemption and the life?"

(In the Temple: Act III.) III. "Moses covered his face from you when he died, that ye might not behold the end of him who gave you the law that yet should end: and that veil remaineth still before you stubborn ones, so that ye refuse to see the end of that which yet shall end; but I remove that veil, since in me the Law shall end that ye may see the death of what ye hypocrites would fain have kept alive: and openly before all eyes will I suffer death for that Love through which I redeem the world to life eternal."

V. "I die through the Law for sake of Love, that ye may know that Love is everlasting and the Life, but Law is of Time and Death. So I break this wall that parteth life, and bring you peace."

(Act IV.) The Disciples: "Now do we understand thee."

Jesus: "Ye have tasted but the milk, not the gall of my doctrine. My death shall give to you the gall, that ye may be steadfast in doing the work that is needful." (See Eph. iv. 13 and 14.)

II. "All men are members of the body of God: each moveth for itself, according to free will; if they strive against each other, however, the body will fall sick, and every several member sicken: but if each one doth bear, support and help the other, the whole body will bloom with living health. This law of life and health ye receive through Love, and whoso keepeth it, what man shall call him slave? for he giveth himself thereby both life and health: but life is freedom, sickness is bondage: Love therefore is the free will of life."

"I am not come to traffic with sin, but to slay it."

I. IV. Judas: "Master, speakest thou of the kingdom of Heaven? or shall it be possible on this sinful earth?" Jesus: "Deem'st thou more possible the laws ye daily break, than that one law wherein ye walk forever justified? —Is the law of life which has been from the beginning, and will be forever, so impossible here on earth, though in it alone ye live? Whereas the law of man, which was broken in the very giving, ye hold imperatively necessary!—O ye sinners and hardened, who fain would hold the truth impossible, and recognise the lie as the necessity. Open your hearts, and see what every child can see!"

(IV.) "I am the Messiah and the son of God: I tell you this that ye may not be led astray and look for any other."

The second coming of Jesus, see II. Thessal. ii., 8-12.

II. "Where there are freemen according to the Law, there are also slaves: but in the law of Love ye all are free and equal."

I. "To the pure all things are pure."

IV. "The milk your mother giveth you: the bread must ye earn for yourselves." "Men are to God what the woman is to the man: the woman receives from the man, and bears, and the fruit of her body becomes man once more; but man and woman are one flesh and blood, and so are we one with God."

Jesus (to Peter, on the road to crucifixion): "Thou followedst me when I was taken,—to deny me:—now that I go to death, stay thou behind,—to testify of me!"

III. IV. "With an offering of blood of bulls and rams the High Priest entered once each year into the sanctuary of the Temple, that yet was made by hand of man: with the offering of my own blood once and forever I go into the holiest sanctuary of the temple that was made by hand of God: but the temple of God is mankind."

I. III. "With cunning have ye put aside the law of God, that ye might keep your precepts!"

Act II. *Jesus*: "Mother, why barest thou these?" *Mary*: "Saith not the law: Let the wife be subject to the husband?" —"Thou sinnedst when thou gavest them life without love, and again thou sinnedst when thou nourishedst and brought them up without love. But I am come to redeem thee, also, from thy sin:* for they shall love me for God's sake, and thank thee that through God thou gavest me to the world. This will I bring to fulness; so attend me to Jerusalem."

I. "Not marriage hallows love,—but love hallows marriage."

II. (Jesus' attitude as Physician towards the degenerate and profoundly-disordered health of the nation:) "the physicians come and boast their science, that yet knows nothing; for where lieth the root of the ill, they overlook, or will not see, that they may rob from the sick and hungering even what preserves his last remains of strength. My medicine is simple: Live after my commandment, and ye need no more physicians. Therefore I say to you, If your bodies are ailing, take care that your children be sound and inherit not your sickness: live steadfast in the common work, say not 'This is mine,' but 'All is ours,'—so none of you will starve, and all grow healthy. The evils that still will befall you through Nature, are light to

* Cf. *Parsifal* act ii., "Erlösung biet' ich auch dir."—Tr.

heal: knows not each beast in the field what herb is good for it?*—and how should ye not know it, when ye once see clearly and with open eyes? But so long as ye go the way of want and gluttony, of usury and starving, your eye is veiled and ye see not what is simpleness itself."—"Why do the beasts in the wilderness not fall sick? They live in strength and joy, and when their hour cometh, they quietly depart and lay them down where their creator lets them end."—

Act III. "Woe be to you, for ye build the Prophets tombs, but your fathers killed them."

(the kingdom of God: Luke xvii., 20, 21.)

II.—"Sell all that thou hast, give it to the poor, and sustain thyself by labour."

Act II. "Your fathers did eat manna in the desert and are dead. I am the bread that cometh down from heaven, that whoso eateth thereof shall not die!"

Gosp. John vii., 1-8 "the world cannot hate you, but me it hateth, because I testify of it that its ways are evil."

(Barabbas, when he gave up Jesus, hurried before him to Jerusalem and stirred up a revolt; it miscarried, however, through the indifference of the people, who knew of Jesus and waited for his coming: but when the people saw themselves deceived in Jesus, they turned back to Barabbas and demanded his release.)

II.—"For Love is Joy."

God was one with the world from the beginning: the earliest races (Adam and Eve) lived and moved in this oneness, innocent, unknowing it: the first step in knowledge was the distinguishing between the helpful and the harmful; in the human heart the notion of the Harmful developed into that of the Wicked: this seemed to be the opposite

(Misunderstanding his own impulses, to himself Man seemed outside God, i.e. wicked: over against themselves men set

* "Weiss doch jedes Thier im Wald, welch' Kraut ihm nützet,"—cf. *Parsifal* act iii.: "Kräuter und Wurzeln findet ein Jeder sich selbst, wir lernten's im Walde vom Thier."—Tr.

of the Good, the Helpful, of God, and that dualism (*Zwiegespaltenheit*) formed the basis of all Sin and Suffering of mankind; upon it was built the idea of man's imperfectness, and that idea itself was bound to swell to doubt of God.

the Law, as come from God, to force themselves to good.)

Human Society next sought deliverance through the *Law*: it fastened the notion of Good to the Law, as to III.
something intelligible and perceptible by us all: but what was bound fast to the Law was only a moment of the Good, and since God is eternally generative, fluent and mobile, the Law thus turned against God's self; for, as man can live and move by none save the ur-law of Motion itself, in pursuance of his nature he needs must clash against the Law, i.e. the binding, standing,—thus grow sinful. This is man's suffering, the suffering of God himself, who has not come as yet to consciousness in men.* That consciousness we finally attain through taking the essence of Man himself for immediate Godhood, through recognising the eternal law whereby the whole creation moves as the positive and ineluctable, and abolishing the distinction between the helpful and the harmful through our recognition that *sub specie æterni* ("im Betracht des Ewigen") the two are the selfsame utterance of creative force: the original oneness of God and the World thus is gained anew to our consciousness, and Sin, therefore Suffering, abolished by our abolition of the clumsy human law—which opposed itself as State to Nature—through recognition that the *only* God indwells in us and in our unity with Nature—the which, again, we recognise itself as undivided. Jesus removed this conflict, and established the oneness of God, by his proclamation of *Love*.

III. *Jesus*: "Between father and son, i.e. the everliving God, ye have placed the Law, and thus set God at variance with himself: I slay the Law, and in its stead proclaim the holy Spirit,—which is eternal Love."—"I am

* Cf. *Parsifal* act iii.: "Ihm seh' ich heil'ges Blut entfliessen, in Sehnsucht nach dem verwandten Quelle."—Tr.

come to bind what ye had loosed, and to loose what ye have bound."

Act II. "Honour your body, keep it clean, fair and healthy, so honour ye God, for your body is God's temple, that in it he may delight."

"On the world no sin lieth, it is perfect as God who made and keepeth it: and pure is each creature that liveth therein, for its life is the love of God, and the law whereby it liveth is the love of God. So lived Man also once in innocence, till the knowledge of good and evil, of what helps and what harms, set him outside himself, and he lived by laws which he himself had made unto death: now I bring Man back into himself, in that he apprehendeth God as in himself, and not outside him: but God is the law of Love, and when once we know it and walk thereby, as every creature walketh without knowing it, we are God himself: for God is the knowledge of self."

"If each unreasoning creature walketh without sin, because unknowingly it walks in Love, how much more may not Man live without sin, who knoweth furthermore the law of Love through me?"

V. "My kingdom is not of this world: I strive against no man, since I fight for all."

II. or IV. "How shall we have joy of the doctrine, if all men do not follow it?"—*Jesus*: "So long as ye are few that know and keep my teaching, will ye suffer and be hated of the world: but the might of that suffering beginneth not from now, it is as old as the law; yet even in your suffering will ye be blessed, for ye know for what ye suffer, in that ye testify of God: so your body alone can suffer, not your soul. Upon you will offence first reach its fulness, but woe to them by whom cometh the offence. Those who know not my doctrine, cannot sin against the Holy Ghost,—but those to whom it is taught, and yet they do not follow it, shall be counted like unto the dogs that return to their vomit. The farther therefore shall my word be taught, and the world yet walketh not thereby, the greater will become the sin and suffering of the world:

nations shall rise against nations, and the mighty of the earth shall lead men forth to slaughter through their covetousness:—but then will I come again and with my faithful people overcome the world, that the kingdom of God may be founded even upon earth: and this will never pass away, for the kingdom of Love endureth for ever."

"The kingdom of God is not without us, but within us: therefore blessed are they who keep my commandment, for theirs is the kingdom of heaven." "When shall these things be?" Jesus: "That is not meet for you to know, but you it behoveth to strive that at all times ye share in the kingdom of heaven, which is everlasting."—"One law alone is right: the more the laws, the more corrupt the world!"

II. "It is more blessed to give than to receive."

*Of Death.**

The last ascension of the individual life into the life of the whole, is Death, which is the last and most definite upheaval of egoism. The plant grows from *one* germ, which is itself: † each evolution of the plant is a manifolding of itself in bloom and seed, and this process of life is a ceaseless progress unto death. Its death is the self-offering of every creature in favour of the maintenance and enrichment of the whole: the creature that fulfils this offering with consciousness, by attuning its free will to the necessity of this offering, becomes a co-creator,—in that it further devotes its free will to the greatest possible moral import of the sacrifice, however, it becomes God himself. This nature-necessity had to lead man to consciousness of itself, so that, for all his seeming to content his egoism by exercise of his free will, he is always advancing on his ascent into an ever more extended generality. This advance is conditioned by Love. Love is the most imperative utterance of life: but as, materially speaking, in it the ego's life-stuff is voided (*entäussert*), so in it takes

* In this and the next few pages it is impossible not to recognise another partial anticipation of the author's Schopenhauerian period.—Tr.

† Cf. Vol. VII. 268.—Tr.

also place the moral process of a riddance of egoism; and the perfect riddance thereof is Death, the giving-up of the body, of the hearth and home of egoism, of the last hindrance to my ascent into the generality.—As man proceeds from a voiding of the life-stuff of his engenderer, is fed by the milk of his mother, and aided in his initial helplessness by the offerings of others, so his growth, his thriving, in fact, the whole maturing of his indivuality is a taking and receiving.

Thus, until his physical maturity, man develops after the principle of the sheerest egoism: the love of the child to its begetters, nourishers and bringers up, is gratitude,—a feeling which is always directed to the thing received; it is the receiver's delight in himself, but no return, for a making good, a paying back, is unthinkable here. So that the individual first fronts the generality as a full-fledged egoist, and his active dealings with it are the gradual abandonment of egoism, ending in his ascent into the generality.

(Gratitude is no love, but a thoroughly unsatisfying feeling, and in itself untrue; it can be no more than praise bestowed on the love-deed of another, the vindication of a benefit conferred on me: love itself it could only be if it returned the boon, for love is giving, not receiving; but a plenary return of the boon could only be a giving-back the gift itself, consequently the abrogation of the love-deed shewn to me. An actual satisfaction of the feeling of gratitude must therefore amount to annulment of the cause of obligation: it thus would be the diametric opposite of Love, namely the denial of her deed; and should it in its turn produce a deed of love, that could not rank as such, since the fulfilment of a duty is an unfree act, whereas the former deed-of-love had sprung from free impulse. Gratitude, therefore, is one of those empty terms which spring from an egoistic feebleness of mind and in their unproductiveness bring forth the most multiform illusions, for it removes the very freedom of action without which Love is inconceivable. Moreover, as Gratitude cannot be conceived without the wish to compensate, a wish that yet stays unfulfilled, from it there grows a duty which is never discharged,—for its fulfilment or discharge would be the actual abrogation of the deed-of-love.)

The first act of surrender-of-oneself is sexual love; it is a giving-away of one's own vital force: in sexual love, and the family, man multiplies himself physically through a riddance of himself, and this undoubtedly involves the physical necessity of his death, as with the plant. This necessity might be countered by the paradox, that man would never die if he did not multiply himself through procreation, but devoted his procreative force, so to say, to the constant reconstruction of his own body: but that would be to establish the most complete and irremediable egoism; and in fact this egoism lies at bottom of the monk's renunciation, against which Nature wreaks her vengeance by letting that procreative force disperse unfruitful, by no means harvesting it for the body's use; for Life is movement along the line of multiplication.—Death therefore amounts, for the unit, to the giving-up himself in favour of the multiplying of himself. If the relationship of the family is pure, if death comes naturally and in advanced old age, with a numerous existing progeny, then death—as we see in patriarchal life—has never seemed bitter or terrible: only after disruption of the natural ties through defilement of the purity of the family, when human egoism set its heart on what lies without the race, on possession and power, must death become terrible, because it cancelled an egoism that could not be fitly imagined as living-on in its multiples. Now in Universal Love-of-man, as taught by Jesus, reconciliation with death is established for all time, since egoism finds through that love its most complete contentment in its most complete repeal. If the Patriarch found contentment in a teeming progeny, that contentment could but grow with the extension of man's love beyond the offspring of his loins. If through his love to his children the father finds the final satisfaction of his egoism in the thriving of his body's fruit, i.e. in the satisfaction of the egoism of his children, he further will wish well to those who help his loved ones to their satisfaction; to know the welfare of oneself and children guaranteed by a social union, at last expands the family-egoism to Patriotism, i.e. to love for the union in which I know my own contentment, or that of my dear ones, ensured through reciprocity. Now, the more definitely and distinctly do I know the welfare of this larger fellowship ensured by the merging of the egoism of the unit in the communism of all, the higher and broader shall I know to be the satisfaction which that egoism finds therein: the nature-necessity of death becomes a moral deed, so soon as I consciously make it a sacrifice to the weal of the community: through my death for the fatherland I obtain the satisfaction of conferring on the fatherland a highest benefit, that of its preservation; therefore the final putting-off of egoism, through death, becomes a magnified contentment of my many-times multiplied Me. But Jesus further teaches us to break through the barriers of patriotism and find our amplest satisfaction in the weal of all the human race. Now, the more intimately do I persuade myself of the blessed truth of this doctrine in course of my individual life; the greater enjoyment do I draw from universal human love by dedicating myself thereto with consciousness; the ampler do I make the satisfaction of my personal need by seeking it in nothing but the satisfaction of universal love to man, so much the more do I destroy my egoism through ascent into the Universal; and the completest—as also the most necessary—annihilation of this me-aloneness is reached in death, the giving up alike of life and self. Through death, however, my individuality is at like time perfected, by the rounding-off of my personal being. So long as a man lives, he belongs (wittingly or unwittingly) to the movement of the generality; let him comport himself as independently as he may, his free will can reasonably be exercised only in harmony with the general movement, for he thereby makes that movement consciously his own, and generates—whereas he could but clog the movement, if he set his will against it; all that moveth changeth, but to us the dead can change no more; through the rounding of his life he steps before us as a sharp-cut, seizable and special object, by which to recognise and judge ourselves.* Through his death the unit certifies his creative concurrence in life, for we know that death, by the law of Nature, is the result of parcelling out a multiple force: in that man shapes, reacts and begets, he annihilates himself, and his life is therefore a continual slaying of himself for the benefit of something new, enriched and diversified, that issues from him; wherefore his ultimate death is but the total parting with the emptied casket of that generative force, and thus a last creation in itself, to wit the upheaval of all unproductive egoism, a making place for life. If we are conscious of this, and act upon that consciousness, we are even God himself, namely the energising of eternal Love; and we set the last sign manual of our godhood on this action through our death, the highest love-offering, to wit the offering of our personal being itself in favour of the universal. Death is accordingly the most perfect deed of love: it becomes such to us through our consciousness of a life consumed in love.—

IV. *Jesus*: "So long as I yet live, ye are in uncertainty about me, for ye are still unclear, and your wishes still at variance, as to what I yet might do: when I shall be no more, will ye come to clearness about me, for then will ye know for certain what I did."

Egoism is taking and receiving—the voidance thereof in love is giving and imparting.

Nothing exists for us, but what is present to man's consciousness.—To the Me the Universal stands opposed: the I is to me the positive, the Universal the negative, for each requirement of the Universal in my regard is a denial of my Me. While *I* am aughtsoever to myself, the universe is naught to me;—only in degree as I rid myself of my

* See Vol. I. 199—"Art-work of the Future"—a parallelism which seems to me an indication that at least this part of the above was not written till 1849-50.—Tr.

Me, and ascend into the universal, does the universal become a fact to me, because with my own Me, the only certain thing to me, I now am in it: the process of putting off my Me in favour of the universal, is Love, is active Life itself: the non-active life, in which I abide by myself, is egoism. Through love I give myself to what lies without me, set my strength in the universal, thus make the cypher something through myself, who now am in it, and that in measure as I rid myself of my Me through love. The most complete divestment of my Me takes place through death;—for inasmuch as I completely upheave my Me, thus make it naught, I mount completely to the Universal, which henceforth is something substantial and stands in the same relation to me through my death as I stood to it through my birth. (A dead father, through his death, has completely passed into the generality of his children, their bodies, customs and deeds.)

Each man lives in love, all his doings are involved therein, for his life itself is the progressive divestment of his Me. Amends for the loss of this Me come only through *consciousness* of his ascent into the generality, for only through knowledge thereof does he find himself again in the Universal, and that enriched and multiplied; this consciousness of self, or better, this becoming-conscious of ourselves in the universal, makes our life creative, just because by our abandonment of self we enrich the generality, and in it our own selves. The ignorance, or non-becoming conscious, of ourselves in the universal brings forth sin, namely the stunting of ourselves: the man who, unconscious of his passing into the generality, could maintain himself as an absolute egoist, that is, would be ever receiving and taking, by his very nature must still submit to the encroachments of the outer world upon himself,—it will take and receive from him what he refuses to give and impart; the motive force of love here turns to hate and robbery, and the loveless egoist will regard the outer world as his most inveterate foe, since he is unable to ascend thereinto with consciousness: in the end he still must bring himself as offering to it, in death; and he is really dead, because he has passed into the universal against his will, without his knowledge, and without having found himself again therein. But enrichment of the universal, also, can only be [i.e. take place through] my knowledge of my ascent into it: from the egoist, therefore, it in truth receives nothing.

Woman. The essence of Woman, like that of children, is egoism: the woman gives not, but receives, or merely re-gives the received. As the child is incomplete in itself until maturity, and the sole activity that it can shew is the return of its parents' love, so the woman in herself is incomplete, and only in returning the love of the man can she attain activity: in her ascent into the man, whose love she receives, she finds the only possibility of yielding up her egoism to the generality, namely in her children and her giving to those children: but the bearing of children and her giving to them are but a re-giving of the already-received. Beyond receipt, the woman's actual share in birth is the travail of bearing: herein lie woman's sufferance and merit, to wit a suffering riddance of her egoism; and this riddance finds its consummation in her love to the children. Thus the woman arrives at activity solely through the man; she rids herself of her egoism through a restitution of the received, not through an actual giving; and only in her recipient ascent into the man, and restituent ascent into the children, can she arrive at conscious ascent into the generality. Therefore the woman is one with the man, and only in her ascent into man can she be deemed as morally established: but the wife is also the completion of the husband, his giving to her is the first divestment of his egoism, without which his productive ascent into the generality would be impossible. Very rightly therefore does Jesus say: Man and wife are one flesh, God (Love) hath knit them into one, and their severance is inadmissible because impossible; for he says: So it was from the beginning,—i.e. this is the law of Nature. The first sin against this law would thus be a marriage without love, for egoism does not dissolve therein, but hardens to indissolubility through constraint.

Innocence is the [state of] absolute egoism, for it receives and gives not. Adam lived in innocence so long as he merely received; the first divestment of his egoism, through procreative love, was the Fall, to wit the unit's step outside itself, and consequent advance towards complete repeal of egoism in death, i.e. self-annihilation. (The state of Innocence could not come to men's consciousness until they had lost it. This yearning back thereto, the struggle for its re-attainment, is the soul of the whole movement of civilisation since ever we learnt to know the men of legend and of history. It is the impulse to depart from a generality that seems hostile to us, to arrive at egoistic satisfaction in ourselves, *et seq.*) This denial of himself must needs appear to man a misery, a harm and evil—and its ultimate consequence, Death, a curse,—so long as he had not become joyfully conscious of his multiple ascent into the generality. The necessity of surcease of the personal being must seem an evil to him who was unaware of the rich indemnification for that loss. This plaint did not exist at the beginning, for in the pure Patriarchate the father feels contented with his passing into his progeny: the Israelites in their slavery and demoralisation in Egypt were the first to raise this cry, because in the disrupted family and captive tribe that riddance of egoism could only be accomplished by submergence in an unloved and squalid generality—that of their captive kinsmen. Only in joy at life can egoism willingly put off itself; if life itself is a joyless thing to me, in its increase and multiplication—the maintenance of this joyless state—I naturally can find no satisfaction, but wish myself back in the state of innocence, namely of inactive, unproductive egoism. In this unjoyful voiding of myself I find my misery increased: my body's fruit becomes to me a burden, which I would rather not have born; so Love withdraws from the field of action, and its most natural contentment in the paternal relation becomes changed into the opposite: the satisfaction of the procreative bent becomes a vulgar lust, the presence of children a burden, life a loveless care, and therefore death a curse, because the abolition of the only thing we comprehend, to wit the Me. In this world of egoistic yearning and dislike arose the Law: in it man was to divest himself of his egoism in favour of a generality from which love, i.e. the blessed consciousness of love, had vanished—to wit, *Possession*. But the Law itself could not make-up for Love, for it was the constraint, the compulsion to benefit the commonalty; only he who found his benefit in its keeping, did according thereto; the lawful act was not the deed of love, for this can only be accomplished of free will, but the deed of egoism, which found itself contented and protected by the law: free Love could only manifest itself outside the law, and thus against it. But Love is mightier than the Law, for it is the Ur-law of life,—yet its utterance must seem a sin, i.e. a breach of the law, so long as the primitive state, in which the law of Love alone prevailed, had not been re-established; and only in the fullest consciousness was *that* to be regained, through Jesus, which we had lost through imperfect consciousness thereof: for through Jesus' proclamation Love was stretched from out the family to cover all the human race.

The loveless constantly abides in egoism, and in death he founders utterly; the movement of life, the riddance of his life-material, takes place against his will; what he wills, he cannot consummate, but what he wills not, he must see fulfilled on him: he therefore remains a sufferer till death. Only he who brings his free will to the divestment of his life-stuff, passes consciously into the universal, and thus lives on therein a multiple and broader life: the divestment of my self is Love, and in the beloved I find myself again. This is the immortality that resides in my free will: for the Egoist sets his will against his necessary putting-off of self, and therefore comes to final end with death,—whereas the Universalist attains through his will to broader living in the generality.

The life of man is evolution in egoism and putting-off thereof again in favour of the generality.

Until maturity, man comprehends Nature only with reference to himself: every impression from Nature goes up into his egoism, for the still-ripening merely receives; only the received is comprehensible to him, and only as regards himself, his Me itself: so far as Nature lies outside him, it therefore is nothing to him, and only his I is something. Only after attained maturity, when man divests himself of self again in love, does Nature become aught to him, in measure as he sinks himself into her; for through love he goes outside himself, and finds himself again in his antithesis. Whence also the understanding of Nature first through love.*

("And if I bestow all my goods to feed the poor, and if I give my body to be burned, but have not love, it profiteth me nothing." (I. Cor. xiii., 3.)

("The spiritual body is not the first, but the natural; afterward the spiritual." (I. Cor. xv., 46.) The spiritual body is my life in the generality.)

(*To be much worked out.*) The Law stands in place of the generality, consequently between me and the universe: thus my ascent into the universal has turned to a dissolution in the Law, accordingly an enrichment of death,—for the Law displaces life. The Law is lovelessness; and even should it command me to love, in keeping it I should not practise love, for Love deals only after itself, not after a commandment. The atonement of the world is therefore to be effected by nothing but upheaval of the Law, which holds the individual back from free bestowal of his Me upon the generality, and parts him from it.—

(Eph. ii., 14.—For he is our peace, who made both (God and Man, i.e. the universal and the individual) one, and
(IV). broke down the middle wall of partition, having abolished through his flesh the enmity,—even the law laid down in commandments; that he might make in himself of twain

* Cf. *Tristan* act iii.—"In des Welt-Athems wehendem All"; and *Parsifal* act iii.—"Sieh! es lacht die Aue."—Tr.

one new man (i.e. the individual consciously finding himself anew in the generality), so bringing peace; and might reconcile them both unto God in one body through the cross, having slain through himself the enmity.)

III.*

For Act I.

Matth. v. 2. That ye may be the children of your Father in heaven; for he maketh his sun to rise on the evil and on the good, and sendeth rain on the just and the unjust. —Ye therefore shall be perfect, even as your Father in heaven is perfect.

(xi.) "What went ye out into the wilderness to see? A reed blown hither and thither by the wind? Or what went ye out for to see? A man clothed in soft raiment? Behold, they that wear soft clothing are in kings' houses. *Et seq.*—But whereunto shall I liken this generation? etc. —John came neither eating nor drinking, and they say, He hath a devil. The son of man came eating and drinking, and they say, Behold a gluttonous man and a winebibber, a friend of publicans and sinners! And wisdom is justified of her children.

I thank thee, O Father, Lord of heaven and earth, that thou didst hide these things from the wise and prudent, and hast revealed them unto babes. (See below, Luke x.)

Come unto me, all ye that labour and are heavy laden, and I will refresh you. Take my yoke upon you and learn of me, for I am meek and lowly in heart; and ye shall find rest unto your souls. For my yoke is easy, and my burden is light.

(xii.) The Son of man is lord even of the sabbath:—

* In this section the text is taken verbatim by Wagner from Luther's New Testament, the 1545 revision; for the English I have gone to the Authorised and the Revised versions, subject to modifications in accordance with the German.—Tr.

"Is it lawful also to heal on the sabbath?" And he said unto them: "Who is there among you that hath a sheep, and if it fall into a pit on the sabbath day, he will not lay hold on it and lift it out? How much then is a man better than a sheep? Wherefore it is lawful to do good on the sabbath."

Then one said unto him: "Behold, thy mother and thy brethren stand without, desiring to speak with thee." Jesus: "Who is my mother? and who are my brethren?" and he stretched forth his hand towards his disciples, and said: "Behold my mother and my brethren. (For whosoever doeth the will of my Father in heaven, the same is my brother, and sister, and mother.)"

(xv.) *Pharisees*: "Why do thy disciples transgress the tradition of the elders? for they wash not their hands when they eat bread." *Jesus*: "Why do ye also transgress the commandment of God because of your traditions? For God commanded, saying, Honour thy father and mother; and, He that curseth father or mother, let him die the death. But ye say, Whosoever shall say to his father or his mother, 'If I offer it up, it is of far more profit to thee,' he doeth well.* Thus it cometh that henceforth no one honoureth his father or his mother, and ye have made void the law of God because of your tradition." "Not that which goeth into the mouth defileth a man; but that which cometh out of the mouth, this defileth a man."—Then came the disciples, and said unto

* "Wenn ich's opfre, so ist's dir viel nützer; der thut wohl"; this is how Luther rendered it in his latest revision, that of 1545. The current German Testament, however, reverts to Luther's original translation of 1522: "Es ist Gott gegeben das dir sollte von mir zunutz kommen," though it adds the "der thut wohl" of the 1545 version. The ellipsis in the Greek construction has made this clause the subject of many a discussion: the meaning assigned by Luther to the "viel nützer" he explains in a marginal note, "Das ist: Gott wird dir viel anders dafür bescheren," so that the son would be saying to his parent: "If I give to God what I ought to have given to thee, God will recompense thee for it many-fold," while the son could still retain possession of the "gift" in God's name. Wycliffe's Bible (1389) has "What euere gifte is of me, it shall profite to thee"; Tyndale's (1526), "Whatsoever thyng I offer, that same doeth profyt the."—Tr.

him, "Knowest thou that the Pharisees were offended, when they heard this saying?" *Jesus*: "Every plant which my heavenly Father hath not planted, shall be rooted up. Let them alone" etc.—

(xix.) Is it lawful also for a man to put away his wife for any cause? Jesus: "Have ye not read that he which made them at the beginning, he made them male and female? For this cause shall a man leave father and mother, and cleave to his wife; and the twain shall be one flesh. What therefore God hath joined together, let not man put asunder."—They say unto him: "Why then did Moses command to give a writing of divorcement, and to put her away?" Jesus: "Moses because of the hardness of your hearts suffered you to put away your wives: but from the beginning it was not so." And following verses.—Verse 16 to the end: scene with the rich young man.

(xxii.) *Master, we know that thou art truthful, and teachest the way of God aright, neither carest thou for any man, for thou regardest not the person of men. Tell us therefore, what thinkest thou? Is it right to give tribute unto Cæsar or not?*

Mark. (ii.) The sabbath was made for man, and not man for the sabbath. (Cf. Matth. xii.)—[Mark iii.] All sins shall be forgiven unto the children of man, even the blasphemies wherewith they blaspheme God; but he that shall blaspheme against the Holy Ghost hath never forgiveness, but is doomed of the eternal judgment.

Luke (iv.) The Spirit of the Lord is upon me, because (Also Act he hath anointed me and sent me to proclaim the gospel II.) to the poor, to heal the broken-hearted, to preach deliverance to the captives, and sight to the blind, to the downtrod that they shall be at liberty, and to preach the acceptable year of the Lord.

(v.) Why do ye eat and drink with publicans and sinners? "They that are whole need not a physician, but they that are sick."—Why do the disciples of John fast often, and make many prayers, and likewise the disciples of the

Pharisees, but thy disciples eat and drink?—Jesus: "Ye may not bid the children of the bridechamber to fast, while the bridegroom is with them. But the days will come, when the bridegroom is taken away from them, and then shall they fast."

(vi. 32.) If ye love them which love you, what thank have ye? for sinners also love those that love them. And if ye do good to them which do good to you, what thank have ye? for sinners also do even the same. And if ye lend to them of whom ye hope to receive, what thank have ye? For sinners also lend to sinners, to receive as much again. (*Et seq.*) Give, and it shall be given unto you. Good measure, pressed down, and shaken together, and running over, shall men give into your bosom; for with the same measure that ye mete withal it shall be given to you again.

Luke. (x.) *Blessed are the eyes which see the things that ye see. For I tell you, that many prophets and kings have desired to see those things which ye see, and have not seen them; and to hear those things which ye hear, and have not heard them.*

(xi.) A woman of the Folk: (M.M.?) "Blessed is the womb that bare thee, and the breasts which thou didst suck!" Jesus: "Yea, blessed are they that hear the word of God and keep it."

(xix.) The Publican: "Behold, Lord, the half of my goods I give to the poor; and if I have surcharged any man, I restore it fourfold." Jesus: "This day is salvation come to this house, for the Son of Man came to seek and to save that which was lost."

John viii. (*Adulteress.*)

Acts Ap. (x.) "Not so, Lord, for I have never eaten anything that is common or unclean." Jesus: "What God hath cleansed, that call not thou common."

(xx.) It is more blessed to give than to receive. (Antithesis to: Thou shalt not steal!)

Romans (xiii.) Every commandment is contained in this: Thou shalt love thy neighbour as thyself. Love doeth no ill to his neighbour. Therefore love is the fulfilment of the law.

I. Cor. (xii. 18.) But now hath God set the members every one of them in the body, as it hath pleased him. (All the following verses very important.) Follow with cap. xiii.: Though I speak with the tongues of men and angels, and have not love, I am become a sounding brass or a tinkling cymbal. Verse 2—then 3: And though I bestow all my goods on the poor and give my body to be burned, and have not love, it profiteth me nothing. (Act I. or II.)

Gal. (*III.*) Wherefore the law was our schoolmaster unto Christ, that we might become just by faith. But now that faith is come, we no longer are under the schoolmaster. For ye all are the children of God through faith in Jesus. (Also Act III.)

Eph. [iv., 6] One God and Father of all, who is above you all and through you all and in you all.

v. So ought husbands also to love their wives as their own bodies. He that loveth his wife, he loveth himself. For no man ever hated his own flesh, but he nourisheth and tendeth it, even as the Lord also the communion. For we are members of his body, of his flesh, and of his bones. *Seq.*

II. Tim. (*iii.*) Traitors, outragers, puffed up, stubborn, unforgiving: who keep the show of godliness, but deny the power thereof. Of these same are they which creep to and fro into houses and lead captive silly women, which are laden with sins and beset by divers lusts, ever learning and never able to come to knowledge of the truth.

Ep. John. [I., ii., iii., iv.] *I bring you not a new commandment, but the old commandment which ye had from the beginning; whosoever is born of God committeth no sin, for his seed remaineth in him, and cannot sin, for he is born of God. But he that loveth not his brother, he is not of God.*

We know that we have come out of death into life, for we love the brethren. He that loveth not his brother, abideth in death.

My little children, let us not love in word, neither in tongue, but in deed and in truth.—But whoso hath this world's goods and seeth his brother in need, and shutteth up his heart to him, how dwelleth the love of God in him?

There is no fear in love, but perfect love casteth out fear, for fear hath torment. He that feareth, is not perfect in his love.

For Act II.

Math. (v.) (See below, Luke.) Blessed are the poor in spirit, for theirs is the kingdom of heaven. Blessed are they that bear suffering, for they shall be comforted. Blessed are the meek, for they shall inherit the earth. Blessed are they which do hunger and thirst after righteousness, for they shall be filled. Blessed are the merciful, for they shall obtain mercy. Blessed are the pure in heart, for they shall see God.—Blessed are they which are persecuted for righteousness' sake, for theirs is the kingdom of heaven. Blessed are ye when men shall revile you and persecute you for my sake, and say all manner of evil against you, if so be that they lie.—Ye are the light of the world. A city that is set on a hill cannot be hid.

(vi.) And when ye pray, use not vain repetitions as the heathen; for they think they shall be heard for their much speaking. Be not ye therefore like unto them. Your Father knoweth what things ye have need of, before ye ask him.—Lay not up for yourselves treasures upon earth, where moth and rust doth devour, and where thieves dig through and steal. But lay up for yourselves treasures in heaven, where neither moth nor rust doth devour, nor thieves dig through and steal; for where your treasure is, there will your heart be also.— —No man can serve two masters; either he will hate the one and love the other, or else he will cleave to the one and despise the other. Ye cannot serve God and mammon. Therefore I say unto you, Have no care for your life, what ye shall eat and drink, nor yet for your body, what ye shall put on. Is not the life more than the food? and the body more than

(Also Act I.)

the raiment? Behold the fowls of the air: they sow not, neither do they reap, nor gather into barns; and yet your heavenly Father feedeth them. Are ye then not much more than they? *Which of you by taking thought can add one cubit unto his stature?* (No man can become richer in himself than he is, but in his brethren he can become more than a thousandfold of what he is.) And the following verses.—

(vii.) Judge not, that ye be not judged. (xviii.) But if thy brother sinneth against thee, go thou and chide him between thee and him alone. If he hear thee, thou hast gained thy brother; if he hear thee not, then take with thee one or two more, that everything may be established at the mouth of two or three witnesses. Will he not hear them, so tell it to the communion; will he not hear the communion, so hold him as a heathen and publican.

(viii.) Jesus said to him: "The foxes have holes, and the birds of the air have nests; but the Son of man hath not where to lay his head."—"Follow thou me, and let the dead bury their dead."

(ix.) And when he saw the multitude, he was grieved thereat; for they were faint and scattered, as sheep that have no shepherd. Then said he unto his disciples: "The harvest is great, but few are the labourers. Pray ye therefore the Lord of the harvest, that he may send labourers into his harvest."

(x.) The disciple is not above his master, nor the servant above his lord. It is enough for the disciple that he be as his master, and the servant as his lord.

And fear ye not them which kill the body, but are not able to kill the soul. But rather fear him which is able to destroy both body and soul in hell.

Think not that I am come to send peace upon earth. I **(Also IV.)**
came not to send peace, but the sword. For I am come to set the man at variance against his father, and the daughter against the mother, and the daughter-in-law against her parent-in-law; and a man's foes shall be they of his own household. He that loveth father or mother

more than me, is not worthy of me; and he that loveth son or daughter more than me, is not worthy of me; and he that doth not take up his cross and follow after me, he is not worthy of me.

(xi.) The blind see and the lame walk, the lepers are cleansed and the deaf hear, the dead arise and to the poor is the evangel preached; and blessed is he, who shall not be offended in me.

(xiii.) Therefore speak I to them in parables, because with eyes to see they see not, and with ears to hear they hear not, for they do not understand.

I will open my mouth in parables, and will utter things secret from the beginning of the world.

(I.) (xviii.) (From the commencement.) Jesus: "Woe unto the world because of tribulation! It must needs be that tribulation cometh, but woe unto that man by whom it cometh! Wherefore if thy hand or thy foot offend thee, cut thou it off and cast it from thee." &c.

(xx.) (Dispute about precedence among the disciples.)

Luke (*vi.*) Blessed are ye that hunger now, for ye shall be filled. Blessed are ye that weep here, for ye shall laugh. Blessed are ye when men hate you and set you aside and reproach you, and cast out your name as evil, for the Son of Man's sake. Rejoice ye in that day and leap for joy, for behold, your reward is great in heaven. In like manner did their fathers to the prophets also. But woe unto you rich, for ye have had your comfort. Woe unto you that are full, for ye shall hunger. Woe unto you that laugh here, for ye shall mourn and weep. Woe unto you, when all men speak fair to you, for so did their fathers to the false prophets.—But I say unto you which hear, Love your enemies *etc.*

(xii.) Take heed and beware of covetousness, for no man's life consisteth in that he hath many possessions!—There was a rich man, whose field had brought forth plentifully; and he reasoned within himself, saying: What shall I do? I have not where to bestow my fruits. And he said: This will I do; I will pull down my barns and build greater, and there will I gather all my fruits and my goods, and will say to my soul: Dear soul, thou hast much goods laid up for many years; take thine *ease*, eat, drink, and be merry. But God said unto him: Thou fool, this night shall thy soul be required of thee, and whose then shall be what thou hast prepared?—

(xii.) I am come to kindle a fire upon the earth; what would I rather, if it burneth already? But first must I be baptised with a baptism, and how am I straitened till it be accomplished! Suppose ye that I came hither to bring peace etc. See the following verses.—

(xvii.) But first must he suffer many things and be rejected of this generation. (Also Act IV.)

"*Remember Lot's Wife!*"

(xxii.) There arose a strife among them, which of them should be accounted the greatest. Jesus: "The kings of this world do rule, and the mighty are called Gracious Master. But not so ye; for he that is greatest among you, let him be as the youngest, and the chief as a servant. For whether is the greater? he that sitteth at table, or he that serveth? Is it not he that sitteth at table? But I am among you as a servant." (Also Act IV.)

John (*i.*) (to the Mother) Which were born, not of blood, nor of the will of the flesh, nor of the will of a man, but of God.

(v.) I receive not honour from men; but I know you, that ye have not the love of God in you.

(vii.) Then said his brethren unto him: "Depart hence and go into Judæa, that thy disciples also may see the works that thou doest. No man doeth anything in secret, and yet himself seeketh to be known openly. If thou doest these things, so reveal thyself before the world."—&c.

Rom. (ii.) For so the heathen, which have not the law, yet do by nature the work of the law; these same, having not the law, are a law unto themselves, in that they shew that the work of the law is written in their hearts, forasmuch as their conscience witnesseth to them, and also their thoughts, which do accuse or else excuse each other *etc.*

(vii.) *But now are we delivered from the law, and dead to that which held us captive, that we should serve in the new order* [*Wesen*] *of the spirit, and not in the old order of the letter. Seq.*

I. Cor. (*i.*) *But that which is foolish before the world, God hath chosen it to confound the wise, and what is weak before the world, God hath chosen it to confound what is strong; and the ignoble before the world, and the despised, hath God chosen, and things that are naught, that he may bring to naught the things that are somewhat, that no flesh should boast itself before him.*

(*iii.*) *Know ye not that ye are the temple of God, and the Spirit of God dwelleth in you? If any man destroy* [*or "defile"*] *the temple of God, him shall God destroy, for the temple of God is holy, which temple ye are.*—Vid. inf. II. Cor. vi.

Wherefore let no man boast of a man. All is yours; whether Paul or Apollo, whether Kephas or the world, whether life or death, whether things present or the things to come; all is yours. But ye are Christ's, and Christ is God's.

(ix.) Every man that striveth in the games is temperate in all things; they do it to receive a perishable crown, but we an imperishable.

I seek not what shall profit myself, but what profiteth many.

II. Cor. (*vi.*) But ye are the temple of the living God, as God hath said: I will dwell in them, will walk with them, and will be their God, and they shall be my people.

(*viii.*) *For if a man is willing, he is acceptable according as he hath, not according as he hath not. I mean not that others may have ease, and ye distress, but that it shall be equal. So let your superfluity supply their want, that thereafter their abundance also may supply your want, and there may be equality, as standeth written: He that had gathered much, had no excess, and he that had gathered little, had no lack.*

Galatians (*v.*). But ye, dear brethren, have been called to freedom. Yet see that through freedom ye do not give way to the flesh, but by love serve one another. (Also Act I.)

Eph. [*iv.*] *Till we all attain to one faith and knowledge, and become a perfect man; so that we no more be children tossed to and fro and swayed by every wind of doctrine and sleight of men, and craftiness, whereby they lie in wait to seduce us.*

Let him that stole, steal no more, but labour and work with his hands a thing that is good, that he may have to give to him that needeth.

(vi.) Put on the armour of God *etc.*

I. Thessal. [iv.] So strive ye to be quiet, and do your own business and labour with your own hands, as we commanded you, that ye may walk honestly toward them that are without, and need nothing of theirs.

I. Tim. (*vi.*) *For we brought nothing into the world, wherefore it is certain we can carry nothing out. But having food and raiment, let us be content. For they that would be rich, they fall into temptation and a snare, and many foolish and hurtful lusts, which drown men in perdition and damnation. For covetousness is a root of all evil, which hath seduced many* etc.

James. (v.) Go to now, ye rich men, weep and howl for your misery that shall come upon you. Your riches are corrupted, your garments are motheaten. Your gold and silver is rusted, and their rust shall be a witness unto you, and shall eat your flesh as a fire. Ye have gathered your treasures for the last days. Ye have condemned and killed the just, and he did not resist you.

For Act III.

Matth. (v.) Think not that I am come to destroy the law and the prophets. I came not to destroy, but to fulfil.

(*ix.*) *No man mendeth an old garment with a patch of new*

cloth, for the patch teareth away from the garment again, and the rent is made worse. Neither do men put new wine into old wine-skins, else the skins do burst and the wine is spilt and the skins are ruined; but put new wine into new wine-skins, the two will hold with one another.

(xvi.) They asked that he would let them see a sign from heaven. Jesus: "At evening ye say, The day will be fine, for the sky is red; and at morning ye say, It will be foul weather to-day, for the sky is red and lowering. Ye hypocrites, the heavens' face ye can discern; can ye not also discern the signs of this time?" *et seq.*

(xxi.) (Entry into Jerusalem.) The stone which the builders rejected, it hath become the head of the corner. —The kingdom of God shall be taken from you, and given to the heathen which do bring forth its fruits. And he that falleth on this stone, shall be broken to pieces; but on whomsoever it shall fall, him will it grind to powder.

(*xxii.*) *Thou shalt love God thy Lord with all thy heart, with all thy soul, with all thy mind. This is the chief and greatest commandment. The other is like unto it: Thou shalt love thy neighbour as thyself. In these two commandments dwell the whole Law and the Prophets.*

(xxiii.) On Moses' seat sit the scribes and pharisees; they speak the law, but do it not. They bind heavy burdens and grievous to be borne, and lay them on men's shoulders, but themselves will not move them with a finger. *Following verses.*

Luke. (xi.) Woe unto you, for ye build the sepulchres of the prophets, but your fathers killed them, *et seq.* Woe unto you scribes, for ye have the key of knowledge; ye enter not therein, and ward them off that fain would enter.

(xiii.) Jerusalem, Jerusalem, thou that killest the prophets and stonest them that are sent to thee, how often would I have gathered thy children together, as a hen her brood under her wings, and ye would not! Behold, your house shall be left unto you desolate. For I say unto you, ye shall not see me till it cometh that ye say, Blessed is he that cometh hither in the name of the Lord.

(*xvii.*) "*When cometh the kingdom of God?*" "*The kingdom of God cometh not with outward tokens. Neither shall they say, Lo here! or Lo there! For behold, the kingdom of God is inward within you.*" (Also Act II.)

(xix.) "Master, rebuke thy disciples!" Jesus: "I tell you, when these shall hold peace, the stones shall cry out."—

John (i.): The true Light, which lighteth every man that cometh into this world. It was in the world, and the world was made by the same, and the world knew it not. He came to his own estate, and his people received him not.

(vii.) My discourse is not mine, but his that sent me. If any man will do his will, he shall become aware whether this teaching be of God, or whether I speak from myself. And foll. (*very important*: from 26. The whole chapter.)

(viii.) It is also written in your law, that the testimony of two is true. I am one, that beareth witness of myself, and the Father, that sent me, beareth witness of me also. Then said they unto him: "Where is thy father?" Jesus: "Ye know neither me, nor my Father; if ye knew me, ye would know my Father also."

Who art thou, then? Jesus: "In the first place he who speaketh with you." &c.

"Made free." (The whole chapter from 31.) (Also for Act I.)

(x.) "*I and the Father are one*!" Following verses.

(xi.) 47 and foll. Council of the Priests and Pharisees.

Acts of Ap. (xvii.) The God whom ye ignorantly worship, him declare I unto you. God who made the world and all that is therein, seeing that he is one Lord of heaven and earth, he dwelleth not in temples made with hands; neither is he tended with man's hands, as though he needed any man, for he himself giveth to each man life and breath and all things, and hath made that of one blood the whole race of men shall dwell on all the face of earth, and hath set bounds beforehand how long and how far they shall dwell, that they should seek the Lord if haply they might feel and find him. And truly he is not far from any one of us, for in him we live, and move, and have our being; as certain also of your own poets have said, We are of his race. Forasmuch then as we are of race divine, we ought not to think that the Godhead is like unto images of gold, or silver, or marble, made by thoughts of man.

Rom. (iii.) We reckon therefore that a man is justified, without the work of the law, through (Love) alone. [The original, of course, has "faith."]

(x.) For, being ignorant of the righteousness that counteth before God, they go about to establish their own righteousness, and have not submitted themselves to the righteousness that counteth in God's eyes. For Christ is the end of the Law; whoso believeth in him, he is righteous.

(For Act IV.) *I. Cor.* (*xv.*) *Thereafter the end, when he shall deliver up the kingdom to God and the Father, when he shall abolish all rule and all supremacy and power. But he must rule till he hath put all his enemies under his feet. The last enemy that shall be abolished, is Death.*—

Galatians (iv.) 22 and following: Hagar-Sinai and Jerusalem (*Important!*)

Timoth. (vi.)—School-wranglings of men deranged of mind and bereft of the truth, *who suppose that godliness is a trade.*

(Also Act II.) *Peter* [II.] (ii.) They count it pleasure to live for the day; spots they are, and blemishes, disporting themselves with your alms, revelling in what is yours; eyes have they full of adultery, not guarding them from sin; entice to themselves unstable souls, have a heart strained through with covetousness; accursed people! They are springs without water, and clouds driven round by a whirlwind, for whom is reserved a darkness, a blackness for ever. For they utter swelling words with naught behind them, and promise freedom while themselves are servants of corruption. For of whom a man is overcome, his servant hath he become. *Et seq.*

Hebr. (viii.) In that he saith: A new, he maketh the

former old; but that which is old and belated, is near to its end.

(x.) For it is impossible to take away sin by the blood of bulls and goats. (Also Act I.)

James (iv.) Ye are greedy, and gain nothing by it; ye hate and envy, and win nothing by it; ye strive and war, and ye have naught.

Revel. John. See the whole chapter xviii.

For Act IV.

Matth. (x.) Behold, I send you forth as sheep into the midst of wolves; be ye therefore wise as serpents, and guileless as doves. But beware of men; for they will deliver you up to their council-chambers, and will scourge you in their schools. And they will bring you before princes and kings for my sake, for a witness over them and over the heathen. And following verses.—

(x.) What I tell you in darkness, that speak ye in the light, and what ye hear in the ear, that preach on the housetops. (Also Act V.)

(xiii.) And that which was sown upon the rocky places, is he that heareth the word and straightway receiveth it with joy; yet he hath no root in him, but is fickle as the weather; when tribulation or persecution ariseth because of the word, he is soon offended.—But that which was sown among the thorns, is he that heareth the word, and the cares of this world and the deceitfulness of riches choke the word, and he bringeth forth no fruit. (Also Act III.)

(xxiv.) "Tell us, when shall this be, and what shall be the token of thy coming and of the end of the world?" —Jesus: "Take heed that no man deceive you. For many shall come in my name and say, I am Christ, and shall deceive many. Ye shall hear wars and outcry of wars; take heed and be not affrighted; all this must first happen, but the end is not yet. For nation shall rise against nation, and kingdom against kingdom, and there shall be pestilence and dear times, and earthquakes in divers places. Then first shall the trouble begin. *Following verses.*

For like as they were in the days of the deluge, they ate, they drank, they married and gave themselves in marriage, until the day that Noa entered into the ark, and they heeded it not until the flood came and took them all away; so also shall the coming of the Son of Man be.

(xxvi.) 9-12. (Anointment of Jesus by M.M.) 33-34 (Peter and Jesus.)

Luke (xxii.) But he that hath a purse, now let him take it, and likewise his wallet. And he that hath none, let him sell his cloak and buy a sword.—But they said: "Lord, see here are two swords." And he said unto them: "It is enough."

Ye have come out as against a murderer, with swords and staves: I was daily with you in the temple, and ye laid no hand on me; but this is your hour, and the power of darkness.

John (*V.*) I say unto you, the Son can do nothing of himself, but what he seeth the Father do; for whatsoever he doeth, that doeth also the Son in like manner.

(xii.) 4 et seq. (Jesus' anointment and Judas.)

(xiii. xiv. xv. xvi. xvii. *Last Supper.*—)

Acts Ap. (i.) It is not for you to know the times and the seasons which the Father hath set for his authority; but ye shall receive the power of the Holy Ghost, who shall come upon you, and ye shall be my witnesses *etc.*

(iv.) The kings of the earth assemble, and the princes are gathered together, against the Lord and against his Christ.

(Also Act II.) *Let none say of his goods that they are his, but let all be in common among you.*

(Also Act III.) *Rom.* (v.) Now, as through the sin of one the condemnation came upon all men, even so through the righteousness of one hath justification of life come to all men.

(viii.) The selfsame Spirit beareth witness to our spirit, that we are children of God. If we are children, then are we also heirs, the heirs of God and joint-heirs with Christ, if so be that we suffer with him, that we may also be exalted to glory together.

For whom he foreknew, he also foreordained, that they should be like unto the image of his son, that the same might be the *firstborn* among many brethren.

Cor. (xv.) I die daily.—Let us eat and drink, for to-morrow we are dead.

(xv.) The last enemy that shall be abolished, is Death.

(46.) The first man, Adam, is sent into natural life, and the last Adam into spiritual life. But the spiritual body is not the first, but the natural, and afterward the spiritual.

Death is swallowed up in victory. Death, where is thy sting? Hell, where is thy victory? But the sting of death is sin, and the strength of sin is the law.

I. Thessal. [v. 3] Then sudden destruction cometh upon them, as travail upon a woman with child, and they shall not escape.

II. Thessal. (*ii*). And then shall that wicked one be revealed, whom the Lord shall bring to naught with the spirit of his mouth, and make an end of him through the manifestment of his coming; *even he whose coming is after the operation of Satan with all manner of lying powers, and* (Also II. perhaps III.) *signs and wonders, and with all kinds of seduction to unrighteousness among those that are lost because they have not accepted the love of truth, that they might be blessed. Therefore God shall send them strong delusions, that they believe in lies, so that all shall be sentenced who believe not the truth but have pleasure in unrighteousness.*

Timothy [I.] (iv.) But the Spirit plainly sayeth, that in the latter times some shall depart from the faith and cleave to seducing spirits and doctrines of devils through the smooth-speaking of liars who have a brand on their conscience, and forbid to be married, and [command] to abstain from the good which God created to be received with thanksgiving by believers and them that know the truth; for every creature of God is good, and nothing to be rejected that is taken with thanksgiving. *Et seq.*

Hebr. (xi.) But Faith is a certain assurance of things hoped for, and not to doubt of that which is not seen.

For Act V.

Matth. (xxviii.) Go ye therefore and instruct all nations, and baptise them in the name of the Father and the Son and the Holy Ghost, and teach them to observe all things that I commanded you. And lo! I am with you always, even unto the end of the world.

Luke (xxii.) "Art thou Christ? tell it us!" Jesus: "If I tell it you, ye will not believe it; but if I ask, ye answer not, and yet will not let me go. Therefore from henceforth" etc.—

(xxiii.) Ye daughters of Jerusalem, weep not for me, but weep for yourselves and for your children. For behold, the days shall come in the which they shall say: Blessed are the barren, and the wombs that never bare, and the breasts which never gave suck *etc.*

Romans (*viii.*) "For the law of the spirit, that maketh living in Christ Jesus, hath made us free from the law of sins and of death."

(Also Act IV.) *Eph.* (vi.) Put on the armour of God, that ye may be able to stand against the wiles of the devil. For we have not to battle with flesh and blood, but with princes and powers, namely with the lords of the world, who rule in the darkness of this world, with the evil spirits under heaven.

POSTHUMOUS

IV.

SKETCHES AND FRAGMENTS.

Entwürfe.

Gedanken. Fragmente.

The following collection of "*Sketches*" *&c. was first published in the German in 1885, two years after the master's death. That edition is prefaced with the following note:* "*I*[A] *is an exact copy of manuscript papers from the years 1849-51, without any alteration whatever. For this reason even unintelligible notes, as on page* 364, *and almost literal repetitions, have been retained. From I*[C] *onwards there were no longer any continuous drafts, all the jottings being found on loose sheets or in notebooks; an attempt has been made to arrange these according to both their inner connection and their chronologic sequence.*"

In course of a long article upon this publication, Freiherr Hans von Wolzogen in the Bayreuther Blätter *for September 1885 gives us further particulars of dates, with regard to individual jottings &c.; these I have incorporated in occasional footnotes etc.*

The collection is introduced by two mottos, as transcribed by Wagner:—

"*The nation that honours not its past, has no future.*"

Lycurgus of Sparta.

"*If a man thinks much himself, he finds much wisdom embodied in the language.*"

Lichtenberg.

TRANSLATOR'S NOTE.

I[A]

SKETCHES

(1849-51).

FUGITIVE NOTES FOR A LARGER ESSAY: THE ARTISTHOOD OF THE FUTURE.

Artisthood of the Future.*

On the principle of Communism.

What ultimate, positive object have all the various efforts, expressed in saga and history, religion and state-constitution, to find divine or other ancient vindication of arbitrary possession and property? Do we ever see a conqueror, a forcible usurper, whether folk or individual, that does not seek to found its wilful annexation on religious, mythical, or other trumped-up covenants? Whence all these surprising fictions, quibbles and so on, to which *alone* we owe the fashioning of religious and civil constitutions? Indisputably hence: because the reasonable man could claim no actual justification, no truly natural right to this or that possession, and therefore, ne'ertheless to satisfy a gnawing need of vindication, must yield himself to the extravagance of phantasy—which even in our modern civil institutions, however sober they may seem, has deposited her bastards to the scorn of common sense. And so on.†

* "*Künstlerthum der Zukunft.*"

† At the end of the German edition there appears a most valuable table of references to parallel, explanatory, or complemental passages in other of the master's writings; for convenience sake I reproduce these references in

* * *

Ye believe that with the foundering of our present conditions and the beginning of the new, the communistic order of the world, history, the historical life of mankind would cease? Precisely the opposite: for then will actual, clear historic life begin, when the so-called historical consequence of hitherto shall cease; which in truth and at bottom is founded on fable, tradition, myth and religion, on customs and observances, titles and assumptions, whose utmost points repose in nowise on historic consciousness, but on mythical, fantastic fiction (deliberate, for the most part), such as monarchy and hereditary possession. And so on.*

* * *

The attempt at ideal vindication of a wrongful possession always arises at the moment when immediate racial or personal right has been washed, so to say, out of the blood of men. In the beginning man derived all title to enjoyment or possession from himself, his need, and his capacity for enjoyment: his might was his right, and in so far as that might passed over to his offspring, did the right also remain, quite logically, with his descendants,—the race took the place of the person; but with this racial constitution it was always the man that stood foremost, and put the thing into the background. The complete opposite arrives at last, when right is conferred by the thing on the man: according to this, the man per se has no right at all, not even that of existence, but obtains it solely through what he possesses, through the thing. To provide this irrational relation with a basis, one grasps at ideal grounds of vindication innate, as it were, in the quality of *things*. And so on.†

* * *

Only the fullest measure shews the true quality of a

footnotes corresponding to each paragraph, with numerals denoting the volume and page of the English translation. The present paragraph is thus brought into connection with Vol. III. 27-8, 167 (first footnote), 354, 382, VII. 273, 277 et seq., VI. 241.—Tr.

* I. 53-7, II. 173-5, 374-5.

† VII. 297 et seq., II. 192, VI. 80, 267-8, 278.

thing, as of a concept; only when no further comparative is thinkable, is the concept pure and vital: the greeks knew no superlative of *free*,—only through the superlative of its antithesis, of dehumanisation, do we come to-day to full knowledge, because the fullest need, of freedom.—Nature gives us simply the positive: history is the first to give the superlative. The hellene * shews us the splendid creature a man can be, but shews us, too, the scandalous: for man to be quite what he should be, he must raise this "should" to the superlative.†

* * *

Consciousness is the end, the dissolution of unconsciousness: but unconscious agency is the agency of nature, of the inner necessity; only when the result of this agency has come to physical appearance, does consciousness set in—and that, of just the physical phenomenon. So ye err when ye seek the revolutionary force in consciousness, and therefore fain would operate through the intelligence: your intelligence is false—i.e. capricious—so long as it is not the apperception of what already has ripened to a physical appearance. Not ye, but the folk—which deals unconsciously—and for that very reason, from a nature-instinct—will bring the new to pass; but the might of the folk is lamed for just so long as it lets itself be led by the chain of an obsolete intelligence, a hindering consciousness: only when this is completely annihilated by and in itself,—only when we all know and perceive that we must yield ourselves, not to our intelligence, but to the necessity of nature, therefore when we have become brave enough to deny our intellect, shall we obtain from natural unconsciousness, from want, the force to produce the new, to bring the stress of nature to our consciousness through its satisfaction.‡

* At this period Wagner avoided *all* capital letters, out of rebellion against the German style of writing, where every noun begins with a capital. See *Letters to Uhlig*, page 15.—Tr.

† II. 360*n*, III. 202*n*, I. 169-70, 177-8, II. 157-8, VI. 231, I. 54, 90, 263-4.

‡ I. 79-82, II. 193-4, 375, IV. 10, VI. 77.

* * *

The most perfect satisfaction of egoism is attained in communism, i.e. through complete denial, upheaval of egoism; for then only is a need satisfied, when it exists no longer,—hunger is satisfied when it is stilled, i.e. is no more there. My *physical* egoism, i.e. my life-need, I satisfy over against nature by consuming, taking; my moral egoism, i.e. my love-need over against man, by giving myself, sinking myself. Modern egoism has the horrible perversity of thinking to still both moral and physical need alike by nothing but consuming, taking,—of classing its fellow-men in the category of extrahuman nature.*—

* * *

What has arrived through natural necessity at physically-demonstrated certainty, alone can be to us an object; with it first enters consciousness. Only what is accomplished, what presents itself to my senses, am I certain of: in it alone, too, does a thing's essence become plain to me, so that I can grasp it, make myself master of it, and represent it to myself as artwork. The artwork is accordingly the conclusion, the end, the fullest confirmation of the essence whereof I have become conscious.†—But the artwork has erroneously been set in place of constantly-becoming and new-creating life, and indeed as state. The state steps in precisely where the artwork ceases: but daily life itself can never be the object of a binding form devised for permanence: the life of the whole (*das gesammtleben*) is just the unconscious course of nature herself, it has its law in necessity: but to wish to represent this necessity in binding political forms of state is a pestilent error, just because consciousness cannot be made to go before, to regulate, as it were, unconsciousness. The unconscious is precisely the involuntary, the necessary and creative,—only when a general need has satisfied itself at behest of this involuntary necessity, does consciousness set in, and the satisfied, the overpassed, can now become an object of conscious treatment by representation; but this it attains

* I. 96-9, 395. † I. 71, 139, II. 5.

in art, not in the state. The state is a dam to necessary life; art is the conscious expression of something life has brought to end, has overcome. So long as I experience hunger, I do not reflect on the nature of hunger: it governs me, not I it; I suffer, and am not free again till I have rid myself thereof,—and not till I am filled, can hunger become an object of thought to me, of consciousness. The state, however, would represent life, need, itself: it would fix the knowledge of the satisfaction of a former need as norm for the satisfying of all future needs: this is its unnatural essence. Art, on the contrary, contents itself with being the direct expression of the consciousness of the satisfaction of a necessity,—but this necessity is life itself, which the state can only hinder, never rule.*

* * *

Art occupies itself with nothing but the accomplished,—the state also—but with the claim to fix it as a standard for the future, which latter does not belong to it, but to life, to spontaneousness (*unwillkür*). Therefore art is true and upright,—the state entangles itself in lies and contradictions,—art wills not to be more than it can be—the expression of truth,—the state wills to be more than it can be;—so art is eternal, because it ever represents the temporal faithfully and honestly,—the state temporal, because it fain would raise the moment to eternity, and therefore is dead in itself before it has so much as entered life.†

* * *

The folk has ever been the only true inventor,—the so-called inventors known to us by name have merely applied the already-discovered to other, kindred objects,—they are nothing but conduits. The unit cannot invent, but simply annexes an invention.‡

* * *

We need but know what we *don't* want, and of instinctive

* I. 24, II. 178-94, I. 203-4, II. 61, 63, IV. 108-11, 114-7, VI. 116, 119, 122-3, 253-5, 264, 235, 331, IV. 8, 9, 11, 33-4, V. 225, I. 252-3.

† See note to last paragraph.

‡ I. 80-1, 89-90, 207, VII. 266-7, I. 335, VI. 235.

natural-necessity we attain quite certainly to what we do want, which never grows quite clear to our consciousness until we have attained it: for the state (*zustand*) in which we have removed what we *don't* want, is the very one at which we wanted to arrive. Thus deals the folk, and therefore it alone deals rightly.—But ye hold it incapable simply because it knows not what it wants: *what* then know *ye*? can ye think out anything besides the actually extant, i.e. attained? Imagine it, ye can—capriciously fancy it, but not know. Only what the folk has brought to pass, can ye know; till then let it content you to perceive quite plainly what ye do not want, to deny what calls for denial, annul what merits annulment.*

* * *

Who, then, is the folk? All those who experience want (*noth*), and recognise their own want as the common want, or feel it involved therein.

* * *

The folk, accordingly, are those who deal instinctively and of necessity; its foes are those who part themselves from this necessity, and deal of caprice egoistically.†

* * *

The modern egoist cannot grasp the inner want, he understands it only as an outer, a want that thrusts in from without: for instance, that the artist would make no art if want, i.e. the want of money, did not drive him to it. So he thinks it good for artists to be badly off, as they otherwise would do no work.‡

* * *

Only a want that of its essence is a *joint* one is also a real want, creative in its longing for satisfaction: therefore only he who feels a want in common, belongs to the folk. The want of the egoist is an isolated need, opposed to the exigence in common,—and unproductive because capricious.§

* I. 79, 81, 155, 273, VI. 24, 35, 119, 129.
† I. 74-6, 207-9, 27-8, 348, 351, VI. 122, 130.
‡ I. 75-6, VII. 21, 137-8, [I. 31].
§ I. 76-7, 262, VI. 204, I. 161, 184-6, 192-3, V. 340.

* * *

Only the sensuous [or "physical"—*sinnlich*] is also sensible (*sinnig*): the non-sensuous is also nonsensical: the sensible is the perfection of the physical;—the senseless the true purport of the non-physical.*

The conscious deed of the poet, is to discover in the stuff selected for artistic representment the necessity of its disposal, and thus to follow nature's ordering: he may choose what stuff, what incident he will,—only in degree as he perceives therein instinctiveness, *i.e.* necessity, and brings that to view, will he furnish an artwork in its presentation.—Therefore only what the folk, what nature produces of itself, can be a subject for the poet; through him, however, the unconscious in the people's product comes to consciousness, and it is he who imparts to the folk this consciousness. Thus in art the unconscious life of the folk arrives at consciousness, and that more definitely and distinctly than in science.†

* * *

Thus the poet cannot create, but only the folk; or the poet only in so far, as he comprehends and utters, represents, the creation of the folk.‡

* * *

Only that science which wholly and completely denies itself and concedes all authenticity to nature, consequently avows nothing but the natural necessity, thereby totally disowning and annulling itself as regulator or ordainer,—only that science is true: so the truth of science begins exactly where its essence ceases and nothing remains but the consciousness of natural necessity. But the representress of this necessity is—art.

* * *

Science has power and interest for only so long as it is *erred* in: so soon as the truth is found therein, it ceases: it therefore is the tool that has weight for only so long as

* I. 72-3, 79-80, 134, 26, II. 89, 69-71, 313, 316-17, 325-6, 121*n*, 269-70.
† VI. 138, II. 265, 146, 351, I. 365-6.
‡ I. 90, 134, 28, 205, II. 153-5, 191, 356*n*, VI. 235.

the stuff, for whose shaping alone it was required, still offers resistance:—when the kernel of the stuff is bared, the tool loses all value for me: so with philosophy.*

* * *

Science is the highest power of the human mind; but the enjoyment of this power is art.†

* * *

The error (christianity) is necessary, but not necessity itself: necessity is the truth, which emerges as the driving force—driving even error—wherever error has attained its goal, annulled itself and come to end. Error therefore is temporal, truth eternal: so science is temporal and art eternal: for where science finds its end, in recognition of the necessary, the true, there enters art as active energy of truth; for it is the image of the true, of life.‡

* * *

I can will anything—but can carry out only what is true and necessary; he who makes himself dependent on community therefore wills nothing but the necessary, he who withdraws from community—the egoist—the arbitrary. But, for this very reason, caprice can produce nothing.§

* * *

From error sprang science: but the error of the greek philosophers had not strength enough to slay itself; the great folk's-error of christianity first had the prodigious ponderance to slay itself. Here, too, the folk is the determinant force.‖

* * *

Out of life grows everything. When polytheism had practically annulled itself through life, and the philosophers had helped to destroy it by science, the new creation arose of itself, in christianity. Christianity was the offspring of the folk; so long as it remained a purely popular expression, everything in it was sturdily honest and true—a necessary error: instinctively this popular phenomenon

* I. 139, 25, 257. † I. 73. § I. 98-9, II. 210, VI. 124.
‡ I. 70, 71, 74, II. 12, 23, 158, V. 93. ‖ I. 74, 59-60, 113-4, II. 166-8, 16.

forced all the intellect and culture of the græco-roman world to be converted to it, and only when it thus had grown in turn an object of intelligence, of science, did the error in it shew itself dishonest, hypocritical, as theology—where theology could go no farther, philosophy stepped in; and this at last destroys itself, inasmuch as it annuls the error at its most unnatural height, denies itself—as science—and relinquishes all honour to nature and necessity:—and lo, when science has advanced thus far, of itself the popular expression of her result appears in communism, which again has sprung from nothing save the folk.*

* * *

But the people's error is merely the practical attestation, the avowal of the degree of general possibility [at the time]; wherefore also it changes and dissolves, because mankind is not the same to-day as it was, e.g., a hundred years ago. This error therefore is honest, because instinctive.†

* * *

What man is to nature, the artwork is to man: all the conditions needful for the existence of man, begat man; man is the product of nature's unconscious, instinctive begetting, but in him, in his being and life—as a thing differentiated from nature—does consciousness make its first appearance. Just so, when from the instinctive, necessarily-shaping life of men the conditions for the existence of the artwork arise, the artwork also arrives quite of itself, as conscious witness of that life: it arises as soon as it can arise, but then with necessity.‡

* * *

Life is the unconscious necessity, art the recognised and consciously set forth, objectified necessity: life is immediate, art immediate.§—

* * *

Only where a life-need is stilled in the only possible way—namely physically—and therefore its essence has come to physical show, will art be possible: for full consciousness

* I. 74, 155, V. 120, I. 55, 166, 179, II. 374-5.
† II. 165, 70-1. ‡ I. 69. § I. 73, 252.

is only in the world of sense (*sinnlichkeit*):—christianity, on the contrary, was unartistic—and the only christian artists, strictly speaking, are the fathers of the church who set forth the naïve, popular, pithy folk's-belief pure and undisfigured.*

* * *

Man, as he stands confronting nature, is wilful and therefore unfree: from his opposition to, his wilful conflict with her, have issued all his errors (in religion and history): only when he comprehends the necessity in the phenomena of nature and his indissoluble connection with her, and becomes conscious of her, fits himself to her laws, does he become free. So the artist confronting life: as long as he chooses, proceeds wilfully, he is unfree; only when he grasps the necessity of life, is he also able to portray it: then, however, he has no more choice, and consequently is free and true.†

* * *

The essence of the understanding (*verstand*) is wilful throughout, because it refers all phenomena to itself alone; only when it ascends into the joint understanding, into reason (*vernunft*), i.e. perceives the general necessity of things, is it free.‡

(: the art of poetry is not the beginning but the end, i.e., the

Modern poetry. Literature.—out of dance and music, by means of speech, the natural artwork grew to drama: the poetic aim appeared as soon as all the antecedent conditions for its realisement were fulfilled; after the severance and egoistic prosecution of the single arts we come at last to this result, that the littérateur writes a play, e.g., and disposes of the actor as a mere tool, just as the sculptor disposes of his clay or stone;—so the actor, excluded in advance from equal title to collabora-

* I. 38, 49, 255-65, II. 159-60, 162, 166-7, I. 160, 162, 333.
† I. 71, 33, 259, II. 201-2, VI. 121-4. ‡ I. 26, II. 206.

tion, and humbled to a tool, revenges himself by his indifference to the poetic aim, inasmuch as he seeks to satisfy his isolated personal vanity, and so forth. (Very important!) Each tries to be all in all to himself.*

apex: it is the conscious agreement of all the arts to give the fullest message to the generality.)

I. The human arts:—dance. music. poetry.—Their inseparability. growth of the one out of the other: yet synchrony—co-conceivability of them all: united earliest in the lyric: the most intelligibly in drama. (natural, patriarchal fellowship:—self-conscious political state-fellowship.):—accessories of drama, architecture (decoration). sculpture,—painting:—reminiscences, notions, i.e. imitations, of the human artwork:—severance of the art-elements, egoistic evolution thereof.†

II. Dance.‡

III. Music.§

IV. Poetry, i.e. literature-poetry.‖

V. Sculpture and plastique. (where these two flourish, as at present, at the renaissance, and in the græco-roman age, there the drama does not flourish; but where this flourishes, must those fade down.)¶

VI. Reunion. (egoism—communism.) To give is more blessed than to receive.**

For VI. In the present state of our whole social system this reunion can be effected only in the individual, through some unusual faculty residing in him: we therefore are living in the time of isolated Genius, of the rich idemnifying individuality of units. In the future this reunion will take place really communistically, through fellowship; Genius no longer will stand isolated, but all will have part in it, the Genius will be an associate one. Will that be a loss,

* II. 121, I. 146-9, V. 224, 258-62, III. 259-60, I. 136-8, 142-6, 193*n*, II. 127-51, III. 8, 11-14, IV. 103-4, III. 51-4, V. 191-4, 195-7, 214, 138-40, VI. 133-42.

† I. 95, 103-4, 134, II. 281-2.

‡ I. 100 et seq.

§ I. 110 et seq.

‖ I. 132 et seq., II. 119-20.

¶ I. 173, V. 120.

** I. 100, 149.

a misfortune? Only to the egoist can it rank as such. (Very important.)*

For V. With painting, more particularly in its present stage, the opposite, the speculative process enters, the idea preceding the execution: in drama the idea—as avowal of the finished life, the life become conscious of itself—grows as it were out of the material, the physical man; with sculpture and painting the opposite process rules, the idea stands first and seeks itself a body. The latter is caprice, then, the former necessity. The finished artistic man has lain hands on the material lying outside him for an end subserving his human artwork: he has raised the treatment and employment of this material to an art by making the human art's requirement a necessity in that treatment and employment, and therewith imparting to the latter the human artwork's necessity. In so far, accordingly, as sculpture and painting have been drawn into the province of the human artwork and employed as its co-operators, have these arts also taken part in necessity; but in so far as they have cut themselves adrift from the human artwork and appeared in isolation, have they fallen victims to caprice and therefore to actual dependence.†

Necessity: i.e. human art.—*Caprice:* i.e. so-called plastic art. Necessity: i.e. freedom.—Caprice: i.e. unfreedom, *choice and limitation.*

For III. Music on the boundary between dance and speech, feeling and thought. She reconciles them in the ancient lyric, where the song, the sung word, gave fire at once and measure to the dance. Dance—and—Song; rhythm—and melody; so she stands both binding and dependent on the two uttermost faculties of man, of physical sensation and of spiritual thought. The *ocean* severs and unites,—so music.‡

* * *

Greek tragedy a religious act: beautiful, human religion, nevertheless captivity: man saw himself as through a mythic veil. In the grecian myth the bond was not yet

* I. 288-91. † I. 174-5. ‡ I. 110.

severed, which fettered man to (in) nature. Mythos and mystery: thence cleaving to the lyric,—masks, speaking-tubes etc. With increasing enlightenment, i.e. dispersal of the nature-ridden core, the religious drama also sank, and the whole naked, unveiled man became the object of plastique, of statuary etc. This man divorced from all religion came down from the cothurnus, put off the veiling mask, and so forth, but lost withal his communistic oneness with a religion-bound community—he developed naked and unveiled—but as egoist—as in the state, which foundered on the egoism of its units,—and with this egoistic, but truthful and enlightened man, did the art of sculpture first mature: to it the man was matter, to the artwork of the future the matter will be *men*. *Very important.**

The genius of communism (*gemeinsamkeit*).

I. 1. *The original communism* of men: family, tribe, nation, creative force of the associate genius: *Speech, religion, state*, according to their spontaneous origin, objectification of one's own essence in the myth—representation thereof in the lyric artwork, *mythos—lyric*. The myth as direct artistic act of life portrayed in the lyric artwork. Namelessness (impersonality) of the poet: the representation—ever afresh, and in manifold variety—is all, the poet but a member of the representing fellowship.—Immeasurable productivity of this genius in common: it seizes all things personal according to the essence of the tribal or national species, identifies them with its view-of-nature, and so begets that inexhaustible wealth in which saga and myth still present themselves to us to-day. Exactly as the stuff forever reproduced itself anew, instinctively, so also did the artwork to which it gave incentive. Invention

* I. 33-5, 52-3, 165 et seq., 160-2, II. 60-1, V. 302, I. 264, 158-9, 186, II. 152-3, III. 306-8.

of every form of purely-human art on the basis of representant motion of the body.—Summary: general characterisation, (racial particularity).

Particularity, i.e. relation to nature; not, however, to general nature, but to the idiosyncrasy of the specific habitation. Restricted view of nature; the particular nature-gods, the particular gods of the stem. Particularity of the hellenic stems: the *sea, shore.* Mountain peoples, arrived at the sea, remained heroic for just so long as the traffic of the sea did not turn to trade.

2. Dissolution of tribal particularity through the individuality, down to the fullest sovereignty of caprice.

Beginning of history. Characteristic difference of history from myth.—Herodom 1°, of the masses, i.e. of the tribal fellowships. Blending, i.e. subjugation of the more cultivated—agricultural—peoples by warrior—mostly mountaineer and hunter, stems.* Characteristics of the subjugated peoples: stationariness, property, individual caprice—(patriarchate)—weakness: final outcome of the subjugation, loss and foundering of nationality; residue: tillers of the field—without property, labourers—without profit from their labour: slaves.—Characteristics of the ruling stems: continued racial community of speech, religion, state, mythos and art. Communality of property: but under this idea of property *men* also are ranged. Agriculture and domestic labour degraded to a penal task for slaves: without natural, necessary activity, the bond of community loses its fertilising fount, becomes unproductive. All activity is now but warlike exploit outwards, and care to maintain the bondage of the subjugated, inwards.† Confusion about oneself, and gradual loss of understanding of one's own essence: artificial (arbitrary) objectification thereof in—*legislation*, i.e. dogged adherence to old instinctive views of the essence of the community at a time when these views themselves have changed with the altered essence. Tyranny of laws. Law and sin.‡ Forcible isolation,—corruption through lack of necessary activity,—shrinkage to an aristocratic caste.—

* I. 51, 96-9, 134-6, 139-40, 164, 201, 262-3, VI. 226-7, 234-5, 247-8.
† I. 49-51, 206.
‡ II. 197, 204.

The subjugated folk-tribes—peasants, labourers—, becoming more and more necessary to their masters, at last form the nucleus of an opposition which finally—with the beginning of history—asserts itself as democracy. (What in Sparta had formerly been Helots and Messenians, at last appears in Athens, the first purely political state, as—democracy.)

Scandinavians—myth of gods
Franks —myth of heroes } Associate artwork of the heroic—conquering tribal fellowships: the *epos*. In it the hero-myth supplants the (nature) gods-myth—which had flourished, in the lyric, for just so long as the tribes had dwelt on the soil of their home and birthplace and remained in close relation with its *natural* attributes. (Blending of both elements in the Odyssey:—) After the migration, however, on an alien soil and as lords of a subjugated folk-stem, the tribal—nature—gods are turned to heroes; in the hero the warrior fellowship portrays itself, extols its strength and its adventures. Strongly pronounced individualisation of man—as in the god-myth individualisation of the nature-powers. Creative share of the whole stem-fellowship in the epos.*—In the subjugated, denationalised people, however, it is rather the nature—gods—myth that survives, in the lyric:

(Gradual detachment of man from nature:) becoming independent of her through subjugation of men who vicariously remain in direct intercourse with nature. (Organisation of the heroic fellowship.)

Constant intercourse of the country-people with nature, the soil and its natural attributes: alternation of the seasons—ur-old festivals: celebration of spring, of vintage, and so on, easter-sports. natural mirthfulness: nature-gods in fantastic shapes, Satyrs, Fauns: goblins, nixies and so on; country games in these fantastic masks; processions: oldest groundwork of the drama: comedy.—On the other hand, decline of epos with the inevitable decay of the ruling hero-races: advent of state-institutions—areopagus. (christianity = inquisition) conservative care.

(Lack of individuality: nature-religion symbolic—hero-religion typic.)

* II. 153-5, 224.

Christian mystery-plays with their comic interludes. Shakespeare and the clown.

The patrician individuality usurps the people's artwork, the drama, stamps it with its stately epic-heroic, conservative tendence: *tragedy*. Marriage of the nobility with the folk: but the tragedy must always be followed by the satyr-play (necessary concession!) when fate had destroyed the hero-races the people celebrated itself in its most peculiar artwork.*

Plastique seeks to preserve the heroic artwork.—Thenceforward constant conservative tendence of Culture-art.

Distinction between the religions of the nobility and of the folk. Complete extermination of the nobility: total reaction of the folk's-artwork against the nobles'-artwork: *comedy*. *Euripides—Aristophanes.* —— Aristophanes and Socrates. —Aristocracy of intellect — (philosophy) and culture-art (statuary and painting). The philosopher and statesman seeks to reconstruct community artificially: but involuntarily he ever keeps the heroic (nobles') community alone in eye: down to the present day the slave, the ignorant, to him seems indispensable. The man of intellect holds himself privileged *because* he is intellectual,—and crushes down the ignorant, whom he prevents from growing intellectual.†—Absolute arbitrariness of everyone: foundering of all community—saving that of the sufferers: religion of the sufferers—Christianity. Error, triumph and corruption of Christianity: as the nature-religion of the first folk foundered in a tyrannical democracy.‡

The more the ruling families made religion their peculiar appanage and means of rule, did the folk in general lose its sense of religion, which became un-understable to it, nay, as favouring the rulers, its natural foe. Roman sacra: patrician means of rule. Conversion of the roman religion into an abstract theory of rights—property. Indifference of the people toward it. Christendom: dominion of the priest—protestant dominion of the prince: irreligiousness of the masses.—What interest had the Helot, the Attic

* I. 52, 135-6.

† I. 35-7, 83-4, 166-7, 178-9, 258, 260, VI. 230.

‡ VI. 230-3.

people etc., in religion at last? *—So the religious meaning of those country festivals was ultimately lost as well. The god of the poor people: Pan. Folk-humour. The fantastic masks—originally representing nature-gods—represented at last the folk itself, just as the hero-gods had turned at last to hero-men. Catholicism and its opposite: the heroic nobility. New individual hero-races: germanic conquests. New community of rank and possession: new Helots and slaves. on the other hand, fictitious universality in catholicism. Crusades: dissolution of catholic communion: monarchic nationalities: basis thereof=the aristocratism of the ruling races. Characteristics of these nationalities: language, arts.—Swift exposure of the lie in this nationalism, faced with the events of recent times: foundering of all religion, luxury of intellect and industry: on the other hand—distress of the labourers: socialism, communism—omnihumanity:—foundering of history, i.e. of the arbitrary gestes of egoistic individualities detached from the community. (General survey.)†

II. What has been the work of the individuality, i.e. the wilful one?—The destruction of all racial and national barriers, and demonstration of the necessity of the individual's redemption into the human generality.‡ Evolution of the political individuality.

political individuality:
Alexander.—
Napoleon.—
(incapacity.)
Artistic. §
Æschylus.—
Goethe.—

III. Standpoint of the individual genius in the present.—Necessity of its redemption into communism. Historic and social trend thereto.—Reason of the ugliness in modern life. Portrayal of the communism of the future. Fellowships. Communes. Distinction of age:—natural manifoldness. —Education. Love. Old age.—Ubiquity of every moment of life through communism. The genius in common.

the monumental.
Time.
*in*felicity—
unproductivity

foundering of the monumental.

I. The original (tribal) communion of men, at one with

* I. 166, VI. 77-8.
† I. 38-9, 48-9, 76, 166-7, 260-3, IV. 7-8.
‡ II. 195-7, 202, I. 276-8.
§ I. 130, 286-9.

nature; its works: speech, religion, customs,—mythos, lyric.—Gradual replacement of the community by the individuality: hero-dom 1., mass—conquering nations. 2., personality—politics.—Art in general: epos, tragedy —comedy.—philosophy: catholicism:—modern nationalism—socialism—communism.

II. Attitude of the individual towards community.—political individuality: Alexander—Napoleon. (starting-point—end-point.) transitionals.—Artistic individuality: Æschylus — Goethe. (Aristophanes — Socrates.) — The monumental. Time. Unproductivity. Infelicity.—

III. The individual genius and modern community.—Characteristics of modern community. Ugliness.—Redemption. Foundering of history and the monumental, consequent on the social thrust of the present.—Conclusions as to the communism of the future.*

In plastic art man learnt to know nature through observation and imitation: his experience was completed when the correct relation between appearance and human apprehensive power was found. In plastic art there therefore was a definite road to take, that from misunderstanding to understanding of nature: this is the reason of its viability as abstract art-variety existing purely for itself: like every other single art-variety, it had to go through a development essential to its particular nature, but which terminates of itself when arrived at the fixed limits of its special faculty, where it has to ascend into general art. As portrayer of nature, plastic art attained her acme when she could see and reproduce nature without any distortion: upon this summit she is brought to a standstill, however, and can invent no further, for what she had to invent she has already discovered: a new subject alone could set her new tasks, but the natural object remains always the same

* VI. 134-41, I. 182-3, II. 372, I. 282-3, 289, 341-3, IV. 251-2, VI. 38-40, 58, 74.

—because she can only depict the done and finished, not growth, not self-engendering. In so far she is throughly monumental, motionless; but ever new invention is only for that art which has an ever new subject; this is the purely-human, dramatic Art, because it represents man's life itself in motion: the subject of drama is not the finished and recorded act, but the representment of unconscious growth, of the engendering of characters and actions. In the representation of this eternal flux, the only source of constant new invention and refreshening of art, plastic art can only participate when as a finished art —i.e. an art equipped for undistorted portraiture of nature —she conforms to the purely human need; and that—advancing from the simplest to the highest need—will accord to her a share in its continually rejuvenate creative power. Apart from that, she is an art that can only imitate herself again and again, technique, mechanism. To-day no isolated art can invent any new thing more; and that not only plastic art, but no less the arts of dance, instrumental music, and poetry. They all have now evolved their highest faculty, to be able in the associate-artwork, the drama, to invent ever newly again; however, not singly for themselves alone, but precisely in the representing of life, of the ever new subject.*

* I. 171 et seq., 183 et seq.

I[B]

A TITLE-PAGE *

[and various jottings connected with the preceding sketches].

I. Art and the revolution.
II. The artisthood of the future.
III. The artwork of the future.

I. Once the rich man lived on the principle "to give is more blessed than to receive"—he enjoyed a happiness which he withheld, alas! from none but the poor. But the modern rich man says: "to take is more blessed than to give."†

II. (man to beast. (Butcher—hunter.) inartistic lovelessness towards the beasts, in whom we see mere wares for commerce. (riding = love of the horse.—touring = steam.) ‡

III. history of music: = christian expression: "where the word can no farther, there music begins:" = *Beethoven*, 9th Symphony, proves on the contrary: "where music can no farther, there comes the word."—(the word stands higher than the tone.) §

(*Written on the back of this Title-Page.*)

While monks and clerics taught us that joy in life and in the living art was evil, then did ye cherish and protect it,

* To the manuscript of *Die Kunst und Die Revolution.*

† I. 99. ‡ VI. 195, 234-46, 115.

§ I. 130-1, II. 106-11, 253, 285, 288-90, V. 79-80, 101-3, 120, 122, VI. 222-3, 249-50.

whereof your wartburg is the witness; if ye princes are but faithful to your fame, now help us free it altogether from the shameful bonds in which it languishes, from the service of commerce.*

*   *   *

Present-day civilisation. As the *monkey* stands between the lion, proud in full assurance of its wild-beast strength, and man, so stands our modern civilised man between the naked, forceful nature-man and the splendid human being of the future: he is hideous and absurd in this irresoluteness both of form and of essence. In nature all well-defined species are beautiful, but the transitions from one to the other rightly seem to us hideous.

(By ill culture I mean that sprung from our civilisation.)†

*   *   *

"Divide and govern"—so said the god of ugliness when he planned our present civilisation. "Divide the harmony of all the senses in joint enjoyment, let each desire enjoyment for itself alone, and of itself thou orderest the worship of the ugly"—so the whole modern concept of dualism, the separateness of body and soul, rests only on the variance, the severance of the belly-man from the brain-man.‡

*   *   *

Aristophanes and Socrates.§

*   *   *

Bakunin's remark that, arrived at the point of disgust with our civilisation, he had felt a longing to become musician.

*   *   *

The art of the future according to climatic conditions. (Is it the fault of our climate, that we are weaklings and psalm-singers (*herjesus-männer*); and does it prevent us from

The Hottentots besmear themselves with fat,

* IV. 42, 50, 108, 124-5, VI. 270, 8, I. 41-3, 188*n*, II. 373-4, IV. 164.

† I. 57, 58, 59, 160-1, 259, III. 56, 62, 63, VI. 44, 60, 70-7, 119, 256, 270-1.

‡ I. 37, 257, 82-3, II. 199.

§ I. 35, 136, II. 284.

being strong and forceful? Only let us be that, and beauty also is ours at once.)*

and so on. Does the European also smear himself with fat when he sojourns in the land of Hottentots; and is this repulsive practice a necessary result of climatic influence?

Are the Turks and modern Greeks the same that the ancient Greeks were in the selfsame climate?

* * *

It is highly characteristic of plastic art—especially of statuary—that its subject is mostly set for it, the artwork consequently ordered.—†

* * *

(For my defence against attacks concerning any inaccuracy in minor matters I appeal to Lessing, Laokoon XXIX.)

* * *

The man who is what he can be (not according to abstract moral theories, but according to his nature), not only appears beautiful to whoever loves him, but really is so: let us all be what we can, and love each other, and we all shall also be beautiful.‡

Story of the snuff-box taken topsy-turvy.

* * *

Town—and country.

* I. 262, 58. † I. 170-1, 76-7, 159-60, 53, VI. 222. ‡ I. 264.

* * *

Byron wishes to write an epic, and hunts for a hero. This is the most candid admission of our abstract, loveless art-producing.

O how small ye think of man, for sake of your dear God.*

* * *

In power of the microscope we can count a thousand muscles in a grub: are they there that we may see and note them? Certainly not: our natural eye grasps nothing but the outward shape, which gives to it the sense of beauty. Thus is the whole relation of science (abstraction) to art.‡

What does the modern ballet-dancer lack of nakedness, except the will?†

* * *

Achilles to Agamemnon: §

Seekest thou pleasure in ruling,
Let prudence then teach thee to love.

* * *

Whoso cannot rejoice, go schl—t [? "schlaget," i.e. slay] him.—; he is not worthy life, for whom it has no charm. ||

* * *

When Wachilde had born a son to Wiking, the three norns came and dowered the child with gifts: the eldest gave wisdom, the younger strength, the third a mind never-satisfied, forever intent on the new. Wiking waxed wroth at this last of gifts, and denied the youngest norn his thanks. Sculd rose and took her gift away. Bitterly did the father rue it. The child grew up a giant in his body's strength, profound in meditative wisdom: but energy entirely failed him; this lack became a matter of his knowledge, though never of his will; he mourned the

Anarchy. Freedom is: to tolerate no rulership that goes against our nature, our knowledge and our will. But if we voluntarily set up a rule that orders naught save what we know and will already, it is superfluous and

* I. 60, 265, VI. 210. † I. 106. ‡ I. 72-3, II. 158, 218-9, VI. 118-9.
§ *Letters to Uhlig*, pp. 35 and 52.—Tr.
|| I. 36-7, 71, II. 371-2, V. 288, VII. 81, 255, III. 224, [VII. 15.—Tr.].

thing he lacked, but nevermore could he replace it. So the strong was scoffed at for a booby: he bore it all, since his reason said how right they were who mocked him: only when they spoke equivocally of his mother, did he grow angry. Never did he build him a boat—but he knew the shallows of rivers and seas, and waded through them: hence his name, Wate.—He is the German folk, upon whom Wiking's sorry bringing-up is practised still each day.*

irrational. Only if we held ourselves for ignorant and arbitrary, could we deem it helpful to endure a rule that ordered what is right for us to know and will: yet the very fact of our thinking it helpful would prove that of ourselves we knew and willed the right, and therefore demonstrate the superfluity of rule. To endure a rulership, however, which we assume not to know and will the right, is slavish.†

* * *

1. Genius. (constant: 1, absorption, denial, extinction, of time by the artwork = dramatic genius. 2, prolongation of time = motionless genius of plastique. 1. communism. 2. egoism.

Worship of a great master lames our own energy: quite rightly do we deem each "perfect" one above us, just because we are not yet perfect: but if we look at the goal of his creative genius, we find it to be art itself, and we need despair of achieving anything higher only when we

* I. 290-1, IV. 165-6, VII. 84-101, 115, 175-7, 182, 202, I. 147-8, II. 52-3, 113-4, 134, 141, 357-62, III. 31-4, 49, 258, 267, 270*n*, IV. 40-50, 62-3, 68-70, 86-93, 100-4, 108, 113, 135, 189-91, 204, 213-5, 253-6, I. xvii., III. 117-8, IV. 338-9, 344, 346, 360, V. 6, 42, 84, 124, 175-6, 180, 213, 279-80, 286, 288, 316-7, 327, 330, 332-3, 339, VI. 7-8, 25-6, IV. 151-69, VI. 46-7, 58, 65-6, 121-4, 127-8, 146, 155, 319, I. 213.

† I. 79, 291, 270*n*, II. 4-5.

look upon art as identical with the work of the single genius. This latter, however, can only apply to the variety, not to the species, of art.

The growing consciousness of void in life first brought forth the idea that time is to be measured by duration, not by animation.

2. The tragic matter (the tragic principle) of antiquity, of the present, and of the future.

3. Man and woman. (or perhaps simply: woman.)

4. The family.

5. Men (i.e. society.)

6. Virtue—vice. Law—sin.*

* * *

1. *The Pianoforte.* (Very important.) progressive abstraction: human voices, instruments = abstract (imitated) human voices: pianoforte, abstraction of the orchestra in behalf of egoism.†

2. *Beethoven* and *Rossini.*‡

3. The recited play (without music.) If absolute music is colour without drawing, absolute poetry is drawing without colour.

* * *

Achilles, after slaying Hector, questioned by the captains whether he now would not join with them in the razing of Troy: "the heart of the eagle I've tasted, the carcass I leave to yourselves!" "What wilt thou do then?" Ach: "Digest!"

Achilles waives the immortality his mother Thetis offers him, an immortality without delight: the delight he is to reap from vengeance allows him to spurn the joys of immortality. (His mother acknowledges that Ach. is greater than the elements (the gods.)

* * *

Man is the completion of god. The eternal gods are the elements for the begetting of man. In man, therefore,

* II. 375-6, I. 146, 155, 160, 162, 166-7, 33-4, 198-201, II. 186-8, 193-201, 204-5.

† II. 122-3, 151, IV. 197-200, II. 253.

‡ II. 45-6.

creation finds its end. Achilles is higher and more perfect than the elemental Thetis.—*

* * *

Reason (*vernunft*) is man's knowledge of nature, as it were the faithful mirror of nature in the human brain: reason can know naught else than nature: a knowledge beyond nature were madness.†

* * *

No unit can be happy before we all are, because no unit can be free before we all are. ‡

Strength.—impulse (*trieb*)—will—enjoyment.
Love.—impulse: sexual love. family-love
love toward men. (the idea)
(society.)
Reason.—reduction of all ideas to nature (truth.)
reason: measure of life.
Freedom. (i.e. reality.)

The more independent and free, the stronger the love: compare the maternal love of a lioness with that of a cow, the conjugal love of wolves with that of sheep etc. §

* * *

Gott: (idee in allen gestalten zum leiden der menschen.) ||
Freedom: resolution of the idea into being.

* * *

The Greek Apollo was the god of beauteous men: Jesus the god of all men; let us make all men beautiful through freedom.¶

* I. 157, 166. † VI. 73, 246. ‡ I. 263, 96-8, 50-1.

§ I. 58-9, 263, II. 352-3, III. 221-4, I. 153, II. 205.

|| In this form the sentence is unintelligible: literally it would be "God: (idea in all shapes to the suffering of men)," though one might read "fashioning" instead of "shapes"; or again, rendered somewhat freely, "abstract idea—perhaps, idée fixe—whatever its form, brings but sorrow to man." However, it is possible that "leiden" is a slip of the pen for "leben"; in which case the sentence could be expanded into "idea that informs all creatures up to human life," thus bringing it into harmony with the paragraph above that commences with "Man is the completion (*vervollkommnung*) of god."—Tr.

¶ I. 264, 65, 79-80.

* * *

Nothing to-day is free but the artwork, which in itself fulfils the beautiful and strong as semblance: no idea is free ere it has been destroyed, i.e. executed, translated into life: real living in beauty and strength alone is free.*—

* * *

The most perfect condition on earth is that wherein human nature, enhanced ad infinitum by society, can experience no longing which it is not in the position to satisfy.

Man's happiness consists in enjoyment: enjoyment is the satisfaction of a longing: the road from desire to satisfaction is deed. Desire in and for itself is suffering; through satisfaction in enjoyment arises joy. The surrounding creation has given man everything to satisfy his desire, for nature herself could not bring forth man before she had produced the means for his sustenance etc.: in a wilderness no man was made.

Society in its multiplicity enhances man's desire, but heightens also his enjoyment, through satisfaction of this enhanced desire, and accordingly his joy. a society which heightens everyone's desire, but does not fulfil it in the same degree to each, is sinful and engenders that awful state of suffering and vice which we have known since ever history began, and now find coming more and more to consciousness. This is despotism, under all its differing forms. Freedom, on the contrary, consists in no obstacle's standing on the path of action, the path from longing to enjoyment, either of the unit or of society; and the one social duty must therefore consist in removing by associate action the natural hindrances which impede the satisfaction of a desire made greater by society itself. The enjoyment reaped through satisfaction of man's physical craving is productive for the individual, since it keeps and feeds the human body. The satisfaction of the desire of love is productive for society, since it increases society. Love, ac-

* I. 35, 97, 107, 183.

cordingly, is the mother of society:—wherefore it can but be its one true principle.*

* * *

Since the beginning of history we perceive but one lever of motion, the longing of human nature intensified to crime: vice, crime, represents in itself the activity of the human race: in it alone is shewn (in great disfigurement) the sincereness of human nature. Virtue, on the contrary, appears as the unstilled longing, renunciation, suffering, sacrifice. Only vice do we see productive in history: virtue, on the contrary, powerless, because it is merely the negation of vice; it has no activity: where virtue girds itself to action, it becomes another vice.†

Note written upside-down between the lines of the above.

A prodigious movement is advancing through the world: it is the storm of european revolution; everyone is taking part in it, and he who does not further it by an onward thrust, but strengthens it through counter-pressure.‡

* * *

In this wise has world-history developed the extraordinary faculties of human nature to their full, and, taken broadly, itself appears as the stupendous energy devoted by the human race to the satisfaction of an infinitely enhanced desire, whose fulfilment accordingly must be the highest enjoyment.§

* * *

Were the earth given over to me, to organise human society to its happiness thereon, I could do no else than grant it fullest liberty to organise itself: that liberty would arise per se from the demolition of everything that stands opposed to it.||—

* * *

Revolution is the movement of the mass toward acquisition and employment of the force which it hitherto had

* I. 69, 201-2, 263, II. 202, 205, 351-3, 355, VI. 259, III. 115*n*.

† I. 76, 193, VI. 227-9, 327-8.

‡ I. 62, 24, 29, [VIII. 232—Tr.].

§ I. 261-2, II. 173-5, VI. 247-9.

|| II. 193n^3, IV. 59-62.

seen with suffering and admiration, then with envy and indignation, in the hands of the unit. The standpoint from which it reacts is that of suffering, renunciation, restraint, i.e. the standpoint of virtue, which it wills to raise triumphant over vice. In movement, however, the action necessarily develops, suffering becomes passion, virtue vice: desire enhanced by conflict can be satisfied only by enhanced enjoyment, and thus are developed the mass's force and faculty, which necessarily must arrive in the end at a standpoint opposite to that where the movement started—that of privation—, i.e. the mass attains to the same force and faculty as the individual (the aristocracy); and only on this standpoint is freedom possible, namely among the equally strong, just as love is possible only among the equally loveworthy.*—

* * *

Where desire is not extant at all, is lifelessness: where the fulfilment of desire is checked unnaturally, i.e. activity is hindered, there is suffering,—where fulfilment is altogether denied to desire, there is death.†

* * *

The Miraculous in Art.

The condensation of the most varied and extended phenomena, where many members harmonise to produce one single, definite effect; the perspicuous presentation of such a harmony, which to us remains unseizable without the deepest research and widest experience, and fills us with amazement when beheld,—in art, which can operate only conformably to certain conditions of time and place, this is to be attained through nothing save the *miraculous.* Here in poetic fiction the tremendous chain of connection embracing the most heterogeneous phenomena is condensed to an easily-surveyed bond of fewer links, yet the force and might of the whole great chain is put into these few: and *in art* this might is miracle.—etc.‡—

* I. 52-6, 208-9. † I. 321-3. ‡ II. 211 et seq., VI. 216, 218-20.

* * *

Lyric and Drama.

(Youth, ripe age. Unconsciousness—consciousness, and so on.) Lyric—enjoyment of art for *oneself*:—Drama—enjoyment offered to others. (morning and evening)—Spring—autumn.—In autumn we enjoy the fruits the spring brought us as blossoms. In spring we all become lyrists—in autumn—(waning—melancholy) dramatists = artistic revival of the spring (winter) = the dramatic reissuing in the Lyric—winter in spring: exit from the artificial dwelling-rooms of man into open nature.—

The same on a larger scale: (world-historically, as it stands before us = evolution of the artwork of the future out of consciousness, i.e. out of the knowledge of nature, i.e. of the mythos and primitive lyric.) Mankind in its distribution over the earth:—tropics = perpetual spring and summer = pre-eminently lyric. Temperate zones = change: predominantly *autumn*: Drama. Mutual fertilisation: constant refreshening of the northern drama by strains of lyric from the south:—strength and firm contour given to the tropical lyric through contact with the drama of the north:—Most manifold transitions.*—

* * *

Genius.

In a favourable event the whole reward of genius in advance of its times could only consist in the exaltation of egoism: deification,—we deify and worship naught save what is unintelligible to us: what we fully understand we love, declare to be a part of us, our equal. This will be the reward of the individual genius of the future.†

* * *

Antique:—out of the chorus into the individual: modern: Shakespeare, commencement with the individual.‡

* I. 103-4 [also *Meistersinger* act. iii.—Tr.].

† II. 375, I. 270, 288-9, VI. 85-6, *Meistersinger* act iii (Sachs and the people).

‡ II. 60-1, I. 53, 46.

* * *

Birth out of music: Æschylus.*

Decadence—Euripides.

—That anything came of Tragedy since then, was simply the deed of a single genius—Shakespeare. Otherwise, as a class of Drama—nothing.

* * *

Opera exactly the same effect as in the Concert-hall: depotencing of the reason.—Conversely in the perfect Drama the full shapes of the dream-vision, the other world, projected before us life-like as by the Magic lantern—as with Ghost-seeing the figures of all times and places distinct before our eyes. Music is the lamp of this lantern.†

* * *

We have said:

in Opera one needs to see something—because its music does not fill us; here accordingly the ear is depotenced—no longer to take in the music intensively. Conversely, a music should be able so to inspire the sight that it shall see the music in shapes.†

* * *

Thus, in our Art-history—the Musician (as *Artist*) is initiated into his art from without; Mozart died when he was just piercing to the mystery. Beethoven was the first to enter wholly in.‡

* * *

Technique.

Technique is the accumulating property of every artist

* V. 196-7, VI. 140, III. 266, II. 282-3, III. 71-2, V. 121, 301-2, 306, 139, IV. 74-5, I. 365-6, 292. [Wolzogen considers that this jotting may perhaps date from 1875-78; should this be the case, the last but two, on "Lyric and Drama," may date from 1861-2, the time of the *Meistersinger* poem, though it partially recalls the end of the first act of *Die Walküre*.—Tr.]

† II. 124-51, V. 107, 110-1, VI. 143, V. 80, 277, 303, VI. [170] 182-3, 327, II. 342-9 [Wolzogen tells us that the first of these two allied paragraphs dates from the sixties, the second from the seventies.—Tr.]

‡ VII. 108-9, I. 120-3, 126, 207-10, III. 317, IV. 193-5, 216-7, III. 116, IV. 317-9, 361-2, V. 78-9, 81-3, 86-90, 103, VI. 89-91, 152, 170-1, 177-8. [This par. dates from the sixties, whereas the succeeding one is evidently from 1849-51.—Tr.]

since the existence of art: it can be accepted, learnt and acquired. That which is to be portrayed by means of technique is in nowise to be learnt, and of it we therefore do not speak.*

* VI. 141, I. 118-9, 127-9, II. 39, III. 48, IV. 76, 261, 348, VI. 222, I. 291.

IC

APHORISMS ON COLOUR, SOUND ETC.

I have met—intelligent—people with no sense at all of music, and for whom tone-forms had no expression, who tried to interpret them by analogy with colour-impressions; but never have I met a musical person to whom sounds conveyed colours, excepting by a figure of speech. [1879, according to Wolzogen.]

* * *

On modulation in purely Instrumental music, and in Drama. Radical difference. Rapid and remote transitions often are as necessary here, as impermissible there for lack of motive.*—[From a note-book of the year 1857.]

* * *

Style.

One would write not only correctly, but in a certain sense even poetically, if with every metaphor one strictly abode by the physical meaning of the principal word [or "noun"], now employed abstractly, in all the epithets and verbs appended to it.

E.g. instead of "His self-reliance (*Selbständigkeit*) breaks through its covering veil" (which is absurd), "His self-reliance stands suddenly revealed (or, bare of its veil)," which would preserve the figure of a statue after its unveiling.† [1869.]

* VI. 175 et seq., II. 291-4, VI. 171.

† IV. 257 et seq., II. 226, 264, 231-2, III. 318, IV. 182, V. 294, 296, IV. 99, 103, V. 332, VI. 57-8.

I^D

FRAGMENTS ON BERLIOZ, ROSSINI, ETC. [1869].

To say nothing but good of a man who all his life heard almost nothing but evil about himself, is just as sacred a duty after his death,* as it becomes a sad necessity to withdraw from one who took the keenest pains to ensure that nothing but good should be said of him during his lifetime the false show which now must misinform posterity. Easy would right judgment be in every case, were the net value of an artist more easy to appraise: but this latter becomes a most difficult task when that artist's influence alike on his age and on posterity seem equally doubtful, whilst on the other hand his pre-eminent artistic qualities themselves are recognisable beyond all doubt. Perhaps in this case it would be best to abide by a faithful recognition of these qualities, since we thence might argue to the character of the artist's contemporary world in a manner that would save us from over-estimating the spirit in which Posterity will approach what the Present bequeaths it; an advantage to those at least who know their judgment narrowed by the influences of no epoch, and free to make acquaintance with the beautiful and significant in all things purely-human.

We now choose Hect. Berlioz, to gain in his case such a judgment uncramped by time and circumstance.†

[Commencement of a discontinued essay, written shortly after Berlioz' death.]

Herr Hiller informs us that, in answer to his question

* II. 89.—Tr.

† VIII. 131, II. 75-80, 332, III. 249-50, VII. 178-82, 187-9, 194, 200, V. 208, I. 15, III. 287 et seq., VII. 139-40, III. 142.

whether poetry and music could ever rouse *an equal interest at the selfsame time*, Rossini replied: "If the magic of tone has really seized the hearer, the word undoubtedly will always come off second best. But if the music doesn't grip (?), what is the good of it? It is useless then, if not superfluous or even detrimental."

We are not surprised at this answer of Rossini's, but rather at his giving any, after a question which Herr Hiller himself might easily have answered in the selfsame terms. However, should Herr H. still be hankering for solutions of problems as to which he is in doubt, we advise him to ask of Rossini next time, "How he accounts for Mozart's music to 'Cosi fan Tutte' not even remotely approaching the effect of that to 'Figaro' or 'Don Juan'? Or, to take an instance nearer home—why 'Der Advocat' failed at Cologne a year ago, notwithstanding that he—Hr Hiller—himself had made the music for it."*

If I never really instigated the various attempts to place my works before the French public, but simply yielded to occasion offered me, I was guided by a feeling which you yourself must have noticed if you kindly paid attention to the Preface to the 4 translated opera-poems ["Music of the Future"] which I let appear in Paris 1861. This feeling of mine was most strikingly corroborated by the truly deterrent ill-will with which my "Tannhäuser" was received at the Paris Grand Opéra. The motives of the hostility then displayed towards my work seemed so multifarious, that it took a longish time to arrive at the principal reason. F. Liszt, I believe, was the first to light upon it: having remained aloof from the heat and passion of the incident itself, he came to the settled conclusion that this or that personal antagonism in the way of myself and my work

* II. 37,—(On Ferd. Hiller), IV. 261 et seq., 310, 345, 350, 360, 363, III. 160-1, IV. 105, VI, 171; (On Rossini), IV. 269 et seq., II. 39-47, 56-7, III. 125-6, 143, VII. 99-100, V. 38, 40, 41, 49, VI. 67-8, 152, 161, 165, 172, IV. 52, 201, VII. 143 et seq., III. 323, II. 89.

might have been conquered with a little patience, if the work itself had stood on a soil where it really could have taken root. He referred to the traditions and idiosyncrasy of this particular theatre, the Paris Grand Opéra, which he compared to those of the Théâtre Français; Shakespeare having always proved an impossibility at the latter, at the former the ideal peculiar to the German genius would remain no less of an inscrutable monstrosity. However, it was no question of the French public's sensibility to the truly characteristic in general, but simply of the expectations which the stranger art-genre had to meet. A Shakespeare-theatre—so Liszt opined—assuredly would interest and progressively attract, if not the whole Parisian public, at least a very substantial part thereof; but before all things, Sh. would be received without a protest *there*—an inconceivability at the Théâtre fr., because the great Briton must here be looked at as an alien and intruder on an unusually well-marked national domain.

About that time Liszt informed me that, asked personally by the Emperor N. III. his opinion of the singular Tannhäuser affair, he had expressed it to the effect that my works ought not to be offered to the French public in any other than their original garb, as avowedly German products, without the least pretence of Frenchifying them, and above all that they should be set on a terrain where every notion of accepting them as French had been abandoned in advance. The Emperor considered this a perfectly intelligible explanation of the case. What ideas it may have contributed to engender in him, I recently discovered when I heard that the Emperor had proposed to his Ministers the inclusion of an *international theatre* in the programme for the last Grand Paris Exhibition. Not one of these ministers understood him: all held their tongues. The Emperor pursued his thought no farther.

Now, I feel disposed to take up this imperial thought, and think it out. Only with great reluctance and timidity, however, can I try to impart my conclusions to others. For I can neither express myself clearly, nor with any hope of being really understood, without openly pointing to two opposite factors which so very few now *wish* to understand; these are the defects of our one-sided development of nationalism, and to their exposure we frequently are more sensitive than to an allusion to personal faults.

To be compassed through the initiative of the French spirit, the realisation of the Emperor's idea of an International Theatre in Paris would have to issue from a need experienced by that spirit itself. We are not supposing the Spaniard, the Englishman, the German or the Italian, to be seized by the wish to found an international theatre in Paris; but we have to imagine the Frenchman taken with a longing to widen his horizon by close acquaintance with the peculiarities of the Theatre of those nations, so as to enable him to remedy some deficiency of his own. Well, if we reflect that ever since the decline of the great Renaissance, i.e. the middle of the 17th century, French Form has governed every cultured nation in the world, above all in respect of the Theatre, and to so notable a degree that almost every native idiosyncrasy of other nations appears to have been remodelled thereby,—such a suggestion will seem wellnigh absurd to address to the French spirit. Our only excuse might be the question, How does this paramount French spirit feel about its own supremacy?*

[Draft for a private letter.]

* * *

If it be a fact that the attention and hope of foreign nations are turned to the unfolding of German Art on the field of Poetry and Music, we must assume that their main concern is with the Originality and unmarred Idiosyncrasy of such unfolding, as they would otherwise obtain no fresh

* VI. 92, VII. 197*n*, III. 269-71, VII. 115-22, I. 16-7, III. 349 seq. II. 131-4, 141, 146, 149-50, 231, 282-3, 359, 369, III. 298-9, I. 153*n*, 147-8, 185, II. 35, 112-4, III. 29, 33, V. 151-2, IV. 175-6, 181-2, 193, 195, 300-1, 352, VI. 64-5, V. 165, 326, VII. 208-10, 219 [222], IV. 37-42, 49, 53-7, 69-70, 82-5, 90, 96, 101-4, 112, V. 84, 85, 114-9, 123-4, 37-9, 42, 44-55, IV. 343, V. 269, 267, III. 384-5, V. 6, III. 267, 115, VI. 57, 45, 114, III. 281, V. 291.

incentive through us. I believe that in this sense it would concern our neighbours no less than ourselves, to see a truly German Style developed by us loyally.*

Beethoven—Schumann.

Music: *intuitions* (Anschauungen)—*concepts* (Begriffe).†

* * *

Goethe a physicist become poet—Schiller a metaphysicist become poet.‡—

* II. 357-8, V. 287-8, 314-5, III. 50-63, V. 84, VI. 25.

† V. 92, 84-5, IV. 27-8, III. 252-3, V. 248, III. 116-8, IV. 339, 348, 350, 363, VI. 167-8, 145.

‡ V. 64-5, 125, II. 144-8, V. 137-8.

II.

PERSONAL.

Why I make no reply to the countless attacks on myself and my art-views.—

No one can expect me to do this in a Musical journal, firstly—because the theme I treat goes far beyond the scope of such a paper, and therefore could only be treated one-sidedly there, with certainty of misconstruction; secondly, because I should be giving myself the look of considering the garbage of other musical journals in my regard as worthy of rejoinder; and that could but flatter them, notwithstanding that from the first I have treated our musical journalists with a contempt than which no greater can ever have been shewn in the world.—

To other voices, that have made themselves heard against me, I have nothing to reply because they belong to persons whose sole desire is to maintain their own opinions, formed or borrowed somewhere about the age of legal majority, against my dissent; an endeavour in which they certainly have exposed their understanding of the matter with sufficient plainness, but never shewn an understanding of my fundamental aims. Only when all this wild and whirling, trivial, and at times malicious chatter about my views on art, which were laid before the public years ago, shall have died away; therefore only when people shall have ceased to await from me a refutation of those who merely want to confute, but not to understand me, can I feel disposed to take my pen again to explain or rectify many an obscure or emotional passage in my earlier writings. Till then, let my friends deem me vanquished by misunderstanding and vulgarity, and put to shame! *

* * *

The Germans are surprised at English critics taking me so seriously and circumstantially, seeking to confute me by placing a literal translation of my principal writings before the public, whereas the Germans think better to pelt me with falsified fragments. The reason of it is, that the Germans stand nearer to an understanding of my writings, and therefore are afraid the latter might be generally understood, which needs must bring about the critics' fall: an English critic, however, feels certain that the musical public, with the whole of pietistic England in the bulk, could never understand me, and shews his cleverness by openly exposing me to this general misunderstanding.†

[From the year 1855, the reference being to the bald translation of *Oper und Drama* published in the *Musical World* during the progress of the series of Philharmonic Concerts conducted by Richard Wagner. —Tr.]

* * *

In the best event these people might arrive at perception that such things are not for them at all, and they simply must abstain from touching them; just as the Police demands of the non-proprietor in respect of Property, and punishes the contravener as a thief. ‡

* * *

If the German public prefers the latrines of its vulgarity to be set up in open street, and even drawn into its pleasure-grounds, as it is doing with the cult of its newspaper-press, one can only let it go its way, but have no more to do with it on account of the stench. §

* I. 205-6*n*, II. 356*n*, III. 51 seq., VI. 3-5, III. 155, 165-6, 253-4, 257, 295-7, 303, 306-9, 311-3, 321-2, IV. 5-9, 222-3, II. 3-7, I. 23-9, V. 55, 129-30, 178, VI. 165, IV. 251-2, VI. 113-6, 255.

† III. 109-10.

‡ II. 13-15, 121, 360, I. 271-3, 275, 342*n*[2], 355*n*, III. 62-3, 363-4, IV. 119, II. 6-7, I. xvi-xvii, V. 123*n*, 162, 213, VI. 62-3, 74, V. 302-4.

§ III. 1-2, 65-6, 264-5, 323, 354-5, IV. 19-21, 217-8, 249-50, III. 77, 109-10, IV. 338, 349, V. 116-7, 297, VI. 5, 46-7, 58-61, 69, 99, 127-9, 142, 143.

* * *

An enemy who is obliged to have recourse to lies and slander, can have no real power; but inasmuch as my enemies use slander and lies against me, they have given me the power over them. They are in my hands, whenever I choose to use it.

[From the year 1867, after the Munich calumnies.]

* * *

The world is taught how to behave itself to every other; only how to behave to a man of my kidney it can never be taught, just because the case occurs too seldom.*

[See the author's long letter of 1865, translated in my preface to Vol. IV.—Tr.]

* * *

Intercourse with Genius has the inconvenience, that the excessive patience without which a genius could never hold out in this world emboldens and spoils us to such a degree, that at last we feel moved to surtax it for once, with results most alarming to us.

[Glasenapp considers that this jotting dates from Richard Wagner's Zurich period, but it has a great likeness to two or three sentences on page 32 of Vol. IV., i.e. of 1864-5.—Tr.]

* * *

He who comes as such a freshman to our time, may possibly espy his profit in it: but he who long has lived therein through ancient blood-relationship, to him it well may seem not so inviting.†

[Referring to the removal of the Jews' civil disabilities. This and the succeeding fragment are from the period between the two Bayreuth Festivals of 1876 and 1882.]

* * *

Artwork of the Future, for none but those awaking from

* VII. 137, 226, 230, 241-3, 321-2, I. 300*n*, 317*n*, 385*n*, III. 3, 257, 261, 287-8, 349, 350, 351-2, 356-8, IV. 227, 233, 247-8, 269, 271, 272, III. 102-6, 111-3, 114-5, IV. 295, 307, 326, 330-2, 335-6, 354, 357-9, 367, V. 5, 80*n*, 177, 263, 265-8, 275-6, 278-81, 286, 303-4, 309-11, 326-9, VI. 15-7, 22-3, 26, 30-3, 36, IV. 168, VI. 53-4, 66, 98-102, 104, 114-5, 117, 120-2, 136, 146-7, 166-9, 172, 184, 295-9, 315, 317-8.

† VI. 44.

the dream of the "Now-time." He who feels not the terrors of that dream sufficiently strongly to drive him to wake, let him dream on! I labour for the wakers.

To have felt, envisaged, willed, the possible "It might be"—enough: what boots possession? That vanishes!*

* VI. 274, II. 376, I. 88-9, 51.

III.

A SKETCH, A REFLECTION, AND FOUR PROGRAMMES.

[Sketch for "Die Sieger"—"The Victors."]

Chakya-Muni. Ananda. Prakriti. (Her Mother.)
Brahmins. Disciples. Folk.

—The *Buddha* on his last journey.—*Ananda* given water from the well by Prakriti, the Tchandala maiden. Her tumult of love for *Ananda*; his consternation.—

Prakriti in love's agony: her mother brings *Ananda* to her: love's battle royal: Ananda, distressed and moved to tears, released by *Chakya* [the Buddha]—

Prakriti goes to *Buddha*, under the tree at the city's gate, to plead for union with *Ananda.* He asks if she is willing to fulfil the stipulations of such union? Dialogue with twofold meaning, interpreted by *Prakriti* in the sense of her passion; she sinks horrified and sobbing to the ground, when she hears at length that she must share Ananda's vow of chastity. *Ananda* persecuted by the *Brahmins.* Reproofs against Buddha's commerce with a Tchandala girl. Buddha's attack on the spirit of Caste. He tells of Prakriti's previous incarnation; she then was the daughter of a haughty Brahmin; the Tchandala King, remembering a former existence as Brahmin, had craved the Brahmin's daughter for his son, who had conceived a violent passion for her; in pride and arrogance the daughter had refused return of love, and mocked at the unfortunate. This she had now to expiate, reborn as Tchandala to feel the torments of a hopeless love; yet to renounce withal, and be led to full redemption by acceptance into Buddha's flock.—*Prakriti* answers Buddha's final question with a joyful Yea. Ananda welcomes her as sister. *Buddha's* last teachings. All are converted by him. He departs to the place of his redemption.

Zurich. May 16, 1856.

Mariafeld. April 1864.

Buddha—Luther.—India—North Germany: between: Catholicism. (South—North.) Middle Ages. By the Ganges gentle, pure renunciation: in Germany monkish impossibility: Luther lays bare this climatic impossibility of carrying out the meek renunciation taught by Buddha: it will not answer here, where we must eat flesh, drink brew, clothe thick, and warmly lodge: here we must compromise; our life here is so plagued, that without "Wine, Woman and Song" we could not possibly hold out, or serve the good old God himself.—

C-sharp minor Quartet:

(Adagio) Melancholy morning-prayer of a deeply suffering heart: (*Allegro*) graceful apparition, rousing fresh desire of life. (Andante and variations). Charm, sweetness, longing, love.—*Scherzo*. Whim, humour, high spirits. —*Finale*. Passing over to resignation. Most sorrowful renunciation.*

[From 1855, when Wagner was superintending a Quartet-union at Zurich.]

Prelude to Tristan und Isolde.†

An old, old tale, exhaustless in its variations, and ever sung anew in all the languages of medieval Europe, tells us of Tristan and Isolde. For his king the trusty vassal had wooed a maid he durst not tell himself he loved, Isolde;

* V. 96-8.

† From the time of the Paris concerts, 1860.—Tr.

as his master's bride she followed him, for, powerless, she needs must do the wooer's bidding. Love's Goddess, jealous of her downtrod rights, avenged herself: the love-drink destined by the careful mother for the partners in this merely political marriage, in accordance with the customs of the age, the Goddess foists on the youthful pair through a blunder diversely accounted for; fired by its draught, their love leaps suddenly to vivid flame, and each avows to each that they belong to none save one another. Henceforth no end to the yearning, longing, bliss and misery of love: world, power, fame, splendour, honour, knighthood, loyalty and friendship, all scattered like a baseless dream; one thing alone left living: desire, desire unquenchable, longing forever rebearing itself,—a fevered craving; one sole redemption—death, surcease of being, the sleep that knows no waking!

Here, in Music's own most unrestricted element, the musician who chose this theme as introduction to his love-drama could have but one care: how to restrain himself, since exhaustion of the theme is quite impossible. So in one long breath he let that unslaked longing swell from first avowal of the gentlest tremour of attraction, through half-heaved sighs, through hopes and fears, laments and wishes, joy and torment, to the mightiest onset, most resolute attempt to find the breach unbarring to the heart a path into the sea of endless love's delight. In vain! Its power spent, the heart sinks back to pine of its desire—desire without attainment; for each fruition sows the seeds of fresh desire, till in its final lassitude the breaking eye beholds a glimmer of the highest bliss: it is the bliss of quitting life, of being no more, of last redemption into that wondrous realm from which we stray the farthest when we strive to enter it by fiercest force. Shall we call it Death? Or is it not Night's wonder-world, whence—as the story says—an ivy and a vine sprang up in lockt embrace o'er Tristan and Isolde's grave? *

* III. 268-9.

Prelude to Act III. "Die Meistersinger." *

With the third strophe of the cobbler-song in the second act the first motive for the strings has been already heard; there it expressed the bitter cry of the man of resignation who shews the world a cheerful, energetic countenance; that smothered cry was understood by Eva, and so deeply did it pierce her heart that she fain would flee away, only to hear this cheerful-seeming song no longer. Now (in the prelude to act iii.) this motive is played alone, and developed till it dies away in resignation: but forthwith, and as from out the distance, the horns intone the solemn song wherewith Hans Sachs greets Luther and the Reformation, the which had won the poet such incomparable popularity. After the first strophe the strings again take single phrases of the genuine cobbler-song, very softly and very much slower, as though the man were turning his gaze from his handiwork heavenwards, and lost in tender musings. Then with redoubled sonority the horns pursue the master's hymn, with which Hans Sachs is greeted on appearance at the festival by the whole populace of Nuremberg in thundrous unison. Next re-appears the strings' first motive, with grandiose expression of the anguish of a deep-stirred soul; calmed and allayed, it attains the utmost cheerfulness of a blest and peaceful resignation.

Prelude to Parsifal. †

"Love—Faith:—Hope?"

First theme: "Love."

"Take ye my body, take my blood, in token of our love!"
(Repeated in faint whispers by angel-voices.)
"Take ye my blood, my body take, in memory of me!"—
(Again repeated in whispers.)—

Second theme: "Faith."

Promise of redemption through faith. Firmly and

* From a letter of the year 1869.

† Drafted for a hearing by the King at Munich 1880.

stoutly faith declares itself, exalted, willing even in suffering.—To the promise renewed Faith answers from the dimmest heights—as on the pinions of the snow-white dove—hovering downwards—usurping more and more the hearts of men, filling the world, the whole of Nature with the mightiest force, then glancing up again to heaven's vault as if appeased. But once more, from out the awe of solitude, throbs forth the cry of loving pity: the agony, the holy sweat of Olivet, the divine death-throes of Golgotha—the body pales, the blood flows forth, and glows now in the chalice with the heavenly glow of blessing, shedding on all that lives and languishes the grace of ransom won by Love. For him who—fearful rue for sin at heart—must quail before the godlike vision of the Grail, for Amfortas, sinful keeper of the halidom, we are made ready: will redemption heal the gnawing torments of his soul? Once more we hear the promise, and—we hope!

IV.

METAPHYSICS, ETHICS AND ART.*

We talk too much,—even hear too much, and—see too little.†

Natura non facit saltus.—

The organ for eventual knowledge of one's self, as Thing-in-itself, did not reach perfection at the outset, even in the human organism; the Intellect the earliest medium, as organ for an individual's preservation. Here lies perhaps the ground of Individuality itself, which—just as it is present only to the intellect—exists for no other end than production of the intellect. By enhancement and abnormal straining of this organ the Will next seeks to arrive at knowledge of the Idea of the species, and finally of itself; which ultimately brings it to the goal, a goal whereat it wills no longer, because it willed no other thing than what it has attained.—Its recognition through the individual intellect of its internecine conflict and dissension is just the moral step toward that enhancement, because it now first feels its misery—its sin.

What utters itself in the Individual, and shews itself to us as Will, is characterised by just the fashion of the individual's intellect. It does not manifest the Thing-in-itself in its purity, but tainted with the individual's mode of apprehension, as Individual Will, which latter—prisoned in principio individuationis—comports itself as the Will-to-live precisely because it feels that this its broken, fugitive appearance is menaced and curtailed at every point by its

* Written, for the most part on loose sheets of paper, during the years 1878 to 1882.

† VI. 325-7.

own counterparts. The purer essence of this Thing-in-itself first shews forth in the geni-al intuition, where the error of the individuality is thrust aside, and pure perception enters; and then we see that this Will is something other than mere Will-to-live, namely the Will-to-know, i.e. to know *Itself.* Hence the high, ecstatic, blessed satisfaction. Accordingly the Intellect is what it *can* be, and to fit the Will it should be, only in the genius. —But the sage [or "Wiser, however"]—morally—Love, Holiness (more instinctive, with decreasing intellectuality).

The great joy of the moment of geni-al beholding (*Anschauung*) comes precisely from final success of the effort to see and know oneself as Species; this is so paramount, that moral pity altogether ceases for the while: the most shocking sight, the most horrible perception, then affects us only in so far as it is the Species' intuition of itself, an overcoming of the personal consciousness: then we shout to ourselves in lofty transport, Ay, that am I (Species—Idea).—From this point, relapse into the common mode of viewing individual life-needs.—Reaction upon morals, up to ethical genius — pity — love — rather instinctive than intellectual.

In the earliest individual contemplation likewise chiefly joy—illusion of taking everything for real. Self-deception of the Will.*

* * *

Reality surely to be explained by Ideality, not the other way round. A religious dogma may embrace the whole real world: let anyone try, on the contrary, to illustrate Religion from the real world.†

* * *

At last the Savant remains alone, entirely for himself, a worthy figure as close of the world-tragedy; but the State, which takes upon itself the general good, is really paying too much for this enjoyment of the unit's.‡

* V. 72-3, VI. 249. [It would be futile to attempt to fill the gaps in the above.—Tr.] † IV. 22-31, V. 66-72, VI. 264, 260-1. ‡ VI. 76.

* * *

By *God*, speaking strictly, man seeks to figure to himself a being not subject to the sorrows of existence (of the world), and consequently above the world—now this is Jesus (Buddha), who overcomes the world.—The world-*Creator* has never been truly currently believed in.*

* * *

Affinities between Religion and Art begin exactly where Religion ceases to be artificial; but if one needs a science for it, then Art is useless.†

* * *

Religion, and Art too ere long — mere rudiments of earlier culture: like the os coccyx on the human body.‡

[An opinion which the master is controverting.—Tr.]

* * *

Chemical knowledge: artificial fodder, trichinæ.§

* * *

All in the long run is done with; even Voltaire's Tragédie could not hold on, and the thing capsized. What has Science not pinned its faith to, and not so very long ago, that to-day lies on the dust-heap? The contrary with works of Art; alter, transform your views and sciences as ye will—there still stands Shakespeare, there Goethe's Faust, there the Beethoven Symphony, with undiminished power! ||

* * *

Physics = Experience (?). Where is this latter? How without this [?,] Physics, to say nothing of what reaches beyond this?—*Physik = Erfahrung* (?) *Wo ist diese? Wie ohne diese Physik, geschweige was über diese hinausgeht?*

Abstract knowledge: beforehand, intuitive; but that needs a proper temperament.¶

* * *

Physics etc. bring truths to light against which there is nothing to say, but which also say nothing to us.—R. W.**

* VI. 244, I. 255, VI. 77-9, 216-9.
† VI. 213.
‡ VI. 76-7.
§ VI. 73, 32, 80.
|| IV. 67, VI. 79.
¶ VI. 236, 75-6.
** II. 157.

* * *

The most crying proof how little the sciences help us, is that the Copernican system has not yet dislodged dear God from heaven, for the great majority of men: here an attempt might haply be made from some other side, to which the God Within might lend his aid! To Him, however, it is quite indifferent how the Church may fret about Copernicus. R. W.*

* * *

In the morality of which would you place greater confidence, seek help from him in misfortune and so on: the man who frees trussed animals, or the man who trusses them to torture them? †—

* * *

[Ills removed through vivisection.]

In the best event, blood-poisonings (mercury)—consequences of excess—for removal of the consequences of bad food and hunger, of over-work etc., ye take but little thought. ‡

* * *

Encouragements to virtue:—

A labourer—found frozen on the highway—finds no compassion, since he had previously got drunk on schnaps.—

Warning to beggars:—but wherefore beggars?—Magistracy. §—

* * *

Why are the proofs of self-sacrificing animal fidelity not more frequent, nay, countless? Simply because of man, who doesn't give the beasts sufficient cause.

* * *

Animals are so good, that they willingly would suffer anything if one only could shew them its utility. ||

* * *

The Disciples understood the Lord almost as little as a faithful dog ourselves; yet—they loved him, obeyed (without understanding) and—founded a new religion.

* VI. 34, 233-4.
† VI. 199-200, 209-10.
‡ VI. 205, 208.
§ VI. 32.
|| VI. 205-6.

* * *

What do we expect from a religion, then, if we exclude compassion with the beasts? *

* * *

Dogma of pity towards the beasts can but repose on a feeling of guilt: that self-preservation obliges us to destroy beasts, albeit we must recognise them as so akin to ourselves, only innocent,—should teach us the guilt of our existence; a guilt which nothing save Pity on the vastest scale can mitigate. R. †

* * *

Very well, existence is no sin; but how if we feel it to be such? ‡

* * *

There's not a century—not a decad of history, that is not almost exclusively filled with the human race's shame.

* * *

It dawned on ancient wisdom, that what breathes in man is the same as in the beast. Already too late—to avert the curse brought down on us by animal food; for—no distinction save through—Pity! §

* * *

Erroneous to seek the fault in the religion, when it lies in the fall of mankind.||—

* * *

The theory of a degeneration of the human race, however opposed it seems to that of constant progress, might yet be the only one, in earnestness, to lead us to some hope.¶

* * *

If we go in search—and so gladly—of every possibility of an ennoblement of the human race, and so forth—we always light upon fresh obstacles. (Blood)**—

* VI. 197-9, 201-2, VII. 48.
† VI. 201-2.
‡ VI. 225-6, 256-7, 203.
§ VI. 201-2.
|| VI. 225.
¶ VI. 237, 73-4, 118.
** VI. 275, 280, 39, 270-1.

* * *

From Hero-dom we have inherited nothing save bloodshed and slaughter—without all heroism—but all with discipline.*

* * *

Two roads for the hero—

Despot, with slavery:
Martyr, with freedom.†

* * *

Every sheer force finds a force still stronger: therefore it cannot be that it is an end in itself (*Jede blosse Kraft findet eine noch stärkere Kraft: sie selbst an sich kann es also nicht sein, worauf es ankommt*).

* * *

The pitiable Weak—impossibly the goal:—per contra, the pitying Strong a force that annuls itself in pity—conclusion—atonement of world-existence.

But only the self-sacrifice of the strong can bring the world's nullity to consciousness of the weak, for the mere preservation of the weak by the strong can never be the object; hence led by *him* to world-renunciation—Christianity.‡—

* III. 221, VI. 277-8, 254-5, 234, 251-2. † VI. 279-80, IV. 25-6.
‡ VI. 279-80, I. 56, 58, 65, 192, VI. 251, 284.

V.

FRAGMENT OF AN ESSAY INTENDED FOR THE "BAYREUTHER BLÄTTER." *

ON THE WOMANLY IN THE HUMAN.
(AS CONCLUSION OF "RELIGION AND ART.")

Vendramin, 11 Feb. 1883.

In all the treatises on the decline of human races with which I am acquainted I find but incidental notice given to the character of the Marriage-bond and its influence upon the attributes of species. It was with the intention of resuming this subject at greater length, that I added to my article on "Hero-dom and Christendom" the following remark: "no blaze of orders can hide the withered heart whose halting beat bewrays its issue from a union pledged without the seal of love, be it never so pure of breed."

If we pause for a moment's deep reflection, we might easily be terrified at the boundless vista opened out by such a thought. Yet, as I lately advocated our searching for the purely Human in its agreement with the ever Natural, mature consideration will shew us the only reasonable, and therefore luminous departure-point, in the relation of man to woman, or rather of male to female.†

Whereas the deterioration of the human races lies plain before us as the day, we see the other animal species preserved in greatest purity, except where man has meddled in their crossing: manifestly because they know no 'marriage of convenience' with a view to property and possession. But they also know no marriage at all; and if it is Marriage that raises man so far above the animal world, to highest evolution of his moral faculties, it is the

* Already published at the end of Volume VI.—Tr. † I. 167-8*n*.

abuse of marriage for ulterior ends that is the cause of our decline below the beasts.

Having thus been brought with perhaps surprising swiftness to the sin and evil that has dogged the progress of our civilisation, excluding us from those advantages which the beasts still retain unimpaired in their breeding, we may consider ourselves as having also reached the ethical crux of our problem.

It is disclosed at once in the difference between the relations of the male to the female in animal, and in human life. However strongly the lust of the male in the highest types of beast may already be directed to the individuality of the female, yet it only protects its mate until she is in the position to teach the young to help themselves, and finally to let them go their way and forget the mother also: here Nature's sole concern is with the species, and she keeps it all the purer by permitting no sexual intercourse save under influence of mutual 'heat.' Man's severance from the animal kingdom, on the other hand, may be said to have been completed by the conversion of 'heat' into passionate affection for the Individual, where the instinct of Species, so powerfully determinant among the beasts, is almost obliterated by the ideal satisfaction of the being loved of this one individual: in the woman alone, the mother, does that instinct seem to retain its force of a natural law; and thus, although transfigured by his ideal love towards her individuality, she preserves a greater kinship to that nature-force than does the man, whose passion now mates the constant mother-love by turning to fidelity. Love's loyalty: marriage; here dwells Man's power over Nature, and divine we call it. 'Tis the fashioner of noble races. Their emergence from the backward lower races might easily be explained by the conversion of polygamy into monogamy; it is certain that the noblest white race is monogamous at its first appearance in saga and history, but marches toward its down-

Only by such a marriage could the races ennoble their breed.

Polygamy (possession) at once among conquerors.

fall through polygamous intercourse with the races which it conquers.

This question of Polygamy versus Monogamy thus brings us to the contact of the purely-human with the ever-natural. Eminent writers have called Polygamy the more natural state, and the monogamous union a perpetual defiance of Nature. Undoubtedly polygamous tribes stand nearer to the state of Nature, and, provided no cross-breedings intervene, thereby preserve their purity of race with the same success as Nature keeps her animal kinds unchanged. Only, a great individual the polygamous cannot breed, save under influence of the ideal canon of Monogamy; a force which does exert its power at times, through passionate affection and love's loyalty, in the very harems of the Orientals. It is here that Woman herself is raised above the natural law of sex, to which in the belief of even the wisest lawgivers she remained so bound that the Buddha himself thought needful to exclude her from the possibility of saint-hood. It is a beautiful feature in the legend, that shews the Victoriously-Perfect at last determined to admit the woman.

Ideality of the man—naturality of the woman —(Buddha)— then—degeneration of the man —etc.

However, the process of emancipation of Woman is only fulfilled amid ecstatic throes.

Love's tragedy.

SUMMARY.

"SIEGFRIED'S DEATH" (52).

ON GERMAN OPERA.

The Germans too learned to create warm human figures. Mozart *v.* Weber and Spohr. Bellini and Italian Song. Gluck's influence on the French; Grétry and Auber. Weber's *Freischütz* and his *Euryanthe.* Bach's vigour; Mozart's command of counterpoint. In the truly learned one never marks his learning. Modern pretence of erudition: none has seized warm life as it is. He will be master, who writes neither French, nor Italian, nor even German (58).

PASTICCIO.

Merits of old Italian mode of writing for the voice, and singing. In Germany good chorus-singing, but dearth of soloists with a well-trained organ, good delivery, correct declamation, pure enunciation, sympathetic expression, and thorough knowledge of music (60). Necessity of dramatic singer's exercising self-control; ensemble to be considered. Italians decline rôles unsuited to their voice etc.; Germans undertake anything, suitable or not. Human voice no lifeless instrument; must be studied by composers (62). Liberty accorded to singer; modifying tempo; the instruments should be a guard of honour to the voice, not its catch-polls. Mozart's orchestration: cantabile and bravura. Bach treats voice as an instrument. Take a lesson from the Italians, and then a man will some day come to re-establish the lost unity of Poetry and Song (64). Pedantic onesidedness of the sect which abjures all ornament. A parliamentary speech should differ from a village sermon; a sumptuous mould etc. may be demanded by æsthetic necessity. Composers have lost touch with the people: essence of dramatic art the Idea behind all human actions; give us passion! One thing needful for Opera—*poesy:* words and tones are simply its expression. The future master (66).

BELLINI.

"Ear-tickling" *v.* "eye-ache." Music-scholars should remove their spectacles, and listen for once; give up their sermonising and learn the lesson of a noble melody. Dramatic passion and its expression: *Norma* and Greek Tragedy (69).

PARISIAN AMUSEMENTS.

Winter turned to summer. Larks and nightingales of the salon; silks and perfumes. Storks and their annual migration to London. Bare necks and eight degrees of frost: what need have the Parisians of a Carnival; have they not their notables and virtuosi? (73).

Rubini's inaudible trill and philosophic calm; the crown of joy on the head of Parisian society. Duprez his follower, doomed to an early death of too much bawling; moonlight laments. What it means to be a Paris idol: claque, press, and public. The Dorus-Gras fading too; C. Heinefetter and young talent (77). Elaborate mounting of *La Juive.* In Paris the word is "make a hit, then enjoy yourself": Dumas and Auber (79). A morning call on despot Scribe; surrounded with authors and composers; the costly puppy and my surprise. Without Scribe no opera, no play: his share of the fees in *Robert* (82). Round of pleasures a mystic part of Louis Philippe's policy: concert-room; three orders, and one beyond all classifying, "more aristocratic than the aristocrats" (84). Characteristics of the Paris virtuoso and amateur: drawingroom piety. Enough! None but a Parisian born can stand the racket, unless he has a country-seat (86).

PARISIAN FATALITIES.

Paris a weariness of flesh to the German: he misses his home customs. But the German wearies the Parisians: because he is honest he must be poor, and therefore stupid. French politeness in taking one for an Englishman: its calamitous effects on a slender purse; a Boulogne hotel-bill upsets the castle in the air; "Pardon, monsieur, vous êtes Anglais?" no longer answered by an unpatriotic "Oui" (92). "Mistresses" not for the German; a failure at the cancan; but much prized as a husband by tradesmen's widows, for his domestic virtues: the vow of abstinence and order of married renunciants (96). How one German fared in Paris: varied talents; explaining *Faust* and proving non-existence of the soul; plans hatched in the hospital; Napoleon's obsequies; two benevolent milliners; the estaminet-widow and her overtures—conflict in the self-disowning soul; now he serves pot-au-feu and draws Strassburg beer. His course was run in six months; would have been shorter, had he stooped to swindling, for Paris has laws against even German strokes of genius (101). Music the German's surest passport in Paris: a drawingroom dilemma; the match-making music-stool. German bankers doff their nationality. Best Germans the poor: their experiences at picture-stalls—Adam and Eve; the lover surprised. These needy Germans the most faithful of friends (104). A seat at the Opéra and the daring wishes it inspires. Spring, and yearning for country air: found at last at Meudon; Legitimist landlord's morning tub; but oh! his talent for inventing musical instruments of torture. Solitude impossible for miles round Paris (107).

LETTERS FROM PARIS.

1. Limits of German acquaintance with Paris. Music to the rescue: musical history of Parisian life to be written (110). Death of good novelties at Grand Opéra; *Robert* as barometer. *Favorite,* and Paris midway between Germany and Italy (112). Sophie Löwe, her disastrous success: a duel averted. Concert of *Gaz. Mus.* and *Columbus* overture; invasion of German music resented by atomic Thomases etc. Opéra Comique run to seed; Halévy may mend matters (115). Théâtre des Italiens and its fashionable

audience: possible to have too much *Cenerentola*; engagement of S. Löwe there (116). Vieuxtemps' Paris début: his concerto nobly conceived and finely executed; death-knell to plaudit-seeking virtuosi. Carnival and bœuf gras (117).

2. The Italians' farewell: heart-breaking scenes; even the box-attendants moved to tears. Last appearance of Mme Mars recalls half a century of his history to the Frenchman (119). Rachel and disputes about salary; the Parisians as much interested in change of Directorate as change of Ministry, which mostly go together. The Royal theatres and traffic in their posts; a director sent as diplomatic envoy to London. Theatre as Mint: Grand Opéra and the two Black Knights; a nightmare ending in overture to *Tell* (123). Comic Opera the true French field: musical conversation. Halévy reversing the usual French procedure by harking back from Grand to Comic; success of his *Guitarrero*. Auber now goes little beyond lathering; notches in his razor; yet the *Diamants* betrays a master's hand and brilliant technique. Scribe and the new line of subject, mostly Portuguese: advantages of an unknown country; Pompadour style out of date (126). Liszt's concert and the Black Knights again; a headache cured by Vieuxtemps: his "epoch." Importance of the Conservatoire concerts; here first have I rightly understood much of Ninth Symphony (129). The "intimate" Schindler's apostolate; he slanders Anders, and apologises that he "did not know him" (131).

3. Berlioz: his music heard nowhere but at his own concerts; his trained orchestra and audience; isolation both outer and inner. Enthusiasm for Beethoven crossed by same blood as Auber's: the *Symphonie Fantastique* a crater of passions; conflict between B.'s inner intuitions and his countrymen's demands, fatal to his future. His sensitiveness to criticism; but does not write for money. July-symphony ideally "popular"; this work must live as long as France (136). Liszt and Berlioz concert for Beethoven memorial; audience insists on Liszt's playing his fantasia on *Robert the Devil*; some day he'll play it to the angels, for last time. Cherubini left out in the cold. Revival of *Joconde*: the old far better than the new French music (138). Début of C. Heinefetter and the director's futile plot against her; Sophie Löwe's unfortunate selection of vocal pieces. Approaching dearth of news, relieved only by coming Concert Monstre; baptism of Comte de Paris, Notre Dame as a set piece in fireworks (140).

4. How *Der Freischütz* has fought its way in Paris; purely musical beauties that strike the French; the Hermit and a modulation. Woe to the work, had it been by an unknown composer and put on *thus*! (143). *Les Willis* ballet and death by dancing: "what strange folk the Germans must be!" Adam the spook (144). Theory and practice: Kastner's *Maschera* a string of fugues. "The two Thieves" and a whole audience fumbling for its watch—with one exception. Rubini's retirement puts society into mourning (146). Heine's talent and significance: German papers rejoicing over his reported thrashing; the French would have behaved better (148).

5. Summer unbearable in Paris: dirt, no air, bad wine and water. Mintings of the journals retailed as truth in Germany; alleged earthquake and Montmartre. Variétés and a topical play with no ending; confederates among the audience (151). Grand Opéra, difference between early and late performances. Novelties at Op. Comique: Boieldieu fils, the burden of a father's name. A text of Scribe's that killed a composer. Preparations for *Reine de Chypre*: fourteen numbers for the prima donna—a physician to be in attendance (153).

6. A premature autumn, but furs must never appear before the Italians. Reopening of their theatre: gloss and mourning; Rubini's trio of replacers. New tenor at the Grand Opéra, cooper Poultier (156). Grétry's *Richard Cœur-de-lion* and Adam's added brass. Cherubini and his hardness of heart. The "Iron Hand" and its invisible characters; Leuven's text, Scribe to the rescue for half the fees; Adam's ghostly music (160). An ill-fated theatre; the Italians' monotonous repertory. The Odéon a "second Th. Français"; to give plays and operas—never a successful scheme in Paris. Boulevard theatres and splendid mounting of sensational pieces (162). Classical severity of the Th. Français; Rachel's rumoured retirement and its cause. Scandal and notoriety. Chateaubriand's fatal blessing (164).

7. Delaroche's great mural painting at the École des Beaux Arts: its skilful grouping of characters and costumes; full light *v.* chiaroscuro; hearty reception by his pupils; a moving little speech. Scribe's new comedy: impossible to get near the box-office. Morals and marriage (167).

8. "Maltese Knight" a provisional title for *Reine de Chypre*: reason for precaution; Charivari's travesty of a piece before its appearance. Halévy's marked success (169). Scribe's *Chaîne*: pity the poor who see this affluence unrolled before their eyes. It is *Paris* itself that makes these plays; Scribe and minor lights merely write them down. Talent and *diligence* of French actors; their ensemble a model for Germans (171).

9. Halévy a slave at the Opéra; frank and honest. Grétry modernised. Illusions about French magnanimity. Berlioz' halfness; sublimity of parts of his work. Falling off in modern French music, due to Italian influence. Paris asks Mendelssohn to write opera: madness for him to accept. Let us give up our belief in Paris (174).

HALÉVY AND "LA REINE DE CHYPRE."

The ideal conditions for writing a perfect opera: complete accord between poet and musician, and simultaneous inspiration by the same idea. Artistic Industry and the droits d'auteur; method of the operatic Director. Aspirants would not envy the famous composer, could they see him on some lovely morning at work on an uncongenial theme; but now and then chance brings him a good textbook, as that of *La Juive* or the *R. de C.* (178). Halévy's talent the opposite of Auber's; solidity, depth, energy and passion. Poetry can never render all that passes in the human heart; music alone reveals the unutterable secrets: exemplified by *Juive*. Breadth and continuity of Halévy's style; care bestowed on every detail (180). He gets the "perfume" of the epoch, and thus his music is more "romantic" than "historic": characteristics of Romantic poetry (181). Auber and the National style: its popular turns and rhythms, alike in poetry and music; more applicable to comedy than tragedy, which should not bear the traces of a local origin; great finish, but lack of variety; cut of the air de danse. But Halévy, while deserting the beaten track, does not throw off respect for Form; dangers before the reckless innovator (184).

Style *v.* mannerism. Artistic degeneration in young French composers; copiers of Auber's forms, without his spirit; too impotent to follow the bolder path of Halévy (187). French music has dethroned Italian in Germany, but neither Auber nor Rossini ever gained followers among German composers. Halévy has already made a greater impression, and the kinship of his aims should shew how German composers may re-enter the field of Musical Drama: an influence more vital than that of passionless Mendelssohn (190). Regret that the younger French school should have taken the easy road of the Italians: no fault of the *public* at Grand Opéra and Op. Comique, whose verdict is a law to the whole musical world. Rossini, and genius good and bad. Unknown composers languishing for lack of opportunity to reach the doors of those great institutes (192).

Happy union of poet and composer in *R. de C.*: an ideal view of the plot. Characterisation of difference in scene of action. Analysis of first two acts (197).

Analysis of last three acts. Musical contrast and continuous flow of melody; perfect rendering of emotion and pathos. Summing up: Halévy's evident aim to simplify his means, yet gain a great variety of definite effects. Significance of his example (200).

JOTTINGS ON THE NINTH SYMPHONY.

About to be performed at Palm Sunday concert by Dresden Kapelle. Hitherto a riddle to many: its misinterpretations; but only needs more frequent hearing. The poor deaf man who yearns to speak to the world in his own language; take him to your heart (203).

ARTIST AND CRITIC.

Seldom allowable for an artist to reply to criticism; but it becomes necessary when a critic of some ability misrepresents. In Dresden I am accused of disdaining Mozart: if I could be allowed for once to get up a Mozart opera entirely afresh, I would consent to be judged by the performance; not otherwise—as I have to accommodate myself to existing habits (207). *Figaro* and the true traditions of its tempi, as preserved by Dionys Weber; Mozart's own rehearsals, his directions not always marked in the score; feeling *v.* metronome; tempi of Susanna's two duets at variance with orchestral rendering (209). Strictures on my beat rebutted by performances of Ninth Symphony and *Armida*. What does Herr C. B. understand of his subject? Dresden compares most favourably with other large German theatres; but our whole stage system needs reforming: different sets of singers required for different classes of opera; plans already considered by Dresden management, but all takes time (212). Evils of ignorant and one-sided criticism: undermining all authority of appointed officers by gratuitous advice to performers; intelligent members of the public despise the Reporter's praise and blame. Personal element (214).

"GREETING TO THE VIENNESE" (*verse*, 217).

DEVRIENT'S "HISTORY OF GERMAN ACTING."

The revolutionary spirit of the day demands more solid food than ballet, Italian opera and trivial farces. National importance of the Theatre: the new free State must recognise its duty here, making the stage independent of all considerations save that of ennobling the taste and manners of the people (219). As yet the Germans have produced no actor-dramatist, like Shakespeare or Molière; but Devrient's experience as actor equips him to point out to the State its highest interest in the Theatre (221).

THEATRE-REFORM.

"Scenophilus" and his attack on Devrient's plan of reform. But which is better qualified to conduct a theatre—the fellowship of artists, or a learned lord-in-waiting? These are the people who have ruined the stage in every way, and chiefly by pitting one performer against the other, destroying all spirit of community. Obedience willingly accorded to a man in whom the company has trust (225).

MAN AND ESTABLISHED SOCIETY.

In the year 1848 Man's fight against Established Society began. Man's destiny and right are one: through perfecting his mental, moral and corporeal faculties to attain an ever higher happiness; but this can only be done by union, not by the unit (229). Society abandons all to chance; the war of Consciousness with Chance the sublimest ever waged (231).

THE REVOLUTION.

Europe fermenting: the coming storm; approach of Goddess Revolution. The prince, statesman, bureaucrat, general, and burgher; their fears and apprehensions (234). Factory-hands and farm-hands, those who have never known joy, encamped on the hills, with eyes strained anxiously towards the dawn; Revolution's address to them, "I will destroy all dominion of Death over Life; to Need alone, belongs what satisfies it; *two* peoples only from henceforth, those who follow and those who withstand me; I am the ever-fashioning Life, that giveth happiness to all." The thousands on the hills arise, with the heaven-shaking cry, "I am a Man" (238).

INVITATION TO THE PRODUCTION OF "TRISTAN" AT MUNICH.

History of former hitches. Carlsruhe project; Paris concerts with view to a "German Opera"; *Tannhäuser* fiasco. To Carlsruhe in person; the Schnorrs had just left for Dresden, where I must not shew myself (241). At Vienna my first hearing of *Lohengrin*; *Tristan* proposed there; Ander's illness. Performance of the whole work in my rooms at Biebrich, with Bülow and the Schnorrs. Vienna again, rehearsals; hostility of the critics; Mme Viardot's "Are German musicians not musical?" Fresh illnesses, and Viennese production abandoned: *T. u. Is.* had become a by-word (244). King Ludwig intervenes: the Schnorrs engaged for Munich, and everything of the best provided; Bülow as conductor, the author of a pianoforte edition which is a marvel to all; a fine orchestra and ample rehearsals—from the desert of theatrical market-driving to the oasis of an artist's studio (246). The performances not offered to idle curiosity, but to serious artistic interest; free to all the friends of my art. An artistic problem, independent of all financial success. Thanks to the Royal author of the Deed (248).

"DIE SARAZENIN"

(*full draft for a five-act opera*—276).

SKETCH FOR "THE APOSTLES' LOVE-FEAST."

Report on Mendelssohn's *St Paul* at Dresden.—Plan of "Love-feast."—Disciples and Apostles assemble; descent of the Holy Ghost; proclamation of the Word (282).

"JESUS OF NAZARETH."

Part I. (*Scenario in five acts*—297).

Part II. (*Exegesis etc.*). Jesus renounces his claim to be the heir of David,—through Adam he is son of God; renounces miracles, since Man must be the help of Man. Political condition of the time; Jesus rejected by both extreme parties of the Jews (299). Faith and knowledge; oaths and their circumvention, crime; the Trinity; the light of the Spirit, for none but yourselves can protect yourselves from evil. The law of Love roots up all Sin (301). Society and its misunderstanding. Marriage and Possession: but marriage becomes a sin when contracted without love, and the parents' right a scourge when exerted on the children against the principle of love: "Thou shalt not marry without love "(303). Property and the starving neighbour: which is the thief—he who took what his neighbour had need of, or he who took from the rich what he needed not? Love one another: all other law is vain and damnable; he who walketh without love is a slave. Only then is love creative, when it is free; through love we are partakers with God in immortality (306). Cæsar's pence and the treasures of love. Moses covered his face when he died, but Jesus removed the veil that we might see the death of the law that parted life. All men are members of one body, which is God (308). Jesus the physician: see that your children inherit not your sickness, nor your neighbour starve (310). The earliest races were one with Nature: development of the idea of Evil from the harmful; then Law arose, and fixed the temporary as eternal; Jesus abolishes the Law and restores man's unity by the knowlege that God is *within* him and the kingdom of Love endureth for ever (313). Death as the last ascent of the individual into the life of the whole, the last upheaval of egoism.—Gratitude a negation of love.—Sexual love the first surrender of self; then family love: universal love at once the most complete contentment and most complete repeal of egoism (315). Patriotism and death for the fatherland, universal love and death for the human race. Life is a continuous act of self-divestment, death the final and creative parting with the emptied casket (317). The Universal opposed to the Me; through death we ascend completely into the Universal; but the egoist is dead forever, since he has passed into the Universal without his knowledge and against his will (319). Woman's ascent into the generality through man and her love for their children. Innocence the state of absolute egoism; the Fall the unit's first step outside himself. The Israelites enslaved in Egypt the first to treat death as a curse, because their life was joyless: in this world of egoistic yearning arose the Law. The immortality that resides in our free will (321). Understanding Nature first through love. Atonement of the world by upheaval of the Law, and free bestowal of the Me upon the generality (322).

Part III. (*Texts from the New Testament in illustration of the above*—340).

SKETCHES AND FRAGMENTS.

I[A]. The principle of communism: no natural right to this or that possession. True historic life will begin when present system of historical title done away with. Right originally was might, and thus passed down to the descendants; but it was the *man* that stood foremost—not, as now, the *thing*. Nature gives the positive, history the superlative; the "should" must be raised to the superlative. Consciousness the end, not the means; the Folk acts instinctively, and therefore brings about the new (345). Modern egoism classes its fellow-men with extrahuman nature. Only the physically accomplished can be an object of consciousness; the artwork grasps its essence and displays it, but the State endeavours to fix it as perpetual norm; thus Art is eternal, but the State temporal, since it is dead as soon as born. The Folk the only true inventor, through necessity; creative through a want in common (348). The poet following nature's plan and the instinct of the folk. Science ceases where it finds the truth; it is the highest power of the human mind, but the enjoyment of this power is art. The folk's error in Christianity; only dishonest when it became Theology (350). What man is to nature, the artwork is to man. Christianity non-artistic. The artist is free only when he no longer chooses, but seizes the necessity of things (352).

The single arts, their evolution, combination and severance. Reunion only possible in the individual at present, but through artistic fellowship in the future. Greek tragedy a beautiful human religion, yet in bondage to nature-powers. Then followed statuary, with naked man as matter: the matter of artwork of the future will be *men* (355).

Communistic genius: speech, religion, state; namelessness of the poet. Nature-myths dependent on particularity of the soil etc. Conquering and subjugated tribes: in former the gods-myth—lingering on in latter—becomes a myth of heroes (357). Conservative tendence of Greek tragedy, but always followed by the people's artwork, the satyr-play. The more the ruling families made religion their means of rule, did the folk in general lose its sense of religion. Germanic conquests and new nationalities; foundering of all religion; socialism; omnihumanity (359). A second draft of the above.—Plastic art had a definite road to take, from misunderstanding to understanding of Nature; it and the other single arts have reached their limit of invention, and can go no farther except at hand of Drama, the representant of eternal flux (361).

I^B. Title-page of *Art and Revolution*: appeal to German princes to liberate art from bonds of commerce.—Ugliness of present civilisation due to its transitional stage: all well-defined species are beautiful; strength and love will give us beauty. Art not dependent on climate,—the Hottentots fat-smeared (364). Byron and his hunt for a hero. Abstraction and the microscope; but it is the outward shape that gives the sense of beauty. The third Norn's gift, a mind never-satisfied: result of its rejection by Wate's father; symbol of German nation. Anarchy and authority (366). Worship of a great master lames our own energy.—Abstract music and absolute poetry.—Achilles rejecting immortality. Man the completion of God. Reason, love, and freedom. Apollo and Jesus (368). Ideal of Society, where every individual's desire shall be elevated and his enjoyment unhindered; love the mother of Society. Vice at present the positive, virtue the negative; revolution develops virtue into vice, till equality is established and all are strong and free. Where fulfilment is wholly denied to desire, is death (371). Lyric and Drama, spring and autumn, south and north. Genius in advance of its age. Greek Tragedy and Shakespeare's; none other. Opera paralyses the reason; in perfect Drama the eye inspired to see the music in shapes. Mozart piercing to the mystery; Beethoven entering in. Technique can be discussed, not that which it expresses (374).

I^C. Colour not conveyed by sound, to the musical. Modulation in dramatic and in purely instrumental music. Literary style and metaphor (375).

I^D. On Berlioz. What influence had he on his age etc.? Count not too much on posterity (376). Hiller's attribution to Rossini of a remark he might easily have made himself (377). *Tannhäuser* in Paris: Liszt's conclusion that the Grand Opéra was wrongly chosen for it; traditions of this house inimical to the German ideal, just as Th. Français has never taken to Shakespeare. Louis Napoleon's idea of an International Theatre in Paris; to be of use, the idea would have to originate in a desire of the French to extend their horizon (379). If German art—poetry and music—is to benefit other nations, it must be through its own creation of an original German style (380).

II. Attacks on person and aims—reasons for leaving unanswered: contempt. Obscurities in my theoretic writings; English and German tactics. Such things are not for these people at all; the reptile press. Goading the patience of genius. The wakers. The ideal: what boots possession? (384).

III. Sketch of *Die Sieger*. Luther *v.* Buddha. Beethoven's C sharp minor quartet (386). Prelude to *Tristan u. Isolde*: old, old tale of love, desire unquenchable—exhaustless theme—the breaking eye espies the infinite bliss of—death?—nay, Night's wonderland (387). Prelude to act iii *Meistersinger*: the attainment of cheerful resignation (388). Prelude to *Parsifal*: love—faith—hope: agony and pity (389).

IV. We *see* too little. The intellect, the individuality, and will-to-live. Genius, saint: beholding, pity. Reality to be explained by the ideal. Religion and art; science and its fallacies (392). Vivisection and animal fidelity. The disciples and their new religion. Pity toward the beasts; tát tvam ási. Degeneration ; blood of heroes and modern war ; the martyr hero. Self-sacrifice of the strong teaches the weak this world's nullity (395).

V. *The Womanly in the human.* Marriage and its elevating influence on the human race ; degeneration through loveless unions. The point of contact of the purely-human with the ever-natural ; animals and propagation. Monogamy and purity of breed ; no great individual sprang from polygamy. Buddha and emancipation of Woman (398).

INDEX

As in previous volumes, the figures denoting tens and hundreds are not *repeated* for one and the same reference unless the numerals run into a fresh line of type. Figures enclosed within brackets refer to my own footnotes etc.—W. A. E.

A.

Abendzeitung, (x, 108), 140, 1, 57, (158, 71, 93), 204.
Abstinence, 93, 5, 104, 89, 332, 9.
Abstraction, 364, 5, 7, 8, 75, 92.
Achilles, 365, 7-8.
Action, dramatic, 194, 361, 71.
Actionnaire, 161.
Actors, 60, 1, 2, 170-1, 219-20, 2, 4, 352-3; in audience, 151.
Adagio, 196, 386.
Adam, 144, 297, 8, 320, 39; and Eve, 104, 310.
Adam, Ad., 144-5, 53, 7-60, 72, 3.
Adelaïde, 113, 39.
Adultery, 286-7, 302, 3, 26, 36.
Advertisements, 84, 111, 40, 61, 92, 246.
Advocat, Der, 377.
ÆSCHYLUS, 359, 60, 73.
Æsthetes, 219, see Connoisseurs etc.
Africaine, 111.
Agamemnon, 365.
Agricultural peoples, 235, 6, 356-7.
Aim, 193, 5, 352-3.
Air varié, 72, 83, 117.
Alberich, 3, 20-2, 50-2.
Alexander, 359, 60.
Alizard (singer), 83.
Alla breve, 209.
Allegory, 56, 150, 1.
Allegretto, 209.
Allegro, 197, 9, 209, 386.
Allgemeine Zeitung (Augsburg, 218).
,, ,, Leipzig, 148.
,, ,, (*Oester.*, 215).
Alliance, Holy, 71, 2.
Alsatian, 145.
Amateur critics, (xvi), 166, 210.
Amateurs, musical, 71, 84-5.
Ambassadors, 121.
Ambition, 75, 105, 13, 77, 95.
Amende honorable, 113, 31.
America, 74.
Amfortas, 389.
Amusements, ix, 70-86, 93, 109, 18.
Ananda, 385-6.
Anarchy, 365.
Ander (Viennese tenor), 242, 4.
Anders, G. E., 130-1.
Andrea Cornaro, 195-6.
Angels: audience of, 137; voices, 388.
"Anglais? Vous êtes," 89-92.
Animals, 6, 11, 8, 101, 5, 263, 362, 393-8.
Anschauung, 133, 380, 91.
Apelles, 165.
Apollo and Jesus, 368.
Apostles, 129, 280-2, 5, 96.
Apotheosis, xviii, 135, 73, 297.
Applause, 57, 60, 9, 76, 83, 4, 118, 138, 41, 52, 73, 80, 7, 98, 251.
Apprehension, 360, 90, see Senses &c.
Apulia, 253, 9, 64, 5, 9, 71.
Arago, 150, 1.
Archæology, 181.
Architecture, 140, 65, 260, 353.
Areopagus, 357.
Arias, 84, 113, 9, 39, 40, 94, 7, 9.
Aristocracy, 84, 170, 95, 216, 27, 98, 356, 8, 9, 71, 96.
Aristophanes, 358, 60, 3.
Armida at Dresden, 210.
Arrangements, oper., (xii), 83, (193), 245.
Art, 347, 60, 6-7, 71, 92; to order, 348, 64.
Art and Life, 55, 7, 8, 65, 6, 207, 19, 349-64.
Art-: history, 184, 239; institutes, 131, 176, 8, 86, 92, 205, 10, 3, 23, 5.
Artesian well, 150.

Artillery etc., 234.
Artist, creative, 133-5, 75-7, 81, 200, 203, 5, 9, 20, 348, 9, 52, 4, 66; and Public, 204-5.
Artisthood of the future, 343, 55, 62, 363, 83-4.
Arts, single, 352-6, 60-1, 7.
Artwork, the, 346, 9, 51-5, 61, 9, 72, 383-4.
Association, 223, 4, 9, 316, 48, 53, 5, 361, 3, 9.
Athens, 357. See Greek.
Atonement of world, 322, 38, 95.
Auber, 56, 75, 9, 110, 4, 24-5, 32, 4, 140, 73, 81-9.
Audry, 149.
Australia, 98-9.
Austria, 227, 8, see Vienna.
Authority *v.* conscience, 365-6.
(Autograph-collectors, xi, 191, 218, 278.)
Autumn, 71, 2, 154, 63, 4, 7, 372.
Ave Maria, 84-5.

B.

B flat, inaudible, 73.
BACH, J. S., 57, 8, 63, 4, 280.
Baden, Grand Duke, 240, 1.
Bakunin, 363.
Ballet, (xiii), 78, 143-4, 83, 218; dancer, 93, 105, 21, 365; master, 223.
Balls, 85, 93, 109, 43, 233.
Balmung, 11, 5, 9, 24, 9-30, 9, 42-3, 9.
Banck, Carl, 204-14.
Bandsmen, 201, 24, 79, 80.
Bankers, 79, 102-3, 5, 7, 26, 7, 223.
Banknotes, 115, 68.
Baptism, 140, 287, 97, 331, 40.
Barabbas, (xvii), 285, 6, 8, 9, 94, 5, 298, 9, 310.
Barbarossa, see *Friedrich.*
Barber, 125.
Barcarole, 196.
Bare head, 253; neck, 72, 105.
Barometer, *Robert* as, 111.
Barricades, Paris, 124, 78.
Barrière du Trône, 140.
(Barroilhet, 123.)
Bats and owls, 146.
Bath in garden, 106; river, 149.
(Bayreuth Theatre, ix.)
(*Bayr. Blätter*, xix, 54, 250, 78, 342, 396.)
(*Bayr. Taschen-Kalender*, 70, 88.)
Beard, 84, 119.
Bears, 38, 101.
Beauty, 55, 6, 64, 7, 133, 42, 66, 84, 197, 354-5, 9, 63-5, 8, 9, 76; fleeting, 118.
Beauty-patches, 117.
Beauvais, 98.
(Becker, 88.)
Beef, price of, 146, cf. 216, 393.
Beer, 87, 96, 101.
BEETHOVEN, 373, 80: *Adelaïde*, 113, 139; and Berlioz, 132-3; biography, 130; deafness, 202; and Halévy, 188; monument, 130, 6, 7; portrait, 129; Quartet, C-sharp minor, 386; and Rossini, 367.
Beethoven's Symphonies, 57, 132, 73, 392: C minor, 133; Eighth, 280; Ninth, 362,—at Dresden, 201-3, 210; Paris, 129.
Beggars, 72, 88, 393.
Beholding, 133, 390, 1.
Believers, 273, 9, 80, 94, 339.
Bellini, 55-6, 67-9, 75, 119.
Bell-ringer of Notre Dame, 140.
Belly-man and brain-man, 363.
Benvenuto Cellini, 143.
Berlin, 112, 45, 6, 211, 8, 25, 43; (Royal Library, 278).
BERLIOZ, 131-7, 42, 3, 72-3, 376: concerts, 132-3, 73; July-Symphony, 110, 35-6, 50, 73; Romeo Sym., 134; *Sym. Fantastique*, 132-3.
Bethlehem, (xviii), 290.
Beust, von, 233.
(*Bianca and Giuseppe*, 176.)
(Bible-criticism, xvii-xix.)
Biebrich on Rhine, 243.
Bills, 88, 91, 126.
Black Knights, 122, 3, 5, 7, 8.
Blackthorn, (Hagen), 26.
Blessing, Chateaubriand's, 164.
Blood, racial, 95, 124, 32, 258, 97, 306, 31, 5, 44, 64, 83, 94, 6-8.
Blood-poisoning, 393.
Bloodshed, 395, see War.
Boar, 25, 31, 4, 47.
Boat-building, 366.
Bodily motion, 356.
Body and members, 306, 8, 23, 7.
Body and spirit, 228-30, 7, 305, 12, 322, 9, 39, 54, 5, 63, 5.
Bœuf gras, 73, 117.
Bohemia, "village in," 144.
Boieldieu, 114, 73; fils, 152.
Bois de Boulogne, 85.
Book-keeping, 94, 8.
Boredom, 173, see Ennui.
(*Botschafter, Wiener*, 239.)

Bouché, Alex., 158.
Bouffe, 149.
Boulanger (tenor), 82.
Boulevards, 72, 3, 87, 170: des Italiens, 70; theatres, 161, 8.
Boulogne, 89-91.
Bouquet-throwing, 119.
Bourgeoisie, 80, 216, 7, 34.
Bourse, 79, 103, 233.
Box-office, 104, 67.
Boxes, 77, 87, 138, 51; Jockey-club, 104-5.
Brahmins, 385.
Brandy, 96, 153.
Brass, modern use, 153, 7, 72.
Bread of Life, 292, 305, 8, 10.
Bread and Wine, 288, cf. 388.
Breath-taking, 63.
Breed, see Blood.
Breslau, 143.
Bridegroom, The, 286, 326.
(British Museum, ix.)
Brotherhood, 13, 30, 3, 84, 91, 5, 105, 36, 234, 8, 61, 87, 98, 9, 301, 305, 24, 39, 86.
Brünnhilde, (viii), 5 et seq.
Buddha, 385-6, 98; and Jesus, 392.
Bull, Ole, 128.
Bülow, Hans von, 243, 5.
Butcher and hunter, 362.
Byron, 365.

C.

Cadenza, 68, 142; see Coloratura.
Cæsar's anger, 289, 95, 300; pence, 286, 90, 307, 25.
Cafés, 92, 109, 70.
Cage: crystal, 183; iron, 233.
Caiaphas, 289, 90, 4, 5.
Calendar, Republican and Russian, 72.
Can and Should, 345, 64, 91.
(Canada, 74.)
Canaille, 150.
Cancan, 93, 172.
Cantabile, 59, 62, 3, 4, 209.
(Capital letters, xx, 345.)
Capitalists, see Bankers.
Caprice, 345, 8, 50, 2, 4, 6.
Capua, (xiii), 251, 65.
Carbonic acid soul, 97.
Care, 321, 57; of life, 234, 7, 328.
Carlsruhe theatre, 240, 1, 2.
Carmagnola, Comte, 138.
Carnival, Paris, 72, 86, 117.
Carriages, 87, 155.
Casket emptied, 317.
Caste, 356, 9, 85.
Castil-Blaze, 157.
Catarina Cornaro, 194-9.
Catholicism, 359, 60, 86.
Cause and Effect, 301.
(*Cavalleria Rusticana*, 123.)
Cellar, 94, 216.
Cenerentola, 115, 6, 61.
Centenarian, 74, 5, 115.
Centime-system, 90-1.
Cerfbeer (theat. dir.), 157.
Certainty, 317, 46.
Chaîne, Une, Scribe's, 167, 9-71.
Chakya-Muni, 385,
Chamber of Deputies, 73, 109, 10, 23.
Champs Elysées, 70, 87, 149.
Chance, 230, 47.
Chandelier, Knights of, 138.
Change, 317, 47, 51, 6, 61, 5, 72; see Motion.
Chanson, 124, see Couplets.
Characterisation, musical, 55, 65, 6, 68, 181, 90, 4-9.
Characters, dramatic, 66, 159, 70-1, 175, 94, 361.
Charivari, (104), 143, 64, 8-9.
Charm, 171, 2, 6, 386.
Chasseurs and attendants, 119.
Chastity, 95, 104, 287, 305, 85, 6.
Chateaubriand, 164.
Chaumière, 93.
Chaussée d'Antin, 146.
Cheating, 95, 101, 233, 7.
Chef d'orchestre, 137, 46, 52.
Chemistry, 97, 392.
CHERUBINI, 134, 7, 57.
Chevalier d'industrie, 101.
Chiaroscuro, 166.
Children, 48, 94, 5, 100, 1, 4, 68, 301, 2, 8, 9, 14, 5, 8, 9, 21, 40.
Chinese, two, 150.
Chioggia, 196.
Chivalry, ancient, 11, 198, 387.
Chocolate, 80.
Choice, 145, 240, 352, 4.
CHOPIN, 105.
Chorale, 280.
Chorus, (xiii, xvi), 84; ensembles, (73), 196, 7; singing, 60, 97, 151, 279.
Chorus, Antique, 372.
Christianity, 139, 63, 244, 52, 350, 7, 358, 93, 5; and Art, 352, 8, 62, 92.
Church, 257, 60, 6, 393; State and Stage, 218-9.
Church-music, 279.
Cities, 105, 63, 211, 37, 99, 364, 85.

Civilisation, 107, 75, 320, 63, 97.
Clapisson, 114, 37, 52, 73.
Claptrap, 60, 117, 36,90, 8.
Claque, the, 76, 138, 51.
Clarinet, 62.
Classical: drama, 162, 218; music, 64, 279.
Cleanliness, 95, 7, 312, 26.
Clergy, 260, 362.
Clerk, 92, 8, 170, 233; a tenor, 157.
Climate, 146, 356, 7, 63, 4, 72, 86.
Clothes, 70-3, 80, 2, 4, 7, 98, 104, 5, 116, 9, 29, 37, 49, 54, 65-6, 323, 386. See Stage-costume.
Clouds, 16, 46, 133, 232, 4, 5, 68, 80.
Coals of fire, 210.
Cobbler, 146, 388.
Cock crows, 294.
Coffee, 91.
Coiffure, 71, 87.
Coiner's caves, 126.
Collaboration, 80, 160, 75.
Collected Works, (ix), 79.
Cologne opera, 377.
Coloratura, 60-5, 77, 139.
Colour, 165; and drawing, 367; and sound, 375.
Columbus overture, (83), 113.
Comedy: early, 357-8, 60; French, 162, 70.
Comfort, 97, 167, 70; see Luxury.
Comic relief, 158, 358.
Commandments, 303, 4, 5, 7, 9, 313, 322, 4, 6, 7.
Commentators, 129-31, 202, see *Faust*.
Commerce, 176, 217, 34, 348, 59, 62, 363.
Community and communism, 213, 9, 224, 80, 2, 7, 8, 9, 97, 309, 16, 21, 327, 9, 38, 42-51, 3, 5-60, 6.
Comparative and superlative, 345.
Composer and singers, 62-6, (73), 173, 191, 8, 243.
Composer's intention, 62, 129, 34, 206, 208-9, 46.
Compromise, 386.
Comte de Paris, 140.
Conception, creative, 133, 75-6, 80, 202.
Concert Monstre, 140, 1.
Concert-room, 201, 79, 373, see Paris.
Concerto, Vieuxtemps', 116-7, 28.
Concierge, 92,
Condensation, poetic, 371.
Conductor, 66, 146, 52, 213, 23, 4: Berlioz, 137; Bülow, 245; Mendelssohn, 279; Mozart, 208; Wagner, (xiv), 205-10, 41, (278).
Confidante, operatic, 159.
Confirmation-coat, 137.
Conflict: inner, 134; dramatic, 193.
Congregational singing, 280.
Connoisseurs, 129, 65, 6, 77, 210, 9, 223.
Conquerors, 343, 56, 7, 9, 60, 97.
Conservative, 357, 8.
Conservatoria, 60, see Paris.
Constantinople, 145.
Consulate, French (Nap.), 119.
Consumption, 120.
Contempt *v.* reply, 381.
Contrast, 66, 166, 80, 94, 5, 7, 8.
Contrition, 85, 287.
Convention, 205; musical, 184, 5.
Conversation-pieces, 80, 124.
Conversion, 85, 129-30, 297, 351.
Cooper tenor, a, 156.
Copernicus, 393.
CORNEILLE, 162.
Cornet-à-piston, 75.
Corpse convulsed, 227.
Correctness of Performance, 129, 61, 171, 201, 7, 9, 40, 5, 79.
Coryphæi, 189.
Cosi fan Tutte, 377.
Coterie, 128, 31.
Cothurnus, 355.
Council of Constance, 199.
" " Ten, 193, 5.
Counterpoint, 57, 8, 64, 96.
Countesses, Parisian, 170.
Country-life, 71, 85-7, 93, 105, 49, 357, 64.
Couplets, musical, 124, 73, 87, 97.
Coupons, 79.
Courage, 184, 98, 217, 80, 2, 93; and perseverance, 166.
Court-festivals, 233.
Court-theatres, 204, 7, 11, 8, 25, 40, 243, 6.
Courtiers, 108, 223, 33, 7.
(Covent Garden Theatre, 110, 23, 39.)
Cowardice, 18, 32, 3, 9, 282, 366.
Cranes and Storks, 71-2.
Cravats and studs, 149.
Creation, 175, 236, 348, 57, 61, see Artist.
Creation (nat.) 71, 136, 80, 238, 81, 301, 10, 1, 7, 39, 68, 9, 92.
Crescendo, 68.
Crime, see Vice.
Criticism (ix, xvi), 56, 66, 134, 77, 92, 204-14, 44, 382.
Cross, The, 252, 96, 323, 30.
Crucifixion, The, (xix), 295-7, 309.
Crusades, The, 252, 359.

Cry, Sachs' bitter, 388.
Culture, 363; Parisian, 107, 379.
Culture-: art, 358; nation, 220, 379.
Curiosity, artistic, 170; vulgar, 246.
Curse, 164, 320, 1, 94; Alberich's, 21, 38-9, 50.
Customs, national etc., 289, 94, 5, 318, 44, 60, 4, 87.
Cuts, 242.
Cyprus, 193, 7.

D.

Dame blanche, 152, 73.
Damoreau-Cinti, 113.
Dance, 144, 251, 352, 3, 4, 61; of Death, 143-4.
Dance-music, 183, 98, 290, see Quadrille.
Dandies, Paris, 104, 24, 78.
Dantan (sculptor), 110.
David, Son of, (xviii), 285, 7, 90, 7, 298, 305.
Dead, the, 286, 317, 76.
Death, 40, 1, 5, 51, 235, 6, 86, 306, 310, 3-9, 20-1, 36, 9, 87; and Birth, 318, 33; sacrificial, 288, 9, 91, 2, 297, 9, 307, 13-4, 6, 89, 95; untimely, 75, 6, 7, 152, 3, 242.
Death-defiance, 40, 218, 27.
Deed, 4, 5, 6, 8, 9, 18, 50, 158, 251, 7, 318, 56, 69; of Art, 245, 8, 349.
Definition, 176, 85, 90.
Degeneration, 114, 86, 357, 73, 94-8.
Dégout, 141, 73, see Ennui.
Deification of artists, 75-6, 366, 72.
Dejazet, 149.
Delanoue, 161.
Delaroche, 164-6.
Demagogues, 55, 285, 90, 8-9.
Democracy, 357, 8, see Commun.
Demoralisation, 320; artistic, 187.
Descente de la Courtille, 73.
Desert, 85, 177, 246, 99, 310.
Desire, 84, 236, 300, 69-70, 86, 7.
Despotism, 81, 195, 236, 369, 95.
Dessauer, 174.
Destiny, 228, 9. See Fate.
Detail, 180, 5, 9, 246, 369.
Dettmer (singer), 279.
Devil, The, 111, 79, 339, 40; German, 57.
Devrient, Eduard, 218-25, 40.
Dialogue, dram., (xvi), 70.
Diamants de la Couronne, 125.
Difficulties in *Tristan*, 240, 2, 3, 5.
Digestive exercises, 115.
Dignity of art, 112, 7, 80, 90, 3, 221-3.
Dilettanti, 71, 84, 223.
Diligence, 166, 71, 90, 234, 43.
(Dinger, Hugo, xvii-xix, 204, 26, 7.)
Dinner, a good, 115, 216.
Diplomats, 79, 121, 49, 233.
Directors, theat., 105, 11-3, 6, 20-1, 138, 45, 52, 5-7, 60-1, 9, 72, 6, 211-2, 218, 22-5, 40, 2, 3.
Disciples, (xviii), 280-2, 6-97, 324, 326, 9, 30, 5, 93; Buddha's, 385.
Discipline, 213-4, 24, 395.
"Divide and govern," 363.
Dividends, 78, 103, 115, 55.
Divorce, 325.
Dogma, relig., 391, 4.
Dogs, 18, 81, 393.
Domestic life, 93-4, 100-1, 21, see Family.
Dominant and minor, 183.
Don Giovanni, 377; in Paris, 122-3.
Dona Maria (Portugal), 125.
Donizetti, 75, 111, 90.
Donna del Lago, 84.
Donner, 25, 31.
Door slammed, 116, 57, 92, cf. 131.
Dorus-Gras, 76-7, 83, 105, 13, 49.
Doubles ententes, 95, cf. 385.
Doucet, 161.
Dove, The white, 389.
Dowry, French, 94.
DRAMA, 65-6, 160, 354, 61, 6, 72:—
  Birth of, 352-3, 7-8, 73.
  Classic *v.* sensational, 162.
  Historical, (xii-xv), 171, 81.
  Literary, 220, 352.
  Musical, (xvi), 66, 124, 45, 76, 80, 189, 92. See Opera.
  Religious, 354-5.
  Spoken, (xv-xvi), 55, 218, 20, (284), 367.
Dramaturgists, 62, 219.
Drapier, Halévy's, 115.
Drawingroom songs, 83, 4, 102.
Dream-image, 373, 86.
Dreamery, 141, 9, 260, 3, 72, 384.
Dreams, 46, 122-3, 7, 75, 235, 57, 9, 273, 387.
DRESDEN, (xi-xv, xix, 105), 127, 164, 240, 1:—
  Anzeiger, (201, 4), 222, 5.
  Critics, 204-5.
  (Frauenkirche, 279).
  Kapelle, 201, 5, 10, 79, 80.
  Tageblatt, 204.
  Theatre, (xiv), 204, 7-12, 41, 2, 3, (278).
Drinking-song (*R. de C.*,) 197.

Droits d'auteur, 81, 138, 60, 76.
Drunken labourer, 393.
Dualism, 311, 63.
Dubarry, 106, 26.
Duelling, 113, 48, 61.
(Düesberg, xi.)
Duets, 194, 9, 209.
Dumas, 79, 162.
Dumersan, 150, 61.
Dupont, 83.
Duprez, 75-6, 105, 9, 11, 49, 73.
Dust and heat, 149.
Duty, 314-5.

E.

Eagle, 367; and sun, 74.
Ear and eye, 67, 155, 373, 90; heart, 203.
Ear-tickling, 67, 191.
Earnestness in art, 178, 245-7.
Earth again, 203.
Earthquake, 297, 337; Paris, 150, 1.
Easter, 294; sports, 357.
Eccentric Beethoven, 202.
Ecole des Beaux Arts, 164-6.
Economy, personal, 90-1.
Ecstasy, 203, 38, 391, 8.
Editors, (xi, xx,) 128, 225, 39.
Education, 227, 30, 334, 58, 9, 66.
Effect, musical, 57, 64, 133, 42, 80, 195-7, 200.
(*Egmont*, xvi.)
Egoism, 103, 93, 224, 306, 13-22, 46, 348, 50, 2-5, 9, 66, 7, 72.
Egypt, 289, 320.
(Eisenach, xii.)
Elders, the Jewish, 289, 91, 4.
Eléazar (*Juive*), 180.
Elector of Hanover, 158.
Elegance, 82, 4, 7, 110, 24, 33, 78, 9.
Elegy, 56, 75, 200.
Elemental, the, 179, 367.
Elf-son, 48.
Embryo of plant, 313, 5.
Emigrant-ship, 98.
Emotion, expression of, 65, 8, 180, 3, 196, 8, 9, 202-3. See Passionate.
Empire, First French, 119.
Energy, 178, 9, 84-9, 365, 6, 88.
English, 74, 89, 91, 3, 100, 9, 18, 21, 128, 228, 379, 82.
Engravings, colouring, 97.
Enjoyment, 236-8, 302, 4, 16, 44, 68-371, 91; artistic, 55, 7, 67-8, 202, 208, 350, 63, 72.
Ennui, 84, 7-8, 105, 41, 73.
Ensemble, 61, 6, 124, 71, 245; -pieces 56, 142, 78, 83, 96, 7, 9, 254, 61, 265, 8, 74.
Entertainment, 80, 2, 133, 71, 251.
Enthusiasm, (xix,) 75, 102, 15, 22, 132, 42, 51, 8, 66, 75, 93, 206, 20, 297, 365.
Entrechats, 143.
Envy, 177, 238, 371.
Epicurean and Stoic, 79.
Epigram, (x,) 143, 58, 64.
Epoch, see New.
Epos, 357, 8, 60, 5.
Equality, 91, 236, 308, 32, 71, 2.
Ernst (violinist), 128.
Error, 301, 46, 9-52, 8, 91, 4.
Esser, H., 243.
Estaminets, 94, 9, 100, 1.
Established, the, 82, 227-31, 5, 311.
Ethics, 391, see Moral.
Euripides, 358, 73.
(*Europa*, Lewald's, 70.)
European, 364, 86; movement, 232, 370.
Euryanthe, 56.
Euthanasia, 315, 20.
Eva (*Meistersinger*), 388.
Ever-natural, the, 396, 8.
Evolution, 313, 22, 59, 67-70: artistic, 124-5, 32, 57, 78, 85, 208, 353, 60, 372; human, 228-9, 351, 90, 7; national, 178, 207, 19, 379.
Exceptional, 131-2, 4, 203, 45, 383.
Excesses, 393.
Exchequer, French deficit, 146.
Excommunication, 255, 6.
Exile, Wagner's, 239-41, 3.
Existing, the, 230, see Established.
Experience, 104, 84, 360, 71, 92; professional, 212-4, 9, 23.
Expression, 66; marks, 206, 9. See Musical.
Extremes, 133.
Eye, 32, 7, 75, 6, 103, 18, 27, 9, 84, 227, 32, 8, 74, 365, 87, 91.

F.

Factory-hands, 235.
Fainting ladies, 119,
Faith, 184, 93, 281, 92, 9, 305, 27, 33, 340, 88, 9.
Falcon, Mme, 77.
Fall, The, 320, 94.
Fame, 78-9, 81, 110, 36, 42, 52, 76, 7, 387.
Familiarity, 91.

Family, 315, 6, 9-20, 9, 55, 67, 8, 97.
Family-influence, 145.
Fanaticism, 140, 79, 80, 98.
Fantaisies brillantes, 83, 117, 37.
Farces, trivial, 218.
Fashionable world, 71, 2, 9, 82, 4-5, 105, 15, 8-9, 46, 54, 73.
Fasting, 286, 325-6.
Fat, 74, 5, 103, 55; smeared, 363.
Fate, 179, 244, 358; question to, (xiv), 118, 36.
Father and: daughter, 118, 285-6; sons, 217, 34, 5, 65, 318, 24, 38.
Fatherland, 90, 1, 316.
Fathers, early Church, 352.
Fatima, 252 seq.; (and Senta, xiii).
Faubourg S. Denis and S. Martin, 82.
,, S. Germain, 146.
Fault-finding, 212-4, see Critic.
Fauns and Satyrs, 357.
FAUST, Goethe's, 127, 392; explaining to French, 96, 8, 100, 1.
Favorite, 111-2, 90.
Fear, 4, 5, 18, 32, 281, 328, 87.
Feeling, 156, 83; understanding by, 203, 8-9. See Heart etc.
Fellowship, 224, 46, 316, 53, 5, 6, 7, 9.
"Fermare, formare, finire," 59.
Fermenting, Europe, 232.
Festivals, country, 357, 9.
(Feuerbach, xvi, xix.)
Few, the, 247, 81, 312.
Fidèle Berger, 159.
Fidelio, recitatives for, 174.
Fifths, forbidden, 58.
Fifth floor, 82, 92.
Figaro, 57, (123), 183, 377; at Dresden, 205-10; overture, 208.
"Filou," 172.
Finales, oper., 56, 142, 96, 9, 255.
Fine, a composer's, 152.
Finish, artistic, 77, 183, 5, 7, 9, 90.
Fire, ,, , 74, 133, 77, 80, cf. Warmth.
Fireworks, 140, 9.
Fish in water, 152.
Fishermen's huts, 287, 8.
Five acts, xii, xiii, xv, xvi, 96, 169, 99.
Flageolet, 109.
Flesh, the, 300, 4, 7, 31, 3; and bone, 238, 327.
Fleshings and feathers, 121.
Flowers, 194, 233; artificial, 70, 1; and fruit, 372.
(FLYING DUTCHMAN, xii, xiii, 113.)
FOLK, 58, 65, 217, 345-51, 88.
Jewish, 285-91, 4-9, 310, 26.
-Plays, 358.
FOLK—*continued*—
and Religion, 343, 50, 2, 8-9.
-Schools, 227, cf. 358.
-Songs, 56, 87, 182.
Spirit of the, 220.
-Wandering, 357.
Food, bad, 216, 35, 392, 3.
Fools, 88; and wise, 22, 332, 7.
Force, 228-9, 36, 98, 363, 95; in Art, 133, 4, 78, 86, 8-9, 96, 364.
Foreign, the, (x), 55, 108, 13-4, 42, 143, 72, 4, 88-90, 247, 378-80.
Forkel, 130.
Form, 133, 4, 365, 79; and Content, 58, 65, 193; musical, 57, 8, 64-9, 184, 7, 90.
(*Fortnightly Review*, viii.)
Fortune, 75, 81, 8, 100, 5, 38, 70.
Fount, inner, 133, 4, 6, 79, 99, 235, 356.
Fountains, Paris etc., 70, 150.
Fourberies de Scapin, 161.
Fra Diavolo, 172.
Franc-tireur, 144.
France and England, 74, 89.
,, ,, Germany, 172, 215, 28, see French.
Francs and sous, 89-92.
(Frankfort Assembly, 215.)
Franks, hero-myths, 357.
Free admittance, 83, 127, 246-7.
Free Will, 236, 305-6, 8, 13, 6, 21, 350.
Freedom, 3, 4, 21, 2, 50, 5, 215-8, 235-8, 99, 301-3, 7, 8, 25, 33, 5, 6, 345, 52, 4, 65, 8-9, 95; artistic, 64, 67, 136, 84, 9, 94, 221, 3, 369.
Freezing, 71, 2, 97-8, 146, 51, 4, 235, 393.
Freia, 23.
Freischütz, Der, 56; Paris, 141-4, 73.
FRENCH:—
Character, 85-9, 92-5, 109, 19, 32, 133, 43-4, 59, 67, 78, 379.
v. Germans, (x), 55-7, 66, 7, 78, 112, 114, 29, 33, 5, 42, 3, 8, 70, 1, 2, 174, 6, 88-9, 220, 378-9.
Government, 82, 110, 20, 40, 64.
History 119.
Language, 95, 7, 8, 103.
Musicians, 78, 135, 44, 5, 52, 73, 181, 5-6, 90, 2. See Opera.
Singers, 75, 7, 151, 72, 243.
("Freudenfeuer, W.," 70.)
Fricka, 15, 23, 6, 30, 5-6.
(*Friedrich Rothbart*, xv, xvi, xx.)
Friedrich II., 252, 6, 7, 61, 5, 6, 8, 275, 6.

Friends of my art, 239, 45-7; personal, (105), 127-8, 239, 40, 1, 5.
Friendship, 104, 28, 34, 75, 387.
Frivolity, 197.
Froh, 25, 31.
Fronde, 119.
Fugue, 57, 8, 64, 145.
Furs, ladies', 70, 154.
Future, the, 135, 86, 92, 343, 7, 55, 359, 60, 2, 3, 72, 6, 83.

G.

Gaiety, 165, 97, 386.
Galilee, 285, 7, 9, 90, 2, 4, 6, 8.
Gallery, the, 170.
Galleys, prisoners on, 162.
Galops d'enfer, 85.
Galvanism, soul as, 97.
Gamins, 80, 103, 35, 49.
Ganges, 386.
Garçons, 80, 91, 2, 4.
Garden and fields, 235, 6, cf. 356.
Garrigues (Frau Schnorr), 242.
Gas, 87, 105.
(Gasperini, 73.)
Gazette Musicale, (xi, 83, 123, 75, 86, 193); concert, 113, 39.
General, milit., 234.
Generality, ascent into the, 313-22, 352, 9, 60.
Geneva, 91.
Genius, 191, 353, 5, 9, 60, 6, 7, 72, 373, 91; goaded too far, 383.
Gennesaret, Lake of, 287.
Geography, 90, 125-6.
Gérard (*R. de C.*), 194-9.
GERMAN:—
  Acting, 61, 171, 220.
  Art, 55, 379.
  Character and capabilities, 56, 7, 67, 87-8, 92-5, 101-3, 8-9, 33, 5, 147-8, 71, 89, 217, 20, 365-6, 82.
  Composers, 55-8, 62-8, 112, 88.
  "High" and "low," 225.
  Officers, army, 148.
  Poets, 96, 147, 220.
  Singers, 60, 1, 138, 9, 209, 11, 41-243, 79.
  Spirit, 190, 216, 378.
  Theatres, 171, 207, 11, 8, 40, 3, 6.
Germanic conquests, 359.
Germany, 87, 90, 103, 44, 88-9, 227-228, 41, 3; North, 386.
Gethsemane, 293.
Ghost-seeing, 102, 44, 55, 8, 60, 257, 373.
Giants (*Ring*), 4, 21, 38.
Gibelinen, 254, 5, 6.
Gibichungen, 7-9, 12, 8, 23-5, 7, 32-3.
Giraffes, 105.
Girard, 146.
Giving *v.* receiving, 313, 4, 7-20, 2, 6, 346, 53, 62.
Gladness, 4, 20, 4, 67, 281, see Joy.
(Glasenapp, C.F., xi, xii, xiii, xvii, xxi, 130, 215, 8, 26, 78.)
Glitter, 71, 5, 87, 108; *v.* glow, 154-155, 79.
Gloire, 136.
GLUCK, 56, 66, 9, 210.
Gluttony, 310, 23.
GOD, 97, 129, 225, 56, 303, 86:—
  Creator, 71, 154, 223, 98, 335, 92.
  and the Devil, 179.
  the Father, 281, 2, 300, 6, 23, 7, 8, 335-6, 8.
  is Love, 301, 3, 4, 5, 17, 9.
  and Man, 308, 65, 7, 8, 92.
  become Man, (viii), 238, 98, 317, 322, 59.
  Son of, 282, 7, 91, 5, 7-301, 4, 6, 8, 327, 38, 9.
  Within, 299, 301, 3, 5, 9, 11, 27, 32, 393.
  and World one, 310-2, 35-6.
Godless, 72, 86.
Gods, the, 4, 5, 7, 21, 2, 6, 7, 9, 31, 35, 9, 42, 9, 51, 81, 136, 232, 52, 9, 356-9, 67, 87.
GOETHE, 359, 60; and Schiller, 220, 380. See *Faust*.
Gold, vein of, 126. See Rhine.
Golgotha, 389.
Gondoliers' song (*R. de C.*), 196.
Good angel, 131, 202, 57, 67.
Good and bad genius, 191.
Good and Evil, 229, 99, 311, 2, 23, 367. See Sin.
Goods, see Property.
(Gospels, The, xix.)
(*Götterdämmerung*, vii-viii.)
Götz von Berlichingen, 160.
Government, 289, see French.
Grâce de Dieu, 162.
Grace, 178, 9, 87, 94, 7, 209, see Charm.
Græco-Roman world, 351, 3.
Grail, Holy, 389.
Grane, 5, 6, 10-1, 5, 6, 44, 9, 50-1.
Gratitude, 120, 8, 314-5.
Graun, 139.
Greek: Art, 165, 355; Philosophers, 350; Tragedy, 69, 354, 8, 72, 3.
Greeks, 345, 56-8, 67; modern, 364; in Palestine, 286, 9.

(Greith, 250.)
GRÉTRY, 56, 153, 7, 72, 91.
Grief, 197, 9 ; and joy, 196.
(Grimm, Jakob, xv, xvii-xviii.)
Grisettes, 80, 7, 92, 9, 170.
Grisi, 74, (110), 139.
Groans and moans, 75.
Grocer, 88, 104.
Gros de Naples, 87.
(Grove's *Dict. of Mus.*, 77, 139, 56.)
Growth, 350, 61, see Evolution.
Guido et Ginevra, 124, 69.
Guitarrero, 115, 24, 5, 6.
Guizot, 72, 3, 97.
Gutter, hearer in, 61, 135.

H.

Habeneck, 137.
Hagar, 336.
Hair, long, 84, 119.
Hair-shirt, 146.
Halévy, 75, 8, 113, 4-5, 24-5, 53, 67-169, 72, 7-200.
Halfness, 172.
Hande, 225.
HANDEL, 58, 145.
Hands, French quivering of, 77.
Hanging, 74, 158.
Hanover, 158, 60.
Happiness, 194, 5, 7, 8, 202, 71-2, 5, 276, 359, 60, 2, 9 ; of Man, 228-31, 233, 7, 8, 368.
Harems, 398.
Harmful and the helpful, the, 224, 9, 299, 306, 10-2.
Harmony, 68, 142, 95, 6, 375.
Harvest and reaper, 235, 329.
Hate, 20, 89, 179, 238, 73, 81, 310, 2, 318, 30, 7.
Head, "washed" *v.* shorn, 95.
Head-ache, 127, 8.
Health, 286, 308, 9, 12.
Heart, 179, 83, 99, 202, 33, 46, 81, 286, 303, 5, 28, 31, 67, 86, 7, 96 ; and brain, 238 ; childlike, 203, 308.
Heart-breaking, 118, 97, 9, 388.
Hearth, 154.
Heaven, 127, 37, 96, 388, 9, 93. See Kingdom.
Hector's body, 367.
Hegel's philosophy, 87, 96, 102.
Heine, Heinrich, 143, 7-8.
Heinefetter, C., 77, 138.
Heir, 34, 40, 8, 50, 152, 217, 34, 97, 338.
Heiterkeit, 165, 6, 386, 8.
Hell, 14, 51, 329, 39.
Helots, 357, 8, 9.
Hereditary rule, 267, 70, 97, 343-4.
Heredity, 152, 309, 44.
Hermit (stage), 122, 42, 59, 63.
Herod, 286, 7, 9, 95.
Heroes, 116, 294, 356-60, 5, 95.
Herold, 114, 72.
Herz, Salle, 71.
Hiller, Ferd., 376-7.
Hills, thousands on, 234, 5, 8.
Hippogryph, Scribe's, 80.
Hissed, 143, 51, 5.
Historians, 100, 40, 220.
History, (xiii), 176, 81, 220, 320, 343-5, 52, 6-9, 70, 94, 7 ; foundering of, 359, 60.
Hoard, the, 8, 11, 2, 21, 2, 34, 43, 4.
Hoffmann, E. A., 154.
Hohenstaufen, 253, 8, 66, 8, 70.
Holding out, 383, 6, 8.
HOLY SPIRIT, 281-2, 92, 7, 300, 11, 312, 25, 32, 8, 9, 40.
Home-sickness, 87, 103, 7, 254, 63, 271.
Honesty and poverty, 88-9, 94, 6, 172, 304.
Hoops, Pompadour, 126.
Hope, 95, 133, 235, 387, 8, 9, 94.
Horns (mus.) 388.
Horror and pity, 162, 391.
Horse, 79, 263, 362, see Grane.
Horsewhipping, a, 148.
Hospitals, Paris, 97, 9.
Hotel, 90-2.
Hôtel : Dieu, 97 ; de Ville, 109.
Hottentots, 363-4.
Hugo, Victor, 120, 40, 62.
Huguenots, Les, 111, 51, 68.
Human nature, 179, 93, 301, 3, 70, 394.
Humanitarian, 127, 393.
Humour, 359, 86 ; sense of (ix), 130.
Hunding, 15 ; sons of, 43.
Hunger, 78, 88, 97, 192, 235, 8, 80, 309, 30, 46, 7, 69, 93.
Hunter, 362 ; races, 356.
Hymns, (xvi), 76, 9, 85, 388.
Hypocrisy, 58, 237, 307, 34, 51.

I.

Icarus, 152.
Ictinus, 165.
Idea, the, 65-6, 134, 75, 85, 354, 68, 369, 90, 1, cf. 346.
Ideal, (a.), 117, 35, 56, 344, 97.

Ideal (n.), 176, 7, 378; realising, 245.
Idealism, 66, 165, (193).
Idols, Paris, 76-7.
Ill-will, 208, 14, 377, 81.
Illusion, 314, 91; dramatic, 183.
Imitators, 173, 87, 9, 90, 379.
Immortality, 105, 11, 5, 6, 252, 306, 321, 67, 92.
Impartiality, 192, 210, 2, 3, 4.
Impotence, 186-7, 90, 2.
Impressions, 185, 219, 322.
Impulse (*Trieb*), 368.
Inaudible singer, 73-5, 155, 6.
Independence, 185, 220, 354, 7, 68.
India, 386.
Indifference, 147, 52, 310, 53, 8.
Individual, the, 302, 56; and Society, 227-31, 6, 313-8, 23, 48, 53, 9, 60, 369.
Individuality, 181, 316, 57, 90-1, 7, 398; artistic, 55, 6, 62, 5, 77, 185, 189, 99, 200, 353, 9, 60, 72.
Industry, 359; art, 176.
Infinite in music, the, 134, 75, 387.
Initiation, 373.
Injustice, 304, 33, 43-4.
Inner being, 133, 89, 203, 390-1.
Innocence, lost, 310, 2, 20, 94.
Innovation, artistic, 184-5, 200.
Inquisition, the, 357.
Inspiration, 238, 58, 9, 80, 97; artistic, 132, 4, 53, 75, 7, 9, 89.
Instinctive, 185, 345-51, 5, 6, 91.
Institute, French, 75, 108.
Instrumental music, 55, 189, 361, 75; and voice, 62-4, 367.
Instruments, a dire assemblage, 106.
Intellect, 173, 89, 219, 345, 51, 8, 9, 365, 90-1.
Intelligibility, artistic, 68, 183, 94, 245, 353, 71, 2.
Intendants, (xiv), 218, 25, 43, 6, (278).
Interest, artistic, 246, 7, 378.
Intonation, purity of, 60.
Intrigue, 80, 8, 101, 50, 77.
Intuition, 133-4, 85, 208, 380, 91, 2.
Invalides, Chapel of, 97, 132.
Invention, 102, 6-7, 347, 55, 60-1; musical, 63, 4, 134, 5, 84.
Invisible princess etc., 159, 60.
"Iron Hand," 158-60, 3.
Isolation, 131-5, 57-8, 73, 6, 203, 29, 318, 20, 48, 52-4, 6, 61, 3.
(Isouard, N., 137.)
Israelites in Egypt, 320.
Italian music, 55, 7, 9, 64, 5, 7-9, 112, 3, 73, 90, 379.
Italian singers, 60, 1, 71, 4, 84, 115, 118-9, 22, 53-6, 60-1, 73.
Italy, 146, 96, 266.
Ivy and vine, 387.

J.

James and Joseph, 285, 7, 8, 95, 306, 309.
Janin, Jules, 113, 64, 7.
Jardin des Plantes, 101, 5.
Jean Paul, 87.
Jerusalem, 282, 8-98, 309, 10, 36; destruction, (xviii), 291, 7, 334, 40.
Jesuits, 218.
JESUS OF NAZARETH, (xv-xix), 280-340, 93; birth, 288, 90, 307; trial, (xix), 294-5, 9; death, 288, 9, 91, 292, 6-7, 9, 308.
Jesus and Apollo, 368; Buddha, 392.
Jeune Homme, Un, 161.
Jews, 103, 63, 285-99, 383.
Jockey Club, Paris, 105.
Joconde, 137-8.
John the Baptist, 287, 97, 9, 323, 5.
,, , Saint, (xix), 288, 92, 5, 6, 297, 338.
Joly, Antenor, 160.
Joseph the Carpenter, 288, 306.
Journal des Débats, 142, 50.
,, ,, *Modes*, 87.
Journalism, 76, 84, 100, 4, 9, 20, 48, 149, 56, 7, 67, 70, 204, 23, 44, 7, 381-3; musical, 83, 113, 28, 243, 381-2.
Journeyman art, 170, 6, 348.
Joy, 175, 94, 6, 8, 202, 3, 33, 4, 5, 7, 282, 310, 69, 91; *Ode to*, 201.
Joy of life, 197, 235, 320, 62, 5, 7, 86.
Judas Iscariot, 285, 8, 90, 1, 2-3, 6-7, 308, 38.
Judgment, æsthetic, 166, 204, 6, 14, 376, 81.
Juive, La, 77, 8, 115, 51, 77, 9-81, 184, 5, 7, 8-90, 8, 9, 200.
July Fête, 150.
,, Revolution, 106, 10, 78.

K.

Kaiser, 252 et seq.
Kapellmeister, 207, (278), see Dresden.
Kaspar (*Freischütz*), 141.
Kastner, Geo., 145.
Kidron, Brook, (xix), 293.
Kietz, Ernst, 164.

King of the French, 115, see Louis.
King of the Jews, 285, 90, 1, 4, 5, 6, 298, 9.
Kingdom of Heaven in Man, 289, 91, 308, 10, 2, 3, 28, 35.
Kinghood, 227, 45, 70, 6, 97, 305, 31.
Kirnberger, 96.
Kiss of Judas, 293.
(Kittl, Johann, 176.)
Know thyself, 298, 312, 56, 90-1.
Know-alls, 212, 381.
Knowledge, 228, 92, 8, 9, 305, 33, 4, 348, 65, 8, see Unconscious.
Kock, Paul de, 71, 150.
Konrad Hohenstaufe, 261, 70.
Konradin ,, , 266, 70, 6.
(Kreuzschule, Dresden, 139.)
(Kürschner, Jos., xii, 54, 108, 10, 3.)
Kurwenal (*Tristan*), 245.

L.

Lablache, 115.
Labour, 236, 310, 31, 3, 56.
Labourers, 92, 157, 235, 7, 356, 7, 393.
Lachner, Franz, 245.
Landsmannschaften, 148.
Language, 342, 55, 6, 9, 60.
Lark, the, 71, 2.
"Last appearance," 74, 119-20, 63.
Last Supper, 280, 1, 91-2, 9, 338, 88.
Lathering, 125.
Latrines, 382.
(Laube, H., 54.)
Laughter, 26, 38, 40, 1, 2, 3, 6, 130, 139, 61, 71, 294, 6, 330.
Laurel wreaths, 115, 65.
Lava stream, 232.
Lay-figures, operatic, 66.
Law, 101, 4, 58, 236, 86, 8, 90, 4, 5, 299-313, 21, 2, 4, 7, 40, 56; eternal, 39, 235, 300, 1, 8, 11, 3, 21; to himself, 39, 305, 31, 3, 6, 66.
Lawyers, 96, 223.
("Laxua," xiii.)
Lear, King, 118.
Learned, the, 55-8, 67-8, 96, 100, 30, 173, 216, 23, 99, 305, 23, 7, 36, 91.
Leathern face, 233.
Leaves, fallen, 154, 233.
Legend, see Saga.
Legion of Honour, 75.
Legitimists, French, 106.
Leipzig, 90, 1, 122.
LEONARDO DA VINCI, 165.
Lessing's *Laokoon*, 364.
Lestocq, 183.
Lethargy, 114, 47.
Letter and spirit, 206, 9, 300, 32.
Leuven, 158-60.
Levity, 124, 97.
(Lewald, 70.)
Liberals, the, 156.
Libretto, (vii, xiii), 66, 176, 9, 92.
Lichtenberg, 342.
Liebesmahl, (xiii-xiv), 277-82.
(*Liebesverbot*, x, 54, 150.)
(Liechtenstein, Prince F., 112.)
Lies, 19, 21, 9, 31, 91, 108, 49, 237, 244, 308, 28, 39, 47, 59, 83.
Life and Death, 235, 6, 8, 86, 300, 7, 313-8, 22, 71, 87. See Art.
Life of everyday, 181, 234, 386, 91.
Life-needs, 346, 51, 91. See N.
Light of the World, 328, 35.
Lighting (pictorial), 166.
Lightning, 133, 232, 97.
Lille, 71, 146.
Lion, 368; and monkey, 363.
(Lipinski, 278.)
LISZT, Franz, (158), 377-8; Paris concerts, 105, 26-7, 36-7, 73; (*Letters to*, xv).
LITERARY WORKS, Wagner's, (xxi, 54), 381-2; (*Ges. Schr.* vii-ix; *Nachgelassene Schr.*, xii-xx, 278):—
Art and Revolution, (284), 362.
Artwork of the Future, (xix, 284, 317), 362.
(*Auber*, xi, 124, 82, 91.)
(*Capitulation*, 88.)
(*Communication*, xii, xv, 284.)
(*End in Paris*, 73.)
Freischütz article, 141.
(*German Musician in Paris*, ix.)
Halévy and R. de C. (x-xii), 175.
Hero-dom and Christendom, 396.
Jesus of Nazareth, (vii, xiv-xx), 283.
(*Memoirs*, unpublished, xxi.)
(*Opera and Drama*, xviii, 104, 24, 175, 382.)
(*Vaterlandsverein Speech*, xiv, 226.)
(*Vienna Opera-house*, 239.)
(*Wibelungen*, xvi.)
Zukunftsmusik, 377.
Literature, 103, 30, 47, 220, 3, 352, 353, 75.
Lobster, 169.
Locality, in drama, 194, 7.
Logic, 131; French, 141, 67.
LOHENGRIN, (xiv, xv, xvi, xviii, 203), 244; at Vienna, 242.
London, 71, 4, 89, 91, 121, 39, 233.
Longevity, 96, 106, 15, 315.

Lot's wife, 331.
Louis XI., 161.
,, , XV., 106, 26.
,, Philippe, 73, 82, 6, 105, 15, 40, 7.
Louvre, concert in the, 140, 1.
Love, 179, 80, 93, 232, 365, 86-9, 91, 393; Doctrine of, 287, 92, 7, 9-313, 321, 2, 6-8, 34, 6; free, 302, 5, 6, 314, 21, 2, 6-8, 71; maternal, 319, 368, 97; sexual, 301-3, 15, 20-1, 59, 368, 9, 87, 96-8,—unfulfilled, 143, 315, 85; universal-human, 315, 6, 321, 2, 46, 64, 8.
Love, Goddess of, 387.
Love-deed, 314, 7, 21, 7.
Love-potion, 9, 12, 49, 273, 5, 387.
Loveless, 305, 18, 20, 1, 62, 5.
Lovers, 159, 94, 264, 72; French, 104, 70; parting, 118, 9, 97.
Löwe, Sophie, 112-3, 6, 39.
Luceria, 255, 8, 60.
Ludwig II., 245, 6, 8.
Lusignan, Jacques, 193.
Lust of the flesh, 321, 7, 33, 6.
Luther, 386, 8; (New Test., 323, 4).
(Lüttichau, von, xiv, 278.)
Luxury, 71, 87, 170, 251, 7, 331, 59.
Lybian desert, 85.
Lycurgus, 342.
Lyon, 71, 146.
Lyric, 353, 4, 5, 7, 60, 72.
Lyric drama, 56, 178-82, 355, see Opera.

M.

Machinist, stage, 78, 122, 223, 353.
Maçon, le, 173.
Mad, 202, 368; -house, 100.
Magic, 18, 31, 2, 4, 180, 257, 8, 377.
Magic lantern, 373.
Main de Fer, 158-60.
Major of Hussars, art-struck, 223.
(Malibran, 110.)
Maltese Knight, 125, 53, 64, 7-8, see *Reine*.
Mammon, 304, 28.
Man and beasts, 228, 9, 30, 301, 10, 312, 62, 3, 93-4, 6-7. See Nature.
Man and Men, 229, 30, 7, 98, 329, 355, 67, 8.
Man and Woman, 301, 8, 19, 67, 96-8.
"Man of the people," 156.
Manfred, (xiii), 251 et seq.
Manna in the desert, 310.
Mannerism, 68, 185-7, 94.
Manners, 70, 2, 93, 103, 24, 9, 56, 383; and taste, public, 219.
Manysidedness, German, 171.
Manuscript, (xix-xx, 284, 342; lost, xi, xiii, 250, 78); play, 168-9; score, Mozart's, 206.
Marchand de vin, 94.
Marengo, 72.
Mariafeld, 386.
Mario, 156.
Market 246; in Temple, 290.
Marriage, 93, 9, 100, 1, 2, 59, 63, 7, 170, 301-3, 5, 6-7, 9, 19, 25, 7, 39, 387, 96-8.
Mars, Mme., 119-20.
Marshal of France, 74, 5, 110.
Martyrs, 395.
Mary Magdalene, 285-8, 91-3, 5, 326, 338.
Mary the Mother, 281, 7-8, 95-7, 306, 309, 24, 31.
Masaniello, see *Muette*.
Maschera, Kastner's, 145.
Masks, ancient, 355, 7, 9.
Masquerade, 72-3, 143, 66.
Mass, the, 182, 90, 230, 47, 356, 8, 70.
Massacre des Innocents, 162.
Masters, great, 137, 58, 200, 366; and performers, 129, 43, 201, 9; pupils, 132, 6, 66.
Masterworks, 115, 25, 42, 58, 86, 206, 279.
Matchbox, 94; covering, 97.
Materialism, 159, 236, 7, 392-3.
Maternity, 159, 63, 8, 368, see Love.
Mathematics, 90, 109, 36.
Matinées, 82.
Matthew Levi, 285-6.
Matthieu Luc, 161.
(McLeod incident, 74.)
Means and end, 64, 195, 8, 200, 4, 345, 50.
Mediocrities, 111, 76, 90.
Meditation, 152, 3, 365, 88.
Meekness, 129-30, 328, 86.
MEISTERSINGER, (154, 372, 3); Prelude to Act III., 388.
Melancholy, 120, 94, 6, 200, 80, 93, 372, 86.
Melismus, 129.
Melody, 59, 68, 175, 82, 354: Berlioz, 135; Halévy, 194, 7-9; Mozart, 55, 57, 66, 183; popular turns, 124, 82, 184, 94.
Melon, 169.
Melting rôles, 155, 6.
Men, Be, 58, 67, 217, 27-30, 8, 345, 64.
MENDELSSOHN, 173, 89-90; *Paulus*, 279.
Mercury (metal), 393.

Messenians, 357.
Messiah, (xviii), 110, 285, 8, 9, 90, 1, 298, 308.
Metaphor, 375.
Metaphysics, 73, 380, 90, see Hegel.
Metronome, 208.
Metternich, 233.
Meudon, 105-6.
MEYERBEER, 75, 102, 72; operas, 78, 81, 110-1, 68.
Mezza voce, 77.
Microscope and grub, 365.
Middle Ages, 181, 98, 386.
Milk, 292, 305, 8, 14; spilt, 48.
Milliners, 71, 99, 146.
Mime (*Ring*), 21, 2, 42-3.
Mine, submarine, 162.
Ministry, 73, 102, 5, 20-1, 61, 3, 4, 233, 378.
Minuet *v.* Cancan, 93.
Miracle, (xviii), 281, 2, 6, 98; in Art, 371. See Signs.
Mirate (tenor), 156.
Mirror, 93, 368.
Mise-en-scène, 78, 111, 21-2, 43, 4, 161-2, 246, 353.
Misquotation, 130, 382.
Mist, 46, 163, 227.
Mistresses, 79, 87, 92-3, 170.
Misunderstood, 129, 202, 6, 88, 92, 9, 378-9, 81-2, 93.
Mitleid, 298, 328, 89, 91, 3-5.
Mitterwurzer, Anton, 245.
Mob, 140, 290, 3, 5, 6, 9.
Mocenigo, 195.
Mockery, 148, 209, 53, 94, 6, 9, 366, 385.
Mode, the, 137, 72, 3, 89, 90.
Models, 66, 114-5, 32, 76, 87, 8, 92, 7.
Modern, 134, 61, 70, 2, 96, 346, 53, 359, 60, 2, 3, 83.
Modulation, 68, 142, 375.
MOLIÈRE, 161, 2, 220.
Monarchy, 227, 344, 59.
Money, (xiv), 75, 9, 81, 9-92, 4, 5, 9, 103, 4, 6, 15, 21, 35, 6, 8, 52, 68, 169, 72, 216, 25, 37, 41, 7, 87, 8, 290, 7, 307, 38, 93.
Monkey, lion and man, 363.
Monks, 95, 166, 99, 256, 315, 62, 86.
Monogamy, 397-8, see Marriage.
Monotony, musical, 68, 183, 7, 90.
Monpou, H., 114, 52-3.
Montmartre, 150.
Monumental, 246, 359, 60, 1, cf. 346.
Moonlight, 20, 46, 257; moans, 75.
(Moore, George, xvii.)
Moral: act, 316; code, 364; lesson, 148; satisfaction, 299, 346, 97; sense, 92, 9, 219, 390, 1, 3, 6.
Morals, public, 72, 167, 219, 29. See Customs.
Mordente (mus.), 60.
Morning and evening, 372; land of, 252, 4, 71.
"Mosaïques," musical, 83.
Moscow, Wagner at, 244.
Moses, 325; death, 307.
Mosque, 260, 5.
Mote and beam, 62.
Mother, 9, 33, 5, 42, 8, 118, 232, 287-8, 301, 9, 14, 24, 66, 85, 97.
Mother-tongue, 103.
Motion, eternal, 301, 11, 5, 7, 46, 50, 351, 61, 6.
Motives, mus., 194, 5, 7, 9, 275, 388.
Mottoes, bonbon, 100.
Mountain tribes, 356.
MOZART, 55, 7, 63, 4, 6, 123, 7, 32, 208, 377; and Beethoven, 129, 373; "disdaining," 206.
Mud, 88, 108.
Muette de Portici, 124, 32, 73, 8, 82, 8.
Muezzin, 265.
Muffs, ladies', 70.
Mule, 288, 90.
Multiplying the Me, 313, 5-7, 20, 1, 359.
Munich (383); theatre, 239-48.
Murat, 162.
Murder, 32, 45, 7, 87, 94, 295.
Musard, 117; and Mozart, 132.
Mushroom operas, 152.
MUSIC, 109, 79, 91, 354, 63, 87:—
  Absolute, 367.
  Copying, 96, 8, 206.
  and Drama, (x, xv-xvi), 55-69, 176, 180, 3, 9-90, 4, 352-3, 72-5, 7.
  "External," 180, 5.
  French and Italian, (x, xi), 56-8, 66, 67, 112, 24, 34, 72-3, 86-92.
  German, 55-68, 102, 13-4, 29, 88, 190, 379.
  "Historic," 181.
  "History of," 109-10, 7, 40, 3, 362.
  Listening to, 55, 67, 127, 9, 42, 202, 373.
  Religious, 58, 84, 189, 279.
  Teachers, 83, 102.
  Understanding, 56, 7, 68, 102, 17, 129, 32, 4, 5, 201-3, 42, 79.
Musical box, 66.
Musical Construction, 134, 83, see Form.
Musical Expression, 55-6, 63, 5, 8-9, 183, 208, 362.

(*Musical World*, London, 382.)
(*Musician*, London, xvii.)
Musician in Paris, German, 102, 4, 8, 109, 40.
MUSICO-DRAMATIC WORKS, Wagner's, 239-48, 377-8, 86-9.
(*Musikalisches Wochenblatt*, 204.)
Mussulman and Christian, 252, 60, 1.
Mystery-plays, 358.
Mystic, 56, 75, 8, 81, 6, 7, 105, 43, 163, 201.
Myth, (xvii-xviii), 160, 343, 4, 54-7, 360, 72.

N.

Naïve in Art, 194, 6, 352.
Naked, 72, 235, 355, 63, 5.
Name, a father's, 152.
Nameless genius, 347, 55.
Naples, 271.
Napoleon I., 72, 81, 162, 359, 60; obsequies, 97-8, 110.
Napoleon III., 241, 378-9.
Narrow streets, 149.
Nathan, Mme., 77.
National: art, 55, 114, 35, 42, 78, 81-182, 8, 9, 94, 355, 78-9; idiosyncrasy, 144, 82, 356, 78, 9.
National, le, 73.
National Guard, French, 104.
Nationality, 58, 66, 90, 1, 103, 237, 313, 37, 42, 55-60, 79.
Naturalism, 61, see Truth.
NATURE:—
  and Art, 154, 349, 55-6, 60-1, 72.
  Gods, 356-9, see G.
  Law, 39, 118, 235, 300, 8, 17, 9, 397, 8.
  Love of, 70-1, 149, 98-9, 203.
  and Man, 193, 7, 203, 36-7, 98, 302, 9, 11, 5, 22, 45, 6, 51, 2, 5, 357, 60, 8, 72, 89, 90, 6-8.
  -Necessity, 313, 6, 45, 6, 8, 9, 52.
  -Powers, 357, 67.
Nau, Mme., 83.
Nazareth, (xix), see Jesus.
Necessity, 118, 311, 3, 5, 21, 47, 50-352; artistic, 65, 208, 9, 349, 51, 4, 361; inner, 202, 345, 8.
Need and satisfaction, 229-30, 6-7, 302, 4, 44, 5, 6-8, 61, 9.
Neidhaid, 8, 28, 43.
Nerves, 127.
Netherlands, 166.
(*Neue Ztft f. Musik*, 54, 108, 71.)
New and old, 137, 57, 8, 232, 7, 334, 336-7, 45, 83.
New epoch, 128, 47, 57, 65, 89, 246.
New path, 66, 184, 6, 7, 241, 365.
Nibelheim, 20.
Nibelungen, the, 3, 11, 20-1, 2, 34, 50; Siegfried as ruler of, 8.
NIBELUNGEN, RING DES, (vii, 195), 239.
(Niemann, Albert, 76.)
(Nietzsche, F., ix.)
Night, 20, 36, 227, 34, 62, 387.
Nightingales and larks, 71, 2.
Ninths and fifths, 58.
Nixies, 37, 357.
Noah, 338.
Noble, 100, 98, 244, 397; art, 68, 108, 117, 28, 35, 66, 94, 201, 11, 20, 42.
(Nohl, Ludwig, 218.)
Noise, 105-7, 10, 23, 49, 72.
Norm, an enduring, 346-7.
Norma, 69.
Norns, 3-5, 21, 39, 50, 365.
North Germany, 386. See South.
Notables, 108, 46, 50.
Notoriety, 83, 163.
Notre Dame de Paris, 140.
"Now-time," the, 384.
Nuances, musical, 60, 8, 209, 46.
Nuremberg greets Sachs, 388.
Nut and old tooth, 59.

O.

Oak, a venerable, 71.
Oaths, 11, 3-4, 9, 29-31, 3, 4, 40, 8, 49, 122, 292, 9.
Object, 346-7, 51, 5, 60.
Odyssey, 357.
(Oesterlein, N., xii.)
Ointment, Precious, 292, 338.
Old age, 234, 315, 59.
Oligarchy, 195, 356, 8.
Olives, Mount of, (xvi,) 293, 389.
Omnibus, 125.
One *v.* Many, 229, 36-7, 306, 15.
One-sidedness, 64, 9, 148, 205, 13, 379, 81.
OPERA, 66, 175-7, 92, 373:—
  Comic, 57, 114, 23-6, 58-9, 78, 81-2.
  French, (x), 56, 7, 67, 78, 9, 81, 114-5, 21, 4-6, 78, 85-6, 90, 2.
  German, 55-69, 144, 69, 73, 88-9, 211; in Paris, 141-3, 60, 240-1, 377-9.
  Grand, (xiii), 124, 53, 78-82, 6, 92.
  Italian, 55-6, 64, 7-9, 115, 8, 218; French aping, 173, 90-1; Germans copying, (x), 65.

OPERA—*continued*—
Numbers, 66, 153, 80, 98, 200.
One-act, 152.
Plot and text, 66, 125-6, 44, 5, 52-153, 8-9, 69, 75-9, 92-3.
Varieties of style, 211-2.
Oratorio, (xiv), 152, 72, 279-80.
Orchestra, 223; Berlioz', 132, 3; Conservatoire, 129; Munich, 245; *v.* Pianoforte, 367; and Singer, 56, 9, 63, 181, 95, 6, 7, 206, 7, 9; Size, 141, 241, 79, 80.
Orchestration, 62, 8; Halévy's, 172, 195-7; modern, 63, 153, 72; Mozart's, 63, 6; Weber's, 56.
Orders, 75, 233, 396.
Organ-grinders, 135.
Organisation, 223, 370, see Assoc.
Oriental, 251, 398.
Originality, 78, 134-5, 52, 3, 75, 96, 379.
Os coccyx, 392.
Owl and bat, 146.

P.

Paganini and Berlioz, 132.
Painting, 106, 64-6, 223, 353, 4, 8.
Palais Royal, 87.
Palestine, 252, 85 et seq.
Palm Sunday concerts, 201, 10, 79.
Palm-trees, 254, 63, 72.
Pan, 359.
Paper world, a, 233.
Paradise lost, 91, 320; regained, 233, 272.
Parents and children, 118, 301-2, 14, 318-20, 4, 9, 97.
PARIS, 70-200:—
Concerts, 71, 82-5, 109, 12, 6, 26-9, 132, 6, 9, 40, 72, 3; Wagner's, 240-1, (386).
Conservatoire, 72, 82, 116, 28-9, 31, 137, 57-8, 72.
"*Don Juan*" in, 122-3.
Exhibition of **1867**, 378.
Fortifications, 109, 46.
Germans in, 87-109, 13-4, 43, 9, 74.
Hospitals, 97, 9.
Opéra (Grand), 71, 6-9, 97, 102, 4-105, 10-3, 6, 20-3, 31, 7, 8-9, 41-143, 9, 51, 6-7, 68, 72, 8, 9, 91-2, 378; Balls, 85, 7, 144; *Tannhäuser* at, (163), 241, 377-8.
Opéra Comique, 80, 114-5, 20, 3-6, 137, 45-6, 52, 3, 7-9, 72, 3, 8, 9, 186, 91-2.
Painters, 164.

PARIS—*continued*—
Royal theatres, 120-1.
Theatres: Ambigu comique, 80, 161; Cirque olympique, 162; Français, 79, 119, 20, 49, 62, 7, 168, 70-1, 378; Gaieté, 161; Guignac, 70; Gymnase, 80, 149; Italien, 71, 115-6, 8, 20, 39, 46, 153-5, 60, 73, 240-1; Odéon, 116, 118, 60-1; Palais Royal, 149; Renaissance, (150), 160-1; Variétés, 73, 149, 50, 61; Vaudeville, 80, 120.
"Parfum allemand," 113.
Parliament, speech in, 65, 110.
Parodies, 168.
PARSIFAL, (viii, 309, 10, 1, 22); Prelude, 388-9.
Part-writing, 84, 142.
Parterre, 104, 16, 51, 70, 7, 91.
Party discord, 110, 289, 99.
Passionate in art, the, 55, 61, 3, 5, 6, 68, 9, 133, 45, 73, 8-80, 5, 9, 93, 5, 196, 9, 203, 372, 5.
Passover, the, 294.
Past, 119, 75; no, 124, 342; Present and Future, 135, 236, 367, 76.
Paste diamonds, 126.
Pastrycook, 144, 58, 9.
Patches, beauty, 73.
Patchouli, 84.
Pathos, 76, 179, 98, 9, see Pass.
Patience, 378, 83.
Patriarchate, 315, 20, 53, 6.
Patricians, 358, see Aristocr.
Patriotism, 87-8, 91, 103, 12, 6, 35, 289, 316.
Patrons, art, 240, 1, 4-6, 362, 4.
Pawnbroker, 109, 26.
Peace, 4, 72, 323, 9, 31.
Pedantry, 67, see Learned.
Peers, French House, 73, 123.
Pendulum beat, 63.
Pension, 106, 20.
Père-la-chaise, 75.
Perfect, the, 323, 8, 33, 66, 98.
Performances, model, 241, 5.
,, , number of, 211, 45, 6; poor, 111, 22-3, 41, 9, 51-2, 61, 208, 210, 2.
Perfume, 70, 1, 84, 105, 15, 6, 46, 292.
Period, mus., 68, 180, 3.
Persecution, relig., 281, 2, 9, 98, 312, 328, 30, 7.
Persiani, 113.
Personalities, 205, 13, 4, 379, 81-3.
Peter, Simon, 288, 91-7, 309.
Phantasy, 104, 33, 49, 76, 94, 343, 8.

Pharisees, 286 seq., 325, 6, 34, 5.
Pheasant, 169.
Phidias, 165.
(Philharmonic, London, 382.)
Philosophy, 350, 1, 8, 60; and music, 87, 96, 102.
Physical, 346, 9, 51, 4, 69, see Sens.
Physician, 96, 8, 153, 70, 285, 7, 9, 309, 25, 30, 93.
Physics, 380, 92-3, see Science.
Physiognomy, 93, 103, 29.
Piano and forte, 155, 6.
Pianoforte, 62, 82-4, 102, 27, 367; rehearsals, 243; score of *Tristan* 245.
Picture-stalls, 103-4.
Piety, 185; worldly, 85, 382.
Pilate, (xvii), 289, 93-9.
Pillet, Léon, 105, 11, 2, 3.
Pirouettes, 143.
Pity, 389, 91, 3, 4, 5.
Pizzicato, 196.
Place de la Concorde, 70.
,, des Invalides, 97.
Plans, 90, 7, 100, 4, 211-2, 44.
Plant, 313, 5, 25.
Plastic art, 165, 353-5, 8, 60-1, 4, 6.
Plays and operas, 161, 367.
Playwrights, 80-1, 96, 161, 70, 223, 352.
Pleasure, love of, 82, 5, 8, 107, 251, 3, 336.
Poesy, 66, 165, 93.
Poet, 79, 96, 148, 349; and actor, 220, 223, 352, 5.
Poet and Musician, 64, 6, 9, 81, 121, 45, 52-3, 75-9, 82, 92-3, 5, 9, 377.
Poetic diction, (xiii), 65.
Poetry, modern, 352-3, 61, 5, 7.
Polacca guerriera, 117, 28.
Police, 103, 47, 59, 60, 218, 382, 93.
Polichinel, 70.
Politeness, 89, 91, 157, 60.
Politics, (xiv), 55, 65, 72, 108, 9, 10, 120, 40, 6, 9, 60, 3, 215-9, 346, 53, 359, 60, 87.
Polygamy, 397-8.
Polytheism, 350.
Pomp, 131, 98.
Pompadour, 106, 26.
Pont Neuf, 117.
Pontons, *Les*, 162.
Poor, the, 71, 82, 8, 103, 4, 5, 70, 235, 7, 8, 88, 310, 22, 5, 7, 8, 32, 362; Pan the god of, 359. See also Poverty.
Pope, 71, 253, 5, 61.
Popular, the, 124, 35, 78, 82, 4, 94, 201, 350, 1, 2, 88. See Folk.
(Porges, H., 250.)
Portamento, 60, 5.
Portrait-painter, 164, 5.
Portugal, 125-6.
Positive and Negative, 317, 70.
Possession, 301, 2, 15, 21, 30, 43, 4, 359, 84, 96, 7. See Property.
Possible, to have felt the, 384.
Posterity, (ix), 376.
Postillon de Lonjumeau, 135, 44, 58.
Pot au feu, 96, 100, 1.
Potpourris, mus., 83.
Poultier (tenor), 156.
Poverty, 78, 88-9, 92, 6, 8, 9, 108, 46, 192, 202, 306.
Powdered wigs, 87, 126.
Power, worldly, 297, 315, 87.
Practical sense, 224, 5. See Theory.
Prado, 93.
Prague Conservatoire, 208.
Praise and blame, worthless, 214.
Prakriti (*Die Sieger*), 385-6.
Prayer, 84-5, 195, 9, 256, 7, 9, 62, 80, 281, 305, 25, 8, 86.
Prejudice, 67, 205; national, 89, 95, 103, 88.
Prelude, orchestral, 3, 7, 271, 386-9.
Priest: Christian, 358; Jewish, 292, 294, 5, 8, 300, 9, 35; and King, 295, 300, 5.
Prima donna quarrels, 112, 38.
Prince and people, 158, 98, 228, 33, 254, 61, 70, 95, 358, 65.
Princes and art, 245, 363.
Princess in trouble, 126, 59, 63.
Private school, 114.
,, view, 164-6.
Privilege, 227, 37, 358.
Prizes, award of, 164-5.
Problems, artistic, 156, 81, 240, 4, 6, 247, 377.
Processions, religious, 199.
Procreation, 313-5, 7, 9-21, 69, 97.
Productivity, 76, 133, 44, 77, 86, 208, 348, 55, 6, 9, 60, 9, 70.
Programmes, 82, 113, 37.
Progress, "constant", 394.
Proof-correcting, 97.
Property, 94-5, 9, 121, 235-7, 53, 80, 282, 7, 8, 301-2, 4, 10, 30, 8, 43, 56, 358, 82, 96; *v.* Man, 236, 344.
Prophesying, (xviii), 291, 2.
Prophetess and wife, 261, 7, 72.
Prophets, The, 330, 3; tombs, 310, 334.
Prose and verse, 79, 101, 10.

Protestant: music, 279; prince, 358.
Proverbs, popular, 182.
Providence, 136, 52, 92.
Prudence, (xiii), 127, 205, 365.
Prussia, 90, 227, 8, see Berlin.
Psalm-singers, 363.
Pseudonym, (70, 171, 222), 222, 5.
Public, musical, 75, 8, 83-4, 116, 32, 134, 6-7, 72, 92, 241, 382; verdict of, 128-9, 43, 91, 213, 4, 47. See Theatre.
Public life, 109, see Art and Life.
Publishers, 113.
Pückler, Prince, 90, 1.
Puget, Dlle., 83, 4, 5, 102.
Pulse-beat and life, 63.
Puns, 146, 82.
Punch and Judy, 70.
Puppy, an expensive, 81.
Pure, the, 308, 12, 28, 86, see Chastity.
Purely Human, 66, 179, 82, 376, 96, 398; arts, 353-4, 6, 61.
Purely Musical, 64, 142, 96, 367.
Puritani, 118, 61.
Pyrenean castle, 90, 1.
,, watering-place, 148.

Q.

Quadrilles, 85, 114, 7, 52, 87.
Quartet, *R. de C.*, 200; Beeth., 386.
Queens, stage, 126, 98.
Queue, 83.
Quiet and order, 217, 33.

R.

Race, 297-8, 310, 20, 36, 44, 56, 9, 396-8; human, 316, 21, 35, 94. See Blood.
Rachel, Dlle., 85, 120, 49, 62-3.
Rachel (*Juive*), 77, 180.
Racine's "transfiguration," 120, 62, 3.
Railways, 362.
Rain, 154, 238, 323.
Ramadan, 260, 2.
Ranting, 61, 75.
RAPHAEL, 165.
(Rationalists, the, xviii.)
Razor, notch in, 125.
Realism, 160, 2.
Reality and ideality, (xviii), 176, 257, 368, 9, 91, 8.
Reason, 228, 312, 43, 52, 68, 73.
Red cap and blouse, 135.
REDEEMER, 285, 7, 97, 8.
Redemption, 97, 107, 234, 5, 89, 91, 300, 4, 5, 7, 9, 59, 60, 85-9.
Reflection, 176, 84, 5, 95, 347, 65-6.
Reform, (xiv), see Theatre.
Reformation, German, 388.
Regisseur, 171, 213, 24.
Rehearsals, 206, 7, 40, 2, 3, 5-6; Mozart's, 208.
Reincarnation, (xv), 385.
Reine de Chypre, 125, 53, 64, 7-9, 72, 177, 84, 92-200.
"Reisebilder," Heine's, 147.
Reissiger, G., (208), 280.
Religion, 86, 95, 140, 343, 4, 52, 5, 356, 8, 60, 91, 4; foundering of, 350, 359; new, 393; Roman, 358. See Christianity.
Religion and Art, 199, 279, 352, 4, 8, 359, 92, 6; State, 218, 358.
Renaissance, the, 165, 353, 79.
Rendering, 59, 61, 2, 3, 206, 9, 43.
Rent, 92, 236-7.
Renunciation, 96, 315, 70, 1, 85, 6, 95.
Repertoire, 121-2, 56, 61, 86, 207, 210-2, 8, 44.
Replacer of Rubini, 155-6.
Reporters, (ix), 108, 27-8, 40, 8-50, 4, 163, 204-5, 13-4, 44, 82-3.
Research, 371; historical, 100.
Residenz, 89, 101;—Theater, 245.
Resignation, 170, 386, 8.
Responsibility, 207-9, 13.
Rest, 78, 85, 95, 105-7, 40, 96, 257, 272, 323, 88.
Restoration, French, 119.
Revolution, (xiv, xv), 72, 82, 105, 19, 124, 6, 40, 6, 7, 50, 215, 8, 27-8, 30, 232-8, 85, 6, 9, 94, 8, 9, 310, 45, 70.
"Revue," theat., 150.
Rhine, 243; songs, 87-8.
Rhine-daughters and gold, 3, 21, 36-40, 50, 2.
Rhythm, 65, 178, 81-4, 96, 354.
Rich, the, 88, 9, 100, 3, 5, 235, 7, 8, 297, 300, 4, 30, 3, 7, 62. See Bankers.
Rich young man, The, 288, 310, 25.
Richard Cœur-de-lion, 153, 7, 72, 91.
Riding *v.* driving, 362.
(*Rienzi*, x, xi, xii, xiii).
Ries' "Notices of Beeth.," 130.
Riga, (54), 69, 72, (116).
Rights, 270, 302, 43, 58; of Man, 228, 30, 7, 344.
Ring, The, 4, 6, 12, 9-22, 7-9, 34, 7-40, 4, 8, 50-2.
Ripening, 189, 322.
River similes, 114, 33, 228, 65.
River-baths, 149.

Robert le diable, 78, 81, 111, (113); Liszt's fantasia, 137.
"Robert mon âme," 76, 83, 4.
Rock: Moses', 235; Peter, 294.
(Roeckel, Aug., xii, 226, 7.)
Roger (tenor), 83.
Roman: legions, (xvii), 285, 8, 9, 93-295, 7, 8; Rights and sacra, 358.
Romances, mus., 152, see Puget.
Romanticism, 56, 66, 72, 80, 150, 81, 196.
Rome, 282, see Pope; Roman.
Romeo e Giul. (Bellini), 55, 119.
Root and soil, 147, 235, 378.
ROSSINI, (xi), 75, 84, 127, 56, 88, 91, 367, 77.
Rothschild, Paris, 103.
Rouen, 156.
Roulades, 60, see Coloratura.
Routine, 60, 81, 177, 246.
RUBENS, 165.
Rubini, 73-6, 9, 105, 15, 9, 42, 6-7, 155-6.
Rudeness, 103.
Rue Lafitte, 103.
,, S. Antoine, 99, 100, 1.
,, S. Honoré, balls, 109.
Ruins, 175, 232, 60.
Rulers, 289, 97, 356, 8, 9, 65-6.
Rules, 67, 224.
Ruoltz, de, 111.
Russia, 72, 146, 244; princesses, 84.

S.

Sabbath, 286, 94, 323-4, 5.
Sachs, Hans, 388.
Sacra, Roman, 358.
Sacrifice, 305, 9, 24, 37, see Death.
Saga, 143, 60, 355; and history, (xii), 175-6, 320, 43, 97.
Saint Georges, de, 169, 77, 93.
S. Petersburg, 145, 6.
Saints, 391, 5, 8.
Salons, 84-5, 157, 70.
Sand and sludge, 114.
Sarazenin, (xii-xiii, xvi), 249 seq.
Satiety, 84, 387.
Satin and silk, 71, 2, 84, 7, 115, 6, 9, 126, 46.
Satyr-plays, 357, 8.
Sauce herbs, 110.
Sauerkraut, 92, 6.
Sauzet, 146.
SAVIOUR, 282, see Jesus.
Saxony, 90, 118, see Dresden.
Scandal-mongers, 147-8, 63, 383.
Scandinavian myths, 357.
Scene-painter, 78, see Mise.
"Scenophilus," 222, 5.
Scherzo, a Beethoven, 386.
SCHILLER, 127, 220, 380; *Maria Stuart*, 111; *Ode*, 201.
Schindler, 129-31.
(Schladebach, Julius, 204.)
Schlesinger, M., (xi, 83), 112-3.
Schnaps, 393.
Schneider's fugues, 58.
Schnorrs, the, 240-3, 5.
Schoolmaster, 37; village, 68.
(SCHOPENHAUER, 66, 313, 90.)
(Schröder-Devrient, Frau, 56, 250.)
SCHUMANN, 380.
Science, 309, 93; and Art, 349-51, 365, 92.
Scores, 67, 206, 9; pfte *Tristan*, 245.
Scribe, A. E., 78-81, 125-6, 52, 3, 8, 160, 2, 7, 70-1, 6.
Sculd, the Norn, 365.
Sculpture, 165, 352, 3, 4, 5.
Sea, 90, 175, 98, 354, 6, 87.
Seat, a good, 104, 67, 70, 246.
Second Advent, 289, 308, 13, 37-8.
Second self, 246.
Second thoughts, 159.
Secret, the, 179, 81, 201, 330, 73.
Seeing *v.* hearing etc., 373, 90.
Self-: Annihilation, 317, 20, 50, 1, 387, 95; Denial, 85, 96; Dependence, 57, 68, 184; Divestment, 315-22; Offering, 49, 272, 96, 9, 313, 6, 7, 9, 46; Preservation, 390, 394; Respect, 204, 6; Sacrifice, 370 —animal, 393 (see Death); Satisfaction, 58, 134; Surrender, 69, 315; Will, 40, 184.
Semblance, 360, 9.
Senses, the, 179, 219, 346, 63.
Sensitiveness, over-, 134.
Sensuous art, 165, 349, 52; music, 55, 179, 88, 98.
Sentimental, 119, 73, 209.
Sermons, 68; village, 65.
(Servais, F., 116.)
Service, 287, 92, 9, 306, 31.
SHAKESPEARE, (xvii), 118, 220, 372, 373, 92; and clown, 358; in Paris, 378.
Shillings and pounds, 90, 2.
Ship, 199, 271; wreck, 95.
Shop, 92; fronts, 87, 93.
Sicily, 258.
Sieger, Die, 385-6.
Siegfried's Tod, (vii-viii, xv, xvi, xx) 1-52, 284.

Sienna, 266, 70.
Sighs, 118.
Significant, the, 129, 72, 8, 84, 9, 200, 12, 28, 39, 46, 376.
Signs and wonders, 291, 2, 7, 334, 9,
Silence, 118, 27, 8, 42, 91, 238, 94, 335, 78, 81, 90.
Silesia, 143, 4.
Silver and gold, 87, 153, 307, 33, 6.
Simon of Cirene, 296.
Simplicity, 56, 142, 70, 2, 94, 5, 6, 198, 200.
Sin, 235, 86, 318, 89, 90, 4, 7; and Law, 300-9, 11, 2, 21, 39, 40, 56, 367.
Sinai, 336.
Singers, 36, 62, 71, 3-7, 82-4, 111, 2, 121, 38-9, 51, 5, 73, 91, 8, 240-5, 251; and conductor, 212-4, 40, 3, 6. See Italian etc.
Singing at sight, 243.
Situations, Dramatic, 59, 80, 144, 59, 183, 95, 7, 9.
Slanders, 204, 383, see Scandal.
Slavery, 3, 8, 15, 21, 50, 215, 7, 36, 305, 7, 8, 20, 56, 8, 9, 66, 95.
Smelling-salts, 233.
Smiles, 73, 81, 146, 233, 40, 73, 94.
Smoke, fiery, 133, 232.
Snuff, 91, 6, 7; box, 364.
Soapsuds, Auber's, 125.
Sobs, 75, 7, 118.
Socialism, 359, 60.
Society, 133, 221, 301, 11, 6, 67, 8, 369-70; high, 108, 18, 70, 233. See Individual.
Socrates, 358, 60, 3.
Soldiers, 216, 7, 34, 7, 85, seq.
Solid, 124, 6, 83, 90, 211, 8.
Soliloquy, 91.
Solitude, (xv), 106-7, 63, 293, 389.
Song and Dance, 354.
Song, Dramatic, 55-69, 178, 82, 94, 198, 9.
Sontag, 63.
Sophistry, 212.
Sorrow, 196, 203, 37, see Suffering.
Sostenuto, 59.
Soul, 134, 203, 27, 80, 1, 2, 303, 12, 329, 31, 63, 88, 9; -denier, 96-8, 100, 1.
Soult, Marshal, 110.
South, 198; *v* North, 266, 372, 86.
Souvenirs of singers, 118.
Spain, 146, 62, 379.
Spark divine, 177.
Sparta, 342, 57.
Speaking, public, 65, 110, 66.
Species, 390, 1, 6; well-marked, 363, 397.
Spectacle, 78, 162, 98-9.
Spectacles and eyes, 67.
Speculation: monetary, 73-4, 127, 233, 7; philosophic, 73-4, 354.
Speech, 352, 5, 6, 60; tone-, 55, 68, 132, 4, 202, 3.
Spener, 222, 5.
Spiders, 234.
Spirit of the age, 58, 66, 185, 228, 372.
Spirits, alcoholic, 153, 393.
Spirituel, 83.
SPOHR, 55, 6.
SPONTINI, 69, 102, 23.
Spring, 72, 118, 357, 72.
Stabat Mater, Rossini's, 173.
Stage-costume, 78, 111, 21, 3, 6, 44, 169, 246.
Stage-music, 271, 4, 90.
Star, good etc., 89, 193, 265, 74.
Stars in heaven, 79, 127.
State, 311, 43, 55, 7, 91; foundering of, 344, 55, 9.
State and Art, 120-1, 32, 218-9, 21, 346-7, 53.
Statesman, 233, 358.
Statuary, 165, 355, 8, 64, 75.
Statutes of Grand Opéra, 120, 41.
Steal, Thou shalt not, 304, 26, 33.
Steam travel, 90, 362.
(Stein, H. von, 284.)
Stem-saga, 356, 7.
Stench, 149, 382.
Stereotyped, 65, 185, 90.
Stoics, 72, 9.
Stoltz, Mme., 77, 112, 53.
Storks and cranes, 71-2, 4.
Storm, 16, 196, 232, 4, 5, 8, 56, 7, 280, 97.
Strassburg, 240; beer, 96, 101.
(Strauss, David, xvii-xix.)
Strauss's waltzes (the older), 87.
Strength, 229, 36, 7, 363, 5, 8, 9, see Strong.
Strings 129; and wind, 196, 388.
Strolling players, 122.
Strong and Weak, 99, 293, 332, 56, 363, 71, 95.
Students, univ., 92, 148, (215).
Studio, artist's, 246.
Stuff, 349, 50, 4, 5, 67.
Style, 185, 7, 8, 9, 211, 375, 80.
Sublime, 173, 290, 1, 3, 28, 30.
Subscribers, theat., 145.
Success, (xiii), 78-9, 81, 111, 2, 5-7, 124, 38, 9, 41, 62, 7, 9, 78, 92, 241, 7.

Suède, Délivrance de la, 168.
Suffering, 77, 175, 234, 5, 7, 81, 98, 311, 2, 9, 21, 5, 8, 39, 58, 69, 70, 1, 386, 9, 93.
Sugar, 91.
Summer and Winter, 372; Paris, 70-2, 87, 140, 9-50.
Sun, 22, 36, 70, 4, 227, 33, 59, 62, 8, 323.
Sunday walk, 94.
Superficial, 124, 9, 246.
Superfluous, 237, 332, 65, 77.
Superiorities, 111.
Superlatives, 345.
Supernatural, 232, 98.
Supersensual entrechats, 143.
Surrounding, natural, 356, 7.
"Susannah, Chaste," 152.
Susanne (*Figaro*,) 209.
Swabia, 266.
Swiss choral-singing, 60.
Sword, 232, 93, 329, 38, see Balmung.
Symbolism, 357.
Sympathy, artistic, 134, 75, 88-9, 94. See *Mitleid*.
Symphony, 172, see Beethoven.
Syrian legions, (xvii), 289, 94, 5, 7, 9.
System, a new, 184, 200.

T.

Tailors, Paris, 109, 46, 9.
Talent, 147, 71, 2, 6, 7, 8, 84, 7, 91, see Young.
Talk, too much, 55, 390.
TANNHÄUSER, (xii, xiii, xiv, xvi), 244; Paris perf.,(83,163),241, 377-8.
Tantièmes, 80, 1, see Droits.
(Tappert, W., 222.)
Tarentum, 253.
Tarnhelm, 11, 3, 7, 21, 2, 3, 4, 32, 5, 44, 52, (195).
Taste, 65, 191, 219; French, 142, 171, 2, 8; ruin of, 173, 86-7.
Tát tvam ási, 391, 4.
Tavern, village, 122, 69.
Taxes, 146, 236.
Tchandala, 385.
Tea, 85, 177.
Tears, 118, 66, 237, 385.
Technique, 117, 25, 361, 73.
Tell, Rossini's, 156; overture, 123—for pfte, 127.
Templars, 252.
Temple, 281, 90-1, 8, 305, 32, 8; veil of, 297, 307.
Tempo, 63, 208-10.
Temporal and eternal, 347, 50. See Law.
Tendence, artistic, 133, 62, 200.
Tenor, operatic, (xiii), 83, 155-7, 242.
THEATRE, 213, 8-25:—
Censorship, 218.
English, 220.
French, 73, 9-81, 109, 62, 70-1, 220, 378-9, 92.
German, see G. and Opera.
International, 378-9.
National influence, 218-9, 21, 47.
Personnel, 211-3, 40, 1.
and Public, 57, 8, 60, 5, 76, 8, 111, 112, 6, 20, 41, 5, 55, 70, 7, 90-2, 246-7, 378.
Reform, (xiv), 211-2, 8-25.
Treasury etc., 121, 6, 38, 45, 247.
Theology, 351.
Theory and practice, 145, 213, 9, 23-4.
Thetis, 367-8.
Thiers, 72, 110, (227).
Thieves, 304, 18, 28, 82; "The two," 146.
Thing-in-itself, 390-1.
Thomas, Ambroise, 114, 38, 73.
Thorns, Crown of, 296.
Thousands on the hills, the, 234-8.
Throat-dexterity, 61, 2, 5, 76, 113.
Thuringia, 144.
Tiberias, 285, 7, 90.
Tichatschek, 242, 79.
Time, 359, 60, 6; and place, 194, 371, 3, 6.
Tips, 80, 92.
TITIAN, 165.
Title, dramatic, 160, 8-9.
Tivoli, Paris, 93.
Tobacco, 91, 4, 6, 7.
Tone, Art of, 362, 77, see Music.
Tone-: figures, 63, 4; shapes, 373, 5.
Tools, 349-50, 2.
Topical pieces, 150-1.
Torch, 232, 93.
Torture-chambers, 233, 393.
Trade in human beings, 235, 356.
Tradition, 305, 24, 44; operatic, 141, 207-9, 378.
Tragedy, 162, 358, 60, 73, 92; "Lyric," 179-82.
Tragic, the, 69, 168-9, 83, 98, 367, 98.
Training artists, 59-60, 156, 7.
Translated writings, (xi), 377, 82.
Travel, 90, 125, 45, 77, 362.
Treasures, 304, 7, 28, 33; hidden, 126.
Trees, 71, 154, 94, 254, 63, 385.
Tribe, 355, 6, 7, see Blood.

Trichinæ, 392.
Trill, 60; Rubini's, 74, 105.
Trinity, The, 282, 300, 6, 40.
TRISTAN UND ISOLDE, (322); at Munich, etc., 239-48; Prelude, 386-7; Vienna rehearsals, 242-4.
Triumvirate of tenors, 156.
Trojan War, 367.
Trombones, 75.
Tropics, etc., 372.
Truth, 327, 39, 49, 50, 68, 92; dramatic etc., 56, 8, 63, 6, 156, 82, 184, 5, 96, 8, 9, 347, 52.
Tuileries, 108, 40; garden, 70, 82, 7.
Turks, 364.
Tutor, private, 100.
Tutti, 68.
Two peoples only, 238.
(Tyndale's Bible, 324.)
Type, large, 158.

U.

Ugliness of modern life, 359, 60, 3.
(Uhl, F., 239.)
(Uhlig, T., 222; *Letters to*, xv, 61, 142, 284, 345, 65.)
Unconscious and Conscious, 147, 85, 228, 9, 30, 98, 300-1, 11, 3, 6-9, 321, 45-9, 51, 2, 72, 91, 5.
Unction, 129.
Understanding (*Verstand*), 352.
Union, 229, 81, 311, 9, 53, 85, 96-8. See Association.
Unison, 388.
Unity, dramatic, 156, 80, cf. 194.
Universality, (x), 58, 66, 103, 82, 3, 189, 94, 315-9, 21, 2, 59.
University students, 148.
Unknown composers, 143, 77, 92.
Unlucky theatre, an, 160-1.
Unutterable, the 179, 374.
Unwillkür, 347, see Instinctive.
Ur-beginning, the, 301.
Ur-forefather, 298.
Ur-law, 39, 321.
Usage, ancient, 216, 89, see Customs.
Useful and Harmful, see H.
Usury, 310, cf. 237.

V.

Valour, 217.
Vanity, actor's, 353, see A.
Variety, 180, 2, 4, 9, 200, 8, 355, 86.
Vaudevilles, (73), 80.
Vegetarian, 386, 94.
Veil, 354, 75. See Temple.
Velvet, 142, 53. See Satin.
Venality, 214.
Vengeance, 11, 3, 22, 6, 9, 32, 4, 43, 45, 8, 51, 137, 266, 72, 3, 4, 98, 367.
Venice, 166, 93, 4, 5, 6.
Ventadour, Salle, 153, 4, 60-1.
Venus, Cyprian, 193.
Vernunft, 368, see Reason.
Véron, 121.
Verre d'eau, Scribe's, 171.
Versailles, 106; fountains, 150.
Verse, 65, 79, 101, 10.
Viardot, Garcia-, Mme, 83, 143.
Vice, 230, 3, 5, 7, 99, 367, 9, 70, 1.
Vienna: insurrection, (xiv), 215, 8; theatre, 160, 242-4.
Vieuxtemps, Henri, 116, 27-9.
View-of-nature, 355-6.
Vindication, 343, 4.
Vintage festivals, 357.
Viola, 197.
Violence, 237, 80, 90, 8.
Violin, 62, 83, 4, 117, 27, 8.
Violoncello, 62, 196, 7.
Virtue, 299, 367, 70, 1, 93.
Virtuosi, 63, 73, 83-4, 102, 5, 13, 7, 128, 36, 73, 98, 222.
Vivacity, artistic, 124, 78, 208.
Vivisection, 393-4.
Vocalisation, 59-65, 75-7, 113, 56, 243.
Voice *v.* Instruments, 59, 62-4, 367.
Volatile on principle, 124.
Volcano, 132, 3, 232.
(*Volksblätter*, xii, 226.)
Voltaire, 392.
Vulgarity, 382.

W.

Wachilde, 365.
Wage, the artist's, 74, 5, 8, 81, 98, 112, 5, 20, 6, 35, 6, 45, 55, 225, 348, 72.
WAGNER, RICHARD; birthplace, 90, 91, 122; character, 127; (death, vii; at Dresden, xii-xv, xix); enemies, (ix), 205-6, 14, 44, 377, 81-3; (hand-writing, xix-xx); landlord, 106; at Munich, 244-8, (383); in Paris, (ix, x), 81, 7, 92, 104-5, 8, 13, 148, 240-1, 377.
(Wagner, Siegfried, 284.)
(*Wagner-Encyclopædie*, xvii.)
(,, *Jahrbuch*, 54, 108, 10, 3.)
(Wagner Museum, xii.)
Wahn, (154), 236.

(Wahnfried archives, 250.)
Waiters, 80, 91, 2, 4.
Wakening, 384.
Walhall, 4, 16, 7, 21, 45, 51.
(*Walküre, Die*, 373.)
Walküren, 4, 15-6, 45, 51.
Wälsungen, 8, 15, 22, 42.
Waltzes of Strauss (older), 87.
Want (*Noth*), 345, 7-8.
War, 25, 39, 45, 72, 96, (227), 234, 313, 37, 56, 7, 95.
Warmth, artistic, 55, 8, 65, 6, 155, 6, 209.
Wartburg, 363.
Washing: feet, 292; hands, 295.
Washing-tub, 106.
Watch, theft of gold, 146, 77.
Watchmakers, 109.
Wate myth, 365-6
Water-Carrier, Cherubini's, 137, 57.
Water, 149, 77, 235, 95, 385.
Waves, 63, 228.
Weather, 70, 2, 3, 154.
WEBER, C. M. von, (x), 55, 6, 60, (61), 62, 123; widow, 143.
Weber, Dionys, 208.
Wedding, 164; double, 80.
Wegeler, 130.
Welfen, 255.
Wheels of State, 233.
Whirlwind, 234, 336.
Whole, the, 180, 224, 9, 30, 313.
Widows, Paris, 94-6.
Wiking, 365-6.
Wild man of the woods, 130.
Wilderness, 287, 97, 9, 310, 23, 69.
Will; individual, 236, 321, 52, 65, 8, 390; Royal, 245. See Free.
Will-to-live, 394; and Intellect, 390-1.
Willis, Les, 143-4.
Wind-instruments, 135, 96, 208.
Winds, the, 70, 154.
Wine, 149, 77, 97, 323, 6; new, 334.
Wine, Woman and Song, 386.
Wings, a father's, 152.
(Winkler, C. G. T., 61, 171.)
Winter, 70, 97, 105, 372.
Wise fool, 22, cf. 332.
Wit, (x), 95, 147, 87.
Within and Without, 132, 3, 4, 79, 185, 365, 73. See God; Kingdom
Wolf and sheep, 368.
Wolf's-gulch (*Freischütz*), 141.
(Wolzogen, Hans von, xx, 342, 73, 5.)
Woman, (xiii), 18, 24, 31, 5, 8, 9, 40, 235, 66, 7, 8, 72, 87, 8, 96, 319, 327, 67, 86, 96-8.
Wonder in Art, the, 144, 371.
Wonder-: fountain, 136; land, 80, 387; man, 127; works, 203, 82.
Wood-birds, 71; language, 41-4.
Woolgathering, 128.
Word, Sacred, 281, 2, 86, 96, 312, 26, 337.
Word more, Not a, 127, 214, 374.
Words and music, 63, 4, 6, 362, 77.
WORLD, 95, 109, 282, 307, 10, 1, 2, 318, 40, 87, 8, 91:—
-City, 171.
-Dominion, 8, 21, 44, 50, 289, 98, 370.
and Genius, 202-3, 383.
-History, (xvi), 370, 2, 94.
Overcoming, 193, 386, 8, 92, 5, 8.
Second, 373, 87.
-Tragedy, 391.
Worm, the, 4, 6, 8, 10, 1, 21, 2, 5, 8, 38, 9, 43.
Wotan, 4, 8, 11, 3, 5, 6, 7, 8, 21, 3, 25, 30, 5, 45, 9, 50, 1.
Wüst, (singer), 279.
(Wycliffe's bible, 324).

Y.

Yawning, 147.
Yearning, 203, 54, 60, 320, 1, 87.
"Young Europe," 147.
Young talents, 77, 116-7, 38, 57, 86, 190, 2, 206.
Youth, 205, 18, 37, 322, 72.

Z.

Zampa, 172.
(*Zeitung f.d. elegante Welt*, 54.)
Zurich, (xix), 386.

In the chronological table of Richard Wagner's writings, volume numbers of the Kegan Paul, Trench, Trübner & Co. edition correspond to Bison Books edition titles as follows:

I	The Art-Work of the Future and Other Works
II	Opera and Drama
III	Judaism in Music and Other Essays
IV	Art and Politics
V	Actors and Singers
VI	Religion and Art
VII	Pilgrimage to Beethoven and Other Essays
VIII	Jesus of Nazareth and Other Writings

GENERAL CHRONOLOGICAL TABLE OF THE CONTENTS OF THE EIGHT VOLUMES.

In his "Richard Wagner" Mr Houston S. Chamberlain has given a "catalogue raisonné" of the prose-writings contained in the master's *Gesammelte Schriften*; the present less ambitious attempt has been undertaken in compliance with the wish of several readers to possess a list enabling them to trace the various works in order of time. The dates given below refer to the time of *writing*, in part ascertained, in part conjectured; the Roman numerals refer to the volumes of this English series of translations, now complete.

		Vol.	
"On German Opera"	Spring, 1834 .	VIII.	(*Die Feen.*)
"Pasticcio" . .	Autumn, „ .	„	(*Das Liebesverbot*: libretto.)
"Bellini: A word in season" . .	Winter, 1837 .	„	
"On German Music"	June or July, 1840	VII.	(*Rienzi* poem.)
"Pergolesi's Stabat Mater" . .	October, 1840 .	„	
"The Virtuoso and the Artist" . .	„ „ .	„	
"A Pilgrimage to Beethoven" . .	November, 1840 .	„	
"On the Overture" .	January, 1841 .	„	
"An End in Paris" .	Jan. or Feb., 1841	„	
Correspondence-letters to the Dresden *Abend-Zeitung* .	Feb. to Dec., „	VIII.	
"The Artist and Publicity" . .	March, 1841 .	VII.	

		Vol.	
"Parisian Amusements"	April, 1841 .	VIII.	
"Der Freischütz" .	May, „ .	VII.	
			(*Der Fliegende Holländer* poem.)
"Le Freischutz" .	June, „ .	„	
"Parisian Fatalities for the German" .	Summer, 1841 .	VIII.	
"A Happy Evening"	October, „ .	VII.	
"Rossini's Stabat Mater" . .	December, 1841 .	„	
"Halévy's Reine de Chypre" . .	„ „ .	„	
Letter to the *Neue Zeitschrift* . .	February, 1842 .	VIII.	
"Halévy and La Reine de Chypre"	Feb. to April, 1842	„	
"Autobiographic Sketch" . .	Winter, 1842 .	I.	
"Die Sarazenin" .	early 1843 . .	VIII.	
"The Apostles' Love-Feast" . . .	April, „ . .	„	
			(*Tannhäuser* poem.)
"Weber's Reinterment," Speech and Chant . . .	December, 1844 .	VII.	
(With "Report" written between 1866 and 1871.)	. .	„	
			(*Lohengrin* poem.)
"On the performance of Beethoven's Ninth Symphony at Dresden": Programme . .	Spring, 1846 .	„	
(With "Report" written between 1866 and 1871.)	.	„	
"Jottings on Ninth Symphony" . .	March, „ .	VIII.	
"Artist and Critic" .	August, „ .	„	

		Vol.
"Plan of Organisation of a German National Theatre for the Kingdom of Saxony" . .	May, 1848 . .	VII.
"Greeting from Saxony to the Viennese" (verse) .	" " . .	VIII.
Vaterlandsverein Speech, and letter to von Lüttichau thereanent . .	June, " . .	IV.
"The Wibelungen" . (revised in summer of 1849 for publication)	Summer, 1848 .	VII.
"The Nibelungen Myth" (first sketch for the *Ring*) . .	" " .	"
"Toast on the Tercentenary of the Royal Kapelle at Dresden" . .	September, " .	"
"Siegfried's Death" .	Oct.-Nov., " .	VIII.
"Jesus of Nazareth".	Winter, 1848-9 .	"
"On E. Devrient's History of German Acting" . .	January, 1849 .	"
"Theatre-Reform" .	" " .	"
"Man and Established Society" .	February, " .	"
"The Revolution" .	April, " .	"
"Art and the Revolution" . . .	Summer, " .	I.
"The Art-work of the Future" . .	Autumn, " .	"
"Art and Climate" .	February, 1850 .	"
"Wieland the Smith"	March, " .	"
"Judaism in Music" (Appendix, New Year 1869)	August, " .	III.

		Vol.	
"Opera and Drama"	Oct. 1850 to Jan. 1851	II.	(*Young Siegfried* poem.)
"A Theatre at Zurich"	April, 1851 .	III.	
"On the Goethe-Stiftung" . . .	May, „ .	„	
"A Communication to my Friends" .	Summer, 1851 .	I.	
"On Musical Criticism" . . .	January, 1852 .	III.	
"Explanatory Programme: Beethoven's Heroic Symphony" . .	prior to Feb., 1852	„	
"Explanatory Programme: Beethoven's Coriolanus Overture" . .	February, 1852 .	„	
"Explanatory Programme: Tannhäuser Overture" .	„ „ .	„	
"On the Performing of Tannhäuser" .	August, „ .	„	(*Der Ring des Nibelungen* poem.)
"Remarks on performing The Flying Dutchman" . .	end of 1852 (or early in '53) .	„	
"Explanatory Programme: The Flying Dutchman Overture" . .	May, 1853 .	„	
"Explanatory Programme: Lohengrin Overture" .	„ „ .	„	
"Gluck's Overture to Iphigenia in Aulis"	June, 1854 .	„	
Sketch for "Die Sieger" . .	May, 1856 .	VIII.	

		Vol.	
"On Liszt's Symphonic Poems" .	February, 1857 .	III.	
"Homage to L. Spohr and W. Fischer" .	November, 1859 .	,,	(*Tristan und Isolde* poem.)
Explanatory Programme: Prelude to "Tristan" .	January, 1860 .	VIII.	
Letter to Hector Berlioz . . .	February, ,, .	III.	
"Music of the Future"	September, ,, .	,,	
"On the Production of Tannhäuser in Paris" . . .	March, 1861 .	,,	
"Preface to the Ring poem" . . .	April, 1863 .	,,	(*Meistersinger* poem.)
"The Vienna Opera-house" . . .	October, ,, .	,,	
"To the Kingly Friend" (verse) .	Summer, 1864 .	IV.	
"On State and Religion" . . .	Winter, 1864-65 .	,,	
"A Music-School for Munich" . .	March, 1865 .	,,	
"Invitation to Tristan in Munich" . .	April, ,, .	VIII.	
"What is German?" (with addendum, Jan., 1878)	Autumn, 1865 .	IV.	
"German Art and German Policy" . .	Autumn, 1867 .	,,	
"Notices: W. H. Riehl" . . .	,, ,, .	,,	
"Notices: Ferdinand Hiller" . . .	,, ,, .	,,	
Dedication of Second Edition, "Opera and Drama" . .	April, 1868 .	II.	
"Recollections of Ludwig Schnorr" .	May, ,, .	IV.	

		Vol.
"Notices: A Remembrance of Rossini"	December, 1868 .	IV.
"Notices: E. Devrient and his Style" .	early 1869 .	,,
Explanatory Programme: Prelude to Act III, "Meistersinger". . .	(?), ,, .	VIII.
Verses on Completion of "Siegfried" .	August ,, .	IV.
Verses on the Munich "Rheingold" .	Oct. (?) ,, .	,,
"About Conducting"	Autumn, 1869 .	,,
Verses on "August 25, 1870" . .	August, 1870 .	,,
"Beethoven" . .	Autumn, ,, .	V.
Verses "To the German army before Paris" . . .	January, 1871 .	
"A Capitulation" (with preface 1873) .	early ,, .	,,
"The Destiny of Opera". . .	Spring, ,, .	,,
Introduction to the "Gesammelte Schriften" . .	July, ,, .	I.
Introduction to Vol. I. "Ges. Schr." .	,, ,, .	VII.
Account of first Performance of "Das Liebesverbot" .	,, ,, .	,,
Introduction to Vol. II. "Ges. Schr." .	Summer (?), 1871 .	,,
"Reminiscences of Auber". . .	Autumn, ,, .	V.
Letter to Boïto on the Production of "Lohengrin" at Bologna . .	November, ,, .	,,

		Vol.
"Epilogue to the Nibelung's Ring" .	December, 1871 .	III.
Introduction to "Art and Revolution" etc. (i.e. Vols. III. and IV. *Ges. Schr.*) .	early 1872 .	I.
Introduction to Vols. V. and VI. "Ges. Schr." . . .	" " .	III.
"Mementoes of Spontini" . .	" " .	"
"Notices: Introduction" . . .	April, " .	IV.
Letter to F. Nietzsche, on Education .	June, " .	V.
"Actors and Singers"	Summer, 1872 .	"
Letter to the Burgomaster of Bologna .	October, " .	"
"On the name Musikdrama". . .	" " .	"
"Letter to an Actor"	November, " .	"
"A Glance at the German Operatic Stage of To-day" .	December, " .	"
"Prologue to a Reading of Götterdämmerung" . .	February, 1873 .	"
"The Rendering of Beethoven's Ninth Symphony" . .	March, " .	"
"Bayreuth: I. Final Report: II. The Playhouse" . .	April, " .	"
"Spohr's Jessonda at Leipzig" . .	December, 1874 .	VI.
"To the Presidents of Wagner-Vereins"	January, 1877 .	" (*Parsifal* poem.)
"Proposed Bayreuth School" (with prospectus of performances) . .	September, 1877 .	"

		Vol.
Introduction to the First Number of the "Bayreuther Blätter" . .	December, 1877 .	VI.
"Modern" . .	February, 1878 .	„
"Public and Popularity" . . .	March to July, 1878	„
"The Public in Time and Space" . .	September, „ .	„
"A Retrospect of the Stage-Festivals of 1876" . . .	November, „ .	„
Introduction to Hans von Wolzogen's "Decay and Rescue of the German Tongue" . .	January, 1879 .	„
"Shall we hope?" .	April, „ .	„
"On Poetry and Composition" . .	June, „ .	„
On Postponement of "Parsifal" . .	July, „ .	„
"On Operatic Poetry and Composition"	August, „ .	„
Letter to E. von Weber "Against Vivisection" . .	October, „ .	„
"On the Application of Music to the Drama" . .	„ „ .	„
"Introduction to the Year 1880" . .	Christmas, „ .	„
"Religion and Art" .	Summer, 1880 .	„
„ „ „ : First Supplement, "What boots this Knowledge?" .	November, „ .	„
Explanatory Programme: Prelude to "Parsifal" .	(?) „ .	VIII.

		Vol.
Announcement of "Parsifal" performances . . .	December, 1880 .	VI.
"Know Thyself" (second supplement to "Religion and Art")	Jan. or Feb., 1881 .	"
Introduction to Count Gobineau's "Ethnological Résumé"	Spring, " .	"
"Hero-dom and Christendom" (third supplement to "Religion and Art") .	Summer, " .	"
"End of the Patronat-Verein" . .	March, 1882 .	"
Open Letter to F. Schön, on the "Stipendiary Fund"	June, " .	"
"Parsifal at Bayreuth, 1882" . . .	November, 1882 .	"
"A Youthful Symphony" . .	December, " .	"
Letter to H. von Stein	January, 1883 .	"
"On the Womanly" (fragment) . .	February, " .	"
Sketches and Fragments (posthumous) . . .	1849 to 1883 .	VIII.